Springmoor Library

Donated
by
Barbara Dechter

A Journey from Prince of Wales's Fort in Hudson's Bay to the Northern Ocean in the Years 1769, 1770, 1771, 1772 New Edition with Introduction, Notes, and Illustrations

by Hearne, Samuel, 1745-1792

ISBN: 9781318021383

HardPress
8345 NW 66TH ST #2561
MIAMI FL 33166-2626
USA
Email: info@hardpress.net

Ordering Information:

Quantity sales. Special discounts are available on quantity purchases by corporations, associations, and others. For details, contact the publisher by email at the address above.

Printed in the United States of America, United Kingdom and Australia

[i]

THE PUBLICATIONS OF
THE CHAMPLAIN
SOCIETY
VI

[ii]

[iii]

THE PUBLICATIONS OF THE CHAMPLAIN SOCIETY

HEARNE:

A JOURNEY FROM PRINCE OF WALES'S FORT IN HUDSON'S BAY TO THE NORTHERN OCEAN

TORONTO
THE CHAMPLAIN SOCIETY

[iv]

*Five Hundred and Twenty Copies of
this Volume have been printed. Twenty
are reserved for Editorial purposes.
The remaining Five Hundred are
supplied only to Members of the
Society and to Subscribing Libraries.*

This copy is No. 229

[v]

A JOURNEY
FROM PRINCE OF WALES'S
FORT IN HUDSON'S BAY TO
THE NORTHERN OCEAN

In the Years 1769, 1770, 1771, and 1772

BY

SAMUEL HEARNE

NEW EDITION
WITH INTRODUCTION, NOTES, AND ILLUSTRATIONS, BY
J. B. TYRRELL, M.A.

TORONTO
THE CHAMPLAIN SOCIETY
1911

[vi]

[vii]

PREFACE

BY SIR EDMUND WALKER

President of the Champlain Society

When the Champlain Society was first organised in 1905 one of the works on its list of proposed publications was the *Journal* of Samuel Hearne. This book, written with great literary charm, is the first account preserved to us of an attempt to explore the interior of far-northern Canada from a base on Hudson Bay. The natives had brought to Fort Prince of Wales glowing reports of a vast store of copper at the mouth of a river which flowed into the Arctic Ocean. An attempt to find it was inevitable. Twice Hearne failed, but his third effort succeeded and, after a laborious journey, he reached the mouth of the Coppermine River. Soon after he was promoted to command at Fort Prince of Wales, now Churchill, on Hudson Bay. France had joined Britain's revolted colonies in their war on the mother land, and one day, in 1782, a French squadron, under the well-known seaman, La Pérouse, dropped anchor before Fort Prince of Wales. Hearne, mightier with the pen than with the sword, surrendered meekly enough in spite of his massive walls from thirty to forty feet thick. Thus ingloriously he dies out of history.

Hearne's *Journal*, published after his early death, has become a rather rare book. Besides the narrative of what he did, it contains copious notes on the natural history of the region which he was the first white man to make known.[viii] A new edition has long been needed. Yet to secure competent editing was a difficult task, since few knew the remote country which Hearne explored. It may be regarded as fortunate that the new edition has been delayed, for only now are we able to present Hearne's story with the annotations necessary to give it the last possible elucidation. The needed knowledge is supplied by Mr. J. B. Tyrrell and Mr. E. A. Preble, two writers pre-eminently suited for their task by journeys in the regions described by Hearne, on parts of which so few white men have set eyes.

Mr. J. B. Tyrrell began his work of exploring in North Western Canada in 1883, and during the ensuing fifteen years he made many important additions to our knowledge of the geology and geography of what is still the least known part of Canada. In 1893, accompanied by his brother, Mr. J. W. Tyrrell, as his assistant, he traversed the so-called Barren Grounds from Lake Athabasca eastward to Chesterfield Inlet, and from there his party paddled in canoes down the west shore of Hudson Bay to Fort Churchill. Of the 3200 miles thus traversed, 1650 were previously unsurveyed and unmapped. From Fort Churchill Mr. Tyrrell walked eight or nine hundred miles on snowshoes to the southern end of Lake Winnipeg. In 1894 he again crossed the Barren Grounds, this time travelling from the north end of Reindeer Lake to a point on Hudson Bay, about 200 miles south-west of Chesterfield Inlet. Thence he went to Churchill as before in canoes along the open coast. From Churchill Mr. Tyrrell again, but by another route, walked on showshoes to the southern end of Lake Winnipeg. On this journey he travelled about 2900 miles, of which 1750 were by canoe and 750 on snowshoes. Almost the whole journey was through previously unexplored country. For the geographical work done in these two years he was awarded the Back Premium by the Royal Geographical Society of London.

In response to an enquiry whether any other white man[ix] has visited the regions described by Hearne, Mr. Tyrrell writes:—

"I happen to be the only one since Hearne who has conducted explorations in the country lying between Fort Churchill and the eastern end of Great Slave Lake and south of latitude 63° N. Except Hearne, I and those who accompanied and assisted me are the only white men who have crossed that great stretch of country, north of a line between the mouth of the Churchill River and Lake Athabasca and a line between the east end of Great Slave Lake and Chesterfield Inlet. Absolutely the only information that I had about the region when I visited it, other than what I had secured in conversation with

Indians, was contained in Hearne's book. My last journey was made sixteen years ago, and no white man has since travelled across that country. With the building of the railroad to Fort Churchill, it will doubtless soon be visited. Since I made a survey of Chesterfield Inlet and its vicinity, my brother, Mr. J. W. Tyrrell, has crossed from the east end of Great Slave Lake by the Hanbury River to Chesterfield Inlet, making a survey as he went, and the Royal North West Mounted Police have sent parties from the Mackenzie River to Hudson Bay along this route, using my brother's maps as their guide. It is hardly necessary to say that a magnificent field for exploration is still left in that far northern country."

So much as to Mr. Tyrrell's work. For the notes explaining Hearne's many observations on natural history we are indebted to Mr. E. A. Preble of Washington. Mr. Preble spent a summer on the west shore of Hudson Bay north of Fort Churchill. He also spent the summers of 1901 and 1903, the winter of 1903-4, and the summers of 1904 and 1907 on the Athabasca and Mackenzie Rivers and on the Barren Grounds north of Great Slave Lake. This most important study of the fauna of Northern Canada was undertaken by Mr. Preble on behalf of the Biological Survey of the United States Department of Agriculture. The various reports and other publications arising from the journeys of Mr. Tyrrell and the investigations of Mr. Preble are mentioned in a bibliographical note at the end of this volume.[x]

This is the first work relating to the West to be published by the Champlain Society. It has already begun an extensive list of the works of early writers on Eastern Canada. The year 1911 will, it is hoped, see the completion of the three volumes of Lescarbot's *History of New France*, now for the first time entirely translated into English. In this as in all other publications of the Society the original text is given with the translation. Nicolas Denys was the first writer to describe in detail the coasts of eastern Canada, and the Society has republished his great book, adequately translated and with copious notes. It has done the same with Le Clercq's account of Gaspé and its interesting natives. The writings of Champlain, entirely translated into English for the first time, will soon appear in six volumes. The regions lying west of Lake Superior have a history as interesting, but the material is scattered. Hearne's *Journal* makes a good beginning. In preparation are the *Journals* of La Vérendrye, the first white man to come in sight of the Rocky Mountains by an overland route. His writings will now for the first time be translated into English. The Society is sparing no pains to provide volumes bearing on the Hudson's Bay Company. Much further work on examining and classifying the papers of the Company will, however, be necessary before anything final can be done. Meanwhile members will enjoy the pleasant narrative of Hearne edited by the competent observers whose services the Society has had the good fortune to secure.

TORONTO, *January 1911.*

[xi]

CONTENTS

	PAGE
PREFACE	vii
LIST OF ILLUSTRATIONS	xiii
EDITOR'S INTRODUCTION	1
AUTHOR'S PREFACE	29
AUTHOR'S CONTENTS	33
AUTHOR'S INTRODUCTION	41
A JOURNEY TO THE NORTHERN OCEAN	61
BIBLIOGRAPHY	419
INDEX	427

[xii]

[xiii]

LIST OF ILLUSTRATIONS

IN ORIGINAL VOLUME

A NORTH-WEST VIEW OF
PRINCE OF WALES'S

FORT IN HUDSON'S BAY,
NORTH AMERICA — *To face p.* 61

INDIAN IMPLEMENTS — " 134

A WINTER VIEW IN
ATHAPUSCOW LAKE — " 232

INDIAN IMPLEMENTS — " 310

A MAP EXHIBITING MR.
HEARNE'S TRACKS

IN HIS TWO JOURNIES FOR
THE DISCOVERY

OF THE COPPER MINE RIVER

IN THE YEARS 1770, 1771,
AND 1772, UNDER

THE DIRECTION OF THE
HUDSON'S BAY

COMPANY — *At end*

PLAN OF THE COPPER MINE
RIVER   "

PLAN OF ALBANY RIVER IN
HUDSON'S BAY   "

PLAN OF MOOS RIVER IN
HUDSON'S BAY   "

PLAN OF SLUDE RIVER   "

ADDITIONS IN PRESENT VOLUME

MAP OF PART OF NORTHERN
CANADA AS

AT PRESENT KNOWN   *At end*

Drawn on the same
projection and scale as
Hearne's

general Map

[xiv]

MAP OF COPPERMINE RIVER   *At end*

As surveyed by Sir John
Franklin in 1821. From

"Franklin's First Journey,"
London, 1823.

MAP OF PART OF NORTH AMERICA

To face *p.* 18

Showing Hearne's course as first published. From

"Cook's Third Voyage," 1784.

MAP OF PART OF NORTH AMERICA, 1787

" 18

From Supplement to "Pennant's Arctic Zoology."

PLAN OF FORT PRINCE OF WALES AS IT

APPEARED IN 1894. By J. B. TYRRELL

page 22

MAP OF YATH-KYED LAKE AND PART OF

KAZAN (CATHAWHACHAGA) RIVER. By

J. B. TYRRELL

To face *p.* 86

MAP OF DUBAWNT LAKE AND PART OF

DUBAWNT RIVER. By J. B. AND J. W.

Tyrrell

" 90

HEARNE'S NAME ON ROCK AT CHURCHILL   "   4

SAMUEL HEARNE   "   25

DUBAWNT LAKE   "   96

DUBAWNT RIVER WHERE HEARNE CROSSED

IT   "   96

A SOUTH-WEST VIEW OF PRINCE OF WALES'S

FORT   "   106

WHOLDIAH LAKE   "   120

GROVE OF SPRUCE WITHIN BARREN LANDS   "   120

ARTILLERY LAKE, LAST WOODS   "   138

ARTILLERY LAKE   "   138

BLOODY FALLS, COPPERMINE RIVER   "   178

From "Franklin's First Journey," p. 360.

COPPER IMPLEMENTS FROM COPPERMINE

RIVER   "   178

[xv]

HERD OF CARIBOU ON
BARREN LANDS NEAR

DUBAWNT RIVER   *To face*
                                p. 234

DRYING CARIBOU MEAT   "   234

WOODS OF SPRUCE AND
LARCH, SOUTH-WEST

OF CHURCHILL, IN WINTER   "   288

STONY BARREN LANDS IN   "   288
SUMMER

CHIPEWYAN INDIANS FROM   "   296
KAZAN RIVER

VALLEY OF THLEWIAZA RIVER   "   296

FORT PRINCE OF WALES,   "   328
GATE

FORT PRINCE OF WALES,   "   328
INTERIOR

[xvi]

[1]

EDITOR'S INTRODUCTION

Samuel Hearne, the author of the book here republished, is one of the most interesting characters to be met with in the annals of exploration in North America. When a young man, only twenty-four years old, he was sent on foot to explore the interior of a great continent. Though he knew nothing of mines or minerals, he, like many a man similarly equipped since his day, was to report on a great mining property. Naturally his report on the "mine" of copper is of little value, but his account of Northern Canada and of the life of the natives who inhabited it is the first published detailed description of any portion of the interior of Western Canada. Very few men of his age accomplished so much, and fewer still have published such admirable narratives of their enterprises.

All that we know of Hearne's early life is contained in an obituary notice which appeared in the *European Magazine and London Review* for June 1797, entitled "Some Account of the late Mr. Samuel Hearne, Author of 'A Journey from Prince of Wales Fort, in Hudson's Bay, to the Northern Ocean, undertaken by order of the Hudson's Bay Company for the discovery of Copper Mines, a North-West Passage, &c., in the years 1769, 1770, 1771, and 1772.'"

"Mr. Samuel Hearne was born in the year 1745. He was the son of Mr. Hearne, Secretary to the Waterworks, London Bridge, a very sensible man, and of a respectable family in Somersetshire; he died of fever in his 40th year, and left Mrs. Hearne with this son, then but three years of age, and a daughter two years older. Mrs. Hearne, [2]finding her income too small to admit her living in town as she had been accustomed to, retired to Bimmester, in Dorsetshire (her native place), where she lived as a gentlewoman, and was much respected. It was her wish to give her children as good an education as the place afforded, and accordingly [she] sent her son to school at a very early period, but his dislike to reading and writing was so great that he made very little progress in either. His masters, indeed, spared neither threats nor persuasion to induce him to learn, but their arguments were thrown away on one who seemed predetermined never to become a learned man; he had, however, a very quick apprehension, and, in his childish sports, showed unusual activity and ingenuity; he was particularly fond of drawing, and though he never had the least instruction in the art, copied with great delicacy and correctness even from nature. Mrs. Hearne's friends, finding her son had no taste for study, advised her fixing on some business, and proposed such as they judged most suitable for him; but he declared himself utterly averse to trade, and begged he might be sent to sea. His mother very reluctantly complied with his request, took him to Portsmouth, and remained with him till he sailed. His captain (now Lord Hood) promised to take care of him, and he kept his word; for he gave him every indulgence his youth required. He was then but eleven years of age. They had a warm engagement soon after he entered, and took several prizes. The captain told him he should have his share, but he begged, in a very affectionate manner, it should be given to his mother, and she should know best what to do with it. He was a midshipman several years under the same commander; but, either on the conclusion of the war, or having no hopes of preferment, he left the navy, and entered into the service of the Hudson's Bay Company as mate of one of their sloops. He was, however, soon distinguished from his associates by his ingenuity, industry, and a wish to undertake some hazardous enterprise by which mankind might be benefited. This was represented to the Company, and they immediately applied to him as a proper person to be sent on an expedition they had long had in view, viz. to find out the North-West Passage. He gladly accepted the proposal, and how far he succeeded is shown to the public in his Journal. On his return he was advanced to a more lucrative post at Prince of Wales Fort, on Hudson Bay, and in a few years was made Commander-in-Chief, in which position he remained till 1782, when the French unexpectedly landed at Prince of Wales Fort, took possession of it, and after having given the governor leave to secure his own property, seized the stock of furs, &c. &c., and blew up [3]the fort. At the Company's request Mr. H. went out the year following, saw it rebuilt,[1] and the new Governor settled in his habitation (which they took care to fortify a little better than formerly), and returned to England in 1787. He had saved a few thousands, the fruits of many years' industry, and might, had he been blessed with prudence, have enjoyed many years of ease and plenty; but he had lived so long where money was of no use that he seemed insensible of its value here, and lent it with little or no security to those he was scarcely acquainted with by name. Sincere and undesigning himself, he was by no means a match for the duplicity of others. His disposition, as may be judged by his writing, was naturally humane; what he wanted in learning and polite accomplishments he made up in native simplicity and innate goodness; and he was so strictly scrupulous with regard to the property of others that he was heard to say a few days before his death, 'He could lay his hand on his heart and say he had never wronged any man of sixpence.'

"Such are the outlines of Mr. Hearne's character, who, if he had some failings, had many virtues to counterbalance them, of which charity was not the least. He died of the dropsy, November 1792, aged 47."

He seems to have entered the service of the Hudson's Bay Company and to have been sent to Fort Prince of Wales, the great stone fortification on the low bare rocky point at the mouth of the Churchill River on Hudson Bay, when he was about twenty years old. For several years he was engaged in the fur trade with the Eskimos, up and down the coast of Hudson Bay, north of Churchill River. One little glimpse is caught of him, on July 1, 1767, for on that day he chiselled his name on the smooth hard rock of Sloops Cove, on the west side of Churchill harbour. When I visited the place, in 1894, the name was as fresh and plain as if his hammer and chisel had just been laid aside.

Being possessed of much more than the average amount of ability and enthusiasm, he was chosen by Moses Norton, the energetic Governor of Fort Prince of Wales, to go out with the Indians into the vast, and as far as that was then known, limitless, territory west of Hudson Bay, in order to find and prospect the place where the native copper had been found which the Indians often brought with them to the fort.

[4]

During the year preceding his departure on his first expedition, he had had an excellent opportunity to perfect himself in a knowledge of astronomical and geodetic work, for in the summer of 1768 the annual ship had brought William Wales, F.R.S., and Joseph Dymond from London, commissioned by the Royal Society to remain at Fort Prince of Wales throughout the ensuing year in order to observe the transit of Venus over the sun on the 3rd of June 1769.[2] They remained at the fort until the ship left again for London in August of the following year (1769). Mr. Wales was one of the foremost astronomers, mathematicians, and litterateurs of his age. Shortly after his return to England he was appointed to accompany Captain Cook on his voyage around the world in the *Resolution* in 1772-74, and again on his last voyage in 1776-79. His presence for more than a year among the little band of white men assembled at this remote fur-trading post on Hudson Bay must have had a helpful influence in preparing Hearne for his great explorations overland to the Arctic Ocean. This book is an account of three journeys which he undertook in rapid succession into the country west of Hudson Bay and north-west of Fort Prince of Wales in search of the fabled bed of copper ore, from which pure copper could be loaded directly into ships at trifling expense. In the first and second journeys he was obliged to turn back before reaching his destination, but in the third journey all difficulties were finally overcome, and he was taken to and shown the "mine" of copper.

It has been my good fortune to travel over parts of the same country through which Hearne had journeyed one hundred and twenty-three years before me, and into which no white man had ventured during the intervening time. The conditions which I found were just such as he describes, except that the inhabitants had changed. The Chipewyan Indians, whom he found occupying advantageous positions everywhere as far as the north end of Dubawnt Lake, had disappeared, and in their places the country had been occupied by scattered bands and families of Eskimos, who had almost forgotten the ocean shores of the north, from which they had come. They were depending entirely, for food and clothing, on the caribou, which they killed on the banks of the inland streams and lakes. Traces of old Indian encampments were seen in a few of the scattered groves that are growing along the banks of Dubawnt and Kazan Rivers, but these camps had evidently not been occupied for many years.[3]

Photo. J. B. Tyrrell, Oakley, 1894.
S. HEARNE'S NAME ON THE SMOOTH GLACIATED ROCK AT SLOOP'S COVE, NEAR CHURCHILL

[5]

Whether Hearne remained at Fort Prince of Wales after his return is not certain, but it is possible that he may have gone to some of the other factories near the southern shore of Hudson Bay, and the plans of Albany, Moos, and Slude (East Main) Rivers, at the end of this book, the first two of which are dated 1774, may have been made by him at this time. In the latter year, however, he was at York Factory, and from there, in May or June, he was sent inland to the Saskatchewan River, where he established Cumberland House on Pine Island Lake, close to a trading-post which had been previously built by Joseph Frobisher, an enterprising merchant from Montreal. The following year he was recalled to Hudson Bay to take charge of his old home, Fort Prince of Wales, in the place of Governor Norton, who had died, and there he remained quietly trading with the Indians till August 1782, when the fort was taken and burnt by the French under Admiral La Pérouse.

As soon as the French with three vessels of war appeared[6] before the fort and demanded its capitulation, Hearne surrendered at discretion, without firing a shot. He was at once taken on board the French ships, and allowed to retain all his private papers and effects, while the furs and other property of the Hudson's Bay Company were either confiscated or burnt. After pillaging and destroying the fort, La Pérouse sailed southward to York Factory, which also surrendered to him as soon as he appeared before it, and then, with all his prisoners on board, including the Governors of Fort Prince of Wales, York, and Severn, he sailed for France.

Hearne does not appear to have been treated by La Pérouse as an enemy who had been taken prisoner at the capture of a hostile fort, but rather as a literary man whom he was anxious to encourage and patronise. While a prisoner on board the French ships he was treated with every consideration, and his generous captor, who was one of the foremost geographers of his time, read his manuscript journal with evident interest, and returned it to him on the express condition that he would print and publish it immediately on his arrival in England.

On the signing of peace with the French in the following year, Hearne was sent back by the Hudson's Bay Company to Churchill. He made no attempt to live again in the fort, which was very unfavourably situated for obtaining both wood and water, but took up his residence on the site of the original trading-post of the Hudson's Bay Company, five miles south of Fort Prince of Wales, where the buildings of the Company stand at the present day.

In 1784, while Hearne was at Churchill, there arrived from England a boy, fourteen years old, named David Thompson, who afterwards became the great geographer of North-Western America. Thompson remained at Churchill for only one year, during which time he copied some of Hearne's Journal, and though he did not carry away any very friendly feelings towards his superior officer, the knowledge which he[7] gained of the interior country, and of the possibilities of travel through it, must have had a stimulating effect on him in after life. His note-books, which are now in possession of the Government of the Province of Ontario, are filled with detailed information about North-Western America, so much of which he subsequently explored. In 1787 Hearne left Churchill and returned to England, and from that date until his death, in 1792, he probably spent most of his time in revising and preparing his Journal for publication.

Before discussing Hearne's character and the extent and value of his work, it will be interesting to recount briefly the circumstances which led up to the expedition to the Coppermine River. In the seventeenth century the search for gold and silver monopolised the thoughts of many of the adventurers in the Southern Seas, but those adventurers who turned their attention to the more northern countries recognised that there were other sources of wealth beside the precious metals. They saw that the furs of many of the wild animals which roamed through the forests might easily be obtained from the natives in exchange for articles of European manufacture of but trifling value, and that these furs might be sold in the markets of Europe and Asia at an enormous profit. In this way what is known as the fur trade had its beginning on the American continent.

The Dutch, French, and English strove for shares in this lucrative trade, and many of the wars and massacres of that time had their origin in the strenuous endeavours of one or other of these nations to outwit its rivals. The Dutch had headquarters on the Hudson River, in what is now the State of New York, the French on the St. Lawrence River, in the present Provinces of Quebec and Ontario, while the English established themselves on the shores of Hudson Bay, founding a fur-trading company, which was destined to survive till the present time, and to be one of the greatest commercial corporations that the world has ever known.[8]

This Company was called "The Governor and Company of Adventurers of England, trading into Hudson's Bay," or in brief, "The Hudson's Bay Company." At first it occupied a few small buildings, called factories or forts, situated at advantageous places near the mouths of rivers on the shore of Hudson Bay, where the Indians, who were accustomed to roam through the great unknown inland country, could come down in canoes to trade their furs for guns, knives, and other commodities brought from England by the white people.

About the beginning of the eighteenth century, some of the Indians who came to the more northern factories or trading-posts, and especially to those situated at the mouths of the Churchill and Nelson Rivers, brought with them rough pieces of native copper, and ornaments and weapons fashioned from this metal. On being asked where the copper came from, they said that they found it on the banks of a river, far away to the north, and that it could be collected from the surface in great abundance, but that the distance through which it was necessary for them to carry it prevented them from bringing much of it to the factories. These stories, along with the specimens which the Indians had in their possession, gradually aroused more and more interest in the minds of the fur-traders. At last they determined that there were far greater riches within their reach than could be obtained by trading with the Indians for furs, and decided to go in search of the copper mines whatever the cost of such a search might be. Among the first to take up this quest was Captain James Knight, a man of about eighty years of age, who had spent most of his life in trading for furs with the Indians, and who for several years had been in charge of York Factory for the Hudson's Bay Company. With him were Captain Barlow, another fur-trader from Fort Albany, and Captain Vaughan.

When the Committee, appointed in 1748 by the British House of Commons to inquire into the state and conditions[9] of the countries adjoining Hudson Bay, was taking evidence, one of the chief witnesses was a Captain Carruthers, who in his evidence stated "that he had heard a good deal of a Copper Mine to the northward of the Churchill River—that the Governor (Knight) was mighty fond of the Discovery, and made great inquiries about it,—that the witness had seen copper which was said to be brought from thence,—that the Governor (Knight) was very earnest in this Discovery, which was always his topic."

Joseph Robson states that "Governor Knight and Captain Barlow being well assured that there were rich mines to the northward, from the accounts of the Indians of those parts who had brought some of the ore to the factory, they were bent upon making the discovery; and the Governor said he knew the way to the place as well as to his bedside."[4] In the year 1719, Captain Knight and his associates sailed from England in two ships, the *Albany* and the *Discovery*, well provided with stores and provisions, and even with strong iron-bound boxes in which to bring back the copper and other precious metals. Unfortunately the expedition was wrecked on Marble Island, and all the officers and crew were lost, although their fate was not definitely known until nearly half a century later.

Three years later, when the two ships had not returned, and no word had been received from them, Captain Scroggs was sent by the Hudson's Bay Company from Churchill to look for them, and at the same time to continue the search for copper. The story of his journey, as given by Dobbs in his "Account of the Countries adjoining to Hudson's Bay" (London, 1744), says nothing about the explorers who had been lost, but comments on the copper deposits as follows:—

"He [Scroggs] had two Northern [Chipewyan] Indians with him, who had wintered at Churchill, and told him of a copper mine somewhere in that country upon the shore near the surface of the earth, and they could direct the sloop so near it, as to lay her side to it, and be soon laden with it; and they brought some pieces of copper from it to Churchill that made it evident there was a mine thereabouts. They had sketched out the country with charcoal upon a skin of parchment before they left Churchill, and so far as they went it agreed very well. One of the Indians desired to leave him, saying he was within three or four days' journey of his own country, but he would not let him go. Captain Norton, late Governor of Churchill, was then with him."

[10]

The Captain Norton here mentioned was the father of Governor Moses Norton who afterwards despatched Hearne to look for the Coppermine River. Captain Carruthers, who is mentioned above, and who, according to his own statement, had "quitted" the service of the Hudson's Bay Company thirty-five years before 1748, said that he "himself carried Mr. Norton, who was afterwards Governor, and two Northern Indians to Churchill where he put them in a canoe, and the purpose of their voyage was to make discoveries and encourage the Indians to come down to trade and bring copper ore."[5]

The journey of Mr. Norton referred to by Captain Carruthers was probably undertaken about 1714, in which year York Factory was restored to the English, after having been occupied by the French for seventeen years. Probably it was on account of this and similar journeys that, in 1719, a gratuity of £15 was voted to Mr. Norton by the Hudson's Bay Company, on account of having endured "great hardships in travelling among the Indians." In 1733 the same Mr. Norton wrote to the directors of the Hudson's Bay Company in London that he had "served your Honors many years and gone through many difficulties and hardships in taking long journeys with the natives to promote your trade with them, even many times to the hazard of my own life."[6]

[11]

In the same Parliamentary Report Alexander Browne, a surgeon who had been for six years in the Company's service, testified "that the Indians brought down the ore at the request of Governor Norton," and also "that he had heard the late Mr. Norton say that he had been at this mine and that a considerable quantity of copper might be brought down."[7] It is not probable that Browne's statement with reference to Norton having visited the Coppermine River is correct, but it would be rash to deny that such a journey had been accomplished until the letters and records of the Hudson's Bay Company are finally made public.

After the unsuccessful voyages of Captains Knight and Scroggs, several other expeditions were sent from Churchill northward along the shore of Hudson Bay. Most of these doubtless more than paid their way by trading for furs with the Eskimos, but to the outside public they were ostensibly to find the North-West Passage to China and the "mine" of copper ore. The most important of these expeditions were those of the *Furnace* and *Discovery* under Captains Middleton and Moor, in 1741-2, and of the *Dobbs* and *California* under Captains Moor and Smith in 1746-7. After these expeditions, interest in the copper may have languished for a while, but the numerous references to it in the Hudson's Bay Report of 1749 show that it was not by any means forgotten.

Meanwhile, Richard Norton of Churchill had died, and his half-breed son Moses Norton had been appointed Governor in his stead. In the year 1767 the remains of Knight's ill-fated expedition were found on Marble Island, and the thoughts of the people on Hudson Bay were undoubtedly again turned to the object for which his voyage had been undertaken. To add to the interest in the copper, the Northern Indians, who came to Churchill in the year 1768, brought with them some fine specimens of ore which they said came from Coppermine River. By this time Governor Moses Norton's interest was thoroughly aroused in the possible value of the copper "mines," and as they were said to be only four hundred miles from Churchill, he determined that, if possible, something definite should be learned about them. Accordingly, that very summer, when the ship came from England, he took passage back in it to London, and laid a plan for the discovery of this supposed great body of copper ore before the directors of the Company and received their approval for its execution. The plan was not to entail any very great expense to the Company. A man was to be sent out with the Indians, who should be supported by them and live as they lived.

[12]

Before that time other men had been sent into the wilderness, in the same way, from factories, especially from York, where, in 1690,

Henry Kelsey had travelled southward until he met the so-called "Naywatamee poets" or Mandan Indians, somewhere near the banks of the Assiniboine or South Saskatchewan Rivers,[8] and in 1754 Anthony Hendry had made a notable journey up the North Saskatchewan River to the great plains, where he had endeavoured to establish friendly relations with the Blackfeet Indians and their allies, and to prevent them from selling their furs to Luc la Corne and the French merchants from Montreal, who had penetrated into the same country several years before. Both these men had been treated with the greatest kindness by the natives and had brought back intelligent accounts of the countries visited by them, though neither of them had the ability of Samuel Hearne to enable them to prepare a report such as the one here published.

[13]

Governor Norton was a man of much more than the ordinary intelligence and strength of character, and he saw that if the expedition was to be a success it must be conducted by some one who would be able to make full and accurate surveys of the route followed, and who could intelligently describe the character and value of the "mine" and determine its latitude and longitude by astronomical observations. For this purpose he chose Samuel Hearne, now a young man twenty-four years of age, who, after his service as a midshipman in the British Navy, was at the time employed as a mate on the *Charlotte*, one of the Company's sloops trading from Churchill with the Eskimos. The story of his journey, the hardships which he endured, and the success which he achieved, form the subject of this book and need not be discussed here.[9]

Hearne's character, which had been moulded to a large extent by his surroundings, can be fairly well understood from a careful reading of his book. He was diligent and reasonably accurate but not strong or forceful. In this latter particular he differed from his great successor, Sir Alexander Mackenzie, who descended the Mackenzie River eighteen years after Hearne had reached its waters at Great Slave Lake. Alexander Mackenzie was a man of masterful temperament, and those who accompanied him, whether white men or natives, were merely so many instruments to be used in the accomplishment of any purpose which he had in hand. Their likes and dislikes, and their habits of life, were merely interesting to him in so far as they affected the results that he wished to attain. His book is a detailed description of the directions and distances which he travelled each day, and of the incidents of travel as they occurred. To Samuel Hearne the natives with whom he travelled were beings whose thoughts and habits of life he found supremely interesting. Their intentions and desires largely controlled the expeditions on which he had embarked. With the exception of the accomplishment of the main object in view, of reaching the Coppermine River, their wishes were everything, his nothing.

[14]

His first expedition was a complete failure, as the Indians simply took him off with them for a couple of hundred miles into the wilderness until they became tired of his company and then robbed him of everything he had and left him to find his own way back to Churchill as best he could. His second expedition was more successful, as the Indians tolerated his company for eight months and supported him as long as food was plentiful, but their enthusiasm, or duty to the Master at Churchill, did not last long enough to carry them to the Coppermine River.

Of his third and successful expedition Hearne was the historian and surveyor, while Matonabbee, a bold and forceful Chipewyan Indian about ten years his senior, was its leader. If at any time Hearne tried to interfere with the arrangements made by the leader he was promptly told to follow instructions if he wished to reach the copper mine. While Matonabbee probably reciprocated, to some extent at least, Hearne's affection for him, he was evidently thinking of and working for Moses Norton, the rough but powerful governor of Fort Prince of Wales, rather than for the quiet and observant young man who was accompanying him. Hearne's sketch of the life of

Matonabbee is one of the most appreciative and sympathetic accounts of a North American Indian that has come to my notice.

Hearne was evidently gifted with a very retentive memory, and had the artist's faculty of seeing the interesting features[15] of his surroundings in their true perspective. Though, like Robert Louis Stevenson and many others, he had not been a brilliant student at school, he possessed the literary ability to present what he saw or knew in an interesting and attractive form. In the ordinary quietude of his tent or office, when thinking of nothing but the subject which he was describing, he undoubtedly recorded his observations with accuracy. But in the warmth of dispute, when endeavouring to overcome the criticisms or objections of others, he was liable to be carried beyond the points of strict accuracy and, in order to strengthen his argument, to fill in blanks in his record from his imagination. He says, for example, that the sun was above the horizon at midnight at the mouth of the Coppermine River. But it is certain either that, on the night which he spent there, the weather was too cloudy to permit of seeing the sun, if it had been above the horizon, or that, even if the weather was clear, the sun must necessarily have been below the horizon at the time. His sketch of Moses Norton also has the appearance of being highly coloured by his evident personal dislike of the man. No one can justly accuse Hearne of lack of personal courage, for the annoyances, hardships, and sufferings, which he endured without complaining, put the thought of personal cowardice entirely out of the question. He had acquired the stoicism of the Indian and he suffered quietly, just as an Indian is prepared to suffer. During the years which Hearne spent among the Indians, living on what they were able to obtain from day to day, as well as in his general intercourse with them as a trader bartering for the furs which they were able to collect and bring to him, he had learned to endure privations, to compromise rather than to fight, and to accomplish his purpose by politic and peaceful, rather than by warlike, methods. Naturally of a complaisant disposition, he had learned to give whatever was demanded of him, no matter who made the demand. Nothing could be more typical of the habits which he had thus acquired than the little experiences[16] in trading, recounted on page <u>285</u>, where, after an Indian had received full payment for the furs which he had brought in, he was given in addition the long list of articles there enumerated. Apparently, the Indian was not refused anything if he persisted in asking.

This habit of acceding to requests to avoid dispute and difficulty, rather than any real fear of personal danger, accounts for Hearne's surrender of Fort Prince of Wales to the French without a struggle. In this case it is quite possible that, in spite of the great strength of the fort which he occupied, he was really not able to make effective resistance against his powerful and determined enemy, who outnumbered him more than ten to one. Although the fort mounted forty heavy guns, and was provided with plenty of ammunition and small arms, it had only thirty-nine men within its walls at the time. But even if Hearne had had a stronger garrison, it is doubtful whether he would have attempted resistance, for his training in the service of the Hudson's Bay Company had taught him to preserve the peace at any price, and it was impossible for him to set aside at a moment's notice what had become second nature to him.

We have seen that Hearne had not the forceful character possessed by Alexander Mackenzie; yet, as a man must be judged by the results which he achieves, it is perhaps all the more creditable to him to have done what he did with his more complaisant and observant disposition. Though he could not control the Indians with whom he travelled, he nevertheless accomplished his purpose of making the journey, and has left a splendid record of it to enrich posterity. He was hardly a great geographer, though he added largely to the geographical knowledge of Northern Canada west of Hudson Bay. It was he who finally set at rest the question of a north-west passage by sea to China and the Orient, south of the mouth of the Coppermine River. He knew nothing of mines or ores, and the information he brought back about the[17] "mine" of copper which he was sent to explore was exceedingly meagre. He verified the report of the existence of native copper on the surface in uncertain quantity. Incidentally he showed that the place where it occurred was too remote and difficult of access to permit of a copper mine being worked at a profit, even if the copper should be found in great abundance. But that was all. In fact, even to the present time, we have very little accurate knowledge of the character and extent of this copper deposit near the Coppermine River, as may be seen by referring to the notes on pages 194 *et seq.*

On Hearne's first and second journeys he had quite adequate scientific apparatus, and so could take astronomical observations to determine his true position. So we find that he occasionally made use of his quadrant and took such observations; consequently the positions given on the map for the principal points in these two journeys are approximately correct. But he started on his third journey with very faulty instruments, and he would appear to have made very little use even of them. The map of the course followed by him on this journey strongly suggests a rough sketch made by his Indian guide, rather than a careful plan worked out by himself, from day to day, or week to week. For example, between Island and Kasba Lakes, near the beginning of his journey, and shortly after he had diverged from his course of the previous year, he began to go wrong. If he was using his compass at all, it is possible that some source of local magnetic attraction was influencing it, for the position of the last-named lake (on his map) is some sixty or seventy miles too far north. It is inconceivable that he could have made any serious effort to correct this faulty course by astronomical observations with his quadrant. His book is chiefly valuable therefore not so much because of its geographical information, but because it is an accurate, sympathetic, and patently truthful record of life among the Chipewyan Indians at that time. Their habits, customs, and general mode of life, however[18] disagreeable or repulsive, are recorded in detail, and the book will consequently always remain a classic in American ethnology.

The manuscript report on Hearne's exploration was submitted to the directors of the Hudson's Bay Company immediately after his return, and they highly commended him for the work he had done, and gave him a handsome bonus.[110] The first account of his journey which seems to have been published was given to the world in 1784 in the "Introduction to Cook's Third Voyage," pp. xlvi-l, written by Dr. John Douglas, Bishop of Salisbury, who later also edited Hearne's own book. The route followed by Hearne on his successful third journey is incorporated in the general map of the world accompanying this book. A Mr. Roberts, who prepared this map, makes the following note with regard to it:—

"The whole of Hudson's Bay I took from a chart compiled by Mr. Marley, from all the most authentic maps he could procure of those parts, with which I was favoured by Samuel Wegg, Esq., F.R.S., and Governor of that Company, who also politely furnished me with Mr. Hearne's Journals and the map of his route to the Coppermine River, which is faithfully inserted in the chart.

"(Sgd.) HENRY ROBERTS.

"SHOREHAM, SUSSEX, *May 18, 1784.*"[111]

Another brief account of Hearne's trip is given in "Pennant's Arctic Zoology," also published in 1784, while his map is incorporated in one of the maps published in "Pennant's Supplement to Arctic Zoology," 1787. Some of the names used on these two maps were continued on the map accompanying Alexander Mackenzie's "Voyages," and also on Arrowsmith's maps up to comparatively recent dates.

MAP OF PART OF NORTH AMERICA
Being a portion of the Map of the World in "Cook's Third Voyage,"
published in 1784 Hearne's route was first published on this map

MAP OF PART OF NORTH AMERICA
Showing General Course of Hearne's Third Journey
From the Second Map of Mr. Pennant's "Arctic Zoology," 1787

[19]

The book here republished appeared first in 1795, three years after Hearne's death, as a large quarto volume of xliv + 458 pages, with five maps, and four full-page illustrations. It was edited by the above-named Dr. John Douglas, who is said to have drawn up the narrative, and to have finished the Introduction, though just how much Hearne's diction was altered by the editor is not known. It is probable, however, that the MS. was published almost exactly as Hearne had written it. An octavo edition, similar in letterpress to the original quarto one, but with some slight omissions or differences in the text and in the general map, was published in Dublin in 1796.

A French translation of the 1795 edition, by Lallemant, one of the secretaries in the French Department of the Marine, was published at Paris in 1799. Dr. Arthur G. Doughty, the Archivist of the Dominion of Canada, has very kindly compared this edition with the English one of 1795, and makes the following remarks with regard to it:—

"The dedication of the English version is omitted in the French. In the Introduction, page 27, there is a note in the English edition which is not translated. Pages 441 to 445 of the English edition are omitted in the French. At the beginning of the French version there is a note on Hearne from the 'Voyage of La Pérouse,' and some remarks by Lallemant. The translation of the whole volume appears to be good."

The note from the "Voyage of La Pérouse" and the remarks of Lallemant are as follows:—

"A LA PÉROUSE.—C'est à vous que l'Europe est redevable de la publication de cet ouvrage, dont le manuscrit fut trouvé parmi les papiers du Gouverneur du fort du Prince de Galles, lorsque vous vous[20] rendîtes maître des établissements anglais dans la Baie de Hudson. En le remettant à son auteur, à la condition expresse de le faire imprimer et publier, jamais vainqueur n'exerça plus utilement son droit de conquête et n'imposa au vaincu une condition plus honorable.[12] Elle était digne du marin aussi généreux qu'éclairé qui devait, quelques années après, entreprendre un voyage non moins important, et dont aujourd'hui nous déplorons la perte.

"Pourquoi faut-il, brave et excellent *Dupetit-Thouars*, que vous nous ayez été aussi ravi! vous qui m'excitâtes avec tant d'ardeur à traduire la relation de *Samuel Hearne*, et qui, après avoir tout sacrifié pour aller redemander *la Pérouse* aux îles de la mer du Sud, soupiriez après la paix pour reprendre vos projets de découvertes. Accablé par le nombre au combat d'*Aboukir*, une mort glorieuse vous a enlevé à votre patrie, à deux sœurs chéries, à l'amitié, aux sciences, et il ne nous est revenu de vous que cette réponse héroïque à l'ennemi: *'Voyez mon pavillon; on ne le déplacera qu'en m'ôtant la vie.'*

"*La Pérouse*, vous l'eussiez pleuré comme nous! il était si attaché à son pays, à son métier, et si passionné pour leur gloire. Il avait une âme si forte et un cœur si sensible; un esprit si cultivé et des dehors si modestes. Il était ami si vrai et frère si tendre. *Perpetue, Félicité*, j'en appèle à votre douleur profonde!

"En associant son nom au vôtre, *la Pérouse*, permettez qu'il partage avec vous l'hommage d'une traduction à laquelle je me suis empressé de consacrer mes veilles pour concourir à vos vues respectives d'utilité. Puisse ce monument être digne de vous deux!

"LALLEMANT,
"l'un des Secrétaires de la Marine."

Hearne[21] intimates on page 32 that the map here reproduced differs slightly from those which he had previously published, a reference doubtless to the one in Cook's "Voyage," but he claims that this one is the most accurate, since he had revised it with great care. Both maps are here given; further explorations in the northern country alone can determine which is the more correct.

Fort Prince of Wales, from which place Hearne started on his expedition, was built by the Hudson's Bay Company in the years 1733 to 1771. It is said to have been designed by English military engineers, and, according to Joseph Robson, was built under the direction of the resident Governor, though Robson himself had much to do with its construction.

The fort, which is one of the most interesting military ruins on the continent, stands on Eskimo Point, just west of the mouth of Churchill River, and though some parts of the walls have fallen, it was, when I visited it, in much the same condition as when built, except that the houses within it had been gutted by fire. It is 310 feet long on the north and south sides, and 317 feet long on the east and west sides, measured from corner to corner of the bastions. The walls are from 37 to 42 feet thick, and 16 feet 9 inches high to the top of the parapet, which is 5 feet high and 6 feet 3 inches wide. On the outside the wall was faced with dressed stone, except towards the river, while on the inside undressed stone was used. The interior of the wall is a rubble of boulders, held together by a poor mortar. In the parapet are forty embrasures and forty guns, from six to twenty-four pounders, are lying on the wall near them, now partly hidden by low[22] willows, currant and gooseberry bushes. The three store-houses and the magazine, which once occupied the centres of the bastions, have disappeared. Within the square enclosure are the stone walls of a house 103 feet long, 33 feet wide, and 17 feet high, which is said to have had a flat roof covered[23] with lead. The small observatory used by Mr. Wales in 1769 was situated on the south-east bastion.

PLAN OF FORT PRINCE OF WALES.

By J. B. Tyrrell. 1894.
Walls, 37 to 42 feet thick, 16 feet 9 inches high.
Scale: 80 feet = 1 inch.

This new edition is a reprint of the quarto edition of 1795. The pagination of the original has been inserted, enclosed within square brackets, at the proper places in the text, and the notes are given as in the original volume. The notes of the present editor are indicated by Arabic numerals.

Most of the photographs here reproduced were taken by the editor in 1893 and 1894, but those of Artillery Lake were taken by Mr. J. W. Tyrrell in 1900, and the Eskimo implements of native copper were obtained by him at that time.

Several additional maps have been added. Among these are the portions of Cook's and Pennant's maps of parts of North America showing the first published records of Hearne's courses; a map of the Coppermine River as surveyed by Sir John Franklin in 1821; and a general map of Northern Canada drawn on the same scale and projection as Hearne's large map, and with his routes laid down as correctly as it has been possible for me to determine them. The latter map is much more easily compared with Hearne's original map than one drawn on the polyconic projection in common use at the present time.

I wish to acknowledge my indebtedness to Mr. Edward A. Preble of the Biological Survey, Washington, D.C., U.S.A., author of "A Biological Investigation of the Hudson Bay Region" and "A Biological Investigation of the Athabaska-Mackenzie Region," who has so kindly annotated Chapter X. on the fauna and flora of Hudson Bay, and has also added the notes to which his initials are attached in other parts of the volume.

J. B. TYRRELL.

TORONTO, *February 1, 1910.*

FOOTNOTES:

[1] This is an error, as the fort was neither rebuilt nor refortified.

[2] The results of their observations were published in the *Philosophical Transactions*, vol. lix. (1769), pp. 467 and 480, and vol. lx. (1770), pp. 100 and 137.

[3] "Report on the Dubawnt, Kazan, and Ferguson Rivers," by J. B. Tyrrell. "Geological Survey of Canada," Part F, vol. ix. 1896. Ottawa, 1897.

[4] "Six Years' Residence in Hudson's Bay," by J. Robson, 1752, p. 15. Robson strongly urged an overland expedition to discover the copper, p. 60.

[5] Hudson's Bay Report, 1749, p. 230.

[6] Ibid., p. 271.

[7] Hudson's Bay Report, 1749, p. 226.

[8] Henry Kelsey's account of this journey has given rise to a good deal of dispute and scepticism. It gives me the impression that it is a story written from memory years after the journey was performed, but his general description of the country on the Red Deer River just north of the Province of Manitoba, and of the plains of Saskatchewan to the south-west of it, is too clear to be mistaken. I am indebted to Professor W. H. Holmes, Director of the United States Bureau of Ethnology, for assistance in identifying the "Naywatamee poets" with the Mandan Indians.

[9] As farther evidence that this expedition was undertaken solely for the purpose of obtaining a knowledge of the whereabouts of the copper deposits, Edward Umfreville, who was employed as a writer at York Factory in Hearne's time, makes the following interesting statement: "Some years since, the Company being informed that the Indians frequently brought fine pieces of copper to their Settlements on Churchill River, they took into consideration, and appointed a person (S. Hearne) with proper assistants, to survey and examine the river where the valuable acquisition was supposed to be concealed."—*The Present State of Hudson's Bay*, by Edward Umfreville, p. 45. London, 1790.

[10] Mr. Beckles Willson, in his book "The Great Company," says, on I know not what authority, that it was £200.

[11] "Cook's Third Voyage," vol. i. Introduction, p. lxxxi. London, 1784. For purposes of comparison, the portion of this map which refers to Hearne is republished at the end of the present volume. It is stated by Beckles Willson in "The Great Company" that short accounts of his journey had been published in 1773 and again in 1778-80, but though diligent search has been made for these accounts in the British Museum and elsewhere, no trace of them can be found.

[12] "Le Gouverneur *Hearne* avait fait, en 1772, un voyage par terre vers le Nord, en partant du fort Churchill dans la Baie de Hudson, '*Samuel Hearne partit du fort du Prince de Galles le 7 Décembre 1770*,' voyage dont on attend les détails avec impatience; le journal manuscrit en fut trouvé par *la Pérouse* dans les papiers de ce Gouverneur, qui insista pour qu'il lui fût laissé comme sa propriété particulière. Ce voyage ayant été fait néanmoins par ordre de la Compagnie de Hudson, dans la vue d'acquérir des connaissances sur la partie du Nord de l'Amérique, le journal pouvait bien être censé appartenir à cette Compagnie, et par conséquent être dévolu au vainqueur; cependant *la Pérouse* céda, par bonté, aux instances du Gouverneur *Hearne*, et lui rendit le manuscrit; mais à la condition expresse de la faire imprimer et publier dès qu'il serait de retour en Angleterre. Cette condition ne paraît pas avoir été remplie jusqu'à present.[A] Espérons que la remarque qui en est faite, rendue publique, produira l'effet attendu ou qu'elle engagera le Gouverneur à faire connaître si la Compagnie de Hudson, qui redoute qu'on ne s'immisce dans ses affaires et son commerce, s'est opposée à sa publication."—Discours préliminaire du Voyage de *la Pérouse* autour du monde, pp. xlvi et xlvii de l'in-4°.

[A] Le Voyage de Samuel Hearne a été publié à Londres en l'an 3, et celui de *la Pérouse* à Paris, en l'an 6. (*Note du Traducteur du Voyage de* Samuel Hearne.)

[24]

M^r. Samuel Hearne
Late Chief at Prince of Wales's Fort.
Hudson's Bay.
Published as the Act directs by J. Sewell, Cornhill Augt. 1st. 1796
From the "European Magazine," June, 1797

[25]

A
JOURNEY
FROM
Prince of Wales's Fort, in
Hudson's Bay,
TO
THE NORTHERN OCEAN.

UNDERTAKEN
BY ORDER OF THE HUDSON'S BAY COMPANY.
**FOR THE DISCOVERY OF
COPPER MINES, A NORTH WEST PASSAGE, &c.**
In the Years 1769, 1770, 1771, & 1772.

By SAMUEL HEARNE.

LONDON:

Printed for A. STRAHAN and T. CADELL:
And Sold by T. CADELL Jun. and W. DAVIES, (Successors to
Mr. CADELL,) in the Strand.

1795

[26]

[27]

TO
SAMUEL WEGG, ESQ., GOVERNOR,
SIR JAMES WINTER LAKE, DEPUTY GOVERNOR,
AND
THE REST OF THE COMMITTEE
OF THE HONOURABLE
HUDSON'S BAY COMPANY.

HONOURABLE SIRS,

As the following Journey was undertaken at your Request and Expence, I feel it no less my Duty than my Inclination to address it to you; hoping that my humble Endeavours to relate, in a plain and unadorned Style, the various Circumstances and Remarks which {iv} occurred during that Journey, will meet with your Approbation.

I am, with much Esteem and Gratitude,
HONOURABLE   SIRS,
Your   most   obedient,   and
most   obliged   humble   Servant,
SAMUEL   HEARNE.
[28]

---

[29]

PREFACE.

Mr. Dalrymple, in one of his Pamphlets relating to Hudson's Bay, has been so very particular in his observations on my Journey, as to remark, that I have not explained the construction of the Quadrant which I had the misfortune to break in my second Journey to the North. It was a Hadley's Quadrant, with a bubble attached to it for a horizon, and made by Daniel Scatlif of Wapping. But as no instrument of the same principle could be procured when I was setting out on my last Journey, an old Elton's Quadrant, which had been upwards of thirty years at the Fort, was the only instrument I could then be provided with, in any respect proper for making observations with on the land.

Mr. Dalrymple also observes, that I only inserted in my last Journal to the Company, one observation for the latitude, which may be true; but I had, nevertheless, several others during that Journey, particularly at Snow-bird Lake, Thelwey-aza-yeth, and Clowey, exclusive of that mentioned in the Journal taken at Conge-cathawhachaga. But when I was on that Journey, and for several {vi} years after, I little thought that any remarks made in it would ever have attracted the notice of the Public; if I had, greater pains might and would have been taken to render it more worthy of their attention than it now is. At that time my ideas and ambition extended no farther than to give my employers such an account of my proceedings as might be satisfactory to them, and answer the purpose which they had in view; little thinking it would ever[30] come under the inspection of so ingenious and indefatigable a geographer as Mr. Dalrymple must be allowed to be. But as the case has turned out otherwise, I have at my leisure hours recopied all my Journals into one book, and in some instances added to the remarks I had before made; not so much for the information of those who are critics in geography, as for the amusement of candid and indulgent readers, who may perhaps feel themselves in some measure gratified, by having the face of a country brought to their view, which has hitherto been entirely unknown to every European except myself. Nor will, I flatter myself, a description of the modes of living, manners, and customs of the natives (which, though long known, have never been described), be less acceptable to the curious.

I cannot help observing, that I feel myself rather hurt at Mr. Dalrymple's rejecting my latitude in so peremptory a manner, and in so great a proportion, as he has done; because, before I arrived at Conge-cathawhachaga, the {vii} Sun did not set during the whole night: a proof that I was then to the Northward of the Arctic Circle. I may be allowed to add, that when I was at the Copper River, on the eighteenth of July, the Sun's declination was but 21°, and yet it was certainly some height above the horizon at midnight; how much, as I did not *then* remark, I will not *now* take upon me to say; but it proves that the latitude was considerably more than Mr. Dalrymple will admit of. His assertion, that no grass is to be found on the (rocky) coast of Greenland farther North than the latitude of 65°, is no proof there should not be any in a much higher latitude in the interior parts of North America. For, in the first place, I think it is more than probable, that the Copper River empties itself into a sort of inland Sea, or extensive Bay, somewhat like that of Hudson's: and it is well known that no part of the coast of Hudson's Straits, nor those of Labradore, at least for some degrees South of them, any more than the East coast of Hudson's Bay, till we arrive[31] near Whale River, have any trees on them; while the West coast of the Bay in the same latitudes, is well clothed with timber. Where then is the ground for such an assertion? Had Mr. Dalrymple considered this circumstance only, I flatter myself he would not so hastily have objected to woods and grass being seen in similar situations, though in a much higher latitude. Neither can the reasoning which Mr. Dalrymple derives from the error I committed in estimating the distance to Cumberland House, any way affect the question under {viii} consideration; because that distance being chiefly in longitude, I had no means of correcting it by an observation, which was not the case here.

I do not by any means wish to enter into a dispute with, or incur the displeasure of Mr. Dalrymple; but thinking, as I do, that I have not been treated in so liberal a manner as I ought to have been, he will excuse me for endeavouring to convince the Public that his objections are in a great measure without foundation. And having done so, I shall quit the disagreeable subject with declaring, that if any part of the following sheets should afford amusement to Mr. Dalrymple, or any other of my readers, it will be the highest gratification I can receive, and the only recompence I desire to obtain for the hardships and fatigue which I underwent in procuring the information contained in them.

Being well assured that several learned and curious gentlemen are in possession of manuscript copies of, or extracts from, my Journals, as well as copies of the Charts, I have been induced to make this copy as correct as possible, and to publish it; especially as I observe that scarcely any two of the publications that contain extracts from my Journals, agree in the dates when I arrived at, or departed from, particular places. To rectify those disagreements I applied to the Governor and Committee of the Hudson's Bay Company, for leave to peruse my original Journals. This was granted with the greatest affability {ix} and politeness; as well as a sight of all[32] my Charts relative to this Journey. With this assistance I have been enabled to rectify some inaccuracies that had, by trusting too much to memory, crept into this copy; and I now offer it to the Public under authentic dates and the best authorities, however widely some publications may differ from it.

I have taken the liberty to expunge some passages which were inserted in the original copy, as being no ways interesting to the Public, and several others have undergone great alterations; so that, in fact, the whole may be said to be new-modelled, by being blended with a variety of Remarks and Notes that were not inserted in the original copy, but which my long residence in the country has enabled me to add.

The account of the principal quadrupeds and birds that frequent those Northern regions in Summer, as well as those which never migrate, though not described in a scientific manner, may not be entirely unacceptable to the most scientific zoologists; and to those who are unacquainted with the technical terms used in zoology, it may perhaps be more useful and entertaining, than if I had described them in the most classical manner. But I must not conclude this Preface, without acknowledging, in the most ample manner, the assistance I have received from the perusal of Mr Pennant's Arctic Zoology, which has enabled me to give several of the birds their proper {x} names; for those by which they are known in Hudson's Bay are purely Indian, and of course quite unknown to every European who has not resided in that country.

To conclude, I cannot sufficiently regret the loss of a considerable Vocabulary of the Northern Indian Language, containing sixteen folio pages, which was lent to the late Mr. Hutchins, then Corresponding Secretary to the Company, to copy for Captain Duncan, when he went on discoveries to Hudson's Bay in the year one thousand seven hundred and ninety. But Mr. Hutchins dying soon after, the Vocabulary was taken away with the rest of his effects, and cannot now be recovered; and memory, at this time, will by no means serve to replace it.

[33]

CONTENTS.

INTRODUCTION

41

CHAP. I.

Transactions from my leaving Prince of Wales's Fort on my first Expedition, till our Arrival there again.

Set off from the Fort; arrive at Po-co-ree-kis-co River—One of the Northern Indians deserts—Cross Seal River, and walk on the barren grounds—Receive wrong information concerning the distance of the woods—Weather begins to be very cold, provisions all expended, and nothing to be got—Strike to the Westward, arrive at the woods, and kill three deer—Set forward in the North West quarter, see the tracks of musk-oxen and deer, but killed none— Very short of provisions—Chawchinahaw wants us to return— Neither he nor his crew contribute to our maintenance—He influences several of the Indians to desert—Chawchinahaw and all his crew leave us—Begin our return to the Factory; kill a few partridges, the first meal we had had for several days—Villany of one of the home Indians and his wife, who was a Northern Indian woman—Arrive at the Seal River, kill two deer; partridges plenty— Meet a strange Northern Indian, accompany him to his tent, usage received there; my Indians assist in killing some beaver—Proceed toward home, and arrive at the Fort

61

CHAP. II.

Transactions from our Arrival at the Factory, to my leaving it again, and during the First Part of my Second Journey, till I had the misfortune to break the Quadrant.

Transactions at the Factory—Proceed on my second journey—
Arrive at Seal River—Deer plentiful for some time—Method of
angling fish under the ice—Set our fishing-nets—Method of setting
nets under the ice—My guide [xii] proposes to stay till the geese
should begin to fly; his reasons accepted—Pitch our tent in the best
[34]manner—Method of pitching a tent in Winter—Fish plentiful for
some time; grow very scarce; in great want of provisions—Manner
of employing my time—My guide killed two deer—Move to the
place they were lying at; there kill several more deer, and three
beavers—Soon in want of provisions again—Many Indians join us
from the Westward—We begin to move towards the barren
ground—Arrive at She-than-nee, there suffer great distress for want
of provisions—Indians kill two swans and three geese—Geese and
other birds of passage plentiful—Leave She-than-nee, and arrive at
Beralzone—One of my companions guns bursts, and shatters his left
hand—Leave Beralzone, and get on the barren ground, clear of all
woods—Throw away our sledges and snow shoes—Each person
takes a load on his back; my part of the luggage—Exposed to many
hardships—Several days without victuals—Indians kill three musk-
oxen, but for want of fire are obliged to eat the meat raw—Fine
weather returns; make a fire; effects of long fasting; stay a day or
two to dry some meat in the Sun—Proceed to the Northward, and
arrive at Cathawhachaga; there find some tents of Indians—A
Northern Leader called Keelshies meets us; send a letter by him to
the Governor—Transactions at Cathawhachaga; leave it and
proceed to the Northward—Meet several Indians—My guide not
willing to proceed; his reasons for it—Many more Indians join us—
Arrive at Doobaunt Whoie River—Manner of ferrying over rivers
in the Northern Indian canoes—No rivers in those parts in a useful
direction for the natives—Had nearly lost the quadrant and all the
powder—Some reflections on our situation, and conduct of the
Indians—Find the quadrant and part of the powder—Observe for
the latitude—Quadrant broke—Resolve to return again to the
Factory

CHAP. III.

Transactions from the time the Quadrant was broken, till I arrived at the Factory.

Several strange Indians join us from the Northward—They plunder me of all I had; but did not plunder the Southern Indians—My guide plundered—We begin our return to the Factory—Meet with other Indians, who join our company—Collect deer-skins for clothing, but could not get them {xiii} dressed—Suffer much hardship from the want of tents and warm clothing—Most of the Indians leave us—Meet with Matonabbee—Some account of him, and his behaviour to me and the Southern Indians—We remain in his company some time—His observations on my two unsuccessful attempts—We leave him, and proceed to a place to which he directed us, in order to make snow-shoes and sledges—Join Matonabbee [35]again, and proceed towards the Factory in his company—Ammunition runs short—Myself and four Indians set off post for the Factory—Much bewildered in a snow storm; my dog is frozen to death; we lie in a bush of willows—Proceed on our journey—Great difficulty in crossing a jumble of rocks—Arrive at the Fort

96

CHAP. IV.

Transactions during our Stay at Prince of Wales's Fort, and the former Part of our third Expedition, till our Arrival at Clowey, where we built Canoes, in May 1771.

Preparations for our departure—Refuse to take any of the home-guard Indians with me—By so doing, I offend the Governor—Leave the Fort a third time—My instructions on this expedition—Provisions of all kinds very scarce—Arrive at the woods, where we kill some deer—Arrive at Island Lake—Matonabbee taken ill—Some remarks thereon—Join the remainder of the Indians' families—Leave Island Lake—Description thereof—Deer plentiful—Meet a strange Indian—Alter our course from West North West to West by South—Cross Cathawhachaga River, Cossed Lake, Snow-Bird Lake, and Pike Lake—Arrive at a tent of strangers, who are employed in snaring deer in a pound— Description of a pound—Method of proceeding—Remarks thereon—Proceed on our journey—Meet with several parties of Indians; by one of whom I sent a letter to the Governor at Prince of Wales's Fort—Arrive at Thleweyazayeth—Employment there— Proceed to the North North West and North—Arrive at Clowey— One of the Indian's wives taken in labour—Remarks thereon— Customs observed by the Northern Indians on those occasions

106

{xiv} CHAP. V.

Transactions at Clowey, and on our Journey, till our Arrival at the Copper-mine River.

Several strange Indians join us—Indians employed in building canoes; description and use of them—More Indians join us, to the amount of some hundreds—Leave Clowey—Receive intelligence that Keelshies was near us—Two young men dispatched for my letters and goods—Arrive at Peshew Lake; cross part of it, and make a large smoke—One of Matonabbee's wives elopes—Some remarks on the natives—Keelshies joins us, and delivers my letters, but the goods were all expended—A Northern Indian wishes to [36]take one of Matonabbee's wives from him; matters compromised, but had like to have proved fatal to my progress—Cross Peshew Lake, when I make proper arrangements for the remainder of my journey— Many Indians join our party, in order to make war on the Esquimaux at the Copper River—Preparations made for that purpose while at Clowey—Proceed on our journey to the North—Some remarks on the way—Cross Cogead Lake on the ice—The sun did not set— Arrive at Congecathawhachaga—Find several Copper Indians there—Remarks and transactions during our stay at Congecathawhachaga—Proceed on our journey—Weather very bad—Arrive at the Stoney Mountains—Some account of them—Cross part of Buffalo Lake on the ice—Saw many musk-oxen—Description of them—Went with some Indians to view Grizzlebear Hill—Join a strange Northern Indian Leader, called O'lye, in company with some Copper Indians—Their behaviour to me—Arrive at the Copper-mine River

133

CHAP. VI.

Transactions at the Copper-mine River, and till we joined all the Women to the South of Cogead Lake.

Some Copper Indians join us—Indians send three spies down the river—Begin my survey—Spies return, and give an account of five tents of Esquimaux—Indians consult the best method to steal on them in the night, and {xv} kill them while asleep—Cross the river—Proceedings of the Indians as they advance towards the Esquimaux tents—The Indians begin the massacre while the poor Esquimaux are asleep, and slay them all—Much affected at the sight of one young woman killed close to my feet—The behaviour of the Indians on this occasion—Their brutish treatment of the dead bodies—Seven more tents seen on the opposite side of the river—The Indians harass them, till they fly to a shoal in the river for safety—Behaviour of the Indians after killing those Esquimaux—Cross the river, and proceed to the tents on that side—Plunder their tents, and destroy their utensils—Continue my survey to the river's mouth—Remarks there—Set out on my return—Arrive at one of the Copper-mines—Remarks on it—Many attempts made to induce the Copper Indians to carry their own goods to market—Obstacles to it—Villany and cruelty of Keelshies to some of those poor Indians—Leave the Copper-mine, and walk at an amazing rate till we join the women, by the side of Cogead Whoie—Much foot-foundered—The appearance very alarming, but soon changes for the better—Proceed to the southward, and join the remainder of the women and children—Many other Indians arrive with them

[37]

CHAP. VII.

Remarks from the Time the Women joined us till our Arrival at the Athapuscow Lake.

Several of the Indians sick—Methods used by the conjurors to relieve one man, who recovers—Matonabbee and his crew proceed to the South West—Most of the other Indians separate, and go their respective ways—Pass by White Stone Lake—Many deer killed merely for their skins—Remarks thereon, and on the deer, respecting seasons and places—Arrive at Point Lake—One of the Indian's wives being sick, is left behind to perish above-ground—Weather very bad, but deer plenty—Stay some time at Point Lake to dry meat, &c.—Winter set in—Superstitious customs observed by my companions, after they had killed the Esquimaux at Copper River—A violent gale of wind oversets my tent and breaks my quadrant—Some Copper and Dog-ribbed Indians join us—Indians propose to go to the Athapuscow Country to kill moose—Leave Point Lake, and arrive at the wood's edge—Arrive at Anawd Lake—Transactions there—Remarkable instance of a man being cured of the palsey by the conjurors—Leave Anawd Lake—Arrive at the great Athapuscow Lake

209

{xvi} CHAP. VIII.

Transactions and Remarks from our Arrival on the South Side of the Athapuscow Lake, till our Arrival at Prince of Wales's Fort on Churchill River.

Cross the Athapuscow Lake—Description of it and its productions, as far as could be discovered in Winter, when the snow was on the ground—Fish found in the lake—Description of the buffalo; of the moose or elk, and the method of dressing their skins—Find a woman alone that had not seen a human face for more than seven months—Her account how she came to be in that situation; and her curious method of procuring a livelihood—Many of my Indians wrestled for her—Arrive at the Great Athapuscow River—Walk along the side of the River for several days, and then strike off to the Eastward—Difficulty in getting through the woods in many places—Meet with some strange Northern Indians on their return from the Fort—Meet more strangers, whom my companions plundered, and from whom they took one of their young women—Curious manner of life which those strangers lead, and the reason they gave for roving so far from their usual residence—Leave the fine level country of the Athapuscows, and arrive at the Stony Hills of the [38]Northern Indian Country—Meet some strange Northern Indians, one of whom carried a letter for me to Prince of Wales's Fort, in March one thousand seven hundred and seventy-one, and now gave me an answer to it, dated twentieth of June following—Indians begin preparing wood-work and birch-rind for canoes—The equinoctial gale very severe—Indian method of running the moose deer down by speed of foot—Arrival at Theeleyaza River—See some strangers—The brutality of my companions—A tremendous gale and snow-drift—Meet with more strangers; remarks on it—Leave all the elderly people and children, and proceed directly to the Fort—Stop to build canoes, and then advance—Several of the Indians die through hunger, and many others are obliged to decline the journey for want of ammunition—A violent storm and inundation, that forced us to the top of a high hill, where we suffered great distress for more than two days—Kill several deer—The Indians' method of preserving the flesh without the assistance of salt—See several Indians that were going to Knapp's Bay—Game of all kinds remarkably plentiful—Arrive at the Factory

252

{xvii} CHAP. IX.

A short Description of the Northern Indians, also a farther Account of their Country, Manufactures, Customs, &c.

An account of the persons and tempers of the Northern Indians—They possess a great deal of art and cunning—Are very guilty of fraud when in their power, and generally exact more for their furs than any other tribe of Indians—Always dissatisfied, yet have their good qualities—The men in general jealous of their wives—Their marriages—Girls always betrothed when children, and their reasons for it—Great care and confinement of young girls from the age of eight or nine years—Divorces common among those people—The women are less prolific than in warmer countries—Remarkable piece of superstition observed by the women at particular periods—Their art in making it an excuse for a temporary separation from their husbands on any little quarrel—Reckoned very unclean on those occasions—The Northern Indians frequently, for the want of firing, are obliged to eat their meat raw—Some through necessity obliged to boil it in vessels made of the rind of the birch-tree—A remarkable dish among those people—The young animals always cut out of their dams, eaten, and accounted a great delicacy—The parts of generation of all animals eat by the men and boys—Manner of passing their time, and method of killing deer in Summer with bows and arrows—Their tents, dogs, sledges, &c.—Snow-shoes—Their partiality to domestic vermin—Utmost extent of the Northern Indian country—Face of the country—Species of [39]fish—A peculiar kind of moss useful for the support of man—Northern Indian method of catching fish, either with hooks or nets—Ceremony observed when two parties of those people meet—Diversions in common use—A singular disorder which attacks some of those people—Their superstition with respect to the death of their friends—Ceremony observed on those occasions—Their ideas of the first inhabitants of the world—No form of religion among them—Remarks on that circumstance—The extreme misery to which old age is exposed—Their opinion of the *Aurora Borealis*, &c.—Some account of Matonabbee, and his services to his country, as well as to the Hudson's Bay Company

{xviii} CHAP. X.

An Account of the principal Quadrupeds found in the Northern Parts of Hudson's Bay: The Buffalo, Moose, Musk-ox, Deer, and Beaver—A capital Mistake cleared up respecting the We-was-kish.

Animals with Canine Teeth: The Wolf—Foxes of various colours—Lynx, or Wild Cat—Polar, or White Bear—Black Bear—Brown Bear—Wolverene—Otter—Jackash—Wejack—Skunk—Pine Martin—Ermine, or Stote.

Animals with cutting Teeth: The Musk Beaver—Porcupine—Varying Hare—American Hare—Common Squirrel—Ground Squirrel—Mice of various kinds—and the Castor Beaver.

The Pinnated Quadrupeds with finlike Feet, found in Hudson's Bay, are but three in number, viz.: The Walrus, or Sea-Horse—Seal—and Sea-Unicorn.

The Species of Fish found in the Salt Water of Hudson's Bay are also few in number: being the Black Whale—White Whale—Salmon—and Kepling.

Shell-fish, and empty Shells of several kinds, found on the Sea Coast near Churchill River.

Frogs of various sizes and colours; also a great variety of Grubbs, and other Insects, always found in a frozen state during Winter, but when exposed to the heat of a slow fire, are soon re-animated.

An account of some of the principal Birds found in the Northern Parts of Hudson's Bay; as well those that only migrate there in Summer, as those that are known to brave the coldest Winters: [40]Eagles of various kinds—Hawks of various sizes and plumage— White or Snowy Owl—Grey or mottled Owl—Cob-a-dee-cooch— Raven—Cinerious Crow—Wood Pecker—Ruffed Grouse— Pheasant—Wood Partridge—Willow Partridge—Rock Partridge— Pigeon—Red-breasted Thrush—Grosbeak—Snow Bunting— White-crowned Bunting—Lapland Finch, two sorts—Lark— Titmouse—Swallow—Martin—Hopping Crane—Brown Crane— Bitron—Carlow, two sorts—Jack Snipe—Red Godwart—Plover— Black Gullemet—Northern Diver—Black-throated Diver—Red-throated Diver—White Gull—Grey Gull—Black-head—Pelican— Goosander—Swans of two species—Common {xix} Grey Goose— Canada Goose—White or Snow Goose—Blue Goose—Horned Wavy—Laughing Goose—Barren Goose—Brent Goose—Dunter Goose—Bean Goose.

The species of Water-Fowl usually called Duck, that resort to those Parts annually, are in great variety; but those that are most esteemed are, the Mallard Duck—Long-tailed Duck—Wigeon, and Teal.

Of the Vegetable Productions as far North as Churchill River, particularly the most useful; such as the Berry-bearing Bushes, &c.: Gooseberry—Cranberry—Heathberry—Dewater-berry—Black

Currans—Juniper-berry—Partridge-berry—Strawberry—Eye-berry—Blue-berry—and a small species of Hips.

Burridge—Coltsfoot—Sorrel—Dandelion.

Wish-a-capucca—Jackashey-puck—Moss of various sorts—Grass of several kinds—and Vetches.

The Trees found so far North near the Sea, consist only of Pines—Juniper—Small Poplar—Bush-willows—and Creeping Birch

335

[41]

INTRODUCTION.

For many years it was the opinion of all ranks of people, that the Hudson's Bay Company were averse to making discoveries of every kind; and being content with the profits of their small capital, as it was then called, did not want to increase their trade. What might have been the ideas of former members of the Company respecting the first part of these charges I cannot say, but I am well assured that they, as well as the present members, have always been ready to embrace every plausible plan for extending the trade. As a proof of this assertion, I need only mention the vast sums of money which they have expended at different times in endeavouring to establish fisheries, though without success: and the following Journey, together with the various attempts made by Bean, Christopher, Johnston, and Duncan,[13] to find a North West passage, are recent proofs that the present members are as desirous of making discoveries, as they are of extending their trade.

That[42] air of mystery, and affectation of secrecy, perhaps, which formerly attended some of the Company's proceedings in the Bay, might give rise to those conjectures; and the unfounded assertions and unjust aspersions of Dobbs, {xxii} Ellis, Robson, Dragge, and the American Traveller,[14] the only Authors that have written on Hudson's Bay, and who have all, from motives of interest or revenge, taken a particular pleasure in arraigning the conduct of the Company, without having any real knowledge of their proceedings, or any experience in their service, on which to found their charges, must have contributed to confirm the public in that opinion. Most of those Writers, however, advance such notorious absurdities, that none except those who are already prejudiced against the Company can give them credit.[B]

Robson, from his six years' residence in Hudson's Bay and in the Company's service, might naturally have been supposed to know something of the climate and soil immediately round the Factories at which he resided; but the whole of his book is evidently written with prejudice, and dictated by a spirit of revenge, because his romantic and inconsistent schemes were rejected by the Company. Besides, it is well known that Robson was no more than a tool in the hand of Mr. Dobbs.

The[43] American Traveller, though a more elegant writer, has still less claim to our indulgence, as his assertions are {xxiii} a greater tax on our credulity. His saying that he discovered several large lumps of the finest virgin copper[C] is such a palpable falsehood that it needs no refutation. No man, either English or Indian, ever found a bit of copper in that country to the South of the seventy-first degree of latitude,[16] unless it had been accidentally dropped by some of the far Northern Indians in their way to the Company's Factory.

The natives who range over, rather than inhabit, the large tract of land which lies to the North of Churchill River, having repeatedly brought samples of copper to the Company's Factory, many of our people conjectured that it was found not far from our settlements; and as the Indians informed them that the mines were not very distant from a large river, it was generally supposed that this river must empty itself into Hudson's Bay; as they could by no means think that any set of people, however wandering their manner of life might be, could ever traverse so large a tract of country as to pass the Northern boundary of that Bay, and particularly without the assistance of water-carriage. The following Journal, however, will show how much those people have been mistaken, and prove also the improbability of putting their favourite scheme of mining into practice.

[44]

{xxiv} The accounts of this grand River, which some have turned into a Strait, together with the samples of copper, were brought to the Company's Factory at Churchill River immediately after its first establishment, in the year one thousand seven hundred and fifteen; and it does not appear that any attempts were made to discover either the river or mines till the year one thousand seven hundred and nineteen, when the Company fitted out a ship, called the *Albany*

Frigate, Captain George Barlow,[D] and a sloop {xxv} called the *Discovery*, Captain David Vaughan. The sole command of this expedition, however, was given to Mr. James Knight, a man of great experience in the Company's service, who had been many years Governor at the different Factories in the Bay, and who had made the first settlement at Churchill River. Notwithstanding the experience Mr. Knight might have had of the Company's business, and his knowledge of those parts of the Bay where he had resided, it cannot be supposed he was well acquainted with the nature of the business in which he then engaged, having nothing to direct him but the slender and imperfect accounts which he had received from the Indians, who at that time were little known, and less understood.

[45]

{xxvi} Those disadvantages, added to his advanced age, he being then near eighty, by no means discouraged this bold adventurer; who was so prepossessed of his success, and of the great advantage that would arise from his discoveries, that he procured, and took with him, some large iron-bound chests, to hold gold dust and other valuables, which he fondly flattered himself were to be found in those parts.

The first paragraph of the Company's Orders to Mr. Knight on this occasion appears to be as follows:

"*To* Captain James Knight.

"*4th June, 1719.*

"Sir,

"From the experience we have had of your abilities in the management of our affairs, we have, upon your application to us, fitted out the *Albany* frigate, Captain George Barlow, and the *Discovery*, Captain David Vaughan, Commander, upon a discovery to the Northward; and to that end have given you power and authority to act and do all things relating to the said voyage, the navigation of the said ship and sloop only excepted; and have given orders and instructions to our said Commanders for that purpose.

"You are, with the first opportunity of wind and weather, to depart from Gravesend on your intended {xxvii} voyage, and by God's permission, to find out the Straits of Anian, in order to discover gold and other valuable commodities to the Northward, &c. &c."

Mr. Knight soon left Gravesend, and proceeded on his [46]voyage; but the ship not returning to England that year, as was expected, it was judged that she had wintered in Hudson's Bay; and having on board a good stock of provisions, a house in frame, together with all necessary mechanics, and a great assortment of trading goods, little or no thoughts were entertained of their not being in safety; but as neither ship nor sloop returned to England in the following year, (one thousand seven hundred and twenty), the Company were much alarmed for their welfare; and, by their ship which went to Churchill in the year one thousand seven hundred and twenty-one, they sent orders for a sloop called the *Whale-Bone*, John Scroggs Master, to go in search of them; but the ship not arriving in Churchill till late in the year, those orders could not be put in execution till the Summer following (one thousand seven hundred and twenty-two).

The North West coast of Hudson's Bay being little known in those days, and Mr. Scroggs finding himself greatly embarrassed with shoals and rocks, returned to Prince of Wales's Fort without making any certain discovery respecting the above ship or sloop; for all the marks he saw among the Esquimaux at Whale Cove scarcely {xxviii} amounted to the spoils which might have been made from a trifling accident, and consequently could not be considered as signs of a total shipwreck.

The strong opinion which then prevailed in Europe respecting the probability of a North West passage by the way of Hudson's Bay, made many conjecture that Messrs. Knight and Barlow had found that passage, and had gone through it into the South Sea, by the way of California. Many years elapsed without any other convincing proof occurring to the contrary, except that Middleton, Ellis, Bean, Christopher, and Johnston, had not been able to find any such passage. And notwithstanding a sloop was annually sent to the Northward on discovery, and to trade with the Esquimaux, it was the Summer of one thousand seven hundred and sixty-seven,[47] before we had positive proofs that poor Mr. Knight and Captain Barlow had been lost in Hudson's Bay.

The Company were now carrying on a black whale fishery, and Marble Island was made the place of rendezvous, not only on account of the commodiousness of the harbour, but because it had been observed that the whales were more plentiful about that island than on any other part of the coast. This being the case, the boats, when on the look-out for fish, had frequent occasion to row close to the island, by which means they discovered a new harbour near the East end of it, at the head {xxix} of which they found guns, anchors, cables, bricks, a smith's anvil, and many other articles, which the hand of time had not defaced, and which being of no use to the natives, or too heavy to be removed by them, had not been taken from the place in which they were originally laid. The remains of the house, though pulled to pieces by the Esquimaux for the wood and iron, are yet very plain to be seen, as also the hulls, or more properly speaking, the bottoms of the ship and sloop, which lie sunk in about five fathoms water, toward the head of the harbour. The figure-head of the ship, and also the guns, &c. were sent home to the Company, and are certain proofs that Messrs. Knight and Barlow had been lost on that inhospitable island, where neither stick nor stump was to be seen, and which lies near sixteen miles from the main land. Indeed the main is little better, being a jumble of barren hills and rocks, destitute of every kind of herbage except moss and grass; and at that part, the woods are several hundreds of miles from the sea-side.

In the Summer of one thousand seven hundred and sixty-nine, while we were prosecuting the fishery, we saw several Esquimaux at this new harbour; and perceiving that one or two of them were greatly advanced in years, our curiosity was excited to ask them some questions concerning the above ship and sloop, which we were the better enabled to do by the assistance of an Esquimaux, who was then in the Company's[48] service as a linguist, and annually sailed in one of their vessels in that character. The {xxx} account which we received from them was full, clear, and unreserved, and the sum of it was to the following purport:

When the vessels arrived at this place (Marble Island) it was very late in the Fall, and in getting them into the harbour, the largest received much damage; but on being fairly in, the English began to build the house, their number at that time seeming to be about fifty. As soon as the ice permitted, in the following Summer, (one thousand seven hundred and twenty), the Esquimaux paid them another visit, by which time the number of the English was greatly reduced, and those that were living seemed very unhealthy. According to the account given by the Esquimaux they were then very busily employed, but about what they could not easily describe, probably in lengthening the long-boat; for at a little distance from the house there is now lying a great quantity of oak chips, which have been most assuredly made by carpenters.

Sickness and famine occasioned such havock among the English, that by the setting in of the second Winter their number was reduced to twenty. That Winter (one thousand seven hundred and twenty) some of the Esquimaux took up their abode on the opposite side of the harbour to that on which the English had built their houses,[E] and {xxxi} frequently supplied them with such provisions as they had, which chiefly consisted of whale's blubber and seal's flesh and train oil. When the Spring advanced, the Esquimaux went to the continent, and on their visiting Marble Island again, in the Summer of one thousand seven hundred and twenty-one, they only found five of the English alive, and those were in such distress for provisions that they eagerly eat the seal's flesh and whale's blubber quite raw, as they purchased it from the natives. This disordered them so much, that three of them died in a few days, and the other two, though very weak, made a shift to bury them. Those two survived many days after the rest, and frequently went to the top of an adjacent rock, and earnestly looked to the South and East, as if in expectation of some vessels coming to their relief. After continuing there a considerable time together, and nothing appearing in sight, they sat down close together, and wept bitterly. At length one of the two died, and the other's strength was so far exhausted, that he fell down and died also, in attempting to dig a grave for his companion. The {xxxii} sculls and other large bones of those two men are now lying above-ground close to the house. The longest liver was, according to the Esquimaux account, always employed in working of iron into implements for them; probably he was the armourer, or smith.

[49]

Some Northern Indians who came to trade at Prince of Wales's Fort in the Spring of the year one thousand seven hundred and sixty-eight, brought farther accounts of the grand river, as it was called, and also several pieces of copper, as samples of the produce of the mine near it; which determined Mr. Norton, who was then Governor at Churchill, to represent it to the Company as an affair worthy of their attention; and as he went that year to England, he had an opportunity of laying all the information he had received before the Board, with his opinion thereon, and the plan which he thought most likely to succeed in the discovery of those mines. In consequence of Mr. Norton's representations, the Committee resolved to send an intelligent person by land to[50] observe the longitude and latitude of the river's mouth, to make a chart of the country he might walk through, with such remarks as occurred to him during the Journey; when I was pitched on as a proper person to conduct the expedition. By the ship that went to Churchill in the Summer of one thousand seven hundred and sixty-nine, the Company sent out some astronomical instruments, very portable, and fit for such observations as they required me {xxxiii} to make, and at the same time requested me to undertake the Journey, promising to allow me at my return, a gratuity proportionable to the trouble and fatigue I might undergo in the expedition.[F]

[51]

{xxxiv} I did not hesitate to comply with the request of the Company, and in the November following, when some Northern Indians came to trade, Mr. Norton, who was then returned to the command of Prince of Wales's Fort, engaged such of them for my guides as he thought were most likely to answer the purpose; but none of them had been at this grand river. I was fitted out with everything thought necessary, and with ammunition to serve two years. I was to be accompanied by two of the Company's servants, two of the Home-guard[G] (Southern) Indians, {xxxv} and a sufficient number of Northern Indians to carry and haul my baggage, provide for me, &c. But for the better stating this arrangement, it will not be improper to insert my Instructions, which, with some occasional remarks thereon, will throw much light on the following Journal, and be the best method of proving how far those orders have been complied with, as well as shew my reasons for neglecting some parts as unnecessary, and the impossibility of putting other parts of them in execution.

[52]

"ORDERS *and* INSTRUCTIONS *for* Mr. SAMUEL HEARNE, *going on an Expedition by Land towards the Latitude 70° North, in order to gain a Knowledge of the Northern Indians Country, &c. on Behalf of the Honourable Hudson's Bay Company, in the Year 1769.*

"Mr. SAMUEL HEARNE,

"SIR,

"Whereas the Honourable Hudson's Bay Company have been informed by the report from Indians, that there is a great probability of considerable advantages to be expected from a better knowledge of their country by us, than what hitherto has been obtained; and as it is the Company's earnest desire to embrace every circumstance that may tend to the benefit of the said Company, or the Nation at large, they have requested you to conduct this Expedition; and as you {xxxvi} have readily consented to undertake the present Journey, you are hereby desired to proceed as soon as possible, with

William Isbester sailor, and Thomas Merriman landsman, as companions, they both being willing to accompany you; also two of the Home-guard Southern Indians, who are to attend and assist you during the Journey; and Captain Chawchinahaw, his Lieutenant Nabyah, and six or eight of the best Northern Indians we can procure, with a small part of their families, are to conduct you, provide for you, and assist you and your companions in every thing that lays in their power, having particular orders so to do.

"2dly, Whereas you and your companions are well fitted-out with every thing we think necessary, as also a sample of light trading goods; these you are to dispose of by way of presents (and not by way of trade) to such far-off Indians as you may meet with, and to smoke your Calimut[1] of Peace with their leaders, in order to establish a friendship with them. You are also to persuade them as much as possible from going to war with each other, to encourage them to exert themselves in procuring furrs and other articles for trade, and to assure them of good payment for them at the Company's Factory.

[53]

"It is sincerely recommended to you and your companions to treat the natives with civility, so as not to give {xxxvii} them any room for complaint or disgust, as they have strict orders not to give you the least offence, but are to aid and assist you in any matter you may request of them for the benefit of the undertaking.

"If any Indians you may meet, that are coming to the Fort, should be willing to trust you with either food or clothing, make your agreement for those commodities, and by them send me a letter, specifying the quantity of each article, and they shall be paid according to your agreement. And, according to the Company's orders, you are to correspond with me, or the Chief at Prince of Wales's Fort for the time being, at all opportunities: And as you have mathematical instruments with you, you are to send me, or the Chief for the time being, an account of what latitude and longitude you may be in at such and such periods, together with the heads of your proceedings; which accounts are to be remitted to the Company by the return of their ships.[I]

"3dly, The Indians who are now appointed your guides, are to conduct you to the borders of the Athapuscow[J] Indians country, where Captain Matonabbee {xxxviii} is to meet you[K] in the Spring of one thousand seven hundred and seventy, in order to conduct you to a river represented by the Indians to abound with copper ore, animals of the furr kind, &c., and which is said to be so far to the Northward, that in the middle of the Summer the Sun does not set, and is supposed by the Indians to empty itself into some ocean. This river, which is called by the Northern Indians Neetha-san-san-dazey, or the Far Off Metal River, you are, if possible, to trace to the mouth, and there determine the latitude and longitude as near as you can; but more particularly so if you find it navigable, and that a settlement can be made there with any degree of safety, or benefit to the Company.

[54] "Be careful to observe what mines are near the river, what water there is at the river's mouth, how far the woods are from the sea-side, the course of the river, the nature of the soil, and the productions of it; and make any other remarks that you may think will be either necessary or satisfactory. And if the said river be likely to be of any utility, take possession of it on behalf of the Hudson's Bay Company, by cutting your {xxxix} name on some of the rocks, as also the date of the year, month, &c.[LI]

[55]

"When you attempt to trace this or any other river, be careful that the Indians are furnished with a sufficient number of canoes for trying the depth of water, the strength of the current, &c. If by any unforeseen accident or disaster you should not be able to reach the before-mentioned river, it is earnestly recommended to you, if possible, to know the event of Wager Strait;[M] for it is represented by the last discoverers to terminate in small rivers and lakes. See how far the woods are from the navigable parts of it; and whether a settlement could with any propriety be made there. If this should prove unworthy of notice, you are to take the same method with Baker's Lake, which is the head of {xl} Bowden's or Chesterfield's Inlet;[N] as also with any other rivers you may meet with; and if likely to be of any utility, you are to take possession of them, as before mentioned, on the behalf of the Honourable Hudson's Bay Company. The draft of Bowden's Inlet and Wager Strait I send with you, that you may have a better idea of those places, in case of your visiting them.

"4thly, Another material point which is recommended to you, is to find out, if you can, either by your own travels, or by information from the Indians, whether there is a passage through this continent.[O] It will be {xli} very useful to clear up this point, if possible, in order to prevent farther doubts from arising hereafter respecting a passage out of Hudson's Bay[P] into the Western Ocean, as hath lately been represented by the American Traveller. The particulars of those remarks you are to insert in your Journal, to be remitted home to the Company.

[56]

"If you should want any supplies of ammunition, or other necessaries, dispatch some trusty Indians to the Fort with a letter, specifying the quantity of each article, and appoint a place for the said Indians to meet you again.

"When on your return, if at a proper time of the year, and you should be near any of the harbours that are frequented by the brigantine *Charlotte*, or the sloop *Churchill*, during their voyage to the Northward, and you should chuse to return in one of them, you are desired to make frequent smokes as you approach those harbours, and they will endeavour to receive you by making smokes in answer to yours; and as one thousand seven hundred and seventy-one will probably be the year in which you will return, the Masters of those vessels at that period shall have particular orders on that head.

[57] {xlii} "It will be pleasing to hear by the first opportunity, in what latitude and longitude you meet the Leader Matonabbee, and

how far he thinks it is to the Coppermine River, as also the probable time it may take before you can return. But in case any thing should prevent the said Leader from joining you, according to expectation, you are then to procure the best Indians you can for your guides, and either add to, or diminish, your number, as you may from time to time think most necessary for the good of the expedition.

"So I conclude, wishing you and your companions a continuance of health, together with a prosperous Journey, and a happy return in safety. Amen.

"MOSES NORTON, Governor.

"Dated at Prince of Wales's Fort, Churchill River, Hudson's "Bay, North America, November 6th, 1769."

Isbester and Merriman, mentioned in my Instructions, actually accompanied me during my first short attempt; but the Indians knowing them to be but common men, used them so indifferently, particularly in scarce times, that I was under some apprehensions of their being starved to death, and I thought myself exceedingly happy when I got them safe back to the Factory. This extraordinary behaviour of the Indians made me determine not to take any Europeans with me on my two last expeditions.

{xliii} With regard to that part of my Instructions which directs me to observe the nature of the soil, the productions thereof, &c., it must be observed, that during the whole time of my absence from the Fort, I was invariably confined to stony hills and barren plains all the Summer, and before we approached the woods in the Fall of the year, the ground was always covered with snow to a considerable depth; so that I never had an opportunity of seeing any of the small plants and shrubs to the Westward. But from appearances, and the slow and dwarfy growth of the woods, &c. (except in the Athapuscow[58] country), there is undoubtedly a greater scarcity of vegetable productions than at the Company's most Northern Settlement; and to the Eastward of the woods, on the barren grounds, whether hills or vallies, there is a total want of herbage except moss, on which the deer feed; a few dwarf willows creep among the moss; some wish-a-capucca and a little grass may be seen here and there, but the latter is scarcely sufficient to serve the geese and other birds of passage during their short stay in those parts, though they are always in a state of migration, except when they are breeding and in a moulting state.

In consequence of my complying with the Company's request, and undertaking this Journey, it is natural to suppose that every necessary arrangement was made for the easier keeping of my reckoning, &c., under the many inconveniences I must be unavoidably obliged to labour in such an expedition. I drew a Map on a large skin of parchment, that contained twelve degrees of latitude {xliv} North, and thirty degrees of longitude West, of Churchill Factory, and sketched all the West coast of the Bay on it, but left the interior parts blank, to be filled up during my Journey. I also prepared detached pieces on a much larger scale for every degree of latitude and longitude contained in the large Map. On those detached pieces I pricked off my daily courses and distance, and entered all lakes and rivers, &c., that I met with; endeavouring, by a strict enquiry of the natives, to find out the communication of one river with another, as also their connections with the many lakes with which that country abounds: and when opportunity offered, having corrected them by observations, I entered them in the general Map. These and several other necessary preparations, for the easier, readier, and more correctly keeping my Journal and Chart, were also adopted; but as to myself, little was required to be done, as the nature of travelling long journies in those countries will never admit of carrying even the most common article of clothing; so[59] that the traveller is obliged to depend on the country he passes through, for that article, as well as for provisions. Ammunition, useful iron-work, some tobacco, a few knives, and other indispensable articles, make a sufficient load for any one to carry that is going a journey likely to last twenty months, or two years. As that was the case, I only took the shirt and clothes I then had on, one spare coat, a pair of drawers, and as much cloth as would make me two or three pair of Indian stockings, which, together with a blanket for bedding, composed the whole of my stock of clothing.[60]

FOOTNOTES:

[13] John Bean was master of the Company's sloop trading to Knapp's Bay and Whale Cove in 1756 and subsequent years, but no more is known of him. Captain Christopher was sent from Churchill in 1761 to examine Chesterfield Inlet, and during that and the following years he explored it to the head of Baker Lake. Magnus Johnson explored Rankin Inlet in 1764. Captain Duncan in 1791 explored Corbett's Inlet, and in the following year made a re-examination of Chesterfield Inlet, and ascended a short distance up Dubawnt River.

[14] "An Account of the Countries adjoining to Hudson's Bay." By Arthur Dobbs. London, 1774.

"A Voyage to Hudson's Bay by the *Dobbs Galley* and *California* in the Years 1746 and 1747." By Henry Ellis. London, 1748.

"An Account of Six Years' Residence in Hudson's Bay." By Joseph Robson. London, 1752.

"An Account of a Voyage for the Discovery of a North-West Passage Performed in the Years 1746 and 1747," 2 vols. By the Clerk of the *California* [T. S. Dragge]. London, 1748.

"The American Traveller." By an Old and Experienced Trader [Alexander Cluny], London, 1769.

[B] Since the above was written, a Mr. Umfreville has published an account of Hudson's Bay, with the same ill-nature as the former Authors; and for no other reason than that of being disappointed in succeeding to a command in the Bay, though there was no vacancy for him.[15]

[15] Umfreville states (p. 3) that he entered the service of the Hudson's Bay Company in the capacity of writer at the salary of £15 a year, and continued in that employ eleven years. But some disagreement arising in point of salary he quitted the service. ("The Present State of Hudson's Bay." By Edward Umfreville. London, 1790.)

[C] American Traveller, p. 23.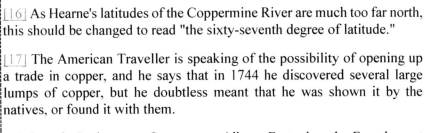

[16] As Hearne's latitudes of the Coppermine River are much too far north, this should be changed to read "the sixty-seventh degree of latitude."

[17] The American Traveller is speaking of the possibility of opening up a trade in copper, and he says that in 1744 he discovered several large lumps of copper, but he doubtless meant that he was shown it by the natives, or found it with them.

[D] Captain Barlow was Governor at Albany Fort when the French went over land from Canada to besiege it in 1704. The Canadians and their Indian guides lurked in the neighbourhood of Albany for several days before they made the attack, and killed many of the cattle that were grazing in the marshes. A faithful Home-Indian, who was on a hunting excursion, discovering those strangers, and supposing them to be enemies, immediately returned to the Fort, and informed the Governor of the circumstance, who gave little credit to it. However, every measure was taken for the defence of the Fort, and orders were given to the Master of a sloop that lay at some distance, to come to the Fort with all possible expedition on hearing a gun fired.

Accordingly, in the middle of the night, or rather in the morning, the French came before the Fort, marched up to the gate, and demanded entrance. Mr. Barlow, who was then on the watch, told them that the Governor was asleep, but he would get the keys immediately. The French, hearing this, expected no opposition, and flocked up to the gate as close as they could stand. Barlow took the advantage of this opportunity, and instead of opening the gate, only opened two port holes, where two six-pounders stood loaded with grape shot, which were instantly fired. This discharge killed great numbers of the French, and among them the Commander, who was an Irishman.

Such an unexpected reception made the remainder retire with great precipitation; and the Master of the sloop hearing the guns, made the best of his way up to the Fort; but some of the French who lay concealed under the banks of the river killed him, and all the boat's crew.

The French retired from this place with reluctance; for some of them were heard shooting in the neighbourhood of the Fort ten days after they were repulsed; and one man in particular walked up and down the platform leading from the gate of the Fort to the Launch for a whole day. Mr. Fullarton, who was then Governor at Albany, spoke to him in French, and offered him kind quarters if he chose to accept them; but to those proposals he made no reply, and only shook his head. Mr. Fullarton then told him, that unless he would resign himself up as a prisoner, he would most assuredly shoot him; on which the man advanced nearer the Fort, and Mr. Fullarton shot him out of his chamber window. Perhaps the hardships this poor man expected to encounter in his return to Canada, made him prefer death; but his refusing to receive quarter from so humane and generous an enemy as the English, is astonishing.

[E] I have seen the remains of those houses several times; they are on the West side of the harbour, and in all probability will be discernible for many years to come.

It is rather surprising, that neither Middleton, Ellis, Christopher, Johnston, nor Garbet, who have all of them been at Marble Island, and some of them often, ever discovered this harbour; particularly the last-mentioned gentleman, who actually sailed quite round the island in a very fine pleasant day in the Summer of 1766. But this discovery was reserved for a Mr. Joseph Stephens! a man of the least merit I ever knew, though he then had the command of a vessel called the *Success*, employed in the whale-fishery; and in the year 1769, had the command of the *Charlotte* given to him, a fine brig of one hundred tons; when I was his mate.

[F] The conditions offered me on this occasion cannot be better expressed than in the Company's own words, which I have transcribed from their private letter to me, dated 25th May 1769:

"From the good opinion we entertain of you, and Mr. Norton's recommendation, we have agreed to raise your wages to £——[18] *per annum* for two years, and have placed you in our Council at Prince of Wales's Fort; and we should have been ready to advance you to the command of the *Charlotte*, according to your request, if a matter of more immediate consequence had not intervened.

"Mr. Norton has proposed an inland Journey, far to the North of Churchill, to promote an extension of our trade, as well as for the discovery of a North West Passage, Copper Mines, &c.; and as an undertaking of this nature requires the attention of a person capable of taking an observation for determining the longitude and latitude, and also distances, and the course of rivers and their depths, we have fixed upon you (especially as it is represented to us to be your own inclination) to conduct this Journey, with proper assistants.

"We therefore hope you will second our expectations in readily performing this service, and upon your return we shall willingly make you any acknowledgment suitable to your trouble therein.

"We highly approve of your going in the *Speedwell*, to assist on the whale-fishery last year, and heartily wish you health and success in the present expedition.

"We remain your loving Friends,

"BIBYE LAKE, Dep. Gov.	"JAMES WINTER LAKE.
"JOHN ANTHONY MERLE.	"HERMAN BERENS.
"ROBERT MERRY.	"JOSEPH SPURREL.
"SAMUEL WEGG.	"JAMES FITZ GERALD."

The Company had no sooner perused my Journals and Charts, than they ordered a handsome sum to be placed to the credit of my account; and in the two first paragraphs of their letter to me, dated 12th May 1773, they express themselves in the following words:

"Mr. SAMUEL HEARNE,

"SIR,—Your letter of the 28th August last gave us the agreeable pleasure to hear of your safe return to our Factory. Your Journal, and the two charts you sent, sufficiently convince us of your very judicious remarks.

"We have maturely considered your great assiduity in the various accidents which occurred in your several Journies. We hereby return you our grateful thanks; and to manifest our obligation we have consented to allow you a gratuity of £——[19] for those services."

As a farther proof of the Company's being perfectly satisfied with my conduct while on that Journey, the Committee unanimously appointed me Chief of Prince of Wales's Fort in the Summer of 1775; and Mr. Bibye Lake, who was then Governor, and several others of the Committee, honoured me with a regular correspondence as long as they lived.

[18] Stated by Beckles Willson to be £130.

[19] Stated by Beckles Willson to be £200.

[G] By the Home-guard Indians we are to understand certain of the natives who are immediately employed under the protection of the Company's servants, reside on the plantation, and are employed in hunting for the Factory.[20]

[20] The Southern or Homeguard Indians here referred to were Crees, one of the most numerous tribes of the Algonquian family. The Northern Indians were Chipewyans, a tribe of the Tinné family.

[H] The Calimut is a long ornamented stem of a pipe, much in use among all the tribes of Indians who know the use of tobacco. It is particularly used in all cases of ceremony, either in making war or peace; at all public entertainments, orations, &c.

[I] No convenient opportunity offered during my last Journey, except one, on the 22d March 1771; and as nothing material had happened during that part of my Journey, I thought there was not any necessity for sending an extract of my Journal; I therefore only sent a Letter to the Governor, informing him of my situation with respect to latitude and longitude, and some account of the usage which I received from the natives, &c.

[J] By mistake in my former Journal and Draft called Arathapefcow.

[K] This was barely probable, as Matonabbee at that time had not any information of this Journey being set on foot, much less had he received orders to join me at the place and time here appointed; and had we accidentally met, he would by no means have undertaken the Journey without first going to the Factory, and there making his agreement with the Governor; for no Indian is fond of performing any particular service for the English, without first knowing what is to be his reward. At the same time, had I taken that rout on my out-set, it would have carried me some hundreds of miles out of my road. See my Track on the Map in the Winter 1770, and the Spring 1771.

[L] I was not provided with instruments for cutting on stone; but for form-sake, I cut my name, date of the year, &c., on a piece of board that had been one of the Indian's targets, and placed it in a heap of stones on a small eminence near the entrance of the river, on the South side.

[M] There is certainly no harm in making out all Instructions in the fullest manner, yet it must be allowed that those two parts might have been omitted with great propriety; for as neither Middleton, Ellis, nor Christopher were able to penetrate far enough up those inlets to discover any kind of herbage except moss and grass, much less woods, it was not likely those parts were so materially altered for the better since their times, as to make it worth my while to attempt a farther discovery of them; and especially as I had an opportunity, during my second Journey, of proving that the woods do not reach the sea-coast by some hundreds of miles in the parallel of Chesterfield's Inlet. And as the edge of the woods to the Northward always tends to the Westward, the distance must be greatly increased in the latitude of Wager Strait. Those parts have long since been visited by the Company's servants, and are within the known limits of their Charter; consequently require no other form of possession.

[N] See the preceding Note.

[O] The Continent of America is much wider than many people imagine, particularly Robson, who thought that the Pacific Ocean was but a few days journey from the West coast of Hudson's Bay. This, however, is so far from being the case, that when I was at my greatest Western distance, upward of five hundred miles from Prince of Wales's Fort, the natives, my guides, well knew that many tribes of Indians lay to the West of us, and they knew no end to the land in that direction; nor have I met with any Indians, either Northern or Southern, that ever had seen the sea to the Westward. It is, indeed, well known to the intelligent and well-informed part of the Company's servants, that an extensive and numerous tribe of Indians, called E-arch-e-thinnews, whose country lies far West of any of the Company's or Canadian settlements, must have traffic with the Spaniards on the West side of the Continent; because some of the Indians who formerly traded to York Fort, when at war with those people, frequently found saddles, bridles, muskets, and many other articles, in their possession, which were undoubtedly of Spanish manufactory.

I have seen several Indians who have been so far West as to cross the top of that immense chain of mountains which run from North to South of the continent of America. Beyond those mountains all rivers run to the Westward. I must here observe, that all the Indians I ever heard relate their excursions in that country, had invariably got so far to the South, that they did not experience any Winter, nor the least appearance of either frost or snow, though sometimes they have been absent eighteen months, or two years.[21]

[21] In the year 1745 Anthony Hendry, under instructions from the Hudson's Bay Company, had travelled inland from York Factory to the upper waters of the Saskatchewan River, where he met the E-arch-e-thinnews or Blackfeet Indians.

[P] As to a passage through the continent of America by the way of Hudson's Bay, it has so long been explored, notwithstanding what Mr. Ellis has urged in its favour, and the place it has found in the visionary Map of the American Traveller, that any comment on it would be quite unnecessary. My latitude only will be a sufficient proof that no such passage is in existence.

A NORTH-WEST VIEW OF PRINCE OF WALES'S FORT IN HUDSON'S BAY, NORTH AMERICA
By Samuel Hearne, 1777

[61]

A
JOURNEY
TO THE
NORTHERN OCEAN.

CHAP. I.

Transactions from my leaving Prince of Wales's Fort on my first expedition, till our arrival there again.

Set off from the Fort—Arrive at Po-co-ree-kis-co River—One of the Northern Indians desert—Cross Seal River, and walk on the barren grounds—Receive wrong information concerning the distance of the woods—Weather begins to be very cold, provisions all expended and nothing to be got—Strike to the Westward, arrive at the woods, and kill three deer—Set forward in the North West quarter, see the tracks of musk-oxen and deer, but killed none—Very short of provisions—Chawchinahaw wants us to return—Neither he nor his crew contribute to our maintenance—He influences several of the Indians to desert—Chawchinahaw and all his crew leave us—Begin our return to the factory; kill a few partridges, the first meal we had had for several days—Villany of one of the home Indians and his wife, who was a Northern Indian woman—Arrive at Seal River, kill two deer; partridges plenty—Meet a strange Northern Indian, accompany him to his tent, usage received there; my Indians assist in killing some beaver—Proceed toward home, and arrive at the Fort.

> 1769. November 6th.

> 1769. November.

Having made every necessary arrangement for my departure on the sixth of November, I took leave of the Governor, and my other friends, at Prince of Wales's Fort, and began my journey, under the salute of seven cannon.[62]

> 8th.

{2} The weather at that time being very mild, made it but indifferent hauling,[0] and all my crew being heavy laden, occasioned us to make but short journeys; however, on the eighth, we crossed the North branch of Po-co-ree-kis-co River,[22] and that night put up in a small tuft of woods, which is between it and Seal River. In the night, one of the Northern Indians deserted; and as all the rest of my crew were heavy laden, I was under the necessity of hauling the sledge he had left, which however was not very heavy, as it scarcely exceeded sixty pounds.

9th.

The weather still continued very fine and pleasant; we directed our course to the West North West, and early in the day crossed Seal River. In the course of this day's journey we met several Northern Indians, who were going to the factory with furs and venison; and as we had not killed any deer from our leaving the Fort, I got several joints of venison from those strangers, and gave them a note on the Governor for payment, which seemed perfectly agreeable to all parties.

1769. November.

When on the North West side of Seal River, I asked Captain Chawchinahaw the distance, and probable time it would take, before we could reach the main woods; which he assured me would not exceed four or five days journey. This put both me and my companions in good {3} spirits, and we continued our course between the West by North and North West, in daily expectation of arriving at those woods, which we were told would furnish us with every thing the country affords. These accounts were so far from being true, that after we had walked double the time here mentioned, no signs of woods were to be seen in the direction we were then steering; but we had frequently seen the looming of woods to the South West.

[63]

> 19th.

The cold being now very intense, our small stock of English provisions all expended, and not the least thing to be got on the bleak hills we had for some time been walking on, it became necessary to strike more to the Westward, which we accordingly did, and the next evening arrived at some small patches of low scrubby woods, where we saw the tracks of several deer,[23] and killed a few partridges. The road we had traversed for many days before, was in general so rough and stony, that our sledges were daily breaking; and to add to the inconveniency, the land was so barren, as not to afford us materials for repairing them: but the few woods we now fell in with, amply supplied us with necessaries for those repairs; and as we were then enabled each night to pitch proper tents, our lodging was much more comfortable than it had been for many nights before, while we were on the barren grounds, where, in general, we thought ourselves well off if we could scrape together as many shrubs as would make a fire; but it {4} was scarcely ever in our power to make any other defence against the weather, than by digging a hole in the snow down to the moss, wrapping ourselves up in our clothing, and lying down in it, with our sledges set up edgeways to windward.

> 21st.

> 1769. November.

[64]

On the twenty-first, we did not move; so the Indian men went a hunting, and the women cut holes in the ice and caught a few fish in a small lake, by the side of which we had pitched our tents. At night the men returned with some venison, having killed three deer, which was without doubt very acceptable; but our number being great, and the Indians having such enormous stomachs, very little was left but fragments after the two or three first good meals. Having devoured the three deer, and given some necessary repairs to our sledges and snow shoes, which only took one day, we again proceeded on toward the North West by West and West North West, through low scrubby pines,[24] intermixed with some dwarf larch,[25] which is commonly called juniper in Hudson's Bay. In our road we frequently saw the tracks of deer, and many musk-oxen,[26] as they are called there; but none of my companions were so fortunate as to kill any of them: so that a few partridges were all we could get to live on, and those were so scarce, that we seldom could kill as many as would amount to half a bird a day for each man; which, considering we had nothing else for the twenty-four hours, was in reality next to nothing.

26th.

{5} By this time I found that Captain Chawchinahaw had not the prosperity of the undertaking at heart; he often painted the difficulties in the worst colours, took every method to dishearten me and my European companions, and several times hinted his desire of our returning back to the factory: but finding I was determined to proceed, he took such methods as he thought would be most likely to answer his end; one of which was, that of not administering toward our support; so that we were a considerable time without any other subsistence, but what our two home-guard (Southern) Indians procured, and the little that I and the two European men could kill; which was very disproportionate to our wants, as we had to provide for several women and children who were with us.

29th.

Chawchinahaw finding that this kind of treatment was not likely to complete his design, and that we were not to be starved into compliance, at length influenced several of the best Northern Indians to desert in the night, who took with them several bags of my ammunition, some pieces of iron work, such as hatchets, ice chissels, files, &c., as well as several other useful articles.

> 30th.

> 1769. November.

[65]

When I became acquainted with this piece of villany, I asked Chawchinahaw the reason of such behaviour. To which he answered, that he knew nothing of the affair: but as that was the case, it would not be {6} prudent, he said, for us to proceed any farther; adding, that he and all the rest of his countrymen were going to strike off another way, in order to join the remainder of their wives and families: and after giving us a short account which way to steer our course for the nearest part of Seal River, which he said would be our best way homeward, he and his crew delivered me most of the things which they had in charge, packed up their awls, and set out toward the South West, making the woods ring with their laughter, and left us to consider of our unhappy situation, near two hundred miles from Prince of Wales's Fort, all heavily laden, and our strength and spirits greatly reduced by hunger and fatigue.

Our situation at that time, though very alarming, would not permit us to spend much time in reflection; so we loaded our sledges to the best advantage (but were obliged to throw away some bags of shot and ball), and immediately set out on our return. In the course of the day's walk we were fortunate enough to kill several partridges, for which we were all very thankful, as it was the first meal we had had for several days: indeed, for the five preceding days we had not killed as much as amounted to half a partridge for each man; and some days had not a single mouthful. While we were in this distress, the Northern Indians were by no means in want; for as they always walked foremost, they {7} had ten times the chance to kill partridges, rabbits, or any other thing which was to be met with, than we had. Beside this advantage, they had great stocks of flour, oatmeal, and other English provisions, which they had embezzled out of my stock during the early part of the journey; and as one of my home Indians, called Mackachy, and his wife, who is a Northern Indian woman, always resorted to the Northern Indians tents, where they got amply supplied with provisions when neither I nor my men had a single mouthful, I have great reason to suspect they had a principal hand in the embezzlement: indeed, both the man and his wife were capable of committing any crime, however diabolical.[66]

> 1769. December. 1st.

This day we had fine pleasant weather for the season of the year: we set out early in the morning, and arrived the same day at Seal River, along which we continued our course for several days. In our way we killed plenty of partridges, and saw many deer; but the weather was so remarkably serene that the Indians only killed two of the latter. By this time game was become so plentiful, that all apprehensions of starving were laid aside; and though we were heavily laden, and travelled pretty good days' journeys, yet as our spirits were good, our strength gradually returned.

> 5th.

In our course down Seal River we met a stranger, a Northern Indian, on a hunting excursion; and though {8} he had not met with any success that day, yet he kindly invited us to his tent, saying he had plenty of venison at my service; and told the Southern Indians, that as there were two or three beaver houses near his tent, he should be glad of their assistance in taking them, for there was only one man and three women at the tent.

> 1769. December.

Though we were at that time far from being in want of provisions, yet we accepted his offer, and set off with our new guide for his tent, which, by a comparative distance, he told us, was not above five miles from the place where we met him, but we found it to be nearer fifteen; so that it was the middle of the night before we arrived at it. When we drew near the tent, the usual signal for the approach of strangers was given, by firing a gun or two, which was immediately answered by the man at the tent. On our arrival at the door, the good man of the house came out, shook me by the hand, and welcomed us to his tent; but as it was too small to contain us all, he ordered his women to assist us in pitching our tent; and in the mean time invited me and as many of my crew as his little habitation could contain, and regaled us with the best in the house. The pipe went round pretty briskly, and the conversation naturally turned on the treatment we had received from Chawchinahaw and his gang; which was always answered[67] by our host with, "Ah! if I had been there, it should not have been so!" when, notwithstanding his hospitality on the present occasion, he {9} would most assuredly have acted the same part as the others had done, if he had been of the party.

Having refreshed ourselves with a plentiful supper, we took leave of our host for a while, and retired to our tent; but not without being made thoroughly sensible that many things would be expected from me before I finally left them.

> 6th.

Early in the morning, my Indians assisted us in taking the beaver houses already mentioned[27]; but the houses being small, and some of the beavers escaping, they only killed six, all of which were cooked the same night, and voraciously devoured under the denomination of a feast. I also received from the Indians several joints of venison, to the amount of at least two deer; but notwithstanding I was to pay for the whole, I found that Mackachy and his wife got all the prime parts of the meat; and on my mentioning it to them, there was so much clanship among them, that they preferred making a present of it to Mackachy, to selling it to me at double the price for which venison sells in those parts: a sufficient proof of the singular advantage which a native of this country has over an Englishman, when at such a distance from the Company's Factories as to depend entirely on them for subsistence.

> 7th.

{10} Thinking I had made my stay here long enough, I gave orders to prepare for our departure; and as I had purchased plenty of meat for present use while we were at this tent, so I likewise procured such a supply to carry with us, as was likely to last us to the Fort.

> 8th.

> 1769. December. 11th.

[68]

Early in the morning we took a final leave of our host, and proceeded on our journey homewards. One of the strangers accompanied us, for which at first I could not see his motive; but soon after our arrival at the Factory, I found that the purport of his visit was to be paid for the meat, said to be given *gratis* to Mackachy while we were at his tent. The weather continued very fine, but extremely cold; and during this part of my journey nothing material happened, till we arrived safe at Prince of Wales's Fort on the eleventh of December, to my own great mortification, and to the no small surprise of the Governor, who had placed great confidence in the abilities and conduct of Chawchinahaw.

FOOTNOTES:

[Q] The colder the weather is, the easier the sledges slide over the snow.

[22] On modern maps this stream is known as Pauk-athakuskow River. The Chipewyan Indians of Fort Churchill and vicinity know it by the name of Beskai dézé or Knife River, while the white people at Churchill know it as North River. Churchill River is called by the Chipewyans 'Tsan dézé, meaning Iron or Metal River.

[23] *Rangifer arcticus* (Rich.).—E. A. P.

[24] *Picea alba* (Ait.).—E. A. P.

[25] *Larix laricina* (Du Roi).—E. A. P.

[26] *Ovibos moschatus* (Zimm.).—E. A. P.

[27] *Castor canadensis* Kuhl. This is the most northerly record near the coast.—E. A. P.

[69]

{11} CHAP. II.

Transactions from our arrival at the Factory, to my leaving it again, and during the first part of my second journey, till I had the misfortune to break the quadrant.

Transactions at the Factory—Proceed on my second journey— Arrive at Seal River—Deer plentiful for some time—Method of angling fish under the ice—Set our fishing nets—Methods of setting nets under the ice—My guide proposes to stay till the geese began to fly; his reasons accepted—Pitch our tent in the best manner— Method of pitching a tent in winter—Fish plentiful for some time; grow very scarce; in great want of provisions—Manner of employing my time—My guide killed two deer—Move to the place they were lying at; there kill several more deer, and three beavers— Soon in want of provisions again—Many Indians join us from the Westward—We begin to move towards the barren ground—Arrive at She-than-nee, and there suffer great distress for want of provisions—Indians kill two swans and three geese—Geese and other birds of passage plentiful—Leave She-than-nee, and arrive at Beralzone—One of my companions guns bursts, and shatters his left hand—Leave Beralzone, and get on the barren ground, clear of all woods—Throw away our sledges and snow shoes—Each person takes a load on his back; my part of the luggage—Exposed to many hardships—Several days without victuals—Indians kill three musk oxen, but for want of fire are obliged to eat the meat raw—Fine weather returns; make a fire; effects of long fasting; stay a day or two to dry some meat in the sun—Proceed to the Northward, and arrive at Cathawhachaga; there find some tents of Indians—A Northern leader called Keelshies meets us; send a letter by him to the Governor—Transactions at Cathawhachaga; leave it, and proceed to the Northward—Meet several Indians—My guide not willing to proceed; his {12} reasons for it—Many more Indians join us—Arrive at Doobaunt Whoie River—Manner of ferrying over rivers in the Northern Indian canoes—No rivers in those parts in a useful direction for the natives—Had nearly lost the quadrant and all the powder—Some reflections on our situation, and the conduct of the Indians—Find the quadrant and part of the [70]powder—Observe for the latitude—Quadrant broke—Resolve to return again to the Factory.

1770. February.

During my absence from Prince of Wales's Fort on my former journey, several Northern Indians arrived in great distress at the Factory, and were employed in shooting partridges for the use of our people at the Fort. One of those Indians called Conne-e-quese, said he had been very near to the famous river I was engaged to go in quest of. Accordingly Mr. Norton engaged him and two other Northern Indians to accompany me on this second attempt; but to avoid all incumbrances as much as possible, it was thought advisable not to take any women,[R] that the Indians might have fewer to provide for. I would not permit any European to go with me, but two of the home-guard (Southern) Indian men were to accompany me as before. Indeed the Indians, both Northern and Southern, paid so little attention to Isbester and Merriman on my former journey, particularly in times of scarcity, that I was determined not to take them with me in future; though the former was very desirous to accompany me again, and was well calculated to encounter the hardships of {13} such an undertaking. Merriman was quite sick of such excursions, and so far from offering his service a second time, seemed to be very thankful that he was once more arrived in safety among his friends; for before he got to the Factory he had contracted a most violent cold.

Having come to the above resolutions, and finally determined on the number of Indians that were to accompany us, we were again fitted out with a large supply of ammunition, and as many other useful articles as we could conveniently take with us, together with a small sample of light trading goods, for presents to the Indians, as before.

[71]

> 1770. February.

My instructions on this occasion amounted to no more than an order to proceed as fast as possible; and for my conduct during the journey, I was referred to my former instructions of November 6th, 1769.

> 23rd.

Every thing being in readiness for our departure, on the twenty-third of February I began my second journey, accompanied by three Northern Indians and two of the home-guard (Southern) Indians. I took particular care, however, that Mackachy, though an excellent hunter, should not be of our party; as he had proved himself, during my former journey, to be a sly artful villain.

The snow at this time was so deep on the top of the ramparts, that few of the cannon were to be seen, {14} otherwise the Governor would have saluted me at my departure, as before; but as those honours could not possibly be of any service to my expedition, I readily relinquished everything of the kind; and in lieu of it, the Governor, officers, and people, insisted on giving me three cheers.

After leaving the Factory, we continued our course in much the same direction as in my former journey, till we arrived at Seal River; when, instead of crossing it, and walking on the barren grounds as before, we followed the course of the river, except in two particular places, where the bends tended so much to the South, that by crossing two necks of land not more than five or six miles wide, we saved the walking of near twenty miles each time, and still came to the main river again.

> 1770. March. 8th.

The weather had been so remarkably boisterous and changeable, that we were frequently obliged to continue two or three nights in the same place. To make up for this inconveniency, deer were so plentiful for the first eight or ten days, that the Indians killed as many as was necessary; but we were all so heavy laden that we could not possibly take much of the meat with us. This I soon perceived to be a great evil, which exposed us to such frequent inconveniences, that in case of not killing any thing for three or four days[72] together, we were in great want of provisions; we seldom, however, went to bed entirely supperless {15} till the eighth of March; when though we had only walked about eight miles that morning, and expended all the remainder of the day in hunting, we could not produce a single thing at night, not even a partridge! nor had we discerned the track of any thing that day, which was likely to afford us hopes of better success in the morning. This being the case, we prepared some hooks and lines ready to angle for fish, as our tent was then by the side of a lake belonging to Seal River, which seemed by its situation to afford some prospect of success.

9th.

Early in the morning we took down our tent, and moved about five miles to the West by South, to a part of the lake that seemed more commodious for fishing than that where we had been the night before. As soon as we arrived at this place, some were immediately employed cutting holes in the ice, while others pitched the tent, got fire-wood, &c.; after which, for it was early in the morning, those who pitched the tent went a hunting, and at night one of them returned with a porcupine,[28] while those who were angling caught several fine trout, which afforded us a plentiful supper, and we had some trifle left for breakfast.

Angling for fish under the ice in winter requires no other process, than cutting round holes in the ice from one to two feet diameter, and letting down a baited hook, which is always kept in motion, not only to {16} prevent the water from freezing so soon as it would do if suffered to remain quite still, but because it is found at the same time to be a great means of alluring the fish to the hole; for it is always observed that the fish in those parts will take a bait which is in motion, much sooner than one that is at rest.

> 19th.

> 1770. March.

> 20th.

[73]

Early in the morning we again pursued our angling, and all the forenoon being expended without any success, we took down our tent and pitched it again about eight miles farther to the Westward, on the same lake, where we cut more holes in the ice for angling, and that night caught several fine pike.[29] The next day we moved about five miles to the South West, down a small river, where we pitched our tent; and having set four fishing nets, in the course of the day we caught many fine fish, particularly pike, trout,[30] tittymeg, and a coarse kind of fish known in Hudson's Bay by the name of Methy.[31][S]

To set a net under the ice, it is first necessary to ascertain its exact length, by stretching it out upon the ice near the part proposed for setting it. This being done, a number of round holes are cut in the ice, at ten or twelve feet distance from each other, and as many in number as will be sufficient to stretch the net at its full length. A line is then passed under the ice, by means {17} of a long light pole, which is first introduced at one of the end holes, and, by means of two forked sticks, this pole is easily conducted, or passed from one hole to another, under the ice, till it arrives at the last. The pole is then taken out, and both ends of the line being properly secured, is always ready for use. The net is made fast to one end of the line by one person, and hauled under the ice by a second; a large stone is tied to each of the lower corners, which serves to keep the net expanded, and prevents it rising from the bottom with every waft of the current. The Europeans settled in Hudson's Bay proceed much in the same manner, though they in general take much more pains; but the above method is found quite sufficient by the Indians.

In order to search a net thus set, the two end holes only are opened; the line is veered away by one person, and the net hauled from under the ice by another; after all the fish are taken out, the net is easily hauled back to its former station, and there secured as before.

[74]

1770. March. 21st.

As this place seemed likely to afford us a constant supply of fish, my guide proposed to stay here till the geese began to fly, which in those Northern parts is seldom before the middle of May. His reasons for so doing seemed well founded: "The weather," he said, "is at this time too cold to walk on the barren grounds, and the woods from this part lead so much {18} to the Westward, that were we to continue travelling in any tolerable shelter, our course would not be better than West South West, which would only be going out of our way; whereas, if we should remain here till the weather permit us to walk due North, over the barren grounds, we shall then in one month get farther advanced on our journey, than if we were to continue travelling all the remainder of the winter in the sweep of the woods."

These reasons appeared to me very judicious, and as the plan seemed likely to be attended with little trouble, it met with my entire approbation. That being the case, we took additional pains in building our tent, and made it as commodious as the materials and situation would admit.

1770. March.

To pitch an Indian's tent in winter, it is first necessary to search for a level piece of dry ground; which cannot be ascertained but by thrusting a stick through the snow down to the ground, all over the proposed part. When a convenient spot is found, the snow is then cleared away in a circular form to the very moss; and when it is proposed to remain more than a night or two in one place, the moss is also cut up and removed, as it is very liable when dry to take fire, and occasion much trouble to the inhabitants. A quantity of poles are then procured, which are generally proportioned both in number and length to the {19} size of the tent cloth, and the number of persons it is intended to contain. If one of the poles should not happen to be forked, two of them are tied together near the top, then raised erect, and their buts or lower ends extended as wide as the proposed diameter of the tent; the other poles are then set round at[75] equal distances from each other, and in such order, that their lower ends form a complete circle, which gives boundaries to the tent on all sides: the tent cloth is then fastened to a light pole, which is always raised up and put round the poles from the weather side, so that the two edges that lap over and form the door are always to the leeward. It must be understood that this method is only in use when the Indians are moving from place to place every day; for when they intend to continue any time in one place, they always make the door of their tent to face the south.

The tent cloth is usually of thin Moose leather, dressed and made by the Indians, and in shape it nearly resembles a fan-mount inverted; so that when the largest curve incloses the bottom of the poles, the smaller one is always sufficient to cover the top; except a hole, which is designedly left open to serve the double purpose of chimney and window.

The fire is always made on the ground in the center, and the remainder of the floor, or bottom of the tent, is covered all over with small branches of the pine tree, {20} which serve both for seats and beds. A quantity of pine tops and branches are laid round the bottom of the poles on the outside, over which the eaves of the tent is staked down; a quantity of snow is then packed over all, which excludes great part of the external air, and contributes greatly to the warmth within. The tent here described is such as is made use of by the Southern Indians, and the same with which I was furnished at the Factory; for that made use of by the Northern Indians is made of different materials, and is of a quite different shape, as shall be described hereafter.

1770. March.

The situation of our tent at this time was truly pleasant,[32] particularly for a spring residence; being on a small elevated point, which commanded an extensive prospect over a large lake, the shores of which abounded with wood of different kinds, such as pine, larch, birch, and poplar; and in many places was beautifully contrasted with a variety of high hills, that shewed their snowy summits above the tallest woods. About two hundred yards from the tent was a fall, or rapid, which the swiftness of the current prevents from freezing in the coldest winters. At the bottom of this fall, which empties itself into the above lake, was a fine sheet of open water near a mile in length, and at least half a mile in breadth; by the margin of which we had our fishing nets set, all in open view from the tent.

[76]

{21} The remaining part of this month passed on without any interruption, or material occurrence, to disturb our repose, worth relating: our fishing nets provided us with daily food, and the Indians had too much philosophy about them to give themselves much additional trouble; for during the whole time not one of them offered to look for a partridge, or anything else which could yield a change of diet.

As the time may now be supposed to have lain heavy on my hands, it may not be improper to inform the reader how I employed it. In the first place, I embraced every favourable opportunity of observing the latitude of the place, the mean of which was 58° 46'

30" North; and the longitude by account was 5° 57' West, from Prince of Wales's Fort. I then corrected my reckoning from my last observation; brought up my journal, and filled up my chart, to the place of our residence. I built also some traps, and caught a few martins; and by way of saving my ammunition, set some snares for partridges. The former is performed by means of a few logs, so arranged that when the martin attempts to take away the bait laid for him, he with very little struggle pulls down a small post that supports the whole weight of the trap; when, if the animal be not killed by the weight of the logs, he is confined till he be frozen to death, or killed by the hunter going his rounds.[77]

> 1770. April.

{22} To snare partridges requires no other process than making a few little hedges across a creek, or a few short hedges projecting at right angles from the side of an island of willows, which those birds are found to frequent. Several openings must be left in each hedge, to admit the birds to pass through, and in each of them a snare must be set; so that when the partridges are hopping along the edge of the willows to feed, which is their usual custom, some of them soon get into the snares, where they are confined till they are taken out. I have caught from three to ten partridges in a day by this simple contrivance; which requires no further attendance than going round them night and morning.

> 1st.

I have already observed that nothing material happened to disturb our repose till the first of April, when to our great surprise the fishing nets did not afford us a single fish. Though some of the preceding days had been pretty successful, yet my companions, like true Indians, seldom went to sleep till they had cleared the tent of every article of provision. As nothing was to be caught in the nets, we all went out to angle; but in this we were equally unsuccessful, as we could not procure one fish the whole day. This sudden change of circumstances alarmed one of my companions so much, that he began to think of resuming the use of his gun, after having laid it by for near a month.

{23} Early in the morning we arose; when my guide Conne-e-quese went a hunting, and the rest attended the nets and hooks near home; but all with such bad success, that we could not procure enough in one day to serve two men for a supper. This, instead of awakening the rest of my companions, sent them to sleep; and scarcely any of them had the prudence to look at the fishing nets, though they were not more than two or three hundred yards from the tent door.

1770. April.

My guide, who was a steady man, and an excellent hunter, having for many years been accustomed to provide for a large family, seemed by far the most industrious of all my crew;[78] he closely pursued his hunting for several days, and seldom returned to the tent till after dark, while those at the tent passed most of their time in smoking and sleeping.

10th.

Several days passed without any signs of relief, till the 10th, when my guide continued out longer than ordinary, which made us conjecture that he had met with strangers, or seen some deer, or other game, which occasioned his delay. We all therefore lay down to sleep, having had but little refreshment for the three preceding days, except a pipe of tobacco and a draught of water; even partridges had become so scarce that not one was to be got; the heavy thaws had driven them all out towards the barren grounds. About midnight, to our {24} great joy, our hunter arrived, and brought with him the blood and fragments of two deer that he had killed. This unexpected success soon roused the sleepers, who, in an instant, were busily employed in cooking a large kettle of broth, made with the blood, and some fat and scraps of meat shred small, boiled in it. This might be reckoned a dainty dish at any time, but was more particularly so in our present almost famished condition.

11th.

After partaking of this refreshment, we resumed our rest, and early in the morning set out in a body for the place where the deer were lying. As we intended to make our stay but short, we left our tent standing, containing all our baggage. On our arrival at the place of destination, some were immediately employed in making a hut or barrocado with young pine trees; while one man skinned the deer, the remainder went a hunting, and in the afternoon returned to the hut, after having killed two deer.

Several days were now spent in feasting and gluttony; during which the Indians killed five more deer and three fine beavers; finding at last, however, that there was little prospect of procuring either more deer or beavers, we determined to return to our tent, with the remains of what we had already obtained.[79]

1770. April. 22d.

The flesh of these deer, though none of the largest, might with frugality have served our small number, (being {25} only six) for some time; but my companions, like other Indians, feasted day and night while it lasted; and were so indolent and unthinking, as not to attend properly to the fishing nets; so that many fine fish, which had been entangled in the nets, were entirely spoiled, and in about twelve or fourteen days we were nearly in as great distress for provisions as ever.

During the course of our long inactivity, Saw-sop-o-kishac, commonly called Sossop, my principal Southern Indian, as he was cutting some birch for spoons, dishes, and other necessary household furniture, had the misfortune to cut his leg in such a manner as to be incapable of walking; and the other Southern Indian, though a much younger man, was so indolent as not to be of any service to me, except hauling part of our luggage, and eating up part of the provisions which had been provided by the more industrious part of my companions.

> 24th.

On the twenty-fourth, early in the day, a great body of Indians was seen in the South West, on the large lake by the side of which our tent stood. On their arrival at our tent we discovered them to be the wives and families of the Northern Indian goose-hunters, who were gone to Prince of Wales's Fort to attend the season. They were bound toward the barren ground, there to wait the return of their husbands and relations from the Fort, after the termination of the goose-season.

> 27th.

{26} My guide having for some days past determined to move toward the barren ground, this morning we took down our tent, packed up our luggage, and proceeded to the Eastward in the same track we came; but Sossop being so lame as to be obliged to be hauled on a sledge, I easily prevailed on two of the Indians who had joined us on the 24th, and who were pursuing the same road, to perform this service for him.[80]

> 1770. April. 29th.

> May. 13th.

After two days good walking in our old track, we arrived at a part of Seal River called She-than-nee,[33] where we pitched our tent and set both our fishing-nets, intending to stay there till the geese began to fly. Though we had seen several swans and some geese flying to the Northward, it was the thirteenth of May before we could procure any. On that day the Indians killed two swans and three geese. This in some measure alleviated our distress, which at that time was very great; having had no other subsistence for five or six days, than a few cranberries, that we gathered from the dry ridges where the snow was thawed away in spots; for though we set our fishing-nets in the best judged places, and angled at every part that was likely to afford success, we only caught three small fish during the whole time. Many of the Northern Indians, who had joined us on the 24th of April, remained in our company for some time; and though I well knew they had had a plentiful winter, and had then good stocks of dried meat by them, and {27} were also acquainted with our distress, they never gave me or my Southern companions the least supply, although they had in secret amply provided for our Northern guides.

19th.

23d.

1770. May.

By the nineteenth, the geese, swans, ducks, gulls, and other birds of passage, were so plentiful, that we killed every day as many as were sufficient for our support; and having stopped a few days to recruit our spirits after so long a fast, on the twenty-third we began once more to proceed toward the barren ground. Sossop having now perfectly recovered from his late misfortune, everything seemed to have a favourable appearance; especially as my crew had been augmented to twelve persons, by the addition of one of my guide's wives, and five others, whom I had engaged to assist in carrying our luggage; and I well knew, from the season of the year, that hauling would soon be at an end for the summer.

[81]

The thaws having been by this time so great as to render travelling in the woods almost impracticable, we continued our course to the East on Seal River, about sixteen miles farther, when we came to a small river, and a string of lakes connected with it, that tended to the North.

June. 1st.

The weather for some time was remarkably fine and pleasant. Game of all kinds was exceedingly plentiful, {28} and we continued our course to the Northward on the above river and lakes till the first of June, when we arrived at a place called Beralzone.[34] In our way thither, beside killing more geese than was necessary, we shot two deer. One of my companions had now the misfortune to shatter his hand very much by the bursting of a gun; but as no bones were broken, I bound up the wound, and with the assistance of some of Turlington's drops, yellow basilicon, &c., which I had with me, soon restored the use of his hand; so that in a very short time he seemed to be out of all danger.

4th.

After stopping a few days at Beralzone, to dry a little venison and a few geese, we again proceeded to the Northward on the barren ground; for on our leaving this place we soon got clear of all the woods.

5th.

6th.

10th.

1770. June.

The snow was by this time so soft as to render walking in snow-shoes very laborious; and though the ground was bare in many places, yet at times, and in particular places, the snow-drifts were so deep, that we could not possibly do without them. By the sixth, however, the thaws were so general, and the snows so much melted, that as our snow-shoes were attended with more trouble than service, we all consented to throw them away. Till the tenth, our sledges proved serviceable, particularly in crossing lakes and ponds on the ice; but that mode of travelling now growing dangerous on account of the great thaws, we {29} determined to throw away our sledges, and every one to take a load on his back.

[82]

This I found to be much harder work than the winter carriage, as my part of the luggage consisted of the following articles, viz. the quadrant and its stand, a trunk containing books, papers, &c., a land-compass, and a large bag containing all my wearing apparel; also a hatchet, knives, files, &c., beside several small articles, intended for presents to the natives. The awkwardness of my load, added to its great weight, which was upward of sixty pounds, and the excessive heat of the weather, rendered walking the most laborious task I had ever encountered; and what considerably increased the hardship, was the badness of the road, and the coarseness of our lodging, being, on account of the want of proper tents, exposed to the utmost severity of the weather. The tent we had with us was not only too large, and unfit for barren ground service, where no poles were to be got, but we had been obliged to cut it up for shoes, and each person carried his own share. Indeed my guide behaved both negligently and ungenerously on this occasion; as he never made me, or my Southern Indians, acquainted with the nature of pitching tents on the barren ground; which had he done, we could easily have procured a set of poles before we left the woods. He took care, however, to procure a set for himself and his wife; and when the tent was divided, though he made shift to get a piece large enough to serve him for {30} a complete little tent, he never asked me or my Southern Indians to put our heads into it.

Beside the inconvenience of being exposed to the open air, night and day, in all weathers, we experienced real distress from the want of victuals. When provisions were procured, it often happened that we could not make a fire, so that we were obliged to eat the meat quite raw; which at first, in the article of fish particularly, was as little relished by my Southern companions as myself.[83]

> 1770. June.

Notwithstanding these accumulated and complicated hardships, we continued in perfect health and good spirits; and my guide, though a perfect niggard of his provisions, especially in times of scarcity, gave us the strongest assurance of soon arriving at a plentiful country, which would not only afford us a certain supply of provisions, but where we should meet with other Indians, who probably would be willing to carry part of our luggage. This news naturally gave us great consolation; for at that time the weight of our constant loads was so great, that when Providence threw any thing in our way, we could not carry above two days provisions with us, which indeed was the chief reason of our being so frequently in want.

> 23d.

From the twentieth to the twenty-third we walked every day near twenty miles, without any other subsistence {31} than a pipe of tobacco, and a drink of water when we pleased: even partridges and gulls, which some time before were in great plenty, and easily procured, were now so scarce and shy, that we could rarely get one; and as to geese, ducks, &c., they had all flown to the Northward to breed and molt.

Early in the morning of the twenty-third, we set out as usual, but had not walked above seven or eight miles before we saw three musk-oxen grazing by the side of a small lake. The Indians immediately went in pursuit of them; and as some of them were expert hunters, they soon killed the whole of them. This was no doubt very fortunate; but, to our great mortification, before we could get one of them skinned, such a fall of rain came on, as to put it quite out of our power to make a fire; which, even in the finest weather, could only be made of moss, as we were near an hundred miles from any woods. This was poor comfort for people who had not broke their fast for four or five days. Necessity, however, has no law; and having been before initiated into the method of eating raw meat, we were the better prepared for this repast: but this was by no means so well relished, either by[84] me or the Southern Indians, as either raw venison or raw fish had been: for the flesh of the musk-ox is not only coarse and tough, but smells and tastes so strong of musk as to make it very disagreeable when raw, though it is tolerable eating when properly cooked. The weather continued so {32} remarkably bad, accompanied with constant heavy rain, snow, and sleet, and our necessities were so great by the time the weather permitted us to make a fire, that we had nearly eat to the amount of one buffalo quite raw.

Notwithstanding I mustered up all my philosophy on this occasion, yet I must confess that my spirits began to fail me. Indeed our other misfortunes were greatly aggravated by the inclemency of the weather, which was not only cold, but so very wet that for near three days and nights, I had not one dry thread about me. When the fine weather returned, we made a fire, though it was only of moss, as I have already observed; and having got my cloaths dry, all things seemed likely to go on in the old channel, though that was indifferent enough; but I endeavoured, like a sailor after a storm, to forget past misfortunes.

None of our natural wants, if we except thirst, are so distressing, or hard to endure, as hunger; and in wandering situations, like that which I now experienced, the hardship is greatly aggravated by the uncertainty with respect to its duration, and the means most proper to be used to remove it, as well as by the labour and fatigue we must necessarily undergo for that purpose, and the disappointments which too frequently frustrate our best concerted plans and most strenuous exertions: it not only enfeebles the body, but depresses the spirits, in spite of {33} every effort to prevent it. Besides, for want of action, the stomach so far loses its digestive powers, that after long fasting it resumes its office with pain and reluctance. During this journey I have too frequently experienced the dreadful effects of this calamity, and more than once been reduced to so low a state by hunger and fatigue, that when[85] Providence threw any thing in my way, my stomach has scarcely been able to retain more than two or three ounces, without producing the most oppressive pain. Another disagreeable circumstance of long fasting is, the extreme difficulty and pain attending the natural evacuations for the first time; and which is so dreadful, that of it none but those who have experienced can have an adequate idea.

To record in detail each day's fare since the commencement of this journey, would be little more than a dull repetition of the same occurrences. A sufficient idea of it may be given in a few words, by observing that it may justly be said to have been either all feasting, or all famine; sometimes we had too much, seldom just enough, frequently too little, and often none at all. It will be only necessary to say that we have fasted many times two whole days and nights; twice upwards of three days; and once, while at She-than-nee, near seven days, during which we tasted not a mouthful of anything, except a few cranberries, water, scraps of old leather, and burnt bones. On those pressing occasions I have frequently seen the Indians examine their wardrobe, {34} which consisted chiefly of skin-clothing, and consider what part could best be spared;

sometimes a piece of an old, half-rotten deer skin, and at others a pair of old shoes, were sacrificed to alleviate extreme hunger. The relation of such uncommon hardships may perhaps gain little credit in Europe; while those who are conversant with the history of Hudson's Bay, and who are thoroughly acquainted with the distress which the natives of the country about it frequently endure, may consider them as no more than the common occurrences of an Indian life, in which they are frequently driven to the necessity of eating one another.[T]

[86]

1770. June.

26th.

30th.

1770. July.

{35} Knowing that our constant loads would not permit us to carry much provisions with us, we agreed to continue a day or two to refresh ourselves, and to dry a little meat in the sun, as it thereby not only becomes more portable, but is always ready for use. On the twenty-sixth, all that remained of the musk-ox flesh being properly dried and fit for carriage, we began to proceed on our journey Northward, and on the thirtieth of June arrived at a small river, called Cathawhachaga,[35] which empties[87] itself into a large lake called Yath-kyed-whoie,[36] or White Snow Lake. Here we found several tents of Northern Indians, who had been some time employed spearing deer in their canoes, as they crossed the above mentioned little river. Here also we met a Northern Indian Leader, or Captain, called Keelshies, and a small party of his crew, who were bound to Prince of Wales's Fort, with furs {36} and other commodities for trade. When Keelshies was made acquainted with the intent of my journey, he readily offered his service to bring me anything from the Factory that we were likely to stand in need of; and though we were then in latitude 63° 4' North, and longitude 7° 12' West from Churchill, yet he promised to join us again, at a place appointed by my guide, by the setting in of the Winter. In consequence of this offer, I looked over our ammunition and other articles; and finding that a little powder, shot, tobacco, and a few knives were likely to be of service before the journey could be completed, I determined to send a letter to the governor of Prince of Wales's Fort, to advise him of my situation, and to desire him to send by the bearer a certain quantity of the above articles; on which Keelshies and his crew proceeded on their journey for the Factory the same day.

MAP OF YATH-KYED LAKE AND PART OF KAZAN RIVER
By J. B. Tyrrell, 1894

1770. July.

Cathawhachaga was the only river we had seen since the breaking up of the ice that we could not ford; and as we had not any canoes with us, we were obliged to get ferried across by the strange Indians. When we arrived on the North side[88] of this river, where the Indians resided, my guide proposed to stop some time, to dry and pound some meat to take with us; to which I readily consented. We also set our fishing-nets, and caught a considerable quantity of very fine fish; such as tittemeg, barble,[37] &c.

6th.

{37} The number of deer which crossed Cathawhachaga, during our stay there, was by no means equal to our expectations, and no more than just sufficient to supply our present wants; so that after waiting several days in fruitless expectation, we began to prepare for moving; and accordingly, on the sixth of July, we set out, though we had not at that time as much victuals belonging to our company as would furnish us a supper. During our stay here, we had each day got as much fish or flesh as was sufficient for present expenditure; but, being in hopes of better times, saved none.

Before we left Cathawhachaga, I made several observations for the latitude, and found it to be 63° 4' North. I also brought up my journal, and filled up my chart to that time. Everything being now ready for our departure, my guide informed me that in a few days a canoe would be absolutely necessary, to enable us to cross some unfordable rivers which we should meet, and could not avoid. This induced me to purchase one at the easy rate of a single knife, the full value of which did not exceed one penny. It must be observed, that the man who sold the canoe had no farther occasion for it, and was glad to take what he could get; but had he been thoroughly acquainted with our necessities, he most assuredly would have had the conscience to have asked goods to the amount of ten beaver skins at least.

> 1770. July.

> 9th.

[89]

{38} This additional piece of luggage obliged me to engage another Indian; and we were lucky enough at that time to meet with a poor forlorn fellow, who was fond of the office, having never been in a much better state than that of a beast of burthen. Thus, provided with a canoe, and a man to carry it, we left Cathawhachaga, as has been observed, on the sixth of July, and continued our course to the North by West, and North North West; and that night put up by the side of a small bay of White Snow Lake,[39] where we angled, and caught several fine trout, some of which weighed not less than fourteen or sixteen pounds. In the night heavy rain came on, which continued three days; but the ninth proving fine weather, and the sun displaying his beams very powerfully, we dried our clothes, and proceeded to the Northward. Toward the evening, however, it began again to rain so excessively, that it was with much difficulty we kept our powder and books dry.

17th.

On the seventeenth, we saw many musk-oxen, several of which the Indians killed; when we agreed to stay here a day or two, to dry and pound[U] some of the carcases to take with us. The flesh of any animal, when it is thus prepared, is not only hearty food, but is always ready for {39} use, and at the same time very portable. In most parts of Hudson's Bay it is known by the name of Thew-hagon,[40] but amongst the Northern Indians it is called Achees.

1770. July. 22d.

Having prepared as much dried flesh as we could transport, we proceeded to the Northward; and at our departure left a great quantity of meat behind us, which we could neither eat nor carry away. This was not the first time we had so done; and however wasteful it may appear, it is a practice so common among all the Indian tribes, as to be thought nothing of. On the twenty-second, we met several strangers, whom we joined in pursuit of the deer, &c. which were at this time so plentiful, that we got every day a sufficient number for our support, and indeed too frequently killed several merely for the tongues, marrow, and fat.

[90]

30th.

1770. August.

After we had been some time in company with those Indians, I found that my guide seemed to hesitate about proceeding any farther; and that he kept pitching his tent backward and forward, from place to place, after the deer, and the rest of the Indians. On my asking him his reason for so doing; he answered, that as the year was too far advanced to admit of our arrival at the Coppermine River that Summer, he thought it more advisable to pass the Winter with some of the Indians then in company, and alleged that there could be no fear of our arriving at that river early in the Summer of one thousand seven hundred and seventy-one. As I could not {40} pretend to contradict him, I was entirely reconciled to his proposal; and accordingly we kept moving to the Westward with the other Indians. In a few days, many others joined us from different quarters; so that by the thirtieth of July we had in all above seventy tents, which did not contain less than six hundred persons. Indeed our encampment at night had the appearance of a small town; and in the morning, when we began to move, the whole ground (at least for a large space all round) seemed to be alive, with men, women, children, and dogs. Though the land was entirely barren, and destitute of every kind of herbage, except wish-a-capucca[v] and moss, yet the deer were so numerous that the Indians not only killed as many as were sufficient for our large number, but often several merely for the skins, marrow, &c. and left the carcases to rot, or to be devoured by the wolves, foxes, and other beasts of prey.

MAP OF DUBAWNT LAKE AND PART OF DUBAWNT RIVER
By J. B. and J. W. Tyrrell, 1893

[91]

In our way to the Westward we came to several rivers, which, though small and of no note, were so deep as not to be fordable, particularly Doobaunt River.[W] On those occasions only, we had recourse to our canoe, which, though of the common size, was too small to carry more {41} than two persons; one of whom always lies down at full length for fear of making the canoe top-heavy, and the other sits on his heels and paddles. This method of ferrying over rivers, though tedious, is the most expeditious way these poor people can contrive; for they are sometimes obliged to carry their canoes one hundred and fifty, or two hundred miles, without having occasion to make use of them; yet at times they cannot do without them; and were they not very small and portable, it would be impossible for one man to carry them, which they are often obliged to do, not only the distance above mentioned, but even the whole Summer.

[92]

1770. August. 6th.

8th.

1770. August.

The person I engaged at Cathawhachaga to carry my canoe proving too weak for the task, another of my crew was obliged to exchange loads with him, which seemed perfectly agreeable to all parties; and as we walked but short days' journies, and deer were very plentiful, all things went on very smoothly. Nothing material happened till the eighth, when we were near losing the quadrant and all our powder from the following circumstance: the fellow who had been released from carrying the canoe proving too weak, as hath been already observed, had, after the exchange, nothing to carry but my powder and his own trifles; the latter were indeed very inconsiderable, not equal in size and weight to a soldier's knapsack. As I intended to have a little sport with the deer, and knowing his load to be much lighter than mine, I gave him the quadrant {42} and stand to carry, which he took without the least hesitation, or seeming ill-will. Having thus eased myself for the present of a heavy and cumbersome part of my load, I set out early in the morning with some of the Indian men; and after walking about eight or nine miles, saw, from the top of a high hill, a great number of deer feeding in a neighbouring valley; on which we laid down our loads and erected a flag, as a signal for the others to pitch their tents there for the night. We then pursued our hunting, which proved very successful. At night, however, when we came to the hill where we had left our baggage, I found that only part of the Indians had arrived, and that the man who had been entrusted with my powder and quadrant, had set off another way, with a small party of Indians that had been in our company that morning. The evening being far advanced, we were obliged to defer going in search of him till the morning, and as his track could not be easily discovered in the Summer, the Southern Indians, as well as myself, were very uneasy, fearing we had lost the powder, which was to provide us with food and raiment the remainder of our journey. The very uncourteous behaviour of the Northern Indians then in[93] company, gave me little hopes of receiving assistance from them, any longer than I had wherewithal to reward them for their trouble and expense; for during the whole time I had been with them, not one of them had offered to give me the least morsel of victuals, without asking something in exchange, which, in general, was three times the value of {43} what they could have got for the same articles, had they carried them to the Factory, though several hundred miles distant.

So inconsiderate were those people, that wherever they met me, they always expected that I had a great assortment of goods to relieve their necessities; as if I had brought the Company's warehouse with me. Some of them wanted guns; all wanted ammunition, iron-work, and tobacco; many were solicitous for medicine; and others pressed me for different articles of clothing; but when they found I had nothing to spare, except a few nick-nacks and gewgaws, they made no scruple of pronouncing me a "poor servant, noways like the Governor at the Factory, who, they said, they never saw, but he gave them something useful." It is scarcely possible to conceive any people so void of common understanding, as to think that the sole intent of my undertaking this fatiguing journey, was to carry a large assortment of useful and heavy implements, to give to all that stood in need of them; but many of them would ask me for what they wanted with the same freedom, and apparently with the same hopes of success, as if they had been at one of the Company's Factories. Others, with an air of more generosity, offered me furs to trade with at the same standard as at the Factory; without considering how unlikely it was that I should increase the enormous weight of my load with articles which could be of no more use to me in my present situation than they were to themselves.

> 1770. August.

{44} This unaccountable behaviour of the Indians occasioned much serious reflection on my part; as it showed plainly how little I had to expect if I should, by any accident,[94] be reduced to the necessity of depending upon them for support; so that, though I laid me down to rest, sleep was a stranger to me that night. The following beautiful lines of Dr. Young I repeated above an hundred times:

"Tired Nature's sweet restorer, balmy Sleep;
He, like the world, his ready visit pays
Where fortune smiles; the wretched he forsakes:
Swift on his downy pinions flies from woe,
And lights on lids unsully'd with a tear."
—NIGHT THOUGHTS.

> 9th.

1770. August.

After passing the night in this melancholy manner, I got up at daybreak, and, with the two Southern Indians, set out in quest of our deserter. Many hours elapsed in fruitless search after him, as we could not discover a single track in the direction which we were informed he had taken. The day being almost spent without the least appearance of success, I proposed repairing to the place where I had delivered the quadrant to him, in hopes of seeing some track in the moss that might lead to the way the Indians were gone whom our deserter had accompanied. On our arrival at that place, we found they had struck down toward a little river which they had crossed the morning before; and there, to our great joy, we found the quadrant and the bag of powder lying on the top of a high stone, but not a human being was to be seen. On {45} examining the powder, we found that the bag had been opened, and part of it taken out; but, notwithstanding our loss was very considerable, we returned with light hearts to the place at which we had been the night before, where we found our baggage safe, but all the Indians gone; they had, however, been so considerate as to set up marks to direct us what course to steer. By the time we had adjusted our bundles, the day was quite spent; seeing, however, a smoke, or rather a fire, in the direction we were ordered to steer, we bent our way towards it; and a little after ten o'clock at night came up with the main body of the Indians;[95] when, after refreshing ourselves with a plentiful supper, the first morsel we had tasted that day, we retired to rest, which I at least enjoyed with better success than the preceding night.

11th.

In the morning of the eleventh we proceeded on to the West, and West by South; but on the twelfth did not move. This gave us an opportunity of endeavouring to ascertain the latitude by a meridian altitude, when we found the place to be in 63° 10' North nearly. It proving rather cloudy about noon, though exceeding fine weather, I let the quadrant stand, in order to obtain the latitude more exactly by two altitudes; but, to my great mortification, while I was eating my dinner, a sudden gust of wind blew it down; and as the ground where it stood was {46} very stoney, the bubble, the sight-vane, and vernier, were entirely broke to pieces, which rendered the instrument useless. In consequence of this misfortune I resolved to return again to the Fort, though we were then in the latitude of 63° 10' North, and about 10° 40' West longitude from Churchill River.[43]

FOOTNOTES:

[R] This was a proposal of the Governor's, though he well knew we could not do without their assistance, both for hauling our baggage, as well as dressing skins for clothing, pitching our tent, getting firing, &c.

[28] *Erethizon dorsatum* (Linn.). Near the extreme northern limit in this quarter.—E. A. P.

[29] *Esox lucius* Linn.—E. A. P.

[30] *Cristivomer namaycush* Walbaum.—E. A. P.

[31] *Lota maculosa* (Le Sueur).—E. A. P.

[S] The Methy are generally caught with a hook; and the best time for that sport is in the night; and if the night be dark, the better.

[32] He appears to have been camped at the rapid at the head or western end of Shethnanei Lake, which, according to the best information at present available, is about latitude 58° 37' and longitude 4° west from Prince of Wales Fort.

[33] She-than-nee is clearly the same word as *Shethnanei*, a Chipewyan word meaning "high hill," and applied to a point on the north shore of Shethnanei Lake. In February 1891, the Rev. J. (Bishop) Lofthouse visited some Indians living at this place, accomplishing the journey out from Churchill in seven days, and the return journey in six days.

[34] *Beralzoa* means Shoal Lake.

[T] It is the general opinion of the Southern Indians, that when any of their tribe has been driven to the necessity of eating human flesh, they become so fond of it, that no person is safe in their company. And though it is well known they are never guilty of making this horrid repast but when driven to it by necessity, yet those who have made it are not only shunned, but so universally detested by all who know them, that no Indians will tent with them, and they are frequently murdered slyly. I have seen several of those poor wretches who, unfortunately for them, have come under the above description, and though they were persons much esteemed before hunger had driven them to this act, were afterward so universally despised and neglected, that a smile never graced their countenances: deep melancholy has been seated on their brows, while the eye most expressively spoke the dictates of the heart, and seemed to say, "Why do you despise me for my misfortunes? the period is probably not far distant, when you may be driven to the like necessity!"

In the Spring of the year 1775, when I was building Cumberland House, an Indian, whose name was Wapoos, came to the settlement, at a time when fifteen tents of Indians were on the plantations: they examined him very minutely, and found he had come a considerable way by himself, without a gun, or ammunition. This made many of them conjecture he had met with, and killed, some person by the way; and this was the more easily credited, from the care he took to conceal a bag of provisions, which he had brought with him, in a lofty pine-tree near the house.

Being a stranger, I invited him in, though I saw he had nothing for trade; and during that interview, some of the Indian women examined his bag, and gave it as their opinion that the meat it contained was human flesh: in consequence, it was not without the interference of some principal Indians, whose liberality of sentiment was more extensive than that in the others, the poor creature saved his life. Many of the men cleaned and loaded their guns; others had their bows and arrows ready; and even the women took possession of the hatchets, to kill this poor inoffensive wretch, for no crime but that of travelling about two hundred miles by himself, unassisted by fire-arms for support in his journey.

[35] After leaving Lake Beralzoa, and before reaching Cathawhachaga River, he had crossed Thlewiaza or Little Fish River, Magnus Lake, and several other lakes and streams which are probably tributaries of the Tha-anne or Rocky-Bank River. Cathawhachaga is evidently the Kazan River

which I descended in 1894, and it is interesting to note that while, in Hearne's time, it was within the hunting grounds of the Chipewyan Indians, at the time of my visit, one hundred and twenty-four years later, these Indians had left it, and its banks were inhabited entirely by Eskimos. Hearne doubtless crossed the river four miles above its discharge into Yath-kyed Lake, at a place called by the Eskimos Paleluah, where the stream is deep and narrow, and has but a moderate current. This is a well-known crossing place for the caribou on their annual migrations from the forest to the Arctic Coast and back again, and the Eskimos wait to spear them while they are swimming across the stream, just as the Indians doubtless waited when they occupied this country. Its position is in latitude 62° 36' north, 28' south of the position assigned to it by Hearne in the text, and the longitude 4° 6' west of Fort Prince of Wales. His map does not here agree with his description, but places this crossing of the Kazan River in latitude 62° 40' north, very nearly in its true position. Cathawhachaga is a Chipewyan word meaning "where fish are plentiful in the river."

[36] Yath-kyed or White Snow Lake, at present known to the Eskimos as Haecoliguah.

[37] Whitefish, suckers, &c.

[38] See note on p. 87.

[39] The bay of Yath-kyed Lake, at which they seem to have stopped, is about eight miles north of Paleluah, where the river was crossed.

[U] To prepare meat in this manner, it requires no farther operation than cutting the lean parts of the animal into thin slices, and drying it in the sun, or by a slow fire, till, after beating it between two stones, it is reduced to a coarse powder.

[40] Théwhagon or Yéwuhikun is the Cree name for meat dried and beaten as above, and it is generally known throughout the fur countries as "pounded meat." When fat is plentiful this shredded dry meat is often packed into a sack made of hide, and boiling fat is poured over and into it. This mixture of dried meat and grease is called pemican.

[V] Wish-a-capucca is the name given by the natives to a plant which is found all over the country bordering on Hudson's Bay; and an infusion of it is used as tea by all the Europeans settled in that country.[41]

[41] This plant, *Ledum palustre*, commonly known as Labrador Tea, is common everywhere in the swamps throughout the forests of the north.

[W] This river, as well as all others deserving that appellation which I crossed during this part of my journey, ran to the East and North-East; and both them and the lakes were perfectly fresh, and inhabited by fish that are well known never to frequent salt water.[42]

[42] The brief description of this portion of his journey here given leaves his course quite indefinite, but his map shows that he travelled northward to the west of Yath-kyed Lake, across Nutarawit River, and thence around the north side of Napashish (Nutarawit) Lake, and westward to within a short distance of the south shore of Aberdeen Lake. Thence he turned south-westward until he reached Dubawnt River, where it flows from Dubawnt Lake. It is there a beautiful stream of clear water flowing between gently sloping grassy banks. The latitude of this place is 63° 33' north, while on his map it is shown as 63° 38' north. As the latitudes of the crossing places of Kazan and Dubawnt Rivers, shown on his map, though differing greatly from his text, are very nearly correct, we may fairly assume that his intermediate positions are also reasonably accurate, and that his northern point of this journey, which he places in latitude 64° 20', is not far from correct.

Dubawnt (properly To' bon') is a Chipewyan word meaning "water-along-the-shore." It is so called because the main body of the lake is at all seasons of the year covered with ice, though for a few days, or possibly weeks, in summer this ice is loosened from the shore, and there is a lane of water between the ice and the land.

[43] The position of the place where he broke his quadrant on the 12th of August is difficult to determine either from the text or from his map. A point in latitude 63° 10' north and longitude 10° 40' west from Churchill, which is the position given in the text, is shown on his map almost in the centre of Dubawnt Lake, and the map shows that after crossing the outlet of the lake his course was at a considerable distance to the north-west and west from it. It is probable therefore that his quadrant was broken on the great plain which lies to the west of the lake, and north-west of the Dubawnt River above the lake.

[96]

{47} CHAP. III.

Transactions from the Time the Quadrant was broken, till I arrived at the Factory

Several strange Indians join us from the Northward—They plundered me of all I had; but did not plunder the Southern Indians—My guide plundered—We begin our return to the Factory—Meet with other Indians, who join our company—Collect deer-skins for clothing, but could not get them dressed—Suffer much hardship from the want of tents and warm clothing—Most of the Indians leave us—Meet with Matonabbee—Some account of him, and his behaviour to me and the Southern Indians—We remain in his company some time—His observations on my two unsuccessful attempts—We leave him, and proceed to a place to which he directed us, in order to make snow-shoes and sledges—Join Matonabbee again, and proceed towards the Factory in his company—Ammunition runs short—Myself and four Indians set off post for the Factory—Much bewildered in a snow storm; my dog is frozen to death; we lie in a bush of willows—Proceed on our journey—Great difficulty in crossing a jumble of rocks—Arrive at the Fort.

1770. August. 13th.

The day after I had the misfortune to break the quadrant, several Indians joined me from the Northward, some of whom plundered me and my companions of almost every useful article we had, among which was my gun; and notwithstanding we were then on the point of returning to the Factory, yet, as one of my companions' guns was a little out of order, the loss was likely to be {48} severely felt; but it not being in my power to recover it again, we were obliged to rest contented.

1770. August.

Nothing can exceed the cool deliberation of those villains; a committee[97] of them entered my tent.[X] The ringleader seated himself on my left-hand. They first begged me to lend them my skipertogan[Y] to fill a pipe of tobacco. After smoking two or three pipes, they asked me for several articles which I had not, and among others for a pack of cards; but on my answering that I had not any of the articles they mentioned, one of them put his hand on my baggage, and asked if it was mine. Before I could answer in the affirmative, he and the rest of his companions (six in number) had all my treasure spread on the ground. One took one thing, and another another, till at last nothing was left but the empty bag, which they permitted me to keep. At length, considering that, though I was going to the Factory, I should want a knife to cut my victuals, an awl to mend my shoes, and a needle to mend my other clothing, they readily gave me these articles, though not without making me understand that I ought to look upon {49} it as a great favour. Finding them possessed of so much generosity, I ventured to solicit them for my razors; but thinking that one would be sufficient to shave me during my passage home, they made no scruple to keep the other; luckily they chose the worst. To complete their generosity, they permitted me to take as much soap as I thought would be sufficient to wash and shave me during the remainder of my journey to the Factory.

Photo: J. B. Tyrrell, August 12, 1893.
CAMP ON THE SHORE OF DUBAWNT LAKE

Photo: J. B. Tyrrell, August 18, 1893.
DUBAWNT RIVER BELOW DUBAWNT LAKE
WHERE HEARNE CROSSED THE RIVER IN JULY 1770

They were more cautious in plundering the Southern Indians, as the relation of such outrages being committed on them might occasion a war between the two nations; but they had nothing of that kind to dread from the English. However, the Northern Indians had address enough to talk my home-guard Indians out of all they had: so that before we left them, they were as clean swept as myself, excepting their guns, some ammunition, an old hatchet, an ice-chissel, and a file to sharpen them.

[98]

It may probably be thought strange that my guide, who was a Northern Indian, should permit his countrymen to commit such outrages on those under his charge; but being a man of little note, he was so far from being able to protect us, that he was obliged to submit to nearly the same outrage himself. On this occasion he assumed a great air of generosity; but the fact was, he gave freely what it was not in his power to protect.

19th.

{50} Early in the morning of the nineteenth, I set out on my return, in company with several Northern Indians, who were bound to the Factory with furrs and other commodities in trade. This morning the Indian who took my gun, returned it to me, it being of no use to him, having no ammunition. The weather for some time proved fine, and deer were very plentiful; but as the above ravagers had materially lightened my load, by taking everything from me, except the quadrant, books, &c., this part of my journey was the easiest and most pleasant of any I had experienced since my leaving the Fort. In our way we frequently met with other Indians, so that scarcely a day passed without our seeing several smokes made by other strangers. Many of those we met joined our party, having furrs and other commodities for trade.

31st.

1770. September.

The deer's hair being now of a proper length for clothing, it was necessary, according to the custom, to procure as many of their skins, while in season, as would make a suit of warm clothing for the Winter: and as each grown person requires the prime parts of from eight to eleven of those skins (in proportion to their size) to make a complete suit, it must naturally be supposed that this addition to my burden was very considerable. My load, however cumbersome and heavy, was yet very bearable; but, after I had carried it several weeks, it proved of no service; for we had not any women properly belonging to our company, consequently had not any {51} person to[99] dress them; and so uncivil were the other Indians, that they would neither exchange them for others of an inferior quality already dressed, nor permit their women to dress them for us, under pretence that they were always employed in the like duty for themselves and families, which was by no means the case; for many of them had sufficient time to have done every little service of that kind that we could have required of them. The truth was, they were too well informed of my poverty to do any acts of generosity, as they well knew I had it not then in my power to reward them for their trouble. I never saw a set of people that possessed so little humanity, or that could view the distresses of their fellow-creatures with so little feeling and unconcern; for though they seem to have a great affection for their wives and children, yet they will laugh at and ridicule the distress of every other person who is not immediately related to them.

15th.

This behaviour of the Indians made our situation very disagreeable; for as the fall advanced, we began to feel the cold very severely for want of proper clothing. We suffered also greatly from the inclemency of the weather, as we had no tent to shelter us. My guide was entirely exempted from all those inconveniences, having procured a good warm suit of clothing; and as one of his wives had long before joined our party, he was provided with a tent, and every other necessary consistent {52} with their manner of living: but the old fellow was so far from interesting himself in our behalf, that he had, for some time before, entirely withdrawn from our company; and though he then continued to carry the greatest part of our little remains of ammunition, yet he did not contribute in the smallest degree towards our support. As deer, however, were in great plenty, I felt little or no inconvenience from his neglect in this respect.

17th.

1770. September.

Provisions still continued very plentiful; which was a singular piece of good fortune, and the only circumstance which at this time could contribute to our happiness or[100] safety; for notwithstanding the early season of the year, the weather was remarkably bad and severely cold, at least it appeared so to us, probably from having no kind of skin-clothing. In this forlorn state we continued our course to the South East; and, to add to the gloominess of our situation, most of the Northern Indians who had been in our company all the first part of the fall, were by this time gone a-head, as we could not keep up with them for want of snow-shoes.

20th.

In the evening of the twentieth, we were joined from the Westward by a famous Leader, called Matonabbee, mentioned in my instructions; who, with his followers, or gang, was also going to Prince of Wales's Fort, with furrs, and other articles for trade. This

Leader, when a youth, resided several years at the above Fort, and was {53} not only a perfect master of the Southern Indian language, but by being frequently with the Company's servants, had acquired several words of English, and was one of the men who brought the latest accounts of the Coppermine River; and it was on his information, added to that of one I-dot-le-ezey, (who is since dead), that this expedition was set on foot.

1770. October.

The courteous behaviour of this stranger struck me very sensibly. As soon as he was acquainted with our distress, he got such skins as we had with us dressed for the Southern Indians, and furnished me with a good warm suit of otter and other skins: but, as it was not in his power to provide us with snow-shoes, (being then on the barren ground), he directed us to a little river which he knew, and where there was a small range of woods, which, though none of the best, would, he said, furnish us with temporary snow-shoes and sledges, that might materially assist us during the remaining part of our journey. We spent several nights in company with this Leader, though we advanced towards the Fort at the rate of ten or twelve miles a day; and as provisions abounded, he made a grand feast for me in the Southern[101] Indian style, where there was plenty of good eating, and the whole concluded with singing and dancing, after the Southern Indian style and manner. In this amusement my home-guard Indians bore no inconsiderable part, as they were both men of some {54} consequence when at home, and well known to Matonabbee: but among the other Northern Indians, to whom they were not known, they were held in no estimation; which indeed is not to be wondered at, when we consider that the value of a man among those people, is always proportioned to his abilities in hunting; and as my two Indians had not exhibited any great talents that way, the Northern Indians shewed them as much respect as they do in common to those of very moderate talents among themselves.

During my conversation with this Leader, he asked me very seriously, If I would attempt another journey for the discovery of the Copper-mines? And on my answering in the affirmative, provided I could get better guides than I had hitherto been furnished with, he said he would readily engage in that service, provided the Governor at the Fort would employ him. In answer to this, I assured him his offer would be gladly accepted; and as I had already experienced every hardship that was likely to accompany any future trial, I was determined to complete the discovery, even at the risque of life itself. Matonabbee assured me, that by the accounts received from his own countrymen, the Southern Indians, and myself, it was very probable I might not experience so much hardship during the whole journey, as I had already felt, though scarcely advanced one third part of the journey.

1770. October.

{55} He attributed all our misfortunes to the misconduct of my guides, and the very plan we pursued, by the desire of the Governor, in not taking any women with us on this journey, was, he said, the principal thing that occasioned all our wants: "for, said he, when all the men are heavy[102] laden, they can neither hunt nor travel to any considerable distance; and in case they meet with success in hunting, who is to carry the produce of their labour? Women," added he, "were made for labour; one of them can carry, or haul, as much as two men can do. They also pitch our tents, make and mend our clothing, keep us warm at night; and, in fact, there is no such thing as travelling any considerable distance, or for any length of time, in this country, without their assistance. Women," said he again, "though they do every thing, are maintained at a trifling expence; for as they always stand cook, the very licking of their fingers in scarce times, is sufficient for their subsistence." This, however odd it may appear, is but too true a description of the situation of women in this country; it is at least so in appearance; for the women always carry the provisions, and it is more than probable they help themselves when the men are not present.

23d.

25th.

November. 1st.

Early in the morning of the twenty-third, I struck out of the road to
the Eastward, with my two companions and two or three Northern
Indians, while Matonabbee and his crew continued their course to
the Factory, promising {56} to walk so slow that we might come up
with them again; and in two days we arrived at the place to which
we were directed. We went to work immediately in making snow-
shoe frames and sledges; but notwithstanding our utmost
endeavours, we could not complete them in less than four days. On
the first of November we again proceeded on our journey toward the
Factory; and on the sixth, came up with Matonabbee and his gang:
after which we proceeded on together several days; when I found
my new acquaintance, on all occasions, the most sociable, kind, and
sensible Indian I had ever met with. He was a man well known, and,
as an Indian, of universal knowledge, and generally respected.

1770. November.

Deer proved pretty plentiful for some time, but to my great surprise,
when I wanted to give Matonabbee a little ammunition for his own
use, I found that my guide,[103] Conreaquefè, who had it all under
his care, had so embezzled or otherways expended it, that only ten
balls and about three pounds of powder remained; so that long
before we arrived at the Fort we were obliged to cut up an ice-chissel
into square lumps, as a substitute for ball. It is, however, rather
dangerous firing lumps of iron out of such slight barrels as are
brought to this part of the world for trade. These, though light and
handy, and of course well adapted for the use of both English and

Indians in long journies, and of sufficient strength for leaden shot or ball, are not strong enough for {57} this kind of shot; and strong fowling-pieces would not only be too heavy for the laborious ways of hunting in this country, but their bores being so much larger, would require more than double the quantity of ammunition that small ones do; which, to Indians at least, must be an object of no inconsiderable importance.

> 20th.

> 21st.

> 1770. November.

> 23rd.

> 1770. November.

I kept company with Matonabbee till the twentieth, at which time the deer began to be so scarce that hardly a fresh track could be seen; and as we were then but a few days walk from the Fort, he advised me to proceed on with all speed, while he and his companions followed at leisure. Accordingly, on the twenty-first, I set out post-haste, accompanied by one of the home-guard (Southern) Tribe, and three Northern Indians. That night we lay on the South side of Egg River; but, long before daybreak the next morning, the weather became so bad, with a violent gale of wind from the North West, and such a drift of snow, that we could not have a bit of fire: and as no good woods were near to afford us shelter, we agreed to proceed on our way: especially as the wind was on our backs, and though the weather was bad near the surface, we could frequently see the moon, and sometimes the stars, to direct us in our course. In this situation

we continued walking the whole day, and it was not till after ten at
night that we could find the smallest tuft of woods to put up in; for
though we well knew we must have passed by several[104]
hummocks of shrubby woods {58} that might have afforded us some
shelter, yet the wind blew so hard, and the snow drifted so
excessively thick, that we could not see ten yards before us the
whole day. Between seven and eight in the evening my dog, a
valuable brute, was frozen to death; so that his sledge, which was a
very heavy one, I was obliged to haul. Between nine and ten at night
we arrived at a small creek, on which we walked about three quarters
of a mile, when we came to a large tuft of tall willows, and two or
three sets of old tent-poles. Being much jaded, we determined not to
proceed any farther that night; so we went to work, and made the
best defence against the weather that the situation of the place and
our materials would admit. Our labour consisted only in digging a
hole in the snow, and fixing a few deer skins up to windward of us;
but the most difficult task was that of making a fire. When this was
once accomplished, the old tent-poles amply supplied us with fuel.
By the time we had finished this business, the weather began to
moderate, and the drift greatly to abate; so that the moon and the
Aurora Borealis shone out with great splendour, and there appeared
every symptom of the return of fine weather. After eating a plentiful
supper of venison, therefore, of which we had a sufficient stock to
last us to the Fort, we laid down and got a little sleep. The next day
proving fine and clear, though excessively sharp, we proceeded on
our journey early in the morning, and at night lay on the South East
side of Seal River. We should have made a much longer day's {59}
journey, had we not been greatly embarrassed at setting out, by a
jumble of rocks, which we could not avoid without going greatly out
of our way. Here I must observe, that we were more than fortunate
in not attempting to leave the little creek where we had fixed our
habitation the preceding night, as the spot where we lay was not
more than two or three miles distant from this dangerous place; in
which, had we fallen in with it in the night, we must unavoidably
have been[105] bewildered, if we had not all perished; as
notwithstanding the advantage of a clear day, and having used every

possible precaution, it was with the utmost difficulty that we crossed it without broken limbs. Indeed it would have been next to an impossibility to have done it in the night.

24th.

25th.

The twenty-fourth and twenty-fifth proved fine, clear weather, though excessively cold; and in the afternoon of the latter, we arrived at Prince of Wales's Fort, after having been absent eight months and twenty-two days, on a fruitless, or at least an unsuccessful journey.[44]

FOOTNOTES:

[X] This only consisted of three walking-sticks stuck into the ground, and a blanket thrown over them.

[Y] Skipertogan is a small bag that contains a flint and steel, also a pipe and tobacco, as well as touchwood, &c. for making a fire. Some of these bags may be called truly elegant; being richly ornamented with beads, porcupine-quills, moose-hair, &c. a work always performed by the women; and they are, with much propriety, greatly esteemed by most Europeans for the neatness of their workmanship.

[44] The text gives very little information from which to follow Hearne's course from the point where he broke his quadrant on August 12th, till he arrived at Churchill on November 25th, so that we must follow him as well as possible from the route laid down on his map.

His route is marked crossing the Dubawnt River in latitude 63° north, near where it flows into an arm or bay of Dubawnt Lake. The river actually flows into the lake from the south-west in latitude 62° 55', and it is probable that he crossed it three miles above this in latitude 62° 53' 30", where, in 1893, we found the most northerly grove of stunted spruce growing on the bank of the river, and where very old remains of Indian camps were plainly to be seen.

From here he turned south-eastward, and travelling around the south end of Dubawnt Lake reached Kazan River just above Angikuni Lake (called on Alexander Mackenzie's map Titmeg Lake), probably just at its western end, where the caribou cross the river in large numbers in their migration southward. This point is in latitude 62° 20' north, while Hearne places his crossing-place in latitude 62° 12'. Thence, keeping south of Angikuni Lake, he turned more to the east, and passing several lakes which cannot be definitely identified, but two of which are probably Magnus and Thaolintoa Lakes, he reached Thlewiaza River east of Island Lake, where he was joined by Matonabbee and a band of Indians, who had left their wives at Island Lake, and were on their way to Fort Prince of Wales to trade.

At the Thlewiaza River he turned eastward down the stream to a grove of timber to obtain wood for snow-shoes. After making snow-shoes he turned southward and rejoined Matonabbee and his band of Indians for a short time, and then pushed on across Egg and Seal Rivers and around the south end of Button's Bay to Fort Prince of Wales.

[106]

{60} CHAP. IV.

Transactions during our Stay at Prince of Wales's Fort, and the former part of our third Expedition, till our Arrival at Clowey, where we built Canoes, in May 1771.

Preparations for our departure—Refuse to take any of the home-guard Indians with me—By so doing, I offend the Governor—Leave the Fort a third time—My instructions on this expedition—Provisions of all kinds very scarce—Arrive at the woods, where we kill some deer—Arrive at Island Lake—Matonabbee taken ill—Some remarks thereon—Join the remainder of the Indians' families—Leave Island Lake—Description thereof—Deer plentiful—Meet a strange Indian—Alter our course from West North West to West by South—Cross Cathawhachaga River, Cossed Lake, Snow-Bird Lake, and Pike Lake—Arrive at a tent of strangers, who are employed in snaring deer in a pound—Description of the pound—Method of proceeding—Remarks thereon—Proceed on our journey—Meet with several parties of Indians; by one of whom I sent a letter to the Governor at Prince of Wales's Fort—Arrive at Thleweyazayeth—Employment there—Proceed to the North North West and North—Arrive at Clowey—One of the Indians' wives taken in labour—Remarks thereon—Customs observed by the Northern Indians on those occasions.

1770. November. 28th.

On my arrival at the Fort, I informed the Governor, of Matonabbee's being so near. On the twenty-eighth of November he arrived. Notwithstanding the many difficulties and hardships which I had undergone during my two unsuccessful attempts, I was so far from being {61} solicited on this occasion to undertake a third excursion, that I willingly offered my service; which was readily accepted, as my abilities and approved courage, in persevering under difficulties, were thought noways inferior to the task.

A SOUTH-WEST VIEW OF PRINCE OF WALES'S FORT, HUDSON'S BAY
Published by J. Sewell, Cornhill, March 1st, 1797
From the "European Magazine", June, 1797

[107]

> 1770. December.

I then determined to engage Matonabbee to be my guide; to which he readily consented, and with a freedom of speech and correctness of language not commonly met with among Indians, not only pointed out the reasons which had occasioned all our misfortunes in my two former attempts, but described the plan he intended to pursue; which at the same time that it was highly satisfactory to me, did honour to his penetration and judgment; as it proved him to be a man of extensive observation with respect to times, seasons, and places; and well qualified to explain everything that could contribute either to facilitate or retard the ease or progress of travelling in those dreary parts of the world.

> 7th.

> 1770. December.

Having engaged Matonabbee, therefore, as my guide, I began to make preparations for our departure; but Mr. Norton, the Governor, having been very fully occupied in trading with a large body of Indians, it was the seventh of December before I could obtain from him my dispatches. It may not be improper to observe, that he again wanted to force some of the home-guard Indians (who were {62} his own relations[Z]) into our company, merely with a view that they might engross all the credit of taking care of{63} me during the journey; but I had round them of so little use in my two former attempts, that I absolutely refused them; and by so doing, offended Mr. Norton to such a degree, that neither time nor absence could ever afterwards eradicate his dislike of me; so that at my return he used every means in his power to treat me ill, and to render my life unhappy. However, to deal with candour on this occasion, it must be acknowledged to his honour, that whatever our private animosities might have been, he did not suffer them to interfere with public business; and I was fitted out with ammunition, and every other article which Matonabbee thought could be wanted. I was also furnished, as before, with a small assortment of light trading goods, as presents to the far distant Indians.

[109]

[108]

1770. December.

At last I succeeded in obtaining my instructions which were as follows:

{64} "ORDERS *and* INSTRUCTIONS *for* Mr. SAMUEL HEARNE, *going on his third Expedition to the North of Churchill River, in quest of a North West Passage, Copper Mines, or any other thing that may be serviceable to the British Nation in general, or the Hudson's Bay Company in particular; in the year 1770.*

"Mr.   SAMUEL   HEARNE.

"SIR,

"As you have offered your service a third time to go in search of the Copper Mine River, &c., and as Matonabbee, a leading Indian, who has been at those parts, is willing to be your guide, we have accordingly engaged him for that service; but having no other instrument on the same construction with the quadrant you had the misfortune to break, we have furnished you with an Elton's quadrant, being the most proper instrument we can now procure for making observations on the land.

"The above Leader, Matonabbee, and a few of his best men, which he has selected for that purpose, are to provide for you, assist you in all things, and conduct you to the Copper Mine River; where you must {65} be careful to observe the latitude and longitude, also the course of the river, the depth of the water, the situation of the Copper Mines, &c., but your first instructions, of November sixth, one thousand seven hundred and sixty-nine, being sufficiently full, we refer you to every part thereof for the better regulation of your conduct during this journey.

1770. December.

"As you and your Indian companions are fitted out with everything that we think is necessary, (or at least as many useful articles as the nature of travelling in those parts will admit of), you are hereby desired to proceed on your journey[110] as soon as possible; and your present guide has promised to take great care of you, and conduct you out and home with all convenient speed.

"I conclude with my best wishes for your health and happiness, together with a successful journey, and a quick return in safety. Amen.

"(Signed) MOSES NORTON, Governor.

"Dated   at   Prince   of   Wales's   Fort, 7th December 1770."

7th.

On the seventh of December I set out on my third journey; and the weather, considering the season of the year, was for some days pretty mild. One of Matonabbee's wives being ill, occasioned us to walk so slow, that {66} it was the thirteenth before we arrived at Seal River; at which time two men and their wives left us, whose loads, when added to those of the remainder of my crew, made a very material difference, especially as Matonabbee's wife was so ill as to be obliged to be hauled on a sledge.

16th.

1770. December.

Finding deer and all other game very scarce, and not knowing how long it might be before we could reach any place where they were in greater plenty, the Indians walked as far each day as their loads and other circumstances would conveniently permit. On the sixteenth, we arrived at Egg River, where Matonabbee and the rest of my crew had laid up some provisions and other necessaries, when on their journey to the Fort. On going to the place where they thought the provisions had been carefully secured from all kinds of wild beasts, they had the mortification to find that some of their countrymen, with whom the Governor had first traded and dispatched from the Fort, had robbed the store of every article, as well as of some of their most useful implements. This loss was more severely felt, as there was a total want of every kind of game; and the Indians, not expecting to meet with so great a disappointment, had not used that[111] economy in the expenditure of the oatmeal and other provisions which they had received at the Fort, as they probably would have done, had they not relied firmly on finding a supply at this place. This disappointment and loss was borne by the Indians with the greatest fortitude; and I did not hear {67} one of them breathe the least hint of revenge in case they should ever discover the offenders; the only effect it had on them was, that of making them put the best foot foremost. This was thought so necessary, that for some time we walked every day from morning till night. The days, however, being short, our sledges heavy, and some of the road very bad, our progress seldom exceeded sixteen or eighteen miles a day, and some days we did not travel so much.

> 18th.

On the eighteenth, as we were continuing our course to the North West, up a small creek that empties itself into Egg River, we saw the tracks of many deer which had crossed that part a few days before; at that time there was not a fresh track to be seen: some of the Indians, however, who had lately passed that way, had killed more than they had occasion for, so that several joints of good meat were found in their old tent-places; which, though only sufficient for one good meal, were very acceptable, as we had been in exceeding straitened circumstances for many days.

> 19th.

> 27th.

> 1770. December.

On the nineteenth, we pursued our course in the North West quarter; and, after leaving the above-mentioned creek, traversed nothing but entire barren ground, with empty bellies, till the twenty-seventh; for though we arrived at some woods on the twenty-sixth, and saw a few deer, four of which the Indians killed, they were {68} at so great a distance from the place on which we lay, that it was the twenty-seventh before the meat was brought to the tents. Here the Indians proposed to continue one day, under pretence of repairing their sledges and snow shoes; but from the little attention they paid to those repairs, I was led to think that the want of food was the chief thing that detained them, as they never ceased[112] eating the whole day. Indeed for many days before we had in great want, and for the last three days had not tasted a morsel of any thing, except a pipe of tobacco and a drink of snow water; and as we walked daily from morning till night, and were all heavy laden, our strength began to fail. I must confess that I never spent so dull a Christmas; and when I recollected the merry season which was then passing, and reflected on the immense quantities, and great variety of delicacies which were then expending in every part of Christendom, and that with a profusion bordering on waste, I could not refrain from wishing myself again in Europe, if it had been only to have had an opportunity of alleviating the extreme hunger which I suffered with the refuse of the table of any one of my acquaintance. My Indians, however, still kept in good spirits; and as we were then across all the barren ground, and saw a few fresh tracks of deer, they began to think that the worst of the road was over for that winter, and flattered me with the expectation of soon meeting with deer and other game in greater plenty than we had done since our departure from the Fort.

> 28th.

{69} Early in the morning of the twenty-eighth, we again set out, and directed our course to the Westward, through thick shrubby woods, consisting chiefly of ill-shaped stunted pines, with small dwarf junipers, intermixed here and there, particularly round the margins of ponds and swamps, with dwarf willow bushes; and among the rocks and sides of the hills were also some small poplars.[46]

> 30th.

> 1770. December.

On the thirtieth, we arrived at the East side of Island Lake,[47] where the Indians killed two large buck deer; but the rutting season was so lately over, that their flesh was only eatable by those who could not procure better food. In the evening, Matonabbee was taken very ill;

and from the nature of his complaint, I judged his illness to have proceeded from the enormous quantity of meat that he had eat on the twenty-seventh, as he had been indisposed ever since that time. Nothing is more common with those Indians, after they have eat as much at a sitting as would serve six moderate men, than to find themselves out of order; but not one of them can bear to hear that it is the effect of eating too much: in defence of which they say, that the meanest of the animal creation knows when hunger is satisfied, and will leave off accordingly. This, however, is a false assertion, advanced knowingly in support of an absurd argument; for it is well known by them, as well as all the Southern Indians, that the black bear, who, for size and the delicacy of its flesh, may justly be called a respectable animal, is so far from knowing {70} when its hunger is satisfied, that, in the Summer, when the berries are ripe, it will gorge to such a degree, that it frequently, and even daily, vomits up great quantities of new-swallowed fruit, before it has undergone any change in the stomach, and immediately renews its repast with as much eagerness as before.

[113]

1770. December.

Notwithstanding the Northern Indians are at times so voracious, yet they bear hunger with a degree of fortitude which, as Mr. Ellis justly observes of the Southern Indians, "is much easier to admire than to imitate." I have more than once seen the Northern Indians, at the end of three or four days fasting, as merry and jocose on the subject, as if they had voluntarily imposed it on themselves; and would ask each other in the plainest terms, and in the merriest mood, if they had any inclination for an intrigue with a strange[114] woman? I must acknowledge that examples of this kind were of infinite service to me, as they tended to keep up my spirits on those occasions with a degree of fortitude that would have been impossible for me to have done had the Indians behaved in a contrary manner, and expressed any apprehension of starving.

31st.

1771. January. 1st.

1771. January.

Early in the morning of the thirty-first, we continued our journey, and walked about fourteen miles to the Westward on Island Lake, where we fixed our residence; but Matonabbee was at this time so ill as to be obliged to be hauled on a sledge the whole day. The {71} next morning, however, he so far recovered as to be capable of walking; when we proceeded on to the West and West by North, about sixteen miles farther on the same Lake, till we arrived at two tents, which contained the remainder of the wives and families of my guides, who had been waiting there for the return of their husbands from the Fort. Here we found only two men, though there were upward of twenty women and children; and as those two men had no gun or ammunition, they had no other method of supporting themselves and the women, but by catching fish, and snaring a few rabbits:[48] the latter were scarce, but the former were easily caught in considerable numbers either with nets or hooks. The species of fish generally caught in the nets are tittemeg, pike, and barble; and the only sorts caught with hooks are trout, pike, burbut, and a small fish, erroneously called by the English tench: the Southern Indians call it the toothed tittemeg, and the Northern Indians call it *saint eah*. They are delicate eating; being nearly as firm as a perch, and generally very fat. They seldom exceed a foot in length, and in shape much resemble a gurnard, except that of having a very long broad fin on the back, like a perch, but this fin is not armed with similar spikes. The scales are large, and of a sooty brown. They are generally most esteemed when broiled or roasted with the scales on, of course the skin is not eaten.

[115]

{72} As the Captain [Matonabbee] and one man were indisposed, we did not move on the second of January; but early in the morning of the third set out, and walked about seven miles to the North Westward, five of which were on the above mentioned Lake; when the Indians having killed two deer, we put up for the night.

Island Lake (near the center) is in latitude 60° 45' North, and 102° 25' West longitude, from London; and is, at the part we crossed, about thirty-five miles wide: but from the North East to the South West it is much larger, and entirely full of islands, so near to each other as to make the whole Lake resemble a jumble of serpentine rivers and creeks; and it is celebrated by the natives as abounding with great plenty of fine fish during the beginning of the Winter. At different parts of this Lake most part of the wives and families of those Northern Indians who visit Prince of Wales's Fort in October and November generally reside, and wait for their return; as there is little fear of their being in want of provisions, even without the assistance of a gun and ammunition, which is a point of real consequence to them. The Lake is plentifully supplied with water from several small rivulets and creeks which run into it at the South West end; and it empties itself by means of other small rivers which run to the North East, the principal of which is Nemace-a-seepee-a-fish, or Little Fish River. Many of the islands, {73} as well as the main land round this Lake, abound with dwarf woods, chiefly pines; but in some parts intermixed with larch and small birch trees. The land, like all the rest which lies to the North of Seal River, is hilly, and full of rocks; and though none of the hills are high, yet as few of the woods grow on their summits, they in general show their snowy heads far above the woods which grow in the vallies, or those which are scattered about their sides.[116]

1771. January.

After leaving Island Lake, we continued our old course between the West and North West, and travelled at the easy rate of eight or nine miles a day. Provisions of all kinds were scarce till the sixteenth, when the Indians killed twelve deer. This induced us to put up, though early in the day; and finding great plenty of deer in the neighbourhood of our little encampment, it was agreed by all parties to remain a few days, in order to dry and pound some meat to make it lighter for carriage.

22d.

1771. January.

Having, by the twenty-second, provided a sufficient stock of provision, properly prepared, to carry with us, and repaired our sledges and snow-shoes, we again pursued our course in the North West quarter; and in the afternoon spoke with a stranger, an Indian, who had one of Matonabbee's wives under his care. He did not remain in our company above an hour, as he only smoked part of a few pipes with his friends, and returned to his tent, which could not {74} be far distant from the place where we lay that night, as the woman and her two children joined us next morning, before we had taken down our tent and made ready for moving. Those people were the first strangers whom we had met since we left the Fort, though we had travelled several hundred miles; which is a proof that this part of the country is but thinly inhabited. It is a truth well known to the natives, and doubtless founded on experience, that there are many very extensive tracts of land in those parts, which are incapable of affording support to any number of the human race even during the short time they are passing through them, in the capacity of migrants, from one place to another; much less are they capable of affording a constant support to those who might wish to make them their fixed residence at any season of the year. It is true, that few rivers or lakes in those parts are entirely destitute of fish; but the uncertainty of meeting with a sufficient supply for any considerable time together, makes the natives very cautious how they put their[117] whole dependance on that article, as it has too frequently been the means of many hundreds being starved to death.

> 23d.

By the twenty-third, deer were so plentiful that the Indians seemed to think that, unless the season, contrary to expectation and general experience, should prove unfavourable, there would be no fear of our being in want of {75} provisions during the rest of the Winter, as deer had always been known to be in great plenty in the direction which they intended to walk.

> February. 3d.

On the third of February, we continued our course to the West by North and West North West,[49] and were so near the edge of the woods, that the barren ground was in sight to the Northward. As the woods trended away to the West, we were obliged to alter our course to West by South, for the sake of keeping among them, as well as the deer. In the course of this day's walk we saw several strangers, some of whom remained in our company, while others went on their respective ways.

> 6th.

> 1771. February.

On the sixth, we crossed the main branch of Cathawhachaga River;[50] which, at that part, is about three quarters of a mile broad; and after walking three miles farther, came to the side of Cossed Whoie,[51] or Partridge Lake; but the day being far spent, and the weather excessively cold, we put up for the night.

[118]

7th.

Early in the morning of the seventh, the weather being serene and clear, we set out, and crossed the above mentioned Lake; which at that part is about fourteen miles wide; but from the South South West to North North East is much larger. It is impossible to describe the intenseness of the cold which we experienced this day; and the dispatch we made in crossing the lake is almost incredible, as it was {76} performed by the greatest part of my crew in less than two hours; though some of the women, who were heavy laden, took a much longer time. Several of the Indians were much frozen, but none of them more disagreeably so than one of Matonabbee's wives, whose thighs and buttocks were in a manner incrusted with frost; and when thawed, several blisters arose, nearly as large as sheeps' bladders. The pain the poor woman suffered on this occasion was greatly aggravated by the laughter and jeering of her companions, who said that she was rightly served for belting her clothes so high. I must acknowledge that I was not in the number of those who pitied her, as I thought she took too much pains to shew a clean heel and good leg; her garters being always in sight, which, though by no means considered here as bordering on indecency, is by far too airy to withstand the rigorous cold of a severe winter in a high Northern latitude. I doubt not that the laughter of her companions was excited by similar ideas.

1771. February.

When we got on the West side of Partridge Lake we[119] continued our course for many days toward the West by South and West South West; when deer were so plentiful, and the Indians killed such vast numbers, that notwithstanding we frequently remained three, four, or five days in a place, to eat up the spoils of our hunting, yet at our departure we frequently left great quantities of good meat behind us, which we could neither eat nor carry with us. {77} This conduct is the more excusable among people whose wandering manner of life and contracted ideas make every thing appear to them as the effect of mere chance. The great uncertainty of their ever visiting this or that part a second time, induces them to think there is nothing either wrong or improvident in living on the best the country will afford, as they are passing through it from place to place; and they seem willing that those who come after them should take their chance, as they have done.

> 21st.

On the twenty-first, we crossed The-whole-kyed Whoie, or Snowbird Lake,[52] which at that part was about twelve or thirteen miles wide, though from North to South it is much larger. As deer were as plentiful as before, we expended much time in killing and eating them. This Matonabbee assured me was the best way we could employ ourselves, as the season would by no means permit us to proceed in a direct line for the Copper-mine River; but when the Spring advanced, and the deer began to draw out to the barren ground, he would then, he said, proceed in such a manner as to leave no room to doubt of our arrival at the Copper-mine River in proper time.

> March. 2d.

> 1771. March. 3d.

[120]

On the second of March, we lay by the side of Whooldyah'd Whoie or Pike Lake,[53] and not far from Doo-baunt Whoie River. On the next day we began to cross the above mentioned Lake, but after walking seven miles on it to the West South West, we arrived at a large tent of Northern {78} Indians, who had been living there from the beginning of the Winter, and had found a plentiful subsistence by catching deer in a pound. This kind of employment is performed in the following manner:

1771. March.

When the Indians design to impound deer, they look out for one of the paths in which a number of them have trod, and which is observed to be still frequented by them. When these paths cross a lake, a wide river, or a barren plain, they are found to be much the best for the purpose; and if the path run through a cluster of woods, capable of affording materials for building the pound, it adds considerably to the commodiousness of the situation. The pound is built by making a strong fence with brushy trees, without observing any degree of regularity, and the work is continued to any extent, according to the pleasure of the builders. I have seen some that were not less than a mile round, and am informed that there are others still more extensive. The door, or entrance of the pound, is not larger than a common gate, and the inside is so crowded with small counter-hedges as very much to resemble a maze; in every opening of which they set a snare, made with thongs of parchment deer-skins well twisted together, which are amazingly strong. One end of the snare is usually made fast to a growing pole; but if no one of a sufficient size can be found near the place where the snare is set, a loose pole is substituted in its room, which is always of such size and length that a deer cannot drag it {79} far before it gets entangled among the other woods, which are all left standing except what is found necessary for making the fence, hedges, &c.

Photo: J. B. Tyrrell, July 19, 1893.
WHOLDIAH LAKE AS SEEN FROM THE HILLS TO THE SOUTH

Photo: J. B. Tyrrell, August 2, 1893.
GROVE OF SPRUCE BESIDE DUBAWNT RIVER,
WITHIN THE BARREN LANDS

[121]

The pound being thus prepared, a row of small brush-wood is stuck up in the snow on each side of the door or entrance; and these hedge-rows are continued along the open part of the lake, river, or plain, where neither stick nor stump besides is to be seen, which makes them the more distinctly observed. These poles, or brush-wood, are generally placed at the distance of fifteen or twenty yards from each other, and ranged in such a manner as to form two sides of a long acute angle, growing gradually wider in proportion to the distance they extend from the entrance of the pound, which sometimes is not less than two or three miles; while the deer's path is exactly along the middle, between the two rows of brush-wood.

Indians employed on this service always pitch their tent on or near to an eminence that affords a commanding prospect of the path leading to the pound; and when they see any deer going that way, men, women, and children walk along the lake or river-side under cover of the woods, till they get behind them, then step forth to open view, and proceed towards the pound in the form of a crescent. The poor timorous deer finding themselves pursued, and at the same time taking the two rows of brushy poles to be two ranks of people stationed {80} to prevent their passing on either side, run straight forward in the path till they get into the pound. The Indians then close in, and block up the entrance with some brushy trees, that have been cut down and lie at hand for that purpose. The deer being thus enclosed, the women and children walk round the pound, to prevent them from breaking or jumping over the fence, while the men are employed spearing such as are entangled in the snares, and shooting with bows and arrows those which remain loose in the pound.[122]

1771. March.

1771. March.

This method of hunting, if it deserves the name, is sometimes so successful, that many families subsist by it without having occasion to move their tents above once or twice during the course of a whole winter; and when the Spring advances, both the deer and Indians draw out to the Eastward, on the ground which is entirely barren, or at least what is so called in those parts, as it neither produces trees or shrubs of any kind, so that moss and some little grass is all the herbage which is to be found on it. Such an easy way of procuring a comfortable maintenance in the Winter months, (which is by far the worst time of the year), is wonderfully well adapted to the support of the aged and infirm, but is too apt to occasion a habitual indolence in the young and active, who frequently spend a whole Winter in this indolent manner: and as those parts of the country are almost destitute of every animal of the furr kind, it cannot be {81} supposed that those who indulge themselves in this indolent method of procuring food can be masters of any thing for trade; whereas those who do not get their livelihood at so easy a rate, generally procure furrs enough during the Winter to purchase a sufficient supply of ammunition, and other European goods, to last them another year. This is nearly the language of the more industrious among them, who, of course, are of most importance and value to the Hudson's Bay Company, as it is from them the furrs are procured which compose the greatest part of Churchill trade. But in my opinion, there cannot exist a stronger proof that mankind was not created to enjoy happiness in this world, than the conduct of the miserable beings who inhabit this wretched part of it; as none but the aged and infirm, the women and children, a few of the more indolent and unambitious part of them, will submit to remain in the parts where food and clothing are procured in this easy manner, because no animals are produced there whose furrs are valuable. And what do the more industrious gain by giving themselves all this additional trouble? The real wants[123] of these people are few, and easily supplied; a hatchet, an ice-chissel, a file, and a knife, are all that is required to enable them, with a little industry, to procure a comfortable livelihood; and those who endeavour to possess more, are always the most unhappy, and may, in fact, be said to be only slaves and carriers to the rest, whose ambition never leads them to any thing beyond the means of procuring food {82} and clothing. It is true, the carriers pride themselves much on the respect which is shewn to them at the Factory; to obtain which they frequently run great risques of being starved to death in their way thither and back; and all that they can possibly get there for the furrs they procure after a year's toil, seldom amounts to more than is sufficient to yield a bare subsistence, and a few furrs for the ensuing year's market; while those whom they call indolent and mean-spirited live generally in a state of plenty, without trouble or risque; and consequently must be the most happy, and, in truth, the most independent also. It must be allowed that they are by far the greatest philosophers, as they never give themselves the trouble to acquire what they can do well enough without. The deer they kill, furnishes them with food, and a variety of warm and comfortable clothing, either with or without the hair, according as the seasons require; and it must be very hard indeed, if they cannot get furrs enough in the course of two or three years, to purchase a hatchet, and such other edge-tools as are necessary for their purpose. Indeed, those who take no concern at all about procuring furrs, have generally an opportunity of providing themselves with all their real wants from their more industrious countrymen, in exchange for provisions, and ready-dressed skins for clothing.

1771. March.

It is undoubtedly the duty of every one of the Company's servants to encourage a spirit of industry among {83} the natives, and to use every means in their power to induce them to procure furrs and other commodities for trade, by assuring them of a ready purchase and good payment for every thing[124] they bring to the Factory: and I can truly say, that this has ever been the grand object of my attention. But I must at the same time confess, that such conduct is by no means for the real benefit of the poor Indians; it being well known that those who have the least intercourse with the Factories, are by far the happiest. As their whole aim is to procure a comfortable subsistence, they take the most prudent methods to accomplish it; and by always following the lead of the deer, are seldom exposed to the griping hand of famine, so frequently felt by those who are called the annual traders. It is true, that there are few of the Indians, whose manner of life I have just described, but have once in their lives at least visited Prince of Wales's Fort; and the hardships and dangers which most of them experienced on those occasions, have left such a lasting impression on their minds that nothing can induce them to repeat their visits: nor is it, in fact, the interest of the Company that people of this easy turn, and who require only as much iron-work at a time as can be purchased with three or four beaver skins, and that only once in two or three years, should be invited to the Factories; because what they beg and steal while there, is worth, in the way of trade, three times the quantity of furrs which they bring. For this reason, it is much more for the interest of the Company that the {84} annual traders should buy up all those small quantities of furrs, and bring them in their own name, than that a parcel of beggars should be encouraged to come to the Factory with scarcely as many furrs as will pay for the victuals they eat while they are on the plantation.

1771. March.

I have often heard it observed, that the Indians who attend the deer-pounds might, in the course of a Winter, collect a vast number of pelts, which would well deserve the attention of those who are called carriers or traders; but it is a truth, though unknown to those speculators, that the deer skins at that season are not only as thin as a bladder, but are also full of warbles, which render them of little or no value.[125] Indeed, were they a more marketable commodity than they really are, the remote situation of those pounds from the Company's Factories, must for ever be an unsurmountable barrier to the Indians bringing any of those skins to trade. The same observation may be made of all the other Northern Indians, whose chief support, the whole year round, is venison; but the want of heavy draught in Winter, and water-carriage in Summer, will not permit them to bring many deer skins to market, not even those that are in season, and for which there has always been great encouragement given.

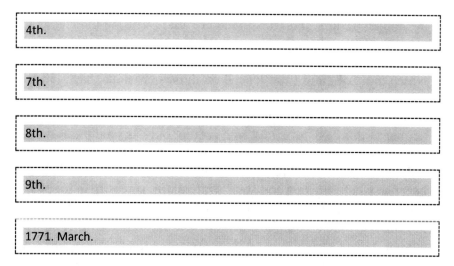

4th.

7th.

8th.

9th.

1771. March.

We stopped only one night in company with the Indians whom we met on Pike Lake, and in the morning of the fourth, proceeded to cross the remainder of that {85} Lake; but, though the weather was fine, and though the Lake was not more than twenty-seven miles broad at the place where we crossed it, yet the Indians lost so much time at play, that it was the seventh before we arrived on the West side of it. During the whole time we were crossing it, each night we found either points of land, or islands, to put up in. On the eighth, we lay a little to the East North East of Black Bear Hill,[54] where the Indians killed two deer, which were the first we had seen for ten days; but having plenty of dried meat and fat with us, we were by no means in want during any part of that time. On the ninth, we proceeded on our course to the Westward, and soon met with as great plenty of deer as we had seen during any part of our journey; which, no doubt, made things go on smooth and easy: and as the Spring advanced, the rigour of the Winter naturally abated, so that at times we had fine pleasant weather over-head, though it was never so warm as to occasion any thaw, unless in such places as lay exposed to the mid-day sun, and were sheltered from all the cold winds.

[126]

> 19th.

> 20th.

On the nineteenth, as we were continuing our course to the West and West by South, we saw the tracks of several strangers; and on following the main path, we arrived that night at five tents of Northern Indians, who had resided there great part of the Winter, snaring deer in the same manner as those before mentioned. Indeed, it should {86} seem that this, as well as some other places, had been frequented more than once on this occasion; for the wood that had been cut down for fewel, and other uses, was almost incredible. Before morning, the weather became so bad, and the storm continued to rage with such violence, that we did not move for several days; and as some of the Indians we met with at this place were going to Prince of Wales's Fort in the Summer, I embraced the opportunity of sending by them a Letter to the Chief at that Fort, agreeably to the tenor of my instructions. By summing up my courses and distances from my last observation, for the weather at that time would not permit me to observe, I judged myself to be in latitude 61° 30' North, and about 19° 60' of longitude to the West of Churchill River. This, and some accounts of the usage I received from the natives, with my opinion of the future success of the journey, formed the contents of my Letter.

> 23d.

> 26th.

> 1771. March.

On the twenty-third, the weather became fine and moderate, so we once more pursued our way, and the next day, as well as on the twenty-sixth, saw several more tents of Northern Indians, who were employed in the same manner as those we had formerly met; but some of them having had bad success, and being relations or acquaintances of part of my crew, joined our company, and proceeded with us to the Westward. Though the deer did not then keep regular paths, so as to enable the Indians to catch them in pounds, yet they were to be[127] met {87} with in great abundance in scattered herds; so that my companions killed as many as they pleased with their guns.

> April. 8th.

We still continued our course to the West and West by South, and on the eighth of April, arrived at a small Lake, called Thelewey-aza-yeth;[55] but with what propriety it is so called I cannot discover, for the meaning of Thelewey-aza-yeth is Little Fish Hill: probably so called from a high hill which stands on a long point near the West end of the Lake. On an island in this Lake we pitched our tents, and the Indians finding deer very numerous, determined to stay here some time, in order to dry and pound meat to take with us; for they well knew, by the season of the year, that the deer were then drawing out to the barren ground, and as the Indians proposed to walk due North on our leaving the Lake, it was uncertain when we should again meet with any more. As several Indians had during the Winter joined our party, our number had now increased to seven tents, which in the whole contained not less than seventy persons.

1771. April.

Agreeably to the Indians' proposals we remained at Thelewey-aza-yeth ten days; during which time my companions were busily employed (at their intervals from hunting) in preparing small staves of birch-wood, about one and a quarter inch square, and seven or eight feet long. These serve as tent-poles all the Summer, {88} while on the barren ground; and as the fall advances, are converted into snowshoe frames for Winter use. Birchrind, together with timbers and other wood-work for building canoes, were also another object of the Indian's attention while at this place; but as the canoes were not to be set up till our arrival at Clowey, (which was many miles distant,) all the wood-work was reduced to its proper size, for the sake of making it light for carriage.

[128]

As to myself, I had little to do, except to make a few observations for determining the latitude, bringing up my journal, and filling up my chart to the present time. I found the latitude of this place 61° 30' North, and its longitude, by my account, 19° West of Prince of Wales's Fort.

18th.

1771. April.

1771. April.

Having a good stock of dried provisions, and most of the necessary work for canoes all ready, on the eighteenth we moved about nine or ten miles to the North North West, and then came to a tent of Northern Indians who were tenting on the North side of Thelewey-aza River. From these Indians Matonabbee purchased another wife; so that he had now no less than seven, most of whom would for size have made good grenadiers. He prided himself much in the height and strength of his wives, and would frequently say, few women would carry or haul heavier loads; and though they had, in general, a very masculine appearance, yet he preferred them to those of a {89} more delicate form and moderate stature. In a country like this, where a partner in excessive hard labour is the chief motive for the union, and the softer endearments of a conjugal life are only considered as a secondary object, there seems to be great propriety in such a choice; but if all the men were of this way of thinking, what would become of the greater part of the women, who in general are but of low stature, and many of them of a most delicate make, though not of the exactest proportion, or most beautiful mould? Take them in a body, the women are as destitute of real beauty as any nation I ever saw, though there are some few of them, when young, who are tolerable; but the care of a family, added to their constant hard labour, soon make the[129] most beautiful among them look old and wrinkled, even before they are thirty; and several of the more ordinary ones at that age are perfect antidotes to love and gallantry. This, however, does not render them less dear and valuable to their owners, which is a lucky circumstance for those women, and a certain proof that there is no such thing as any rule or standard for beauty. Ask a Northern Indian, what is beauty? he will answer, a broad flat face, small eyes, high cheek-bones, three or four broad black lines across each cheek, a low forehead, a large broad chin, a clumsy hook-nose, a tawny hide, and breasts hanging down to the belt. Those beauties are greatly heightened, or at least rendered more valuable, when the possessor is capable of dressing all kinds of skins, converting them into the different parts {90} of their clothing, and able to carry eight or ten[AA] stone in Summer, or haul a much greater weight in Winter. These, and other similar accomplishments, are all that are sought after, or expected, of a Northern Indian woman. As to their temper, it is of little consequence; for the men have a wonderful facility in making the most stubborn comply with as much alacrity as could possibly be expected from those of the mildest and most obliging turn of mind; so that the only real difference is, the one obeys through fear, and the other complies cheerfully from a willing mind; both knowing that what is commanded must be done. They are, in fact, all kept at a great distance, and the rank they hold in the opinion of the men cannot be better expressed or explained, than by observing the method of treating or serving them at meals, which would appear very humiliating, to an European woman, though custom makes it sit light on those whose lot it is to bear it. It is necessary to observe, that when the men kill any large beast, the women are always sent to bring it to the tent: when it is brought there, every operation it undergoes, such as splitting, drying, pounding, &c. is performed by the women. When any thing is to be prepared for eating, it is the women who cook it; and when it is done, the wives and daughters of the greatest Captains in the country are never served, till all the males, even those who are in the capacity of servants, have eaten what they think proper; {91} and in times of scarcity it is frequently their lot to be left without a single morsel. It is, however, natural to think they take the liberty of helping themselves in secret; but this must be done with great prudence, as capital embezzlements of provisions in such times are looked on as affairs of real consequence, and frequently subject them to a very severe beating. If they are practised by a woman whose youth and inattention to domestic concerns cannot plead in her favour, they will for ever be a blot in her character, and few men will chuse to have her for a wife.

[130]

20th.

Finding plenty of good birch growing by the side of Theley-aza River, we remained there for a few days, in order to complete all the wood-work for the canoes, as well as for every other use for which we could possibly want it on the barren ground, during our Summer's cruise. On the twentieth, Matonabbee sent one of his brothers, and some others, a-head, with birch-rind and wood-work for a canoe, and gave them orders to proceed to a small Lake near the barren ground called Clowey, where they were desired to make all possible haste in building the canoe, that it might be ready on our arrival.

1771. April.

Having finished such wood-work as the Indians thought would be necessary, and having augmented our stock of dried meat and fat, the twenty-first was appointed for moving; but one of the women having been taken in labour, and it being rather an extraordinary case, we {92} were detained more than two days. The instant, however, the poor woman was delivered, which was not until she had suffered all the pains usually felt on those occasions for near fifty-two hours, the signal was made for moving when the poor creature took her infant on her back and set out with the rest of the company;[131] and though another person had the humanity to haul her sledge for her, (for one day only,) she was obliged to carry a considerable load beside her little charge, and was frequently obliged to wade knee-deep in water and wet snow. Her very looks, exclusive of her moans, were a sufficient proof of the great pain she endured, insomuch that although she was a person I greatly disliked, her distress at this time so overcame my prejudice, that I never felt more for any of her sex in my life; indeed her sighs pierced me to the soul, and rendered me very miserable, as it was not in my power to relieve her.

When a Northern Indian woman is taken in labour, a small tent is erected for her, at such a distance from the other tents that her cries cannot easily be heard, and the other women and young girls are her constant visitants: no male, except children in arms, ever offers to approach her. It is a circumstance perhaps to be lamented, that these people never attempt to assist each other on those occasions, even in the most critical cases. This is in some measure owing to delicacy, but more probably to an opinion they entertain that nature is {93} abundantly sufficient to perform every thing required, without any external help whatever. When I informed them of the assistance which European women derive from the skill and attention of our midwives, they treated it with the utmost contempt; ironically observing, "that the many hump-backs, bandy-legs, and other deformities, so frequent among the English, were undoubtedly owing to the great skill of the persons who assisted in bringing them into the world, and to the extraordinary care of their nurses afterward."

> 1771. April.

A Northern Indian woman after child-birth is reckoned unclean for a month or five weeks; during which time she always remains in a small tent placed at a little distance from the others, with only a female acquaintance or two; and during the whole time the father never sees the child. Their reason for this practice is, that children when first born are sometimes not very sightly, having in general large heads, and[132] but little hair, and are, moreover, often discoloured by the force of the labour; so that were the father to see them to such great disadvantage, he might probably take a dislike to them, which never afterward could be removed.

The names of the children are always given to them by the parents, or some person near of kin. Those of the boys are various, and generally derived from some place, season, or animal; the names of the girls are chiefly {94} taken from some part or property of a Martin; such as, the White Martin, the Black Martin, the Summer Martin, the Martin's Head, the Martin's Foot, the Martin's Heart, the Martin's Tail, &c.[AB]

> 23d.

May. 3d.

On the twenty-third, as I hinted above, we began to move forward, and to shape our course nearly North; but the weather was in general so hot, and so much snow had, in consequence, been melted, as made it bad walking in snow-shoes, and such exceeding heavy hauling, that it was the third of May before we could arrive at Clowey,[56] though the distance was not above eighty-five miles from Thelewey-aza-yeth. In our way we crossed part of two small Lakes, called Tittameg Lake and Scartack Lake; neither of which are of any note, though both abound with fine fish.

FOOTNOTES:

[Z] Mr. Norton was an Indian;[45] he was born at Prince of Wales's Fort, but had been in England nine years, and considering the small sum which was expended in his education, had made some progress in literature. At his return to Hudson's Bay he entered into all the abominable vices of his countrymen. He kept for his own use five or six of the finest Indian girls which he could select; and notwithstanding his own uncommon propensity to the fair sex, took every means in his power to prevent any European from having intercourse with the women of the country; for which purpose he proceeded to the most ridiculous length. To his own friends and country he was so partial, that he set more value on, and shewed more respect to one of their favourite dogs, than he ever did to his first officer. Among his miserable and ignorant countrymen he passed for a proficient in physic, and always kept a box of poison, to administer to those who refused him their wives or daughters.

With all these bad qualities, no man took more pains to inculcate virtue, morality, and continence on others; always painting, in the most odious colours, the jealous and revengeful disposition of the Indians, when any attempt was made to violate the chastity of their wives or daughters. Lectures of this kind from a man of established virtue might have had some effect; but when they came from one who was known to live in open defiance of every law, human and divine, they were always heard with indignation, and considered as the hypocritical cant of a selfish debauchee, who wished to engross every woman in the country to himself.

His apartments were not only convenient but elegant, and always crowded with favourite Indians: at night he locked the doors, and put the keys under his pillow; so that in the morning his dining-room was generally, for the want of necessary conveniences, worse than a hog-stye. As he advanced in years his jealousy increased, and he actually poisoned two of his women because he thought them partial to other objects more suitable to their ages. He was a most notorious smuggler; but though he put many thousands into the pockets of the Captains, he seldom put a shilling into his own.

An inflammation in his bowels occasioned his death on the 29th of December 1773; and though he died in the most excruciating pain, he retained his jealousy to the last; for a few minutes before he expired, happening to see an officer laying hold of the hand of one of his women who was standing by the fire, he bellowed out, in as loud a voice as his situation would admit, "God d——n you for a b——h, if I live I'll knock out your brains." A few minutes after making this elegant apostrophe, he expired in the greatest agonies that can possibly be conceived.

This I declare to be the real character and manner of life of the late Mr. Moses Norton.

[45] He was a son of Richard Norton, an Englishman, and a former Governor of Fort Prince of Wales, by an Indian woman. He was undoubtedly a man of forceful character, and was able to retain the confidence of the directors of the Company in London, but whether he was the moral degenerate described by Hearne is uncertain.

[46] *Populus tremuloides* (Michx.).

[47] The name by which the Chipewyan Indians of Fort Churchill know this lake is Nueltin (meaning Frozen-Island) Lake, which name seems to have been corrupted on Mackenzie's map into "North Lined Lake." On the Cook map it is marked Menishtick Lake, which is simply the Cree name for Island Lake. There is no record of any one having visited Island Lake since Hearne's time, but in 1894, while on the way to the Kazan River, I explored two of the upper branches of the Thlewiaza River, which flows into the lake, and was told by the Indians that the distance north-eastward

down the river to this lake was not very great. This information, if correct, would place the lake rather farther south than it is placed by Hearne.

[48] *Lepus americanus* (Erxleben).

[49] Between Island Lake and the Cathawhachaga River, the map indicates that he crossed Fatt Lake, which is probably the lake now known to the Indians of Reindeer Lake as Twal-kai-tua or Fat-fish Lake, and said by them to lie east of Kasba Lake, though its exact position has not been determined. On the Pennant and Mackenzie maps it is called Wiethen Lake.

[50] The Cathawhachaga or Kazan River would appear to have been crossed about five miles below where it leaves Kasba Lake, as it is here about a quarter of a mile wide, while between this place and the lake it is for the most part a swift stream varying from one to three hundred yards in width. His crossing-place would therefore be in latitude 60° 37' N., while his own latitude for the crossing-place, as given on his map, is 61° 32' N., which would be far out on the barren lands, beyond the northern limit of the woods. Thus, almost as soon as he left the track followed by him on his former journey, his surveys become very inaccurate. This is so much at variance with the approximate accuracy of his surveys on his second journey, that either the Elton quadrant carried by him was quite useless, or else he did not make use of it at all.

[51] Cossed Whoie, spelt Cassad on the Cook map, and Cassed on the Pennant map. This lake lies at the source of the Kazan River, and is now known as Kasba Lake. He crossed it north of the point where the Kazan River flows from its eastern side. My survey of the lake, made in 1894, did not extend north of its outlet, but, judging from what I could see of it, and from the information obtainable from the Chipewyan Indians of the vicinity, the width here given for the lake is much too great.

[52] The-whole-kyed (Whoie) or Snowbird Lake, known to the Indians of Lake Athabasca as Thel-wel-ky Lake. The course from Kasba Lake is given in the text as W. by S. and W.S.W., and the time occupied in travelling it as thirteen days, while on Hearne's map the course is shown as westward and the distance twenty miles.

[53] The name Whooldyah'd Lake had been applied to the lake at the source of Dubawnt River, which I explored in the summer of 1893. The

lake was known to the Indians of the vicinity as Pelican Lake, and they assured me that there was no lake on the river of the name of Whooldyah'd or Pike Lake. The identification of this lake with the one crossed by Hearne is reasonably, but not perfectly, certain.

[54] It had taken him thirteen days to travel from Wholdiah Lake to this camp, and, assuming a rate of four miles a day, he was fifty-two miles west of that lake. As his course was about westerly, his position would be in latitude 60° 20' north and longitude 11° 30' west of Churchill.

[55] The exact position of this lake (Thelewey-aza-yeth) has not yet been determined. In the text it is given in latitude 61° 30' north, longitude 19° west of Prince of Wales Fort, while on the map it is placed in latitude 61° 15' and 19° 30' west of Prince of Wales Fort, or one hundred and fifty miles west of Wholdiah Lake. The direction travelled from the crossing of Wholdiah Lake is shown as a little south of west, and as the south end of the latter lake is in latitude 60° 20', it is reasonable to suppose that Thelewey-aza-yeth Lake is at least a degree farther south than it is shown on the map, and, judging from the known approximate position of Hill Island Lake, which he crossed on his way back from the Coppermine, it is much farther east than the position assigned to it on the map.

[AA] The stone here meant is fourteen pounds.

[AB] Matonabbee had eight wives, and they were all called Martins.

[56] Lake Clowey is marked on the map as discharging by a stream into Great Slave Lake, but its exact position is not known. On the map it is placed in latitude 62° 50', which is probably not very far from its correct position. From the description here given, it would appear to be near the divide between the watershed of Great Slave Lake and Thelon River. L'Abbé Petitot in *Géographie de L'Athabaskaw-Mackenzie* identifies the Clowey River, which flows from this lake into Great Slave Lake, with the T'ézus-dèssé or Poudrerie (Snowdrift) River, which flows into Christie Bay of Great Slave Lake.

CHAP. V.

Transactions at Clowey, and on our Journey, till our Arrival at the Copper-mine River.

Several strange Indians join us—Indians employed building canoes; description and use of them—More Indians join us, to the amount of some hundreds—Leave Clowey—Receive intelligence that Keelshies was near us—Two young men dispatched for my letters and goods—Arrive at Peshew Lake; cross part of it, and make a large smoke—One of Matonabbee's wives elopes—Some remarks on the natives—Keelshies joins us, and delivers my letters, but the goods were all expended—A Northern Indian wishes to take one of Matonabbee's wives from him; matters compromised, but had like to have proved fatal to my progress—Cross Peshew Lake, when I make proper arrangements for the remainder of my journey—Many Indians join our party, in order to make war on the Esquimaux at the Copper River—Preparations made for that purpose while at Clowey—Proceed on our journey to the North—Some remarks on the way—Cross Cogead Lake on the ice—The Sun did not set— Arrive at Congecathawhachaga—Find several Copper Indians there—Remarks and transactions during our stay at Congecathawhachaga—Proceed on our journey—Weather very bad—Arrive at the Stoney Mountains—Some account of them— Cross part of Buffalo Lake on the ice—Saw many musk-oxen— Description of them—Went with some Indians to view Grizzlebear Hill—Join a strange Northern Indian Leader, called O'lye, in company with some Copper Indians—Their behaviour to me— Arrive at the Coppermine River.

1771. May.

The Lake Clowey is not much more than twelve miles broad in the widest part. A small river which runs into it on the West side, is said by the Indians to join the Athapuscow Lake.

{96} On our arrival at Clowey on the third of May, we found that the Captain's brother, and those who were sent[134] a-head with him from Theley-aza River, had only got there two days before us; and, on account of the weather, had not made the least progress in building the canoe, the plan of which they had taken with them. The same day we got to Clowey several other Indians joined us from different quarters, with intent to build their canoes at the same place. Some of those Indians had resided within four or five miles, to the South-East of Clowey, all the Winter; and had procured a plentiful livelihood by snaring deer, in the manner which has been already described.

18th.

19th.

20th.

Immediately after our arrival at Clowey, the Indians began to build their canoes, and embraced every convenient opportunity for that purpose: but as warm and dry weather only is fit for this business, which was by no means the case at present, it was the eighteenth of May before the canoes belonging to my party could be completed. On the nineteenth we agreed to proceed on our journey; but Matonabbee's canoe meeting with some damage, which took near a whole day to repair, we were detained till the twentieth.

Those vessels, though made of the same materials with the canoes of the Southern Indians, differ from them both in shape and construction; they are also much smaller and {97} lighter; and though very slight and simple in their construction, are nevertheless the best that could possibly be contrived for the use of those poor people, who are frequently obliged to carry them a hundred, and sometimes a hundred and fifty miles at a time, without having occasion to put them into the water. Indeed, the chief use of these canoes is to ferry over unfordable rivers; though sometimes, and at a few places, it must be acknowledged, that they are of great service in killing deer, as they enable the Indians to cross rivers and the narrow parts of lakes; they are also useful in killing swans, geese, ducks, &c. in the moulting season.

1771. May.

All the tools used by an Indian in building his canoe, as well as in making his snow-shoes, and every other kind of wood-work, consist of a hatchet, a knife, a file, and an awl; in the use of which they are so dextrous, that every thing they make is executed with a neatness not to be excelled by the most expert mechanic, assisted with every tool he could wish.

INDIAN IMPLEMENTS

Reference

A The Bottom of the Canoe
B The Forepart
C The Frame compleat
D A set of Timbers bent and lashed in their proper shape for drying
E A Canoe compleat
F A Paddle
G A spear to kill Deer with in the Water

H The method of carrying the Canoe in Summer

S. H. delin.

Reference to the Skeleton

1 The Stem
2 The Stern Post
3 Two forked Sticks supporting the Stem and Stern
4 The Gunwalls
5 Small Rods placed between the Timbers and the Birchrind
6 The Timbers
7 The Kelsin
8 Large Stones to keep the Bottom steady, till the sides are sewed to

In[135] shape the Northern Indian canoe bears some resemblance to a weaver's shuttle; being flat-bottomed, with straight upright sides, and sharp at each end; but the stern is by far the widest part, as there the baggage is generally laid, and occasionally a second person, who always lies down at full length in the bottom of the canoe. In this manner they carry one another across rivers and the narrow {98} parts of lakes in those little vessels, which seldom exceed twelve or thirteen feet in length, and are from twenty inches to two feet broad in the widest part. The head, or fore part, is unnecessarily long, and narrow; and is all covered over with birch-bark, which adds considerably to the weight, without contributing to the burthen of the vessel. In general, these Indians make use of the single paddle, though a few have double ones, like the Esquimaux: the latter, however, are seldom used, but by those who lie in wait to kill deer as they cross rivers and narrow lakes.[AC]

1771. May.

[136]

During our stay at Clowey we were joined by upward of two hundred Indians from different quarters, most of whom built canoes at this place; but as I was under the protection of a principal man, no one offered to molest {99} me, nor can I say they were very clamorous for any thing I had. This was undoubtedly owing to Matonabbee's informing them of my true situation; which was, that I had not, by any means, sufficient necessaries for myself, much less to give away. The few goods which I had with me were intended to be reserved for the Copper and Dogribbed Indians, who never visit the Company's Factories. Tobacco was, however, always given away; for every one of any note, who joined us, expected to be treated with a few pipes, and on some occasions it was scarcely possible to get off without presenting a few inches[AD] to them; which, with the constant supplies which I was obliged to furnish my own crew, decreased that article of my stock so fast, that notwithstanding I had yet advanced so small a part of my journey, more than one half of my store was expended. Gun-powder and shot also were articles commonly asked for by most of the Indians we met; and in general these were dealt round to them with a liberal hand by my guide Matonabbee. I must, however, do him the justice to acknowledge, that what he distributed was all his own, which he had purchased at the Factory; to my certain knowledge he bartered one hundred and fifty martins' skins for powder only; besides a great number of beaver, and other furrs, for shot, ball, iron-work, and tobacco, purposely to give away among his countrymen; as he had certainly as many of these articles given to him as were, in {100} his opinion, sufficient for our support during our journey out and home.

> 20th.

> 1771. May.

Matonabbee's canoe having been repaired, on the twentieth we left Clowey, and proceeded Northward. That morning a small gang of strangers joined us, who informed my guide, that Captain Keelshies was within a day's walk to the Southward. Keelshies was the man by whom I had sent a letter to Prince of Wales's Fort, from Cathawhachaga, in the beginning of July one thousand seven hundred and seventy; but not long after that, having the misfortune to break my quadrant, I was obliged to return to the Fort a second time; and though we saw many smokes, and spoke with several Indians on my return that year, yet he and I missed each other on the barren ground, and I had not seen or heard of him since that time.

[137]

21st.

As Matonabbee was desirous that I should receive my letters, and also the goods I had written for, he dispatched two of his young men to bring them. We continued our journey to the Northward; and the next day saw several large smokes at a great distance to the Eastward on the barren ground, which were supposed to be made by some parties of Indians bound to Prince of Wales's Fort with furrs and other commodities for trade.

22d.

1771. May.

On the twenty-second and twenty-third, we proceeded to the North, at the rate of fourteen or fifteen miles a day; and in the evening of the latter, got clear of all {101} the woods, and lay on the barren ground.[57] The same evening the two young men who were sent for my letters, &c. returned, and told me that Keelshies had promised to join us in a few days, and deliver the things to me with his own hand.

[138]

> 24th.

The twenty-fourth proved bad and rainy weather, so that we only walked about seven miles, when finding a few blasted stumps of trees, we pitched our tents. It was well we did so, for toward night we had excessively bad weather, with loud thunder, strong lightning, and heavy rain, attended with a very hard gale of wind from the South West; toward the next morning, however, the wind veered round to the North West, and the weather became intensely cold and frosty. We walked that day about eight miles to the Northward, when we were obliged to put up, being almost benumbed with cold. There we found a few dry stumps, as we had done the day before, which served us for fewel.[AE]

> 26th.

> 1771. May. 27th.

> 28th.

{102} The weather on the twenty-sixth was so bad, with snow[139] and thick drifting sleet, that we did not move; but the next morning proving fine and pleasant, we dried our things, and walked about twelve miles to the Northward; most of the way on the ice of a small river which runs into Peshew Lake.[AF][58] We then saw a smoke to the Southward, which we judged to be made by Keelshies, so we put up for the night by the side of the above-mentioned Lake, where I expected we should have waited for his arrival; but, to my great surprise, on the morrow we again set forward, and walked twenty-two miles to the Northward on Peshew Lake, and in the afternoon pitched our tents on an island, where, by my desire, the Indians made a large smoke, and proposed to stay a day or two for Captain Keelshies.

Photo: J. W. Tyrrell, 1900.
LAST WOODS ON EAST SHORE, ARTILLERY LAKE

Photo: J. W. Tyrrell, 1900.
WEST SHORE, ARTILLERY LAKE
IN LAT. 62° 56'

1771. May.

1771. May.

[140]

In the night, one of Matonabbee's wives and another woman eloped: it was supposed they went off to the Eastward, in order to meet their former husbands, from {103} whom they had been sometime before taken by force. This affair made more noise and bustle than I could have supposed; and Matonabbee seemed entirely disconcerted, and quite inconsolable for the loss of his wife. She was certainly by far the handsomest of all his flock, of a moderate size, and had a fair complexion; she apparently possessed a mild temper, and very engaging manners. In fact, she seemed to have every good quality that could be expected in a Northern Indian woman, and that could render her an agreeable companion to an inhabitant of this part of the world. She had not, however, appeared happy in her late situation; and chose rather to be the sole wife of a sprightly young fellow of no note, (though very capable of maintaining her,) than to have the seventh or eighth share of the affection of the greatest man in the country. I am sorry to mention an incident which happened while we were building the canoes at Clowey, and[141] which by no means does honour to Matonabbee: it is no less a crime than that of having actually stabbed the husband of the above-mentioned girl in three places; and had it not been for timely assistance, would certainly have murdered him, for no other reason than because the poor man had spoken disrespectfully of him for having taken his wife away by force. The cool deliberation with which Matonabbee committed this bloody action, convinced me it had been a long premeditated design; for he no sooner heard of the man's arrival, than he opened one of his wives' bundles, and, with the greatest {104} composure, took out a new long box-handled knife, went into the man's tent, and, without any preface whatever, took him by the collar, and began to execute his horrid design. The poor man anticipating his danger, fell on his face, and called for assistance; but before any could be had he received three wounds in the back. Fortunately for him, they all happened on the shoulder-blade, so that his life was spared. When Matonabbee returned to his tent, after committing this horrid deed, he sat down as composedly as if nothing had happened, called for water to wash his bloody hands and knife, smoked his pipe as usual, seemed to be perfectly at ease, and asked if I did not think he had done right?

1771. May.

It has ever been the custom among those people for the men to wrestle for any woman to whom they are attached; and, of course, the strongest party always carries off the prize. A weak man, unless he be a good hunter and well-beloved, is seldom permitted to keep a wife that a stronger man thinks worth his notice: for at any time when the wives of those strong wrestlers are heavy-laden either with furrs or provisions, they make no scruple of tearing any other man's wife from his bosom, and making her bear a part of his luggage. This custom prevails throughout all their tribes, and causes a great spirit of emulation among their youth, who are upon all occasions, from their childhood, trying their strength and skill in wrestling. This enables them to protect their property,[142] and particularly their wives, {105} from the hands of those powerful ravishers; some of whom make almost a livelihood by taking what they please from the weaker parties, without making them any return. Indeed, it is represented as an act of great generosity, if they condescend to make an unequal exchange; as, in general, abuse and insult are the only return for the loss which is sustained.

The way in which they tear the women and other property from one another, though it has the appearance of the greatest brutality, can scarcely be called fighting. I never knew any of them receive the least hurt in these rencontres; the whole business consists in hauling each other about by the hair of the head: they are seldom known either to strike or kick one another. It is not uncommon for one of them to cut off his hair and to grease his ears, immediately before the contest begins. This, however, is done privately; and it is sometimes truly laughable, to see one of the parties strutting about with an air of great importance, and calling out, "Where is he? Why does he not come out?" when the other will bolt out with a clean shorned head and greased ears, rush on his antagonist, seize him by the hair, and though perhaps a much weaker man, soon drag him to the ground, while the stronger is not able to lay hold on him. It is very frequent on those occasions for each party to have spies, to watch the other's motions, which puts them more on a footing of equality. For want of hair to pull, they {106} seize each other about the waist, with legs wide extended, and try their strength, by endeavouring to vie who can first throw the other down.

1771. May.

On these wrestling occasions the standers-by never attempt to interfere in the contest; even one brother offers not to assist another, unless it be with advice, which, as it is always delivered openly on the field during the contest, may, in fact, be said to be equally favourable to both parties. It sometimes happens that one of the wrestlers is superior in strength to the other; and if a woman be the cause of the contest, the[143] weaker is frequently unwilling to yield, notwithstanding he is greatly overpowered. When this happens to be the case, the relations and friends, or other bye-standers, will sometimes join to persuade the weaker combatant to give up the contest, lest, by continuing it, he should get bruised and hurt, without the least probability of being able to protect what he is contending for. I observed that very few of those people were dissatisfied with the wives which had fallen to their lot, for whenever any considerable number of them were in company, scarcely a day passed without some overtures being made for contests of this kind; and it was often very unpleasant to me, to see the object of the contest sitting in pensive silence watching her fate, while her husband and his rival were contending for the prize. I have indeed not only felt pity for those poor wretched victims, but the utmost indignation, when I {107} have seen them won, perhaps, by a man whom they mortally hated. On those occasions their grief and reluctance to follow their new lord has been so great, that the business has often ended in the greatest brutality; for, in the struggle, I have seen the poor girls stripped quite naked, and carried by main force to their new lodgings. At other times it was pleasant enough to see a fine girl led off the field from a husband she disliked, with a tear in one eye and a finger on the other: for custom, or delicacy if you please, has taught them to think it necessary to whimper a little, let the change be ever so much to their inclination. I have throughout this account given the women the appellation of girls, which is pretty applicable, as the objects of contest are generally young, and without any family: few of the men chuse to be at the trouble of maintaining other people's children, except on particular occasions, which will be taken notice of hereafter.

1771. May.

Some of the old men, who are famous on account of their supposed skill in conjuration, have great influence in persuading the rabble from committing those outrages; but the humanity of these sages is seldom known to extend beyond[144] their own families. In defence of them they will exert their utmost influence; but when their own relations are guilty of the same crime, they seldom interfere. This partial conduct creates some secret, and several open enemies; but the generality of their neighbours are deterred, through fear or superstition, from {108} executing their revenge, and even from talking disrespectfully of them, unless it be behind their backs; which is a vice of which almost every Indian in this country, without exception, is guilty.

1771. May.

Notwithstanding the Northern Indians are so covetous, and pay so little regard to private property as to take every advantage of bodily strength to rob their neighbours, not only of their goods, but of their wives, yet they are, in other respects, the mildest tribe, or nation, that is to be found on the borders of Hudson's Bay: for let their affronts or losses be ever so great, they never will seek any other revenge than that of wrestling. As for murder, which is so common among all the tribes of Southern Indians, it is seldom heard of among them. A murderer is shunned and detested by all the tribe, and is obliged to wander up and down, forlorn and forsaken even by his own relations and former friends. In that respect a murderer may truly be compared to Cain, after he had killed his brother Abel. The cool reception he meets with by all who know him, occasions him to grow melancholy, and he never leaves any place but the whole company say "There goes the murderer!" The women, it is true, sometimes receive an unlucky blow from their husbands for misbehaviour, which occasions their death; but this is thought nothing of: and for one man or woman to kill another out of revenge, or through jealousy, or on any other account, is so extraordinary, that very few are now {109} existing who have been guilty of it. At the present moment I know not one, beside Matonabbee, who ever made an attempt of that nature; and he is, in every other respect, a man of such universal good sense, and, as an Indian, of such great humanity, that I am at a loss how to[145] account for his having been guilty of such a crime, unless it be by his having lived among the

Southern Indians so long, as to become tainted with their blood-thirsty, revengeful, and vindictive disposition.

> 29th.

Early in the morning of the twenty-ninth, Captain Keelshies joined us. He delivered to me a packet of letters, and a two-quart keg of French brandy; but assured me, that the powder, shot, tobacco, knives, &c. which he received at the Fort for me, were all expended. He endeavoured to make some apology for this, by saying, that some of his relations died in the Winter, and that he had, according to their custom, thrown all his own things away; after which he was obliged to have recourse to my ammunition and other goods, to support himself and a numerous family. The very affecting manner in which he related this story, often crying like a child, was a great proof of his extreme sorrow, which he wished to persuade me arose from the recollection of his having embezzled so much of my property; but I was of a different opinion, and attributed his grief to arise from the remembrance of his deceased relations. However, as a small recompence for my loss, he presented me with four {110} ready-dressed moose-skins, which was, he said, the only retribution he could then make. The moose-skins, though not the twentieth part of the value of the goods which he had embezzled, were in reality more acceptable to me, than the ammunition and the other articles would have been, on account of their great use as shoe-leather, which at that time was a very scarce article with us, whereas we had plenty of powder and shot.

> 1771. May.

On the same day that Keelshies joined us, an Indian man, who had been some time in our company, insisted on taking one of Matonabbee's wives from him by force, unless he complied with his demands, which were, that Matonabbee should give him a certain quantity of ammunition, some pieces of iron-work, a kettle, and several other articles; every one of which, Matonabbee was obliged to deliver, or lose the woman;[146] for the other man far excelled him in strength. Matonabbee was more exasperated on this occasion, as the same man had sold him the woman no longer ago than the nineteenth of the preceding April. Having expended all the goods he then possessed, however, he was determined to make another bargain for her; and as she was what may be called a valuable woman in their estimation; that is, one who was not only tolerably personable, but reckoned very skilful in manufacturing the different kinds of leather, skins, and furrs, and at the same time very clever in the performance of every other domestic duty required of the sex in this part of the {111} world; Matonabbee was more unwilling to part with her, especially as he had so lately suffered a loss of the same kind.

1771. May.

29th.

This dispute, which was after some hours decided by words and presents, had like to have proved fatal to my expedition; for Matonabbee, who at that time thought himself as great a man as then lived, took this affront so much to heart, especially as it was offered in my presence, that he almost determined not to proceed any farther toward the Coppermine River, and was on the point of striking off to the Westward, with an intent to join the Athapuscow Indians, and continue with them: he being perfectly well acquainted with all their leaders, and most of the principal Indians of that country, from whom, during a former residence among them of several years, he said he had met with more civility than he ever did from his own countrymen. As Matonabbee seemed resolutely bent on his design, I had every reason to think that my third expedition would prove equally unsuccessful with the two former. I was not, however, under the least apprehension for my own safety, as he promised to take me with him, and procure me a passage to Prince of Wales's Fort, with some of the Athapuscow Indians, who at that time annually visited the Factory in the way of trade. After waiting till I thought Matonabbee's passion had a little abated, I used every argument of which I was master in favour of his proceeding on the[147] journey; assuring him {112} not only of the future esteem of the present Governor of Prince of Wales's Fort, but also of that of all his successors as long as he lived; and that even the Hudson's Bay Company themselves would be ready to acknowledge his assiduity and perseverance, in conducting a business which had so much the appearance of proving advantageous to them. After some conversation of this kind, and a good deal of intreaty, he at length consented to proceed, and promised to make all possible haste. Though it was then late in the afternoon, he gave orders for moving, and accordingly we walked about seven miles that night, and put up on another island in Peshew Lake. The preceding afternoon the Indians had killed a few deer; but our number was then so great, that eight or ten deer would scarcely afford us all a taste. These deer were the first we had seen since our leaving the neighbourhood of Thelewey-aza-yeth; so that we had lived all the time on the dried meat which had been prepared before we left that place in April.

> 30th.

> 1771. May.

The thirtieth proved bad, rainy weather; we walked, however, about ten miles to the Northward, when we arrived on the North side of Peshew Lake, and put up. Here Matonabbee immediately began to make every necessary arrangement for facilitating the executing of our design; and as he had promised to make all possible haste, he thought it expedient to leave most of his wives and all his children in the care of some Indians, then in our company, who had his orders to proceed to the {113} Northward at their leisure; and who, at a particular place appointed by him, were to wait our return from the Copper-mine River. Having formed this resolution, Matonabbee selected two of his young wives who had no children, to accompany us; and in order to make their loads as light as possible, it was agreed that we should not take more ammunition with us than was really necessary for our support, till we might expect again to join those Indians and the women and children. The same measures were also[148] adopted by all the other Indians of my party; particularly those who had a plurality of wives, and a number of children.

> 31st.

As these matters took some time to adjust, it was near nine o'clock in the evening of the thirty-first before we could set out; and then it was with much difficulty that Matonabbee could persuade his other wives from following him, with their children and all their lumber; for such was their unwillingness to be left behind, that he was obliged to use his authority before they would consent, consequently they parted in anger; and we no sooner began our march, than they set up a most woeful cry, and continued to yell most piteously as long as we were within hearing. This mournful scene had so little effect on my party, that they walked away laughing, and as merry as ever. The few who expressed any regret at their departure from those whom they were to leave behind, {114} confined their regard wholly to their children, particularly to the youngest, scarcely ever mentioning their mother.

Though it was so late when we left the women, we walked about ten miles that night before we stopped. In our way we saw many deer; several of which the Indians killed. To talk of travelling and killing deer in the middle of the night, may at first view have the appearance of romance; but our wonder will speedily abate, when it is considered that we were then to the Northward of 64° of North latitude, and that, in consequence of it, though the Sun did not remain the whole night above the horizon, yet the time it remained below it was so short, and its depression even at midnight so small at this season of the year, that the light, in clear weather, was quite sufficient for the purpose both of walking, and hunting any kind of game.[50]

1771. May.
---

[149]

It should have been observed, that during our stay at Clowey a great number of Indians entered into a combination with those of my party to accompany us to the Copper-mine River; and with no other intent than to murder the Esquimaux, who are understood by the Copper Indians to frequent that river in considerable numbers. This scheme, notwithstanding the trouble and fatigue, as well as danger, with which it must be obviously attended, was nevertheless so universally approved by those people, that for some time almost every man who joined {115} us proposed to be of the party. Accordingly, each volunteer, as well as those who were properly of my party, prepared a target, or shield, before we left the woods of Clowey. Those targets were composed of thin boards, about three quarters of an inch thick, two feet broad, and three feet long; and were intended to ward off the arrows of the Esquimaux. Notwithstanding these preparations, when we came to leave the women and children, as has been already mentioned, only sixty volunteers would go with us; the rest, who were nearly as many more, though they had all prepared targets, reflecting that they had a great distance to walk, and that no advantage could be expected from the expedition, very prudently begged to be excused, saying, that they could not be spared for so long a time from the maintenance of their wives and families; and particularly, as they did not see any then in our company, who seemed willing to encumber themselves with such a charge. This seemed to be a mere evasion, for I am clearly of opinion that poverty on one side, and avarice on the other, were the only impediments to their joining our party; had they possessed as many European goods to squander away among their countrymen as Matonabbee and those of my party did, in all probability many might have been found who would have been glad to have accompanied us.

When I was acquainted with the intentions of my companions, and saw the warlike preparations that were carrying on, I endeavoured as much as possible to persuade {116} them from putting their inhuman design into execution; but so far were my intreaties from having the wished-for effect, that it[150] was concluded I was actuated by cowardice; and they told me, with great marks of derision, that I was afraid of the Esquimaux. As I knew my personal safety depended in a great measure on the favourable opinion they entertained of me in this respect, I was obliged to change my tone, and replied, that I did not care if they rendered the name and race of the Esquimaux extinct; adding at the same time, that though I was no enemy to the Esquimaux, and did not see the necessity of attacking them without cause, yet if I should find it necessary to do it, for the protection of any one of my company, my own safety out of the question, so far from being afraid of a poor defenceless Esquimaux, whom I despised more than feared, nothing should be wanting on my part to protect all who were with me. This declaration was received with great satisfaction; and I never afterwards ventured to interfere with any of their war-plans. Indeed, when I came to consider seriously, I saw evidently that it was the highest folly for an individual like me, and in my situation, to attempt to turn the current of a national prejudice which had subsisted between those two nations from the earliest periods, or at least as long as they had been acquainted with the existence of each other.

June. 1st.

16th.

Having got rid of all the women, children, dogs, heavy baggage, and other incumbrances, on the first of June we {117} pursued our journey to the Northward with great speed; but the weather was in general so precarious, and the snow, sleet, and rain so frequent, that notwithstanding we embraced every opportunity which offered, it was the sixteenth of June before we arrived in the latitude of 67° 30', where Matonabbee had proposed that the women and children should wait our return from the Copper-mine River.

1771. June.

1771. June.

In our way hither we crossed several lakes on the ice; of which Thoy-noy-kyed Lake[60] and Thoy-coy-lyned Lake[61] were the principal. We also crossed a few inconsiderable creeks and rivers,[62] which were only useful as they furnished a small supply of fish to the natives. The weather, as I have before observed, was in general disagreeable, with a great deal of rain and snow. To make up for that inconvenience, however, the deer were so plentiful, that the Indians killed not only a sufficient quantity for our daily support, but frequently great numbers merely for the fat, marrow and tongues. To induce them to desist from this practice, I often interested myself, and endeavoured, as much as possible, to convince them in the clearest terms of which I was master, of the great impropriety of such waste; particularly at a time of the year when their skins could not be of any use for clothing, and when the anxiety to proceed on our journey would not permit us to stay long enough in one place to eat up half the spoils of their hunting. As national customs, however, are not easily {118} overcome, my remonstrances proved ineffectual; and I was always answered, that it was certainly right to kill plenty, and live on the best, when and where it was to be got, for that it would be impossible to do it where every thing was scarce: and they insisted on it, that killing plenty of deer and other game in one part of the country, could never make them scarcer in another. Indeed, they were so accustomed to kill every thing that came within their reach, that few of them could pass by a small bird's nest, without slaying the young ones, or destroying the eggs.

[152]

[151]

20th.

From the seventeenth to the twentieth, we walked between seventy and eighty miles to the North West and North North West; the greater part of the way by Cogead Lake[63]; but the Lake being then frozen, we crossed all the creeks and bays of it on the ice.

21st.

On the twenty-first we had bad rainy weather, with so thick a fog that we could not see our way: about ten o'clock at night, however, it became fine and clear, and the Sun shone very bright; indeed it did not set all that night, which was a convincing proof, without any observation, that we were then considerably to the North of the Arctic Polar Circle.

22d.

1771. June.

As soon as the fine weather began, we set out and walked about seven or eight miles to the Northward, when we {119} came to a branch of Conge-ca-tha-wha-chaga River[64]; on the North side of which we found several Copper Indians, who were assembled, according to annual custom, to kill deer as they cross the river in their little canoes.

[153]

The ice being now broken up, we were, for the first time this Summer, obliged to make use of our canoes to ferry across the river:

which would have proved very tedious, had it not been for the kindness of the Copper Indians, who sent all their canoes to our assistance. Though our number was not much less than one hundred and fifty, we had only three canoes, and those being of the common size, could only carry two persons each, without baggage. It is true, when water is smooth, and a raft of three or four of those canoes is well secured by poles lashed across them, they will carry a much greater weight in proportion, and be much safer, as there is scarcely a possibility of their oversetting; and this is the general mode adopted by the people of this country in crossing rivers when they have more than one canoe with them.

1771. June.

Having arrived on the North side of this river, we found that Matonabbee, and several others in our company, were personally acquainted with most of the Copper Indians whom we found there. The latter seemed highly pleased at the interview with our party, and endeavoured, by every means in their power, to convince our company of their readiness to serve us to the utmost; so that by the {120} time we had got our tents pitched, the strangers had provided a large quantity of dried meat and fat, by way of a feast, to which they invited[154] most of the principal Indians who accompanied me, as well as Matonabbee and myself, who were presented with some of the very best.

It is natural to suppose, that immediately after our arrival the Copper Indians would be made acquainted with the nature and intention of our journey. This was no sooner done than they expressed their entire approbation, and many of them seemed willing and desirous of giving every assistance; particularly by lending us several canoes, which they assured us would be very useful in the remaining part of our journey, and contribute both to our ease and dispatch. It must be observed, that these canoes were not entirely entrusted to my crew, but carried by the owners themselves who accompanied us; as it would have been very uncertain where to have found them at our return from the Copper River.

Agreeably to my instructions, I smoked my calumet of peace with the principal of the Copper Indians, who seemed highly pleased on the occasion; and, from a conversation held on the subject of my journey, I found they were delighted with the hopes of having an European settlement in their neighbourhood, and seemed to have no idea that any impediment could prevent such a scheme from being carried into execution. Climates and {121} seasons had no weight with them; nor could they see where the difficulty lay in getting to them; for though they acknowledged that they had never seen the sea at the mouth of the Copper River clear of ice, yet they could see nothing that should hinder a ship from approaching it; and they innocently enough observed, that the water was always so smooth between the ice and shore, that even small boats might get there with great ease and safety. How a ship was to get between the ice and the shore, never once occurred to them.

1771. June.

Whether it was from real motives of hospitality, or from the great advantages which they expected to reap by my discoveries, I know not; but I must confess that their civility[155] far exceeded what I could expect from so uncivilized a tribe, and I was exceedingly sorry that I had nothing of value to offer them. However, such articles as I had, I distributed among them, and they were thankfully received by them. Though they have some European commodities among them, which they purchase from the Northern Indians, the same articles from the hands of an Englishman were more prized. As I was the first whom they had ever seen, and in all probability might be the last, it was curious to see how they flocked about me, and expressed as much desire to examine me from top to toe, as an European Naturalist would a non-descript animal. They, however, found and pronounced me to be a perfect human being, except in the colour of my hair {122} and eyes: the former, they said, was like the stained hair of a buffaloe's tail, and the latter, being light, were like those of a gull. The whiteness of my skin also was, in their opinion, no ornament, as they said it resembled meat which had been sodden in water till all the blood was extracted. On the whole, I was viewed as so great a curiosity in this part of the world, that during my stay there, whenever I combed my head, some or other of them never failed to ask for the hairs that came off, which they carefully wrapped up, saying, "When I see you again, you shall again see your hair."

> 23d.

The day after our arrival at Congecathawhachaga, Matonabbee dispatched his brother, and several Copper Indians, to Copper-mine River, with orders to acquaint any Indians they might meet, with the reason of my visiting those parts, and also when they might probably expect us at that river. By the bearers of this message I sent a present of tobacco and some other things, to induce any strangers they met to be ready to give us assistance, either by advice, or in any other way which might be required.

> 1771. June.

As Matonabbee and the other Indians thought it advisable to leave all the women at this place, and proceed to the Copper-mine River without them, it was thought necessary[156] to continue here a few days, to kill as many deer as would be sufficient for their support during {123} our absence. And notwithstanding deer were so plentiful, yet our numbers were so large, and our daily consumption was so great, that several days elapsed before the men could provide the women with a sufficient quantity; and then they had no other way of preserving it, than by cutting it in thin slices and drying it in the Sun. Meat, when thus prepared, is not only very portable, but palatable; as all the blood and juices are still remaining in the meat, it is very nourishing and wholesome food; and may, with care, be kept a whole year without the least danger of spoiling. It is necessary, however, to air it frequently during the warm weather, otherwise it is liable to grow mouldy: but as soon as the chill air of the fall begins, it requires no farther trouble till next Summer.

1771. June.

We had not been many days at Congecathawhachaga before I had reason to be greatly concerned at the behaviour of several of my crew to the Copper Indians. They not only took many of their young women, furrs, and ready-dressed skins for clothing, but also several of their bows and arrows, which were the only implements they had to procure food and raiment, for the future support of themselves, their wives, and families. It may probably be thought, that as these weapons are of so simple a form, and so easily constructed, they might soon be replaced, without any other trouble or expense than a little labour; but this supposition can only hold good in places where proper materials are easily procured, which was not the case here: {124} if it had, they would not have been an object of plunder. In the midst of a forest of trees, the wood that would make a Northern Indian a bow and a few arrows, or indeed a bow and arrows ready made, are not of much value; no more than the man's trouble that makes them: but carry that bow and arrows several hundred miles from any woods and place where those are the only weapons in use, their intrinsic value will be found to increase, in[157] the same proportion as the materials which are made are less attainable.[AG]

To do Matonabbee justice on this occasion, I must say that he endeavoured as much as possible to persuade his countrymen from taking either furrs, clothing, or bows, from the Copper Indians, without making them some satisfactory return; but if he did not encourage, neither did he endeavour to hinder them from taking as many women as they pleased. Indeed, the Copper Indian women seem to be much esteemed by our Northern traders; for what reason I know not, as they are in reality the same people in every respect;

and their language differs not so much as the dialects of some of the nearest counties in England do from each other.

1771. June.

It is not surprising that a plurality of wives is customary among these people, as it is so well adapted to {125} their situation and manner of life. In my opinion no race of people under the Sun have a greater occasion for such an indulgence. Their annual hunt, in quest of furrs, is so remote from any European settlement, as to render them the greatest travellers in the known world; and as they have neither horse nor water carriage, every good hunter is under the necessity of having several persons to assist in carrying his furrs to the Company's Fort, as well as carrying back the European goods which he receives in exchange for them. No persons in this country are so proper for this work as the women, because they are inured to carry and haul heavy loads from their childhood, and to do all manner of drudgery; so that those men who are capable of providing for three, four, five, six, or more women, generally find them humble and faithful servants, affectionate wives, and fond and indulgent mothers to their children. Though custom makes this way of life sit apparently easy on the generality of the women, and though, in general, the whole of their wants seem to be comprized in food and clothing only, yet nature at times gets the better of custom, and the spirit of jealousy makes its appearance among them: however, as the husband is always arbitrator, he soon settles the business, though perhaps not always to the entire satisfaction of the parties.

[158]

Much does it redound to the honour of the Northern Indian women when I affirm, that they are the mildest and most virtuous females I have seen in any part of North {126} America; though some think this is more owing to habit, custom, and the fear of their husbands, than from real inclination. It is undoubtedly well known that none can manage a Northern Indian woman so well as a Northern Indian man; and when any of them have been permitted to remain at the Fort, they have, for the sake of gain, been easily prevailed on to deviate from that character; and a few have, by degrees, become as abandoned as the Southern Indians, who are remarkable throughout all their tribes for being the most debauched wretches under the Sun. So far from laying any restraint on their sensual appetites, as long as youth and inclination last, they give themselves up to all manner of even incestuous debauchery; and that in so beastly a manner when they are intoxicated, a state to which they are peculiarly addicted, that the brute creation are not less regardless of decency. I know that some few Europeans, who have had little opportunity of seeing them, and of enquiring into their manners, have been very lavish in their praise; but every one who has had much intercourse with them, and penetration and industry enough to study their dispositions, will agree, that no accomplishments whatever in a man, is sufficient to conciliate the affections, or preserve the chastity of a Southern Indian woman.[AH]

[159]

1771. June.

{127} The Northern Indian women are in general so far from being like those I have above described, that it is very {128} uncommon to hear of their ever being guilty of incontinency, not even those who are confined to the sixth or even eighth part of a man.

It is true, that were I to form my opinion of those women from the behaviour of such as I have been more particularly acquainted with, I should have little reason to say much in their favour; but impartiality will not {129} permit me to make a few of the worst characters a standard for the general conduct of all of them. Indeed it is but reasonable to think that travellers and interlopers will be always served with the worst commodities, though perhaps they pay the best price for what they have.

It may appear strange, that while I am extolling the chastity of the Northern Indian women, I should acknowledge that it is a very common custom among the men of[160] this country to exchange a night's lodging with each other's wives. But this is so far from being considered as an act which is criminal, that it is esteemed by them as one of the strongest ties of friendship between two families; and in case of the death of either man, the other considers himself bound to support the children of the deceased. Those people are so far from viewing this engagement as a mere ceremony, like most of our Christian god-fathers and god-mothers, who, notwithstanding their vows are made in the most solemn manner, and in the presence of both God and man, scarcely ever afterward remember what they have promised, that there is not an instance of a Northern Indian having once neglected the duty which he is supposed to have taken upon himself to perform. The Southern Indians, with all their bad qualities,[161] are remarkably humane and charitable to the widows and children of departed friends; and as their situation and manner of life enable them to do more acts of charity with less trouble {130} than falls to the lot of a Northern Indian, few widows or orphans are ever unprovided for among them.

Though the Northern Indian men make no scruple of having two or three sisters for wives at one time, yet they are very particular in observing a proper distance in the consanguinity of those they admit to the above-mentioned intercourse with their wives. The Southern Indians are less scrupulous on those occasions; for among them it is not at all uncommon for one brother to make free with another brother's wife or daughter;[A] but this is held in abhorrence by the Northern Indians.

1st.

1771. July.

{131} By the time the Indians had killed as many deer as they thought would be sufficient for the support of the women during our absence, it was the first of July; and during this time I had two good observations, both by meridional and double altitudes; the mean of which determined the latitude of Congecathawhachaga[65] to be 68° 46' North; and its longitude, by account, was 24° 2' West from Prince of Wales's Fort, or 118° 15' West of the meridian of London.

[162]

2d.

On the second, the weather proved very bad, with much snow and sleet; about nine o'clock at night, however, it grew more moderate, and somewhat clearer, so that we set out, and walked about ten miles to the North by West, when we lay down to take a little sleep. At our departure from Congecathawhachaga, several Indians who had entered the war list, rather chose to stay behind with the women; but their loss was amply supplied by Copper Indians, who accompanied us in the double capacity of guides and warriors.

3d.

On the third the weather was equally bad with that of the preceding day; we made shift, however, to walk ten or eleven miles in the same direction we had done the day before, and at last were obliged to put up, not being able to see our way for snow and thick drift. By putting up, no more is to be understood than that we got to leeward of a {132} great stone, or into the crevices of the rocks, where we regaled ourselves with such provisions as we had brought with us, smoked our pipes, or went to sleep, till the weather permitted us to proceed on our journey.

> 4th.

> 1771. July.

On the fourth, we had rather better weather, though constant light snow, which made it very disagreeable under foot. We nevertheless walked twenty-seven miles to the North West, fourteen of which were on what the Indians call the Stony Mountains; and surely no part of the world better deserves that name. On our first approaching these mountains, they appeared to be a confused heap of stones, utterly inaccessible to the foot of man: but having some Copper Indians with us who knew the best road, we made a tolerable shift to get on, though not without being obliged frequently to crawl on our hands and knees. Notwithstanding the intricacy of the road, there is a very visible path the whole way across these mountains, even in the most difficult parts: and also on the smooth rocks, and those parts which are[163] capable of receiving an impression, the path is as plain and well-beaten, as any bye foot-path in England. By the side of this path there are, in different parts, several large, flat, or table stones, which are covered with many thousands of small pebbles. These the Copper Indians say have been gradually increased by passengers going to and from the mines; and on its being observed to us that it was the {133} universal custom for every one to add a stone to the heap, each of us took up a small stone in order to increase the number, for good luck.

Just as we arrived at the foot of the Stony Mountains, three of the Indians turned back; saying, that from every appearance, the remainder of the journey seemed likely to be attended with more trouble than would counterbalance the pleasure they could promise themselves by going to war with the Esquimaux.

5th.

6th.

1771. July.

On the fifth, as the weather was so bad, with constant snow, sleet, and rain, that we could not see our way, we did not offer to move: but the sixth proving moderate, and quite fair till toward noon, we set out in the morning, and walked about eleven miles to the North West; when perceiving bad weather at hand, we began to look out for shelter among the rocks, as we had done the four preceding nights, having neither tents nor tent-poles with us. The next morning fifteen more of the Indians deserted us, being quite sick of the road, and the uncommon badness of the weather. Indeed, though these people are all enured to hardships, yet their complaint on the present occasion was not without reason: for, from our leaving Congecathawhachaga we had scarcely a dry garment of any kind, or any thing to screen us from the inclemency of the weather, except rocks and {134} caves; the best of which were but damp and unwholesome lodging. In some the water was constantly dropping from the rock that formed the roof, which made our place of retreat little better than the open air; and we had not been able to make one spark of fire (except what was sufficient to light a pipe) from the[164] time of our leaving the women on the second instant; it is true, in some places there was a little moss, but the constant sleet and rain made it so wet, as to render it as impossible to set fire to it as it would be to a wet sponge.

We had no sooner entered our places of retreat, than we regaled ourselves with some raw venison which the Indians had killed that morning; the small stock of dried provisions we took with us when we left the women being now all expended.

Agreeably to our expectations, a very sudden and heavy gale of wind came on from the North West, attended with so great a fall of snow, that the oldest Indian in company said, he never saw it exceeded at any time of the year, much less in the middle of Summer. The gale was soon over, and by degrees it became a perfect calm: but the flakes of snow were so large as to surpass all credibility, and fell in such vast quantities, that though the shower only lasted nine hours, we were in danger of being smothered in our caves.

> 7th.

> 1771. July.

{135} On the seventh, we had a fresh breeze at North West, with some flying showers of small rain, and at the same time a constant warm sunshine, which soon dissolved the greatest part of the new-fallen snow. Early in the morning we crawled out of our holes, which were on the North side of the Stony Mountains, and walked about eighteen or twenty miles to the North West by West. In our way we crossed part of a large lake on the ice, which was then far from being broken up. This lake I distinguished by the name of Buffalo, or Musk-Ox Lake,[66] from the number of those animals[67] that we found grazing on the margin of it; many of which the Indians killed, but finding them lean, only took some of the bulls' hides for shoe-soals. At night the bad weather returned, with a strong gale of wind at North East, and very cold rain and sleet.

[165]

> 1771. July.

This was the first time we had seen any of the musk-oxen since we left the Factory. It has been observed that we saw a great number of them in my first unsuccessful attempt, before I had got an hundred miles from the Factory; and indeed I once perceived the tracks of two of those animals within nine miles of Prince of Wales's Fort. Great numbers of them also were met with in my second journey to the North: several of which my companions killed, particularly on the seventeenth of July one thousand seven hundred and seventy. They are also found at times in considerable numbers near the sea-coast of Hudson's Bay, {136} all the way from Knapp's Bay to Wager Water, but are most plentiful within the Arctic Circle. In those high latitudes I have frequently seen many herds of them in the course of a day's walk, and some of those herds did not contain less than eighty or an hundred head. The number of bulls is very few in proportion to the cows; for it is rare to see more than two or three full-grown bulls with the largest herd: and from the number of the males that are found dead, the Indians are of opinion that they kill each other in contending for the females. In the rutting season they are so jealous of the cows, that they run at either man or beast who offers to approach them; and have been observed to run and bellow even at ravens, and other large birds, which chanced to light near them. They delight in the most stony and mountainous parts of the barren ground, and are seldom found at any great distance from the woods. Though they are a beast of great magnitude, and apparently of a very unwieldy inactive structure, yet they climb the rocks with great ease and agility, and are nearly as sure-footed as a goat: like it too, they will feed on any thing; though they seem fondest of grass, yet in Winter, when that article cannot be had in sufficient quantity, they will eat moss, or any other herbage they can find, as also the tops of willows and the[166] tender branches of the pine tree. They take the bull in August, and bring forth their young the latter end of May, or beginning of June; and they never have more than one at a time.

> 1771. July.

{137} The musk-ox, when full grown, is as large as the generality, or at least as the middling size, of English black cattle;[A] but their legs, though large, are not so long; nor is their tail longer than that of a bear; and, like the tail of that animal, it always bends downward and inward, so that it is entirely hid by the long hair of the rump and hind quarters: the hunch on their shoulders is not large, being little more in proportion than that of a deer: their hair is in some parts very long, particularly on the belly, sides, and hind quarters; but the longest hair about them, particularly the bulls, is under the throat, extending from the chin to the lower part of the chest, between the fore-legs; it there hangs down like a horse's mane inverted, and is full as long, which makes the animal have a most formidable appearance. It is of the hair from this part that the Esquimaux make their musketto {138} wigs, and not from the tail, as is asserted by Mr. Ellis;[AK] their tails, and the hair which is on them, being too short for that purpose. In Winter they are provided with a thick fine wool, or furr, that grows at the root of the long hair, and shields them from the intense cold to which they are exposed during that season; but as the Summer advances, this furr loosens from the skin, and, by frequently rolling themselves on the ground, it works out to the end of the hair, and in time drops off, leaving little for their Summer clothing except the long hair. The season is so short in those high latitudes, that the new fleece begins to appear, almost as soon as the old one drops off; so that by the time the cold becomes severe, they are again provided with a Winter-dress.

[167]

The flesh of the musk-ox noways resembles that of the Western buffalo, but is more like that of the moose or elk; and the fat is of a clear white, slightly tinged with a light azure. The calves and young heifers are good eating; but the flesh of the bulls both smells and tastes so strong of musk, as to render it very disagreeable: even the knife that cuts the flesh of an old bull will smell so strong of musk, that nothing but scouring the blade quite bright can remove it, and the handle will retain the scent for a long time. Though no part of a bull is free from this smell, yet the parts of generation, in particular the *urethra*, are by far the most strongly impregnated. The {139} urine itself must contain the scent in a very great degree; for the sheaths of the bull's *penis* are corroded with a brown gummy substance, which is nearly as high-scented with musk as that said to be produced by the civet cat; and after having been kept for several years, seems not to lose any of its quality.

8th.

1771. July.

On the eighth, the weather was fine and moderate, though not without some showers of rain. Early in the morning we set out, and walked eighteen miles to the Northward. The Indians killed some deer; so we put up by the side of a small creek, that afforded a few willows, with which we made a fire for the first time since our leaving Congecathawhachaga;[168] consequently it was here that we cooked our first meal for a whole week. This, as may naturally be supposed, was well relished by all parties, the Indians as well as myself. And as the Sun had, in the course of the day, dried our clothing, in spite of the small showers of rain, we felt ourselves more comfortable than we had done since we left the women. The place where we lay that night, is not far from Grizzled Bear Hill; which takes its name from the numbers of those animals that are frequently known to resort thither for the purpose of bringing forth their young in a cave that is found there. The wonderful description which the Copper Indians gave of this place exciting the curiosity of several of my companions as well as myself, we went to view it; but on our arrival at it {140} found little worth remarking about it, being no more than a high lump of earth, of a loamy quality, of which kind there are several others in the same neighbourhood, all standing in the middle of a large marsh, which makes them resemble so many islands in a lake. The sides of these hills are quite perpendicular; and the height of Grizzled Bear Hill, which is the largest, is about twenty feet above the level ground that surrounds it. Their summits are covered with a thick sod of moss and long grass, which in some places projects over the edge; and as the sides are constantly mouldering away, and washing down with every shower of rain during the short Summer, they must in time be levelled with the marsh in which they are situated. At present those islands, as I call them, are excellent places of retreat for the birds which migrate there to breed; as they can bring forth their young in perfect safety from every beast except the Quiquehatch,[68] which, from the sharpness of its claws and the amazing strength of its legs, is capable of ascending the most difficult precipices.

> 1771. July.

[169]

On the side of the hill that I went to survey, there is a large cave which penetrates a considerable way into the rock, and may probably have been the work of the bears, as we could discover visible marks that some of those beasts had been there that Spring. This, though deemed very curious by some of my companions, did not appear so to me, as it neither engaged my attention, nor raised my {141} surprise, half so much as the sight of the many hills and dry ridges on the East side of the marsh, which are turned over like ploughed land by those animals, in searching for ground-squirrels,[69] and perhaps mice, which constitute a favourite part of their food. It is surprising to see the extent of their researches in quest of those animals, and still more to view the enormous stones rolled out of their beds by the bears on those occasions. At first I thought these long and deep furrows had been effected by lightning; but the natives assured me they never knew anything of the kind happen in those parts, and that it was entirely the work of the bears seeking for their prey.

> 9th.

> 10th.

> 1771. July.

On the ninth, the weather was moderate and cloudy, with some flying showers of rain. We set out early in the morning, and walked about forty miles to the North and North by East. In our way we saw plenty of deer and musk-oxen: several of the former the Indians killed, but a smart shower of rain coming on just as we were going to put up, made the moss so wet as to render it impracticable to light a fire. The next day proving fine and clear, we set out in the morning, and walked twenty miles to the North by West and North North West; but about noon the weather became so hot and sultry as to render walking very disagreeable; we therefore put up on the top of a high hill, and as the moss was then dry, lighted a fire, and should have made a comfortable meal, and been otherwise tolerably happy, had it not been {142} for the muskettoes, which were uncommonly numerous, and their stings almost insufferable. The same day Matonabbee sent several Indians a-head, with orders to proceed to the Copper-mine River as fast as possible, and acquaint any Indians they might meet, of our approach. By those Indians I also sent some small presents, as the surest means to induce any strangers they found, to come to our assistance.

[170]

11th.

The eleventh was hot and sultry, like the preceding day. In the morning we walked ten or eleven miles to the North West, and then met a Northern Indian Leader, called Oule-eye, and his family, who were, in company with several Copper Indians, killing deer with bows and arrows and spears, as they crossed a little river, by the side of which we put up, as did also the above-mentioned Indians.[AL] That afternoon I smoked my calumet of peace with these strangers, and found them a quite different set of people, at least in principle, from those I had seen at Congecathawhachaga: for though they had great plenty of provisions, they neither offered me nor my companions a mouthful, and would, if they had been permitted, have taken the last garment from off my back, and robbed me of every article I possessed. Even my Northern companions could not help taking notice of such unaccountable behaviour. Nothing but their poverty {143} protected them from being plundered by those of my crew; and had any of their women been worth notice, they would most assuredly have been pressed into our service.

> 12th.

> 13th.

> 1771. July.

The twelfth was so exceedingly hot and sultry, that we did not move; but early in the morning of the thirteenth, after my companions had taken what dry provisions they chose from our unsociable strangers, we set out, and walked about fifteen or sixteen miles to the North and North by East, in expectation of arriving at the Copper-mine River that day; but when we had reached the top of a long chain of hills, between which we were told the river ran, we found it to be no more than a branch of it which empties itself into the main river about forty miles from its influx into the sea. At that time all the Copper Indians were dispatched different ways, so that there was not one in company, who knew the shortest cut to the main river. Seeing some woods to the Westward, and judging that the current of the rivulet ran that way, we concluded that the main river lay in that direction, and was not very remote from our present situation. We therefore directed our course by the side of it, when the Indians met with several very fine buck deer, which they destroyed; and as that part we now traversed afforded plenty of good fire-wood, we put up, and cooked the most comfortable meal to which we had sat down for some months. As such favourable opportunities of indulging the appetite happen but seldom, it is a general {144} rule with the Indians, which we did not neglect, to exert every art in dressing our food which the most refined skill in Indian cookery has been able to invent, and which consists chiefly in boiling, broiling, and roasting: but of all the dishes cooked by those people, a *beeatee*, as it is called in their language, is certainly the most delicious, at least for a change, that can be prepared from a deer only, without any other ingredient. It is a kind of haggis, made with the blood, a good quantity of fat shred small, some of the tenderest of the flesh, together with the heart and lungs cut, or more commonly torn into small shivers; all which is put into the stomach, and roasted, by being suspended before the fire by a string. Care must be taken that it does not get too much heat at first, as the bag would thereby be liable to be burnt, and the contents be let out. When it is sufficiently done, it will emit steam, in the same manner as a fowl or a joint of meat; which is as much as to say, Come, eat me now: and if it be taken in time, before the blood and other contents are too much done, it is certainly a most delicious morsel, even without pepper, salt, or any other seasoning.

[171]

1771. July.

After regaling ourselves in the most plentiful manner, and taking a few hours rest, (for it was almost impossible to sleep for the muskettoes,) we once more set forward, directing our[172] course to the North West by West; and after walking about nine or ten miles, arrived at that long wished-for spot, the Copper-mine River.[70]

FOOTNOTES:

[AC] See the Plate, where Fig. A represents the bottom of the canoe, Fig. B being the fore-part. Fig. C is the complete frame of one before it is covered with the bark of the birch-tree; it is represented on an artificial bank, which the natives raise to build it on. Fig. D is an end-view of a set of timbers, bent and lashed in their proper shape, and left to dry. Fig. E is the representation of a complete canoe. Fig. F represents one of their paddles. Fig. G a spear with which they kill deer; and Fig. H, their mode of carrying the canoe.

The following references are to the several parts of the canoe: Fig. C. 1. The stem. 2. The stern-post. 3. Two forked sticks supporting the stem and stern-post. 4. The gunwales. 5. Small rods placed between the timbers and birch-bark that covers them. 6. The timbers. 7. The keelson. 8. Large stones placed there to keep the bottom steady till the sides are sewed on.

[AD] The tobacco used in Hudson's Bay is the Brasil tobacco; which is twisted into the form of a rope, of near an inch diameter, and then wound into a large roll; from which it is taken by measures of length, for the natives.

[57] Thus, four days after leaving Clowey, travelling in a northerly direction, they passed out of the wooded region and reached the barren grounds, though it is evident that there had been open barren grounds to the east of them for most of the way. Their course probably lay along the height of land east of Artillery Lake. The northern edge of the forest and southern line of the barren grounds crosses this lake near the middle, the most northern woods on its eastern shore being in latitude 63° 4' N., while on its western side the woods extend north to latitude 63° 11' N.

Artillery Lake is thus described by J. W. Tyrrell, who visited it in May 1900:—

"Artillery Lake was reached by our outfit on the 26th of May, more than two weeks after it had been first visited by Fairchild and Acres, when exploring and 'brushing' the trail for our voyageurs. Then its ice had been as solid as in winter, showing no signs of disruption or decay, whereas now it was rapidly decomposing, forming what is known as candle-ice, and making much open water along the shores. It lies in a north-easterly and south-westerly direction, and is fifty-five miles in length, ... and the superficial area of the lake is about one hundred and ninety square miles. Its shores are bold and high, in some places about two hundred feet above the lake, and for the most part they present a bare, desolate appearance, especially on the easterly shore where few trees of any kind can be seen.

"Such small groves as were found are shown on the map, but on the westerly side, about ten miles from the south end, the shore is quite well timbered with small spruce, and they continue northerly, although thinly scattered, for a distance of twenty miles, eight miles farther north than the last grove on the east shore. There the woods cease entirely." (Report on an Exploratory Survey between Great Slave Lake and Hudson Bay. By J.

W. Tyrrell. Ann. Report, Dept. of the Interior, Ottawa, 1901. App. 26, Part III., pp. 17-18.)

[AF] I have observed, during my several journies in those parts, that all the way to the North of Seal River the edge of the wood is faced with old withered stumps, and trees which have been blown down by the wind. They are mostly of the sort which is called here Juniper, but were seldom of any considerable size. Those blasted trees are found in some parts to extend to the distance of twenty miles from the living woods, and detached patches of them are much farther off; which is a proof that the cold has been increasing in those parts for some ages. Indeed, some of the older Northern Indians have assured me, that they have heard their fathers and grandfathers say, they remembered the greatest part of those places where the trees are now blasted and dead, in a flourishing state; and that they were remarkable for abounding with deer. It is a well-known fact, that many deer are fond of frequenting those plains where the juniper trees abound near barren grounds, particularly in fine weather during the Winter; but in heavy gales of wind they either take shelter in the thick woods, or go out on the open plains. The Indians, who never want a reason for any thing, say, that the deer quit the thin straggling woods during the high winds, because the nodding of the trees, when at a considerable distance from each other, frightens them; but in the midst of a thick forest, the constant rustling of the branches lulls them into security, and renders them an easy prey to a skilful hunter.

[This appears to have been the last wood seen before reaching the Coppermine River.

The wood known as juniper on Hudson Bay is the American larch, *Larix laricina* (Du Roi) which extends to the edge of the barren grounds.]

[AF] Probably the same with Partridge Lake in the Map.

[58] Between Clowey and Peshew or Cat Lake, the map shows that their course was across Partridge Lake. The exact position of this lake was made known by Mr. Warburton Pike and afterwards by James W. Tyrrell, who crossed from Great Slave Lake to Hudson Bay in 1900. It is a small lake on the river between Artillery and Clinton-Colden Lakes, and lies just a little north of the southern edge of the barren lands. The name given to it on the Cook map is Cossadgath and on the Mackenzie map Cassandgath Lake, which are evidently modifications of the Chipewyan word for

Ptarmigan or "White Partridge." With regard to the limits of Hearne's course in an east and west direction, it is quite clear that he passed to the east of Great Slave Lake and to the west of the belt of timber on Hanbury River, so that he must have passed in the vicinity of this lake if he did not pass over it.

Peshew is the Cree word for Wild Cat or Lynx, and therefore Peshew Lake should be the Cat Lake of the map, and not Partridge Lake as stated in the note, which was evidently inserted by Dr. Douglas after the author's death. Peshew or Cat Lake has been identified by Sir George Back, and following him by Sir John Richardson, as Artillery Lake, but this identification is almost certainly wrong. The shores of the southern half of Artillery Lake are wooded, while the Cat Lake of Hearne was three days' journey at least north of the southern edge of the barren lands. I think, therefore, that the Peshew or Cat Lake of this map is the lake which was named by Sir George Back, Clinton-Colden Lake, and which is known by this name on our present maps. Besides, though this argument may have little weight, Hearne's map shows Partridge and Cat Lakes in approximately the same positions in latitude as Partridge Lake (Kasba) and Clinton-Colden Lake respectively. On the Cook and Mackenzie maps, Cat Lake is shown as Cheesadawd Lake, which is certainly the same word as Tchizè-ta, which Abbé Petitot says means Gîte-du-Lynx or Home-of-the-Wild-Cat Lake. Petitot, however, states that this is the name of the lake which is now known as Walmsley Lake. Rt. Rev. J. Lofthouse, Bishop of Keewatin, also informs me that the Chipewyan name for Wild Cat or Lynx Lake is Seeza-tua. Another complication is brought in by the Pennant map, which leaves Hearne's Cat Lake unnamed, and applies the name Peshew (Cat) Lake to the Lake known on Hearne's map as No-name Lake. This is much more nearly in the position of Walmsley Lake of the present maps. It is therefore difficult to avoid the conclusion that Hearne trusted to his memory for the names of these lakes, and that his memory failed him here. It is quite possible that after crossing Partridge Lake the Indians changed their course, for some reason or other, and turned west or south of west to Walmsley Lake, and that in the excitement of meeting Keelshies, just from Churchill with a two-quart keg of brandy, Hearne neglected to make note of the change in the course.

[59] Some of the women and children were thus left on the north side of Peshew, probably Clinton-Colden Lake, and in that case he is correct in saying that they were north of latitude 64°. At the town of Dawson, in the

Yukon territory, which is in about the same latitude, there is sufficient light to work and travel at midnight between the 10th of May and the 1st of August.

[60] The map shows that he changed his course a little more to the west from the north shore of Clinton-Colden Lake, but actually he altered his course more than is there shown, and, while his map is reasonably correct thus far, it here becomes very inaccurate, and his distances are greatly exaggerated from this point to the mouth of the Coppermine River, during the time when the party was hurrying, with the lightest equipment possible, across the barren lands. The first lake crossed is said to have been Thoy-noy-kyed Lake, which is identified by Sir John Richardson as Tha-na-koi or Sand Hill Mount or Aylmer Lake. This lake is placed by Hearne about seventy-five miles from Cat (Clinton-Colden) Lake, while actually it is only a very few miles from it, forming, with it, but one body of water with a rapid between them. On the Cook map it is shown as having its discharge in a stream flowing south-westward into the east end of Great Slave Lake. If his Cat Lake should prove to be Walmsley Lake his distances would not be quite so inaccurate, for Walmsley and Aylmer Lakes are about fifty miles apart.

[61] Thoy-coy-lyned Lake has not been definitely located, and as there are very many lakes still unknown in that country, there is little use in making a guess at its position. Between it and Cogead Lake, the women of the party were all left behind at a point which he places in latitude 67° 30', but which must have been much farther south, as we shall see.

[62] One of these streams, just north of Thoy-coy-lyned Lake, is called on the map Thlewey-chuck, which means Great-fish River. This can hardly be the Great Fish River which rises in Sussex Lake and empties into the Arctic Ocean south of King William Island, but it may be a river mentioned by Petitot under the name *L'uétchôr des tchègè*, which is said by him to flow southward into Great Slave Lake. Or it may be some other stream known by the same name to the Chipewyan Indians.

[63] COGEAD LAKE.—This lake has been identified by Sir J. Richardson with Contwoy-to or Rum Lake of Franklin, the name which it bore in his day among the Copper Indians. Sir J. Franklin says of it: "The lake is called by them Contwoy-to or Rum Lake, in consequence of Mr. Hearne having here given the Indians who accompanied him some of that liquor." It lies

in N. latitude 65° 50', a long way south of the Arctic circle, and therefore Hearne is in error in the next paragraph when he says that the sun "did not set all that night." Mr. Frank Russell visited this district in 1894, and he speaks of a large lake called by the Indians Ko-ă-kă-tcai-tĭ which he thinks must be the Rum Lake of Franklin, and consequently the Cogead Lake of Hearne ("Explorations in the Far North," by Frank Russell, 1898, p. 113).

[64] This place has also been identified by Sir John Franklin, who says: "We subsequently learned from the Copper Indians that the part at which we had crossed the (Anatessy) river was the Congecathawhachaga of Hearne, of which I had little idea at the time" ("First Journey," p. 405). Sir John Richardson ("Polar Regions," p. 126) makes the following statement with regard to the identification of this place:

"Travelling without incumbrance, the war-party, with Hearne in company, reached a river of some size called Congecawthawhachaga, on the 21st of June, and there they met a large body of the Copper Indians or Red Knives, one of whom, then a boy named Cascathry, was well known in 1820-21 to Sir John Franklin. This boy joined the war-party, and in his old age remembered the circumstances well. Hearne says that he ascertained with his Elton's quadrant the position of the ferry over the river to be 68° 46' north, and 118° 15' west of London. According to Sir John Franklin's observations it lies in 66° 14' N., long. 112° W."

[AG] See Postlethwayt on the article of Labour.

[AH] Notwithstanding this is the general character of the Southern Indian women, as they are called on the coasts of Hudson's Bay, and who are the same tribe with the Canadian Indians, I am happy to have it in my power to insert a few lines to the memory of one of them, whom I knew from her infancy, and who, I can truly affirm, was directly the reverse of the picture I have drawn.

MARY, the daughter of MOSES NORTON, many years Chief at Prince of Wales's Fort, in Hudson's Bay, though born and brought up in a country of all others the least favourable to virtue and virtuous principles, possessed them, and every other good and amiable quality, in a most eminent degree.

Without the assistance of religion, and with no education but what she received among the dissolute natives of her country, she would have shone with superior lustre in any other country: for, if an engaging person, gentle manners, an easy freedom, arising from a consciousness of innocence, an amiable modesty, and an unrivalled delicacy of sentiment, are graces and virtues which render a woman lovely, none ever had greater pretensions to general esteem and regard: while her benevolence, humanity, and scrupulous adherence to truth and honesty, would have done honour to the most enlightened and devout Christian.

Dutiful, obedient, and affectionate to her parents; steady and faithful to her friends; grateful and humble to her benefactors; easily forgiving and forgetting injuries; careful not to offend any, and courteous and kind to all; she was, nevertheless, suffered to perish by the rigours of cold and hunger, amidst her own relations, at a time when the griping hand of famine was by no means severely felt by any other member of their company; and it may truly be said that she fell a martyr to the principles of virtue. This happened in the Winter of the year 1782, after the French had destroyed Prince of Wales's Fort; at which time she was in the twenty-second year of her age.

Human nature shudders at the bare recital of such brutality, and reason shrinks from the task of accounting for the decrees of Providence on such occasions as this: but they are the strongest assurances of a future state, so infinitely superior to the present, that the enjoyment of every pleasure in this world by the most worthless and abandoned wretch, or the most innocent and virtuous woman perishing by the most excruciating of all deaths, are matters equally indifferent. But,

"Peace to the ashes, and the virtuous mind,
Of her who lived in peace with all mankind;
Learn'd from the heart, unknowing of disguise,
Truth in her thoughts, and candour in her eyes;
Stranger alike to envy and to pride,
Good sense her light, and Nature all her guide;
But now removed from all the ills of life,
Here rests the pleasing friend and faithful wife."—WALLER.

Her father was, undoubtedly, very blamable for bringing her up in the tender manner which he did, rendering her by that means not only incapable of bearing the fatigues and hardships which the rest of her countrywomen think little of, but of providing for herself. This is, indeed, too frequent a practice among Europeans in that country, who bring up their children in so indulgent a manner, that when they retire, and leave their offspring behind, they find themselves so helpless, as to be unable to provide for the few wants to which they are subject. The late Mr. Ferdinand Jacobs, many years Chief at York Fort, was the only person whom I ever knew that acted in a different manner; though no man could possibly be fonder of his children in other respects, yet as there were some that he could not bring to England, he had them brought up entirely among the natives; so that when he left the country, they scarcely ever felt the loss, though they regretted the absence of a fond and indulgent parent.

[Al] Most of the Southern Indians, as well as the Athapuscow and Neheaway tribes, are entirely without scruple in this respect. It is notoriously known, that many of them cohabit occasionally with their own mothers, and frequently espouse their sisters and daughters. I have known several of them who, after having lived in that state for some time with their daughters, have given them to their sons, and all parties been perfectly reconciled to it.

In fact, notwithstanding the severity of the climate, the licentiousness of the inhabitants cannot be exceeded by any of the Eastern nations, whose luxurious manner of life, and genial clime, seem more adapted to excite extraordinary passions, than the severe cold of the frigid Zone.

It is true, that few of those who live under the immediate protection of the English ever take either their sisters or daughters for wives, which is probably owing to the fear of incurring their displeasure; but it is well known that acts of incest too often take place among them, though perhaps not so frequently as among the foreign Indians.

[65] As seen on page 153, the latitude given for this place is 2° 32' too far north. Almost any quadrant, however bad, would permit of taking an observation closer than this; but as the error is approximately two and a half degrees, his mistake in observing the double altitude would be five degrees, and if he took an observation at all it is possible that this error was in making the calculations or in transcribing, rather than in taking, the observation.

[66] The position of this lake has not since been determined, and as the name Musk-Ox Lake seems to be one given by Hearne himself, and as the Indian name is not given, it will be difficult at any time to identify it.

[67] *Ovibos moschatus* (Zimm.).

[AJ] Mr. Dragge says, in his Voyage ["An Account of a Voyage for the Discovery of a North-West Passage," by the Clerk of the *California*, London, 1748], vol. ii. p. 260, that the musk-ox is lower than a deer, but larger as to belly and quarters; which is very far from the truth; they are of the size I have here described them, and the Indians always estimate the flesh of a full-grown cow to be equal in quantity to three deer. I am sorry also to be obliged to contradict my friend Mr. Graham, who says that the flesh of this animal is carried on sledges to Prince of Wales's Fort, to the amount of three or four thousand pounds annually. To the amount of near one thousand pounds may have been purchased from the natives in some particular years, but it more frequently happens that not an ounce is brought one year out of five. In fact, it is by no means esteemed by the Company's servants, and of course no great encouragement is given to introduce it; but if it had been otherwise, their general situation is so remote from the settlement, that it would not be worth the Indians while to haul it to the Fort. So that, in fact, all that has ever been carried to Prince of Wales's Fort, has most assuredly been killed out of a herd that has been accidentally found within a moderate distance of the settlement; perhaps an hundred miles, which is only thought a step by an Indian.

[AK] Voyage to Hudson's Bay, p. 232.

[68] *Gulo luscus* Linn. See p. 346.

[69] *Citellus parryi* Richardson.—E. A. P.

[AL] This river runs nearly North East, and in all probability empties itself into the Northern Ocean, not far from the Copper River.

[70] He reached the Coppermine River at Sandstone Rapids, having travelled one hundred and forty-five miles north-westward from Congecathawhachaga in thirteen days, making an average of eleven miles a day, or, omitting the two days on which the party did not travel, an average of thirteen miles a day. The distance stated in the text is one hundred and eighty-eight miles. Considering the very rough nature of the country over which he was travelling, this is not a very extravagant estimate nor a very unreasonable error. While his estimate of distance is not very bad, his direction should have been N. 58° W. instead of N. 23° W., as shown on his map. Mr. Frank Russell, who crossed the Coppermine

River in the spring of 1894 while on a hunt for musk oxen, says that its present Chipewyan name is Tson Te ("Explorations in the Far North," p. 112).

In 1821 Sir John Franklin explored and surveyed this river from Point Lake to the Arctic Ocean, a distance of about two hundred and seventy-five miles. Its length above Point Lake is not known, but it is probably about two hundred miles. A short distance below Point Lake Franklin says that it "is about two hundred yards wide and ten feet deep, and flows very rapidly over a rocky bottom" ("First Journey," p. 327).

Sir John Richardson writes of the river farther north as follows: "The river contracting to a width of a hundred and twenty yards at length forces itself through the *Rocky Defile*, a narrow channel which it has cut during a lapse of ages in the shelving foot of a hill" ("First Journey," p. 527).

[173]

{145} CHAP. VI.

Transactions at the Copper-mine River, and till we joined all the women to the South of Cogead Lake.

Some Copper Indians join us—Indians send three spies down the river—Begin my survey—Spies return, and give an account of five tents of Esquimaux—Indians consult the best method to steal on them in the night, and kill them while asleep—Cross the river— Proceedings of the Indians as they advance towards the Esquimaux tents—The Indians begin the massacre while the poor Esquimaux are asleep, and slay them all—Much affected at the sight of one young woman killed close to my feet—The behaviour of the Indians on this occasion—Their brutish treatment of the dead bodies— Seven more tents seen on the opposite side of the river—The Indians harass them, till they fly to a shoal in the river for safety—Behaviour of the Indians after killing those Esquimaux—Cross the river, and proceed to the tents on that side—Plunder their tents, and destroy their utensils—Continue my survey to the river's mouth—Remarks there—Set out on my return—Arrive at one of the Coppermines— Remarks on it—Many attempts made to induce the Copper Indians to carry their own goods to market—Obstacles to it—Villany and cruelty of Keelshies to some of those poor Indians—Leave the Copper-mine, and walk at an amazing rate till we join the women, by the side of Cogead Whoie—Much foot-foundered—The appearance very alarming, but soon changes for the better— Proceed to the Southward, and join the remainder of the women and children—Many other Indians arrive with them.

> 1771. July. 14th

We had scarcely arrived at the Copper-mine River when four Copper Indians joined us, and brought with them two canoes. They had seen all the Indians who were sent from us at various times, except Matonabbee's {146} brother, and three others that were first dispatched from Congecathawhachaga.[174]

1771. July.

On my arrival here I was not a little surprised to find the river differ so much from the description which the Indians had given of it at the Factory; for, instead of being so large as to be navigable for shipping, as it had been represented by them, it was at that part scarcely navigable for an Indian canoe, being no more than one hundred and eighty yards wide, every where full of shoals, and no less than three falls were in sight at first view.

Near the water's edge there is some wood; but not one tree grows on or near the top of the hills between which the river runs. There appears to have been formerly a much greater quantity than there is at present; but the trees seem to have been set on fire some years ago, and, in consequence, there is at present ten sticks lying on the ground, for one green one which is growing beside them. The whole timber appears to have been, even in its greatest prosperity, of so crooked and dwarfish a growth as to render it of little use for any purpose but fire-wood.

Soon after our arrival at the river-side, three Indians were sent off as spies, in order to see if any Esquimaux were inhabiting the river-side between us and the sea. After walking about three-quarters of a mile by the side of the river, we put up, when most of the Indians went a {147} hunting, and killed several musk-oxen and some deer. They were employed all the remainder of the day and night in splitting and drying the meat by the fire. As we were not then in want of provisions, and as deer and other animals were so plentiful, that each day's journey might have provided for itself, I was at a loss to account for this unusual œconomy of my companions; but was soon informed, that those preparations were made with a view to have victuals enough ready-cooked to serve us to the river's mouth, without being obliged to kill any in our way, as the report of the guns, and the smoke of the fires, would be liable to alarm the natives, if any should be near at hand, and give them an opportunity of escaping.[175]

1771. July. 15th.

Early in the morning of the fifteenth, we set out, when I immediately began my survey, which I continued about ten miles down the river, till heavy rain coming on we were obliged to put up; and the place where we lay that night was the end, or edge of the woods, the whole space between it and the sea being entirely barren hills and wide open marshes. In the course of this day's survey, I found the river as full of shoals as the part which I had seen before; and in many places it was so greatly diminished in its width, that in our way we passed by two more capital falls.

16th.

Early in the morning of the sixteenth, the weather being fine and pleasant, I again proceeded with my survey, and continued it for ten miles farther down the river; {148} but still found it the same as before, being every where full of falls and shoals. At this time (it being about noon) the three men who had been sent as spies met us on their return, and informed my companions that five tents of Esquimaux were on the west side of the river. The situation, they said, was very convenient for surprising them; and, according to their account, I judged it to be about twelve miles from the place we met the spies. When the Indians received this intelligence, no farther attendance or attention was paid to my survey, but their whole thoughts were immediately engaged in planning the best method of attack, and how they might steal on the poor Esquimaux the ensuing night, and kill them all while asleep. To accomplish this bloody design more effectually, the Indians thought it necessary to cross the river as soon as possible; and, by the account of the spies, it appeared that no part was more convenient for the purpose than that where we had met them, it being there very smooth, and at a considerable distance from any fall. Accordingly, after the Indians had put all their guns, spears, targets, &c. in good order, we crossed the river, which took up some time.

1771. July.

When we arrived on the West side of the river, each painted the front of his target or shield; some with the figure of the[176] Sun, others with that of the Moon, several with different kinds of birds and beasts of prey, and many with the images of imaginary beings, which, {149} according to their silly notions, are the inhabitants of the different elements, Earth, Sea, Air, &c.

On enquiring the reason of their doing so, I learned that each man painted his shield with the image of that being on which he relied most for success in the intended engagement. Some were contented with a single representation; while others, doubtful, as I suppose, of the quality and power of any single being, had their shields covered to the very margin with a group of hieroglyphics, quite unintelligible to every one except the painter. Indeed, from the hurry in which this business was necessarily done, the want of every colour but red and black, and the deficiency of skill in the artist, most of those paintings had more the appearance of a number of accidental blotches, than "of any thing that is on the earth, or in the water under the earth"; and though some few of them conveyed a tolerable idea of the thing intended, yet even these were many degrees worse than our country sign-paintings in England.

1771. July.

When this piece of superstition was completed, we began to advance toward the Esquimaux tents; but were very careful to avoid crossing any hills, or talking loud, for fear of being seen or overheard by the inhabitants; by which means the distance was not only much greater than it otherwise would have been, but, for the sake of keeping in the lowest grounds, we were obliged to walk through {150} entire swamps of stiff marly clay, sometimes up to the knees. Our course, however, on this occasion, though very serpentine, was not altogether so remote from the river as entirely to exclude me from a view of it the whole way: on the contrary, several times (according to the situation of the ground) we advanced so near it, as to give me an opportunity of convincing myself that it was as unnavigable as it was in those parts which I had surveyed[177] before, and which entirely corresponded with the accounts given of it by the spies.

It is perhaps worth remarking, that my crew, though an undisciplined rabble, and by no means accustomed to war or command, seemingly acted on this horrid occasion with the utmost uniformity of sentiment. There was not among them the least altercation or separate opinion; all were united in the general cause, and as ready to follow where Matonabbee led, as he appeared to be ready to lead, according to the advice of an old Copper Indian, who had joined us on our first arrival at the river where this bloody business was first proposed.

Never was reciprocity of interest more generally regarded among a number of people, than it was on the present occasion by my crew, for not one was a moment in want of any thing that another could spare; and if ever the spirit of disinterested friendship expanded the heart of a Northern Indian, it was here exhibited in the most {151} extensive meaning of the word. Property of every kind that could be of general use now ceased to be private, and every one who had any thing which came under that description, seemed proud of an opportunity of giving it, or lending it to those who had none, or were most in want of it.

The number of my crew was so much greater than that which five tents could contain, and the warlike manner in which they were equipped so greatly superior to what could be expected of the poor Esquimaux, that no less than a total massacre of every one of them was likely to be the case, unless Providence should work a miracle for their deliverance.

1771. July.

The land was so situated that we walked under cover of the rocks and hills till we were within two hundred yards of the tents. There we lay in ambush for some time, watching the motions of the Esquimaux; and here the Indians would have advised me to stay till the fight was over, but to this I could by no means consent; for I considered that when the Esquimaux came to be surprised, they would try every way to[178] escape, and if they found me alone, not knowing me from an enemy, they would probably proceed to violence against me when no person was near to assist. For this reason I determined to accompany them, telling them at the same time, that I would not have any hand in the murder they were about to commit, {152} unless I found it necessary for my own safety. The Indians were not displeased at this proposal; one of them immediately fixed me a spear, and another lent me a broad bayonet for my protection, but at that time I could not be provided with a target; nor did I want to be encumbered with such an unnecessary piece of lumber.

While we lay in ambush, the Indians performed the last ceremonies which were thought necessary before the engagement. These chiefly consisted in painting their faces; some all black, some all red, and others with a mixture of the two; and to prevent their hair from blowing into their eyes, it was either tied before and behind, and on both sides, or else cut short all round. The next thing they considered was to make themselves as light as possible for running; which they did, by pulling off their stockings, and either cutting off the sleeves of their jackets, or rolling them up close to their armpits; and though the muskettoes at that time were so numerous as to surpass all credibility, yet some of the Indians actually pulled off their jackets and entered the lists quite naked, except their breech-cloths and shoes. Fearing I might have occasion to run with the rest, I thought it also advisable to pull off my stockings and cap, and to tie my hair as close up as possible.

17th.

By the time the Indians had made themselves thus completely frightful, it was near one o'clock in the {153} morning of the seventeenth; when finding all the Esquimaux quiet in their tents, they rushed forth from their ambuscade, and fell on the poor unsuspecting creatures, unperceived till close at the very eves of their tents, when they soon began the bloody massacre, while I stood neuter in the rear.

From "Franklin's First Journey."
BLOODY FALLS, COPPERMINE RIVER

COPPER IMPLEMENTS FROM COPPERMINE RIVER

[179]

1771. July.

In a few seconds the horrible scene commenced; it was shocking beyond description; the poor unhappy victims were surprised in the midst of their sleep, and had neither time nor power to make any resistance; men, women, and children, in all upward of twenty, ran out of their tents stark naked, and endeavoured to make their escape; but the Indians having possession of all the land-side, to no place could they fly for shelter. One alternative only remained, that of jumping into the river; but, as none of them attempted it, they all fell a sacrifice to Indian barbarity!

1771. July.

The shrieks and groans of the poor expiring wretches were truly dreadful; and my horror was much increased at seeing a young girl, seemingly about eighteen years of age, killed so near me, that when the first spear was stuck into her side she fell down at my feet, and twisted round my legs, so that it was with difficulty that I could disengage myself from her dying grasps. As two Indian men pursued this unfortunate victim, I solicited very hard for her life; but the murderers made no reply till they had {154} stuck both their spears through her body, and transfixed her to the ground. They then looked me sternly in the face, and began to ridicule me, by asking if I wanted an Esquimaux wife; and paid not the smallest regard to the shrieks and agony of the poor wretch, who was twining round their spears like an eel! Indeed, after receiving much abusive language from them on the occasion, I was at length obliged to desire that they would be more expeditious in dispatching their victim out of her misery, otherwise I should be obliged, out of pity, to assist in the friendly office of putting an end to the existence of a fellow-creature who was so cruelly wounded. On this request being made, one of the Indians hastily drew his spear from the place where it was first lodged, and pierced it through her breast near the heart. The love of life, however, even in this most miserable state, was so predominant, that though this might justly be called the most merciful act that could be done for[180] the poor creature, it seemed to be unwelcome, for though much exhausted by pain and loss of blood, she made several efforts to ward off the friendly blow. My situation and the terror of my mind at beholding this butchery, cannot easily be conceived, much less described; though I summed up all the fortitude I was master of on the occasion, it was with difficulty that I could refrain from tears; and I am confident that my features must have feelingly expressed how sincerely I was affected at the barbarous scene I then {155} witnessed; even at this hour I cannot reflect on the transactions of that horrid day without shedding tears.

The brutish manner in which these savages used the bodies they had so cruelly bereaved of life was so shocking, that it would be indecent to describe it; particularly their curiosity in examining, and the remarks they made, on the formation of the women; which, they pretended to say, differed materially from that of their own. For my own part I must acknowledge, that however favourable the opportunity for determining that point might have been, yet my thoughts at the time were too much agitated to admit of any such remarks; and I firmly believe, that had there actually been as much difference between them as there is said to be between the Hottentots and those of Europe, it would not have been in my power to have marked the distinction. I have reason to think, however, that there is no ground for the assertion; and really believe that the declaration of the Indians on this occasion, was utterly void of truth, and proceeded only from the implacable hatred they bore to the whole tribe of people of whom I am speaking.

1771. July.

When the Indians had completed the murder of the poor Esquimaux, seven other tents on the East side of the river immediately engaged their attention: very luckily, however, our canoes and baggage had been left at a little distance up the river, so that they had no way of {156} crossing to get at them. The river at this part being little more than eighty yards wide,[181] they began firing at them from the West side. The poor Esquimaux on the opposite shore, though all up in arms, did not attempt to abandon their tents; and they were so unacquainted with the nature of fire-arms, that when the bullets struck the ground, they ran in crowds to see what was sent them, and seemed anxious to examine all the pieces of lead which they found flattened against the rocks. At length one of the Esquimaux men was shot in the calf of his leg, which put them in great confusion. They all immediately embarked in their little canoes, and paddled to a shoal in the middle of the river, which being somewhat more than a gun-shot from any part of the shore, put them out of the reach of our barbarians.

1771. July.

When the savages discovered that the surviving Esquimaux had gained the shore above mentioned, the Northern Indians began to plunder the tents of the deceased of all the copper utensils they could find; such as hatchets, bayonets, knives, &c. after which they assembled on the top of an adjacent high hill, and standing all in a cluster, so as to form a solid circle, with their spears erect in the air, gave many shouts of victory, constantly clashing their spears against each other, and frequently calling out *tima! tima!*[AM] by way of derision to the poor surviving {157} Esquimaux, who were standing on the shoal almost knee-deep in water. After parading the hill for some time, it was agreed to return up the river to the place where we had left our canoes and baggage, which was about half a mile distant, and then to cross the river again and plunder the seven tents on the East side. This resolution was immediately put in force; and as ferrying across with only three or four canoes[AN] took a considerable time, and as we were, from the crookedness of the river and the form of the land, entirely under cover, several of the poor surviving Esquimaux, thinking probably that we were gone about our business, and meant to trouble them no more, had returned from the shoal to their habitations. When we approached their tents, which we did under cover of the rocks, we found them busily employed tying up bundles. These the Indians seized with their usual ferocity; on which, the Esquimaux having their canoes lying ready in the water, immediately embarked, and all of them got safe to the former shoal, except an old man, who was so intent on collecting his things, that the Indians coming upon him before he could reach his canoe, he fell a sacrifice to their fury: I verily believe not less than twenty had a hand in his death, as his whole body was like a cullender. It is here necessary to observe that the spies {158} when on the look-out, could not see these seven tents, though close under them, as the bank, on which they stood, stretched over them.

[182]

1771. July.

1771. July.

17th.

It ought to have been mentioned in its proper place, that in making our retreat up the river, after killing the Esquimaux on the West side, we saw an old woman sitting by the side of the water, killing salmon,[171] which lay at the foot of the fall as thick as a shoal of herrings. Whether from the noise of the fall, or a natural defect in the old woman's hearing, it is hard to determine, but certain it is, she had no knowledge of the tragical scene which had been so lately transacted at the tents, though she was not more than two hundred yards from the place. When we first perceived her, she seemed perfectly at ease, and was entirely surrounded with the produce of her labour. From her manner of behaviour, and the appearance of her eyes, which were as red as blood, it is more than probable that her sight was not very good; for she scarcely discerned that the Indians were enemies, till they were within twice the length of their spears of her. It was in vain that she attempted to fly, for the wretches of my crew transfixed her to the ground in a few seconds, and butchered her in the most savage manner. There was scarcely a man among them who had not a thrust at her with his spear; and many in doing this, aimed at torture, rather than immediate death, as they not only poked out her eyes, {159} but stabbed her in many parts very remote from those which are vital.

[183]

It may appear strange, that a person supposed to be almost blind should be employed in the business of fishing, and particularly with any degree of success; but when the multitude of fish is taken into the account, the wonder will cease. Indeed they were so numerous at the foot of the fall, that when a light pole, armed with a few spikes, which was the instrument the old woman used, was put under water, and hauled up with a jerk, it was scarcely possible to miss them. Some of my Indians tried the method, for curiosity, with the old woman's staff, and seldom got less than two at a jerk, sometimes three or four. Those fish, though very fine, and beautifully red, are but small, seldom weighing more (as near as I could judge) than six or seven pounds, and in general much less. Their numbers at this place were almost incredible, perhaps equal to any thing that is related of the salmon in Kamschatka, or any other part of the world. It does not appear that the Esquimaux have any other method of catching the fish, unless it be by spears and darts; for no appearance of nets was discovered either at their tents, or on any part of the shore. This is the case with all the Esquimaux on the West side of Hudson's Bay; spearing in Summer, and angling in Winter, are the only methods they have yet devised to catch fish, though at {160} times their whole dependence for support is on that article.[AO]

[184]

{161} When the Indians had plundered the seven tents of all the copper utensils, which seemed the only thing worth {162} their notice, they threw all the tents and tent-poles into the river, destroyed a vast quantity of dried salmon, musk-oxen flesh, and other provisions; broke all the stone kettles; and, in fact, did all the mischief they possibly could to distress the poor creatures they could not murder, and who were standing on the shoal before mentioned, obliged to be woeful spectators of their great, or perhaps irreparable loss.

After the Indians had completed this piece of wantonness we sat down, and made a good meal of fresh salmon, which were as numerous at the place where we now rested, as they[185] were on the West side of the river. When we had finished our meal, which was the first we had enjoyed for many hours, the Indians told me that they were again ready to assist me in making an end of my survey. It was then about five o'clock in the morning of the seventeenth, the sea being in sight from the North West by West to the North East, about eight miles distant. I therefore set instantly about commencing my survey, and pursued it to the mouth of the river, which I found all the way so full of shoals and falls that it was not navigable even for a boat, and that it emptied itself into the sea over a ridge or bar. {163} The tide was then out; but I judged from the marks which I saw on the edge of the ice, that it flowed[186] about twelve or fourteen feet, which will only reach a little way within the river's mouth. The tide being out, the water in the river was perfectly fresh; but I am certain of its being the sea, or some branch of it, by the quantity of whalebone and seal-skins which the Esquimaux had at their tents, and also by the number of seals[72] which I saw on the ice. At the mouth of the river, the sea is full of islands and shoals, as far as I could see with the assistance of a good pocket telescope. The ice was not then broke up, but was melted away for about three quarters of a mile from the main shore, and to a little distance round the islands and shoals.

18th.

By the time I had completed this survey, it was about one in the morning of the eighteenth; but in those high latitudes, and at this season of the year, the Sun is always at a good height above the horizon, so that we had not only day light, but sunshine the whole night: a thick fog and drizzling rain then came on, and finding that neither the river nor sea were likely to be of any use, I did not think it worth while to wait for fair weather to determine the latitude exactly by an observation; but by the extraordinary care I took in observing the courses and distances when I walked from Congecathawhachaga, where I had two good observations, the latitude may be depended upon within twenty miles at the utmost. For the sake of form, {164} however, after having had some consultation with the Indians, I erected a mark, and took possession of the coast, on behalf of the Hudson's Bay Company.[73]

[187]

1771. July.

Having finished this business, we set out on our return, and walked about twelve miles to the South by East, when we stopped and took a little sleep, which was the first time that any of us had closed our eyes from the fifteenth instant, and it was now six o'clock in the morning of the eighteenth. Here the Indians killed a musk-ox, but the moss being very wet, we could not make a fire, so that we were obliged to eat the meat raw, which was intolerable, as it happened to be an old beast.

1771. July.

Before I proceed farther on my return, it may not be improper to give some account of the river, and the country adjacent; its productions, and the animals which constantly inhabit those dreary regions, as well as those that only migrate thither in Summer, in order to breed and rear their young, unmolested by man. That I may do this to better[188] purpose, it will be necessary to go back to the place where I first came to the river, which was about forty miles from its mouth.

Beside the stunted pines already mentioned, there are some tufts of dwarf willows; plenty of Wishacumpuckey,[74] (as the English call it, and which they use as tea); some {165} jackasheypuck, which the natives use as tobacco; and a few cranberry and heathberry bushes; but not the least appearance of any fruit.

The woods grow gradually thinner and smaller as you approach the sea; and the last little tuft of pines that I saw is about thirty miles from the mouth of the river, so that we meet with nothing between that spot and the sea-side but barren hills and marshes.

1771. July.

The general course of the river is about North by East; but in some places it is very crooked, and its breadth varies from twenty yards to four or five hundred. The banks are in general a solid rock, both sides of which correspond so exactly with each other, as to leave no doubt that the channel of the river has been caused by some terrible convulsion of nature; and the stream is supplied by a variety of little rivulets, that rush down the sides of the hills, occasioned chiefly by the melting of the snow. Some of the Indians say, that this river takes its rise from the North West side of Large White Stone Lake, which is at the distance of near three hundred miles on a straight line; but I can scarcely think that is the case, unless there be many intervening lakes, which are supplied by the vast quantity of water that is collected in so great an extent of hilly and mountainous country: for were it otherwise, I should imagine that the multitude of small rivers, which must empty themselves into the main stream in the course of so {166} great a distance, would have formed a much deeper and stronger current than I discovered, and occasioned an annual deluge at the breaking up of the ice in the Spring, of which there was not the least appearance, except at Bloody Fall, where the river was contracted to the breadth of about twenty yards. It was at the foot of this fall that my Indians killed the Esquimaux; which was the reason why I distinguished it by that appellation. From this fall, which is about eight miles from the sea-side, there are very few hills, and those not high. The land between them is a stiff loam and clay, which, in some parts, produces patches of pretty good grass, and in others tallish dwarf willows: at the foot of the hills also there is plenty of fine scurvy-grass.

[189]

The Esquimaux at this river are but low in stature, none exceeding the middle size, and though broad set, are neither well-made nor strong bodied. Their complexion is of a dirty copper colour; some of the women, however, are more fair and ruddy. Their dress much resembles that of the Greenlanders in Davis's Straits, except the women's boots, which are not stiffened out with whalebone, and the tails of their jackets are not more than a foot long.

Their arms and fishing-tackle are bows and arrows, spears, lances, darts, &c. which exactly resemble those made use of by the Esquimaux in Hudson's Straits, and {167} which have been well described by Crantz[AP]; but, for want of good edge-tools, are far inferior to them in workmanship. Their arrows are either shod with a triangular piece of black stone, like slate, or a piece of copper; but most commonly the former.

> 1771. July.

The body of their canoes is on the same construction as that of the other Esquimaux, and there is no unnecessary prow-projection beyond the body of the vessel; these, like their arms and other utensils, are, for the want of better tools, by no means so neat as those I have seen in Hudson's Bay and Straits. The double-bladed paddle is in universal use among all the tribes of this people.

[190]

Their tents are made of parchment deer-skins in the hair, and are pitched in a circular form, the same as those of the Esquimaux in Hudson's Bay. These tents are undoubtedly no more than their Summer habitations, for I saw the remains of two miserable hovels, which, from the situation, the structure, and the vast quantity of bones, old shoes, scraps of skins, and other rubbish lying near them, had certainly been some of their Winter retreats. These houses were situated on the South side of a hill; one half of them were under-ground, and the upper parts closely set round with poles, meeting at the top in a conical form, like their Summer-houses or tents. These tents, {168} when inhabited, had undoubtedly been covered with skins; and in Winter entirely overspread with the snow-drift, which must have greatly contributed to their warmth. They were so small, that they did not contain more than six or eight persons each; and even that number of any other people would have found them but miserable habitations.

Their household furniture chiefly consists of stone kettles, and wooden troughs of various sizes; also dishes, scoops, and spoons, made of the buffalo or musk-ox horns. Their kettles are formed of a pepper and salt coloured stone; and though the texture appears to be very coarse, and as porous as a dripstone, yet they are perfectly tight, and will sound as clear as a china bowl. Some of those kettles are so large as to be capable of containing five or six gallons; and though it is impossible these poor people can perform this arduous work with any other tools than harder stones, yet they are by far superior to any that I had ever seen in Hudson's Bay; every one of them being ornamented with neat mouldings round the rim, and some of the large ones with a kind of flute-work at each corner. In shape they were a long square, something wider at the top than bottom, like a knife-tray, and strong handles of the solid stone were left at each end to lift them up.[191]

> 1771. July.

Their hatchets are made of a thick lump of copper, about five or six inches long, and from one and a half to two inches square; they are bevelled away at one end like a {169} mortice-chissel. This is lashed into the end of a piece of wood about twelve or fourteen inches long, in such a manner as to act like an adze: in general they are applied to the wood like a chissel, and driven in with a heavy club, instead of a mallet. Neither the weight of the tool nor the sharpness of the metal will admit of their being handled either as adze or axe, with any degree of success.

The men's bayonets and women's knives are also made of copper; the former are in shape like the ace of spades, with the handle of deers horn a foot long, and the latter exactly resemble those described by Crantz. Samples of both these implements I formerly sent home to James Fitzgerald, Esq. then one of the Hudson's Bay Committee.

Among all the spoils of the twelve tents which my companions plundered, only two small pieces of iron were found; one of which was about an inch and a half long, and three eighths of an inch broad, made into a woman's knife; the other was barely an inch long, and a quarter of an inch wide. This last was rivetted into a piece of ivory, so as to form a man's knife, known in Hudson's Bay by the name of *Mokeatoggan*, and is the only instrument used by them in shaping all their wood-work.

Those people had a fine and numerous breed of dogs, with sharp erect ears, sharp noses, bushy tails, &c. {170} exactly like those seen among the Esquimaux in Hudson's Bay and Straits. They were all tethered to stones, to prevent them, as I suppose, from eating the fish that were spread all over the rocks to dry. I do not recollect that my companions killed or hurt one of those animals; but after we had left the tents, they often wished they had taken some of those fine dogs with them.

1771. July.

Though the dress, canoes, utensils, and many other articles belonging to these people, are very similar to those of Hudson's[192] Bay, yet there is one custom that prevails among them—namely, that of the men having all the hair of their heads pulled out by the roots—which pronounces them to be of a different tribe from any hitherto seen either on the coast of Labradore, Hudson's Bay, or Davis's Straits. The women wore their hair at full length, and exactly in the same stile as all the other Esquimaux women do whom I have seen.

When at the sea-side, (at the mouth of the Copper River,) besides seeing many seals on the ice, I also observed several flocks of sea-fowl flying about the shores; such as, gulls, black-heads, loons, old wives, ha-ha-wie's, dunter geese, arctic gulls, and willicks. In the adjacent ponds also were some swans and geese in a moulting state, and in the marshes some curlews and plover; plenty of hawks-eyes, (i.e. the green plover,) and some yellow-legs;[75] also several other small birds, that visit those Northern parts in the {171} Spring to breed and moult, and which doubtless return Southward as the fall advances. My reason for this conjecture is founded on a certain knowledge that all those birds migrate in Hudson's Bay; and it is but reasonable to think that they are less capable of withstanding the rigour of such a long and cold Winter as they must necessarily experience in a country which is so many degrees within the Arctic Circle, as that is where I now saw them.

> 1771. July.

That the musk-oxen, deer, bears, wolves, wolvarines, foxes, Alpine hares,[76] white owls, ravens, partridges, ground-squirrels, common squirrels, ermins, mice, &c. are the constant inhabitants of those parts, is not to be doubted. In many places, by the sides of the hills, where the snow lay to a great depth, the dung of the musk-oxen and deer was lying in such long and continued heaps, as clearly to point out that those places had been their much-frequented paths during the preceding Winter. There were also many other similar appearances on the hills, and other parts, where the snow was entirely thawed away, without any print of a foot being visible in the moss; which is a certain proof that these long ridges of dung must have been dropped in the snow as the beasts were passing and repassing over it in the Winter. There are likewise similar proofs that the Alpine hare[77] and the partridge[78] do not migrate, but remain there the whole year: the latter we found in considerable flocks among the tufts of willows which grow near the sea.

[193]

{172} It is perhaps not generally known, even to the curious, therefore may not be unworthy of observation, that the dung of the musk-ox, though so large an animal, is not larger, and at the same time so near the shape and colour of that of the Alpine hare, that the difference is not easily distinguished but by the natives, though in general the quantity may lead to a discovery of the animal to which it belongs.

1771. July.

I did not see any birds peculiar to those parts, except what the Copper Indians call the "Alarm Bird," or "Bird of Warning."[79] In size and colour it resembles a Cobadekoock, and is of the owl genus. The name is said to be well adapted to its qualities; for when it perceives any people, or beast, it directs its way towards them immediately, and after hovering over them some time, flies round them in circles, or goes a-head in the same direction in which they walk. They repeat their visits frequently; and if they see any other moving objects, fly alternately from one party to the other, hover over them for some time, and make a loud screaming noise, like the crying of a child. In this manner they are said sometimes to follow passengers a whole day. The Copper Indians put great confidence in those birds, and say they are frequently apprized by them of the approach of strangers, and conducted by them to herds of deer and musk-oxen; which, without their assistance, in all probability, they never could have found.

[194]

{173} The Esquimaux seem not to have imbibed the same opinion of those birds; for if they had, they must have been apprized of our approach toward their tents, because all the time the Indians lay in ambush, (before they began the massacre,) a large flock of those birds were continually flying about, and hovering alternately over them and the tents, making a noise sufficient to awaken any man out of the soundest sleep.

After a sleep of five or six hours we once more set out, and walked eighteen or nineteen miles to the South South East, when we arrived at one of the copper mines, which lies, from the river's mouth about South South East, distant about twenty-nine or thirty miles.

This mine, if it deserve that appellation, is no more than an entire jumble of rocks and gravel, which has been rent many ways by an earthquake. Through these ruins there runs a small river; but no part of it, at the time I was there, was more than knee-deep.[80]

[195]

1771. July.

1771. July.

1771. July.

The Indians who were the occasion of my undertaking this journey, represented this mine to be so rich and valuable, that if a factory were built at the river, a ship might be ballasted with the ore, instead of stone; and that with the same ease[196] and dispatch as is done with stones at Churchill River. By their account the hills were entirely composed of that metal, all in handy lumps, like {174} a heap of pebbles. But their account differed so much from the truth, that I and almost all[197] my companions expended near four hours in search of some of this metal, with such poor success, that among us all, only one piece of any size could be found. This, however, was remarkably good, and weighed above four pounds.[AQ] I believe the copper has formerly been in much greater plenty; for in many places, both on the surface and in the cavities and crevices of the rocks, the stones are much tinged with verdigrise.

It may not be unworthy the notice of the curious, or undeserving a place in my Journal, to remark, that the Indians imagine that every bit of copper they find resembles some object in nature; but by what I saw of the large piece, and some smaller ones which were found by my companions, it requires a great share of invention to make this out. I found that different people had different ideas on the subject, for the large piece of copper above mentioned had not been found long before it had twenty different names. One saying that it resembled this animal, and another that it represented a particular part of another; at last it was generally allowed to resemble an Alpine hare couchant: for my part, I must confess that I could not see it had the least resemblance to any thing to which they compared it. It would be endless to {175} enumerate the different parts of a deer, and other animals, which the Indians say the best pieces of copper resemble: it may therefore be sufficient to say, that the largest pieces, with the fewest branches and the least dross, are the best for their use; as by the help of fire, and two stones, they can beat it out to any shape they wish.

1771. July.

[198]

Before Churchill River was settled by the Hudson's Bay Company, which was not more than fifty years previous to this journey being undertaken, the Northern Indians had no other metal but copper among them, except a small quantity of iron-work, which a party of them who visited York Fort about the year one thousand seven hundred and thirteen, or one thousand seven hundred and fourteen, purchased; and a few pieces of old iron found at Churchill River, which had undoubtedly been left there by Captain Monk. This being the case, numbers of them from all quarters used every Summer to resort to these hills in search of copper; of which they made hatchets, ice-chissels, bayonets, knives, awls, arrow-heads, &c. [AP] The many {176} paths that had been beaten by the Indians on these occasions, and which are yet, in many places, very perfect, especially on the dry ridges and hills, is surprising; in the vallies and marshy grounds, however, they are mostly grown over with herbage, so as not to be discerned.

1771. July.

The Copper Indians set a great value on their native metal even to this day; and prefer it to iron, for almost every use except that of a hatchet, a knife, and an awl: for these three necessary implements, copper makes but a very poor substitute. When they exchange copper for iron-work with our trading Northern Indians, which is but seldom, the standard is an ice-chissel of copper for an ice-chissel of iron, or an ice-chissel and a few arrow-heads of copper, for a half-worn hatchet; but when they barter furrs with our Indians, the established rule is to give ten times the price for every thing they purchase that is given for them at the Company's Factory. Thus, a hatchet that is bought at the Factory for one beaver-skin, or one cat-skin, or three ordinary martins' skins, is sold to {177} those people at the advanced price of one thousand *per cent.*; they also pay in proportion, for knives, and every other smaller piece of iron-work. For a small brass kettle of two pounds, or two pounds and a half weight, they pay sixty martins, or twenty beaver in other kinds of furrs.[AS] If the kettles are not bruised, or ill-used in any other respect, the Northern traders have the conscience at times to exact something more. It is at this extravagant price that all the Copper and Dog-ribbed Indians, who traffic with our yearly traders, supply themselves with iron-work, &c.

[199]

1771. July.

From those two tribes our Northern Indians used formerly to purchase most of the furrs they brought to the Company's Factory; for their own country produced very few of those articles, and being, at that time, at war with the Southern Indians, they were prevented from penetrating far enough backwards to meet with many animals of the furr kind; so that deer-skins, and {178} such furrs as they could extort from the Copper and Dog-ribbed Indians, composed the whole of their trade; which, on an average of many years, and indeed till[200] very lately, seldom or ever exceeded six thousand *Made Beaver per annum.*

> 1771. July.

At present happy it is for them, and greatly to the advantage of the Company, that they are in perfect peace, and live in friendship with their Southern neighbours. The good effect of this harmony is already so visible, that within a few years the trade from that quarter has increased many thousands of Made Beaver annually; some years even to the amount of eleven thousand skins.[AT] Besides {179} the advantage arising to the Company from this increase, the poor Northern Indians reap innumerable benefits from a fine and plentiful country, with the produce of which thcy annually load themselves for trade, without giving the least offence to the proper inhabitants.

[201]

> 1771. July.

Several attempts have been made to induce the Copper and Dog-ribbed Indians to visit the Company's Fort at Churchill River, and for that purpose many presents have been sent, but they never were attended with any success. And though several of the Copper Indians have visited Churchill, in the capacity of servants to the Northern Indians, and were generally sent back loaded with presents for their countrymen, yet the Northern Indians always plundered them of the whole soon after they left the Fort. This kind of treatment, added to the many inconveniences that attend so long a journey, are great obstacles in their way; otherwise it would be as possible for them to bring their own goods to market, as for the Northern Indians to go so far to purchase them on their own account, {180} and have the same distance to bring them as the first proprietors would have had. But it is a political scheme of our Northern traders to prevent such an intercourse, as it would greatly lessen their consequence and emolument. Superstition, indeed, will, in all probability, be a lasting barrier against those people ever having a settled communication with our Factory;[202] as few of them chuse to travel in countries so remote from their own, under a pretence that the change of air and provisions (though exactly the same to which they are accustomed) are highly prejudicial to their health; and that not one out of three of those who have undertaken the journey, have ever lived to return. The first of these reasons is evidently no more than gross superstition; and though the latter is but too true, it has always been owing to the treachery and cruelty of the Northern Indians, who took them under their protection.

It is but a few years since, that Captain Keelshies, who is frequently mentioned in this Journal, took twelve of these people under his charge, all heavy laden with the most valuable furrs; and long before they arrived at the Fort, he and the rest of his crew had got all the furrs from them, in payment for provisions for their support, and obliged them to carry the furrs on their account.

On their arrival at Prince of Wales's Fort, Keelshies laid claim to great merit for having brought those strangers, {181} so richly laden, to the Factory, and assured the Governor that he might, in future, expect a great increase in trade from that quarter, through his interest and assiduity. One of the strangers was dubbed with the name of Captain, and treated accordingly, while at the Fort; that is, he was dressed out in the best manner; and at his departure, both himself and all his countrymen were loaded with presents, in hopes that they would not only repeat the visit themselves, but by displaying so much generosity, many of their countrymen would be induced to accompany them.

There seems to be great propriety in the conduct of the Governor[AU] on this occasion; but however well-intended, it had quite the contrary effect, for Keelshies and the rest of his execrable gang, not content with sharing all the furrs those poor people had carried to the Fort, determined to get also all the European goods that had been given to them by the Governor. As neither Keelshies nor any of his gang had the courage to kill the Copper Indians, they concerted a deep-laid scheme for their destruction; which was to leave them on an island. With this view, when they got to the proposed spot, the Northern Indians took care to have all the baggage belonging to the Copper Indians ferried across to the main, and having stripped them of such parts of their clothing as they {182} thought worthy their notice, went off with all the canoes, leaving them all behind on the island, where they perished for want. When I was on my journey to the Fort in June one thousand seven hundred and seventy two, I saw the bones of those poor people, and had the foregoing account from my guide Matonabbee; but it was not made known to the Governor for some years afterward, for fear of prejudicing him against Keelshies.

[203]

A similar circumstance had nearly happened to a Copper Indian who accompanied me to the Fort in one thousand seven hundred and seventy-two: after we were all ferried across Seal River, and the poor man's bundle of furrs on the South-side, he was left alone on the opposite shore; and no one except Matonabbee would go over for him. The wind at that time blew so hard, that Matonabbee stripped himself quite naked, to be ready for swimming in case the canoe should overset; but he soon brought the Copper Indian safe over, to the no small mortification of the wretch who had the charge of him, and who would gladly have possessed the bundle of furrs at the expence of the poor man's life.

When the Northern Indians returned from the Factory that year, the above Copper Indian put himself under the protection of Matonabbee, who accompanied him as far North, as the latitude 64°, where they saw some Copper Indians, among whom was the young man's father, into {183} whose hands Matonabbee delivered him in good health, with all his goods safe, and in good order.[204]

1771. July.

Soon after we had left the Coppermine, there came on a thick fog with rain, and at intervals heavy showers of snow. This kind of weather continued for some days; and at times it was so thick, that we were obliged to stop for several hours together, as we were unable to see our way, and the road was remarkably rocky and intricate.

22d.

At three o'clock in the morning of the twenty-second, Matonabbee's brother and one of the Copper Indians, who had been first dispatched a-head from Congecathawhachaga, overtook us. During their absence they had not discovered any Indians who could have been serviceable to my expedition. They had, however, been at the Copper River, and seeing some marks set up there to direct them to return, they had made the best of their way, and had not slept from the time they left the river till they joined us, though the distance was not less than a hundred miles. When they arrived we were asleep, but we soon awakened, and began to proceed on our journey. That day we walked forty-two miles; and in our way passed Buffalo Lake: at night, we put up about the middle of the Stony Mountains. The weather was excessively hot and sultry.

23d.

{184} On the twenty-third, the weather continued much the same as on the preceding day. Early in the morning we set out, and walked forty-five miles the first day, during which the Indians killed several fine fat buck deer.

24th.

1771. July.

About one o'clock in the morning of the twenty-fourth, we stopped and took a little refreshment, as we had also done about noon the preceding day; but the Indians had been so long from their wives and families, that they promised not to sleep till they saw them, especially as we were then in sight of the hills of Congecathawhachaga,[83] where we had left the last of them. After resting about an hour, we proceeded on our way, and at six in the morning arrived at Congecathawhachaga; when, to our great disappointment, we found that all our women had got set across the river before the Copper Indians left that part; so that when we arrived, not an Indian was to be found, except an old man and his family, who had arrived in our absence, and was waiting at the crossing-place with some furrs for Matonabbee, who was so nearly related to the old man as to be his son-in-law, having one of his daughters for a wife. The old man had another with him, who was also offered to the great man, but not accepted.

[205]

Our stay at this place may be said to have been of very short duration; for on seeing a large smoke to the Southward, we immediately crossed the river, and walked towards it, {185} when we found that the women had indeed been there some days before, but were gone; and at their departure had set the moss on fire, which was then burning, and occasioned the smoke we had seen. By this time the afternoon was far advanced; we pursued, however, our course in the direction which the women took, for their track we could easily discover in the moss. We had not gone far, before we saw another smoke at a great distance, for which we shaped our course; and, notwithstanding we redoubled our pace, it was eleven o'clock at night before we reached it; when, to our great mortification, we found it to be the place where the women had slept the night before; having in the morning, at their departure, set fire to the moss which was then burning.

25th.

The Indians, finding that their wives were so near as to be within one of their ordinary day's walk, which seldom exceeded ten or twelve miles, determined not to rest till they had joined them. Accordingly we pursued our course, and about two o'clock in the morning of the twenty-fifth, came up with some of the women, who had then pitched their tents by the side of Cogead Lake.[x4]

[206]

1771. July.

From our leaving the Copper-mine River to this time we had travelled so hard, and taken so little rest by the way, that my feet and legs had swelled considerably, and I had become quite stiff at the ankles. In this situation I had {186} so little power to direct my feet when walking, that I frequently knocked them against the stones with such force, as not only to jar and disorder them, but my legs also; and the nails of my toes were bruised to such a degree, that several of them festered and dropped off. To add to this mishap, the skin was entirely chafed off from the tops of both my feet, and between every toe; so that the sand and gravel, which I could by no means exclude, irritated the raw parts so much, that for a whole day before we arrived at the women's tents, I left the print of my feet in blood almost at every step I took. Several of the Indians began to complain that their feet also were sore; but, on examination, not one of them was the twentieth part in so bad a state as mine.

This being the first time I had been in such a situation, or seen anybody foot-foundered, I was much alarmed, and under great apprehensions for the consequences. Though I was but little fatigued in body, yet the excruciating pain I suffered when walking, had such an effect on my spirits, that if the Indians had continued to travel two or three days longer at that unmerciful rate, I must unavoidably have been left behind; for my feet were in many places quite honey-combed, by the dirt and gravel eating into the raw flesh.

1771. July.

As soon as we arrived at the women's tents, the first thing I did, was to wash and clean my feet in {187} warm water; then I bathed the swelled parts with spirits of wine, and dressed those that were raw with Turner's cerate; soon after which I betook myself to rest. As we did not move on the following day, I perceived that the swelling abated, and the raw parts of my feet were not quite so much inflamed. This change for the better gave me the strongest assurance that rest was the principal thing wanted to effect a speedy and complete cure[207] of my painful, though in reality very simple disorder, (foot-foundering,) which I had before considered to be an affair of the greatest consequence.

27th.

Rest, however, though essential to my speedy recovery, could not at this time be procured; for as the Indians were desirous of joining the remainder of their wives and families as soon as possible, they would not stop even a single day; so that on the twenty-seventh we again began to move; and though they moved at the rate of eight or nine miles a day, it was with the utmost difficulty that I could follow them. Indeed the weather proved remarkably fine and pleasant, and the ground was in general pretty dry, and free from stones; which contributed greatly to my ease in walking, and enabled me to keep up with the natives.

31st.

August. 1st.

5th.

1771. July.

On the thirty-first of July, we arrived at the place[85] where the wives and families of my companions had been ordered to wait our return from the Copper-mine River. Here we found several tents of Indians; but those {188} belonging to Matonabbee, and some others of my crew, had not arrived. We saw, however, a large smoke to the Eastward, which we supposed had been made by them, as no other Indians were expected from that quarter. Accordingly, the next morning, Matonabbee sent some of his young men in quest of them, and on the fifth, they all joined us; when, contrary to expectation, a great number of other Indians were with them; in all, to the amount of more than forty tents. Among those Indians, was the man who Matonabbee stabbed when we were at Clowey. With the greatest submission he led his wife to Matonabbee's tent, set her down by his side, and retired, without saying a word. Matonabbee took no notice of her, though she was bathed in tears; and by degrees, after reclining herself on her elbow for some time, she lay down, and, sobbing, said, *see'd dinne, see'd dinne!* which is, My husband, my husband! On which Matonabbee told her, that if she had respected him as such, she would not have run away from him; and that she was at liberty to go where she pleased. On which she got up, with seeming reluctance, though most assuredly with a light heart, and returned to her former husband's tent.

[208]

FOOTNOTES:

[AM] *Tima* in the Esquimaux language is a friendly word similar to *what cheer?*

[AN] When the fifteen Indians turned back at the Stony Mountains, they took two or three canoes with them; some of our crew that were sent a-head as messengers had not yet returned, which occasioned the number of our canoes to be so small.

[71] Probably some form of the wide-ranging *Salmo alpinus.*—E. A. P.

[AO] When the Esquimaux who reside near Churchill River travel in Winter, it is always from lake to lake, or from river to river, where they have formed magazines of provisions, and heaps of moss for firing. As some of those places are at a considerable distance from each other, and some of the lakes of considerable width, they frequently pitch their tents on the ice, and instead of having a fire, which the severity of the climate so much requires, they cut holes in the ice within their tents, and there sit and angle for fish; if they meet with any success, the fish are eaten alive out of the water; and when they are thirsty, water, their usual beverage, is at hand.

When I first entered into the employment of the Hudson's Bay Company, it was as Mate of one of their sloops which was employed in trading with the Esquimaux: I had therefore frequent opportunities of observing the miserable manner in which those people live. In the course of our trade with them we frequently purchased several seal-skin bags, which we supposed were full of oil; but on opening them have sometimes found great quantities of venison, seals, and sea-horse paws, as well as salmon: and as these were of no use to us, we always returned them to the Indians, who eagerly devoured them, though some of the articles had been perhaps a whole year in that state; and they seemed to exult greatly in having so over-reached us in the way of trade, as to have sometimes one third of their bargain returned.

This method of preserving their food, though it effectually guards it from the external air, and from the flies, does not prevent putrefaction entirely, though it renders its progress very slow. Pure train oil is of such a quality that it never freezes solid in the coldest Winters; a happy circumstance for those people, who are condemned to live in the most rigorous climate without the assistance of fire. While these magazines last, they have nothing more to do when hunger assails them, but to open one of the bags, take out a side of venison, a few seals, sea-horse paws, or some half-rotten salmon, and without any preparation, sit down and make a meal; and the lake or river by which they pitch their tent, affords them water, which is their constant drink. Besides the extraordinary food already mentioned, they have several other dishes equally disgusting to an European palate; I will only mention one, as it was more frequently part of their repast when I visited their tents, than any other, except fish. The dish I allude to, is made of the raw liver of a deer, cut in small pieces of about an inch square, and mixed up with the contents of the stomach of the same animal; and the farther digestion has taken place, the better it is suited to their taste. It is impossible to describe or conceive the pleasure they seem to enjoy when eating such unaccountable food: nay, I have even seen them eat whole handfuls of maggots that were produced in meat by fly-blows; and it is their constant custom, when their noses bleed by any accident, to lick their blood into their mouths, and swallow it. Indeed, if we consider the inhospitable part of the globe they are destined to inhabit, and the great distresses to which they are frequently driven by hunger in consequence of it, we shall no longer be surprized at finding they can relish any thing in common with the meanest of the animal creation, but rather admire the wisdom and kindness of Providence in forming the palates and powers of all creatures in such a manner as is best adapted to the food, climate, and every other circumstance which may be incident to their respective situations.

It is no less true, that these people, when I first knew them, would not eat any of our provisions, sugar, raisins, figs, or even bread; for though some of them would put a bit of it into their mouths, they soon spit it out again with evident marks of dislike; so that they had no greater relish for our food than we had for theirs. At present, however, they will eat any part of our provisions, either fresh or salted; and some of them will drink a draft of porter, or a little brandy and water; and they are now so far civilized, and attached to the English, that I am persuaded any of the Company's servants who could habituate themselves to their diet and manner of life, might now live as secure under their protection, as under that of any of the tribes of Indians who border on Hudson's Bay.

They live in a state of perfect freedom; no one apparently claiming the superiority over, or acknowledging the least subordination to another, except what is due from children to their parents, or such of their kin as take care of them when they are young and incapable of providing for themselves. There is, however, reason to think that, when grown up to manhood, they pay some attention to the advice of the old men, on account of their experience.

[72] Several species inhabit the region; the commonest is the ringed or fetid seal (*Phoca hispida*).—E. A. P.

[73] In the summer of 1821, fifty years after Hearne's visit, Sir John Franklin, accompanied by Sir John Richardson and Sir George Back, descended and surveyed the Coppermine River from Point Lake to the sea. He was at the Bloody Falls from the 15th to the 18th of July, exactly fifty years after Hearne, and found the latitude to be 67° 42' 35" N. He speaks of it as follows:

"Several human skulls which bore the marks of violence, and many bones were strewed about the ground near the encampment, and as the spot exactly answers the description, given by Mr. Hearne, of the place where the Chipewyans who accompanied him perpetrated the dreadful massacre on the Esquimaux, we had no doubt of this being the place. This rapid is a sort of shelving cascade, about three hundred yards in length, having a descent of from ten to fifteen feet. It is bounded on each side by high walls of red sandstone, upon which rests a series of lofty green hills. The surrounding scenery was accurately delineated in a sketch taken by Mr. Hood" ("First Journey," pp. 349-350).

In 1838 Thomas Simpson determined the latitude of Bloody Falls as 67° 42' 52" ("Narrative of Discoveries," Thomas Simpson, p. 261).

Sir John Richardson revisited the lower part of the Coppermine River in 1826, and again in 1848, and he knew it better than any other white man. Speaking of Hearne, he says: "His description of the lower part of the Coppermine River is evidently that of one who has been on the spot."

"He appears to have fallen on the Coppermine River first at the Sandstone rapids of Franklin, and to have traced it to Bloody Falls; but as, contrary to his usual practice, he under-rates the distance from thence to the coast, we are led to conclude that he did not actually go down to the sea, but was content to view it from the top of the hill which overhangs the falls; and, indeed, it is not very probable that he could have induced the Indians, over whom he had little influence, to accompany him on his survey, after they had completed the massacre which was the object of their long and laborious journey; nor, had he gone actually to the mouth of the river, would he have mentioned marks of a tide fourteen feet high" (Back, pp. 147-151).

Hearne's description of the occurrence of the timber on the banks of the river, is particularly accurate, and I am inclined to give him credit for having been at or near the mouth of the river, even though his statement in regard to the rise and fall of the tide is inaccurate.

[74] Wishacumpuckey is one of the species of *Ledum*; jackasheypuck = *Arctostaphylos uvaursi* Spreng.; cranberry = *Vaccinium vitisidœa* Linn.; heathberry probably = *Empetrum nigrum* Linn.—E. A. P.

[AP] See Hist. of Greenland, vol. i. pp. 132-156.

[75] Gull = *Larus*; blackhead = *Sterna paradisœa* Brünn; loon = *Gavia*; old-wife = *Harelda hyemalis* Linn.; ha-ha-wie = *Harelda hyemalis* Linn.; hawks-eye = *Charadrius dominicus* Müll.; yellow-legs = *Totanus flavipes* Gmel.—E. A. P.

[76] For descriptions of these mammals see Chapter X.

[77] *Lepus arcticus canus* Preble.

[78] *Lagopus lagopus* (Linn.)

[79] The Alarm bird is probably the Short-eared Owl, *Asio flammeus* (Pontoppidan), a common summer inhabitant of the Barren Grounds. The Cobadekoock is the Hawk Owl, which seldom goes north of the woods.—E. A. P.

[80] The exact locality here described does not appear to have been visited by any white man since 1771, but Sir John Richardson visited the Copper Mountains in 1821, and the following description by him will give some idea of their character:

"The Copper Mountains appear to form a range running S.E. and N.W. The great mass of rock in the mountains seems to consist of felspar in various conditions; sometimes in the form of felspar rock or claystone, sometimes coloured by hornblende, and approaching to greenstone, but most generally in the form of dark reddish-brown amygdaloid. The amygdaloidal masses, contained in the amygdaloid, are either entirely pistacite, or pistacite enclosing calc-spar. Scales of native copper are very generally disseminated through this rock, through a species of trap tuff which nearly resembled it, and also through a reddish sandstone on which it appears to rest. When the felspar assumed the appearance of a slaty claystone, which it did towards the base of the mountains on the banks of the river, we observed no copper in it. The rough and in general rounded and more elevated parts of the mountain, are composed of the amygdaloid; but between the eminences there occur many narrow and deep valleys, which are bounded by perpendicular mural precipices of greenstone. It is in these valleys, amongst the loose soil, that the Indians search for copper. Amongst the specimens we picked up in these valleys, were plates of native copper; masses of pistacite containing native copper; of trap rock with associated native copper, green malachite, copper glance or variegated copper ore and iron-shot copper green; and of greenish-grey prehnite in trap (the trap is felspar, deeply coloured with hornblende), with disseminated native copper; the copper, in some specimens, was crystallized in rhomboidal dodecahedrons. We also found some large tabular fragments, evidently portions of a vein consisting of prehnite, associated with calcareous spar, and native copper. The Indians dig wherever they observe the prehnite lying on the soil, experience having taught them that the largest pieces of copper are found associated with it. We did not observe the vein in its original repository, nor does it appear that the Indians have found it, but judging from the specimens just mentioned, it most probably traverses felspathose trap. We also picked up some fragments of a greenish-grey coloured rock, apparently sandstone, with disseminated variegated copper ore and copper glance; likewise rhomboidal fragments of white calcareous spar, and some rock crystals. The Indians report that they have found copper in every part of this range, which they have examined for thirty or forty miles to the N.W., and that the Esquimaux come hither to search for that metal. We afterwards found some ice-chisels in possession of the latter people twelve or fourteen inches long, and half-an-inch in diameter, formed of pure copper.

"To the northward of the Copper Mountains, at the distance of ten miles, in a direct line, a similar range of trap hills occurs, having, however, less altitude. The intermediate country is uneven, but not hilly, and consists of a deep sandy soil, which, when cut through by the rivulets, discloses extensive beds of light-brownish red sandstone, which appears to belong to the new red sandstone formation. The same rock having a thin slaty structure, and dipping to the northward, forms perpendicular walls to the river, whose bed lies a hundred and fifty feet below the level of the plain. The eminences in the plain are well clothed with grass, and free from the large loose stones so common on the Barren Grounds, but the ridges of trap are nearly destitute of vegetation.

"Beyond the last-mentioned trap range, which is about twenty miles from the sea, the country becomes still more level, the same kind of sandstone continuing as a subsoil. The plains nourish only a coarse short grass, and the trees which had latterly dwindled to small clumps, growing only on low points on the edge of the river under shelter of the high bank, entirely disappear. A few ranges of trap hills intersect this plain also, but they have much less elevation than those we passed higher up the stream.

"The river in its section of the plain, as far as Bloody Fall, presents alternately cliffs of reddish sandstone, and red-coloured slaty indurated clay or marl, and shelving white clay banks. At Bloody Fall, the stream cuts through a thick bed of dark, purplish-red felspar rock, similar to that observed at the Rocky Defile (page 527), and associated, as at that place, with a rock composed principally of light red felspar and quartz, but which is probably a species of red secondary granite. At the Bloody Fall, the felspar rock is covered to the depth of six or seven hundred feet with a bed of greyish white, and rather tenacious clay, which being deeply intersected with ravines, forms steep hills. Nearer the sea, the river is bounded by very steep cliffs of yellowish-white sand; and on the sea-coast, the above-mentioned red granite reappears on the west bank of the river, forming a rugged ridge about two hundred and fifty feet high" ("First Journey," pp. 528-530).

Sir John Franklin makes the following reference to the Copper Mountains, which he visited in July 1821:

"We rejoined our hunters at the foot of the Copper Mountains, and found they had killed three musk-oxen. This circumstance determined us on encamping to dry the meat, as there was wood at the spot. We availed ourselves of this delay to visit the Copper Mountains in search of specimens of the ore, agreeably to my instructions; and a party of twenty-one persons, consisting of the officers, some of the voyagers, and all the Indians, set off on that excursion. We travelled for nine hours over a considerable space of ground, but found only a few small pieces of native copper. The range we ascended was on the west side of the river, extending W.N.W. and E.S.E. The mountains varied in height from twelve to fifteen hundred feet. The uniformity of the mountains is interrupted by narrow valleys, traversed by small streams. The best specimens of metal we procured were among the stones in these valleys, and it was in such situations that our guides desired us to search most carefully. It would appear, that when the Indians see any sparry substance projecting above the surface, they dig there; but they have no other rule to direct them, and have never found the metal in its original repository. Our guides reported that they had found copper in large pieces in every part of this range, for two days' walk to the north-west, and that the Esquimaux come hither to search for it. The annual visits which the Copper Indians were accustomed to make to these mountains, when most of their weapons and utensils were made of copper, have been discontinued since they have been enabled to obtain a supply of ice-chisels and other instruments of iron by the establishment of trading posts near their hunting grounds. That none of those who accompanied us had visited them for many years was evident, from their ignorance of the spots most abundant in metal.

"The impracticability of navigating the river upwards from the sea, and the want of wood for forming an establishment, would prove insuperable objections to rendering the collection of copper at this part worthy of mercantile speculation" ("First Journey," p. 340-1).

[AQ] This piece of Copper is now in the possession of the Hudson's Bay Company.

[AR] There is a strange tradition among those people, that the first person who discovered those mines was a woman, and that she conducted them to the place for several years; but as she was the only woman in company, some of the men took such liberties with her as made her vow revenge on them; and she is said to have been a great conjurer. Accordingly when the men had loaded themselves with copper, and were going to return, she refused to accompany them, and said she would sit on the mine till she sunk into the ground, and that the copper should sink with her. The next year, when the men went for more copper, they found her sunk up to the waist, though still alive, and the quantity of copper much decreased; and on their repeating their visit the year following, she had quite disappeared, and all the principal part of the mine with her; so that after that period nothing remained on the surface but a few small pieces, and those were scattered at a considerable distance from each other. Before that period they say the copper lay on the surface in such large heaps, that the Indians had nothing to do but turn it over, and pick such pieces as would best suit the different uses for which they intended it.[81]

[81] A slightly different version of this tradition is given by Sir John Franklin, who heard it at Fort Chipewyan in 1820 from an old Chipewyan Indian named "Rabbit's Head," a stepson of Matonabbee. See Franklin's "First Journey," pp. 145-7.

[AS] What is meant by Beaver in other kind of furrs, must be understood as follows: For the easier trading with the Indians, as well as for the more correctly keeping their accounts, the Hudson's Bay Company have made a full-grown beaver-skin the standard by which they rate all other furrs, according to their respective values. Thus in several species of furrs, one skin is valued at the rate of four beaver-skins; some at three, and others at two; whereas those of an inferior quality are rated at one; and those of still less value considered so inferior to that of a beaver, that from six to twenty of their skins are only valued as equal to one beaver skin in the way of trade, and do not fetch one-fourth of the price at the London market. In this manner the term "Made Beaver" is to be understood.

[AT] Since this Journal was written, the Northern Indians, by annually visiting their Southern friends, the Athapuscow Indians, have contracted the small-pox, which has carried off nine-tenths of them, and particularly those people who composed the trade at Churchill Factory. The few survivors follow the example of their Southern neighbours, and all trade with the Canadians, who are settled in the heart of the Athapuscow country: so that a very few years has proved my short-sightedness, and that it would have been much more to the advantage of the Company, as well as have prevented the depopulation of the Northern Indian country, if they had still remained at war with the Southern tribes, and never attempted to better their situation. At the same time, it is impossible to say what increase of trade might not, in time, have arisen from a constant and regular traffic with the different tribes of Copper and Dog-ribbed Indians. But having been totally neglected for several years, they have now sunk into their original barbarism and extreme indigence; and a war has ensued between the two tribes, for the sake of a few remnants of iron-work which was left among them; and the Dog-ribbed Indians were so numerous, and so successful, as to destroy almost the whole race of the Copper Indians.

While I was writing this Note, I was informed by some Northern Indians, that the few which remain of the Copper tribe have found their way to one of the Canadian houses in the Athapuscow Indians' country, where they get supplied with every thing at less, or about half the price they were formerly obliged to give; so that the few surviving Northern Indians, as well as the Hudson's Bay Company, have now lost every shadow of any future trade from that quarter, unless the Company will establish a settlement with the Athapuscow country, and undersell the Canadians.[82]

[82] In 1778 Peter Pond, a fur trader from Montreal, had built a trading post on the east bank of Athabasca River, about thirty miles up-stream from Athabasca Lake, and in 1786, after the formation of the North-West Company, Laurent Leroux and Cuthbert Grant, two of the employees of this Company, had descended Slave River to Great Slave Lake and had established a trading post on its southern shore. The Copper Indians traded at the latter post, while the Northern or Chipewyan Indians resorted to the more southern and older post on the Athabasca River. Among the members of this latter tribe, who had been accustomed to make long pilgrimages to Churchill in order to procure implements and utensils of various kinds in exchange for furs, but who afterwards found that they could buy such goods as they needed more advantageously from the traders on the Athabasca River, very much nearer home, was a man known to those traders as "English Chief." This Indian accompanied Sir Alexander Mackenzie, one of the partners of the North-West Company, and one of those who would have been spoken of by Hearne as *Canadians*, on his journey from Lake Athabasca to the Arctic Ocean in 1789.

This note also throws an interesting light on the date on which the journal was written, for the first outbreak of small-pox, which swept off the Indians of Western Canada, occurred in 1781, and therefore the journal itself was written before that date, while Hearne was living as Governor at Fort Prince of Wales. The note would appear to have been written about 1787, after the destruction of Fort Prince of Wales, and while Hearne was living at Fort Churchill, five miles south of the old fort, and before he finally returned to England.

[AU] Mr. Moses Norton.

[83] The party had thus reached Congecathawhachaga on the morning of the seventh day after leaving Bloody Falls or the mouth of the Coppermine River, the distance in a direct line being about one hundred and sixty miles. If they travelled in a direct line they averaged twenty-five miles a day, but the windings of the journey would add something to this distance.

[84] Contwoito Lake, described on page 152.

[85] The exact position of this place, to which the women and children had moved from the north shore of Cat or Clinton-Colden Lake, is not certain, but it was evidently on some of the lakes or streams marked on his map as lying between Cogead (Contwoito) and Point Lakes.

[209]

{189} CHAP. VII.

Remarks from the Time the Women joined us till our Arrival at the Athapuscow Lake.

Several of the Indians sick—Method used by the conjurers to relieve one man, who recovers—Matonabbee and his crew proceed to the South West—Most of the other Indians separate, and go their respective ways—Pass by White Stone Lake—Many deer killed merely for their skins—Remarks thereon, and on the deer, respecting seasons and places—Arrive at Point Lake—One of the Indian's wives being sick, is left behind to perish above-ground—Weather very bad, but deer plenty—Stay some time at Point Lake to dry meat, &c.—Winter set in—Superstitious customs observed by my companions, after they had killed the Esquimaux at Copper River—A violent gale of wind oversets my tent and breaks my quadrant—Some Copper and Dog-ribbed Indians join us—Indians propose to go to the Athapuscow Country to kill moose—Leave Point Lake, and arrive at the wood's edge—Arrive at Anawd Lake—Transactions there—Remarkable instance of a man being cured of the palsey by the conjurers—Leave Anawd Lake—Arrive at the great Athapuscow Lake.

1771. August.

1771. August.

Several of the Indians being very ill, the conjurers, who are always the doctors, and pretend to perform great cures, began to try their skill to effect their recovery. Here it is necessary to remark, that they use no medicine either for internal or external complaints, but perform all their cures by charms. In ordinary cases, sucking the part affected, blowing, and singing to it; {190} haughing, spitting, and at the same time uttering a heap of unintelligible jargon, compose the whole process of the cure. For some inward complaints; such as, griping in the intestines, difficulty of making water, &c., it is very common to see those jugglers[210] blowing into the *anus*, or into the parts adjacent, till their eyes are almost starting out of their heads: and this operation is performed indifferently on all, without regard either to age or sex. The accumulation of so large a quantity of wind is at times apt to occasion some extraordinary emotions, which are not easily suppressed by a sick person; and as there is no vent for it but by the channel through which it was conveyed thither, it sometimes occasions an odd scene between the doctor and his patient; which I once wantonly called an engagement, but for which I was afterward exceedingly sorry, as it highly offended several of the Indians; particularly the juggler and the sick person, both of whom were men I much esteemed, and, except in that moment of levity, it had ever been no less my inclination than my interest to shew them every respect that my situation would admit.

I have often admired the great pains these jugglers take to deceive their credulous countrymen, while at the same time they are indefatigably industrious and persevering in their efforts to relieve them. Being naturally not very delicate, they frequently continue their windy process so long, that I have more than once seen the doctor quit his patient with his face and breast in a very disagreeable condition. However {191} laughable this may appear to an European, custom makes it very indecent, in their opinion, to turn any thing of the kind to ridicule.

When a friend for whom they have a particular regard is, as they suppose, dangerously ill, beside the above methods, they have recourse to another very extraordinary piece of superstition; which is no less than that of pretending to swallow hatchets, ice-chissels, broad bayonets, knives, and the like; out of a superstitious notion that undertaking such desperate feats will have some influence in appeasing death, and procure a respite for their patient.

1771. August.

On such extraordinary occasions a conjuring-house is erected, by driving the ends of four long small sticks, or[211] poles, into the ground at right angles, so as to form a square of four, five, six, or seven feet, as may be required. The tops of the poles are tied together, and all is close covered with a tent-cloth or other skin, exactly in the shape of a small square tent, except that there is no vacancy left at the top to admit the light. In the middle of this house, or tent, the patient is laid, and is soon followed by the conjurer, or conjurers. Sometimes five or six of them give their joint-assistance; but before they enter, they strip themselves quite naked, and as soon as they get into the house, the door being well closed, they kneel round the sick person or persons, and begin to suck {192} and blow at the parts affected, and then in a very short space of time sing and talk as if conversing with familiar spirits, which they say appear to them in the shape of different beasts and birds of prey. When they have had sufficient conference with those necessary agents, or shadows, as they term them, they ask for the hatchet, bayonet, or the like, which is always prepared by another person, with a long string fastened to it by the haft, for the convenience of hauling it up again after they have swallowed it; for they very wisely admit this to be a very necessary precaution, as hard and compact bodies, such as iron and steel, would be very difficult to digest, even by the men who are enabled to swallow them. Besides, as those tools are in themselves very useful, and not always to be procured, it would be very ungenerous in the conjurers to digest them, when it is known that barely swallowing them and hauling them up again is fully sufficient to answer every purpose that is expected from them.

1771. August. 6th.

At the time when the forty and odd tents of Indians joined us, one man was so dangerously ill, that it was thought necessary the conjurers should use some of those wonderful experiments for his recovery; one of them therefore immediately consented to swallow a broad bayonet. Accordingly, a conjuring-house was erected in the manner above described, into which the patient was conveyed, and he was[212] soon followed by the conjurer, who, after a long preparatory discourse, and the necessary {193} conference with his familiar spirits, or shadows, as they call them, advanced to the door and asked for the bayonet, which was then ready prepared, by having a string fastened to it, and a short piece of wood tied to the other end of the string, to prevent him from swallowing it. I could not help observing that the length of the bit of wood was not more than the breadth of the bayonet; however, as it answered the intended purpose, it did equally well as if it had been as long as a handspike.

Though I am not so credulous as to believe that the conjurer absolutely swallowed the bayonet, yet I must acknowledge that in the twinkling of an eye he conveyed it to—God knows where; and the small piece of wood, or one exactly like it, was confined close to his teeth. He then paraded backward and forward before the conjuring-house for a short time, when he feigned to be greatly disordered in his stomach and bowels; and, after making many wry faces, and groaning most hideously, he put his body into several distorted attitudes, very suitable to the occasion. He then returned to the door of the conjuring-house, and after making many strong efforts to vomit, by the help of the string he at length, and after tugging at it some time, produced the bayonet, which apparently he hauled out of his mouth, to the no small surprize of all present. He then looked round with an air of exultation, and strutted into the conjuring-house, where he renewed his incantations, and continued them without intermission twenty-four hours. {194} Though I was not close to his elbow when he performed the above feat, yet I thought myself near enough (and I can assure my readers I was all attention) to have detected him. Indeed I must confess that it appeared to me to be a very nice piece of deception, especially as it was performed by a man quite naked.

1771. August.

Not long after this slight-of-hand work was over, some of the Indians asked me what I thought of it; to which I answered,[213] that

I was too far off to see it so plain as I could wish; which indeed was no more than the strictest truth, because I was not near enough to detect the deception. The sick man, however, soon recovered; and in a few days afterwards we left that place and proceeded to the South West.

> 9th.

On the ninth of August, we once more pursued our journey, and continued our course in the South West quarter, generally walking about seven or eight miles a day. All the Indians, however, who had been in our company, except twelve tents, struck off different ways. As to myself, having had several days rest, my feet were completely healed, though the skin remained very tender for some time.

> 19th-25th.

From the nineteenth to the twenty-fifth, we walked by the side of Thaye-chuck-gyed Whoie,[80] or Large Whitestone Lake, which is about forty miles long from the North {195} East to the South West, but of very unequal breadth. A river from the North West side of this lake is said to run in a serpentine manner a long way to the Westward; and then tending to the Northward, composes the main branch of the Copper-mine River, as has been already mentioned; which may or may not be true. It is certain, however, that there are many rivulets which empty themselves into this lake from the South East; but as they are all small streams, they may probably be no more than what is sufficient to supply the constant decrease occasioned by the exhalations, which, during the short Summer, so high a Northern latitude always affords.

Deer were very plentiful the whole way; the Indians killed great numbers of them daily, merely for the sake of their skins; and at this time of the year their pelts are in good season, and the hair of a proper length for clothing.

[214]

The great destruction which is made of the deer in those parts at this season of the year only, is almost incredible; and as they are never known to have more than one young one at a time, it is wonderful they do not become scarce; but so far from being the case, that the oldest Northern Indian in all their tribe will affirm that the deer are as plentiful now as they ever have been; and though they are remarkably scarce some years near Churchill River, yet it is said, and with great probability of truth, that they are {196} more plentiful in other parts of the country than they were formerly. The scarcity or abundance of these animals in different places at the same season is caused, in a great measure, by the winds which prevail for some time before; for the deer are supposed by the natives to walk always in the direction from which the wind blows, except when they migrate from East to West, or from West to East, in search of the opposite sex, for the purpose of propagating their species.

It requires the prime part of the skins of from eight to ten deer to make a complete suit of warm clothing for a grown person during the Winter; all of which should, if possible, be killed in the month of August, or early in September; for after that time the hair is too long, and at the same time so loose in the pelt, that it will drop off with the slightest injury.

Beside these skins, which must be in the hair, each person requires several others to be dressed into leather, for stockings and shoes, and light Summer clothing; several more are also wanted in a parchment state, to make *clewla* as they call it, or thongs to make netting for their snow-shoes, snares for deer, sewing for their sledges, and, in fact, for every other use where strings or lines of any kind are required: so that each person, on an average, expends, in the course of a year, upwards of twenty deer skins in {197} clothing and other domestic uses, exclusive of tent cloths, bags, and many other things which it is impossible to remember, and unnecessary to enumerate.

All skins for the above-mentioned purposes are, if possible, procured between the beginning of August and the middle of October; for when the rutting season is over, and the Winter[215] sets in, the deer-skins are not only very thin, but in general full of worms and warbles[87]; which render them of little use, unless it be to cut into fine thongs, of which they make fishing-nets, and nets for the heels and toes of their snow-shoes. Indeed the chief use that is made of them in Winter is for the purpose of food; and really when the hair is properly taken off, and all the warbles are squeezed out, if they are well-boiled, they are far from being disagreeable. The Indians, however, never could persuade me to eat the warbles, of which some of them are remarkably fond, particularly the children. They are always eaten raw and alive, out of the skin; and are said, by those who like them, to be as fine as gooseberries. But the very idea of eating such things, exclusive of their appearance, (many of them being as large as the first joint of the little finger,) was quite sufficient to give me an unalterable disgust to such a repast; and when I acknowledge that the warbles out of the deers backs, and the domestic lice, were the only two things I ever saw my {198} companions eat, of which I could not, or did not, partake, I trust I shall not be reckoned over-delicate in my appetite.

The month of October is the rutting season with the deer in those parts, and after the time of their courtship is over, the bucks separate from the does; the former proceed to the Westward, to take shelter in the woods during the Winter, and the latter keep out in the barren ground the whole year. This, though a general rule, is not without some exceptions; for I have frequently seen many does in the woods, though they bore no proportion to the number of bucks. This rule, therefore, only stands good respecting the deer to the North of Churchill River; for the deer to the Southward live promiscuously among the woods, as well as in the plains, and along the banks of rivers, lakes, &c. the whole year.

[216]

The old buck's horns are very large, with many branches, and always drop off in the month of November, which is about the time they begin to approach the woods. This is undoubtedly wisely ordered by Providence, the better to enable them to escape from their enemies through the woods; otherwise they would become an easy prey to wolves and other beasts, and be liable to get entangled among the trees, even in ranging about in search of food. The same opinion may probably be admitted of the Southern deer, which always reside among {199} the woods; but the Northern deer, though by far the smallest in this country, have much the largest horns, and the branches are so long, and at the same time spread so wide, as to make them more liable to be entangled among the under-woods, than any other species of deer that I have noticed. The young bucks in those parts do not shed their horns so soon as the old ones: I have frequently seen them killed at or near Christmas, and could discover no appearance of their horns being loose. The does do not shed their horns till the Summer; so that when the buck's horns are ready to drop off, the horns of the does are all hairy, and scarcely come to their full growth.

1771. August.

The deer in those parts are generally in motion from East to West, or from West to East, according to the season, or the prevailing winds; and that is the principal reason why the Northern Indians are always shifting their station. From November till May, the bucks continue to the Westward, among the woods, when their horns begin to sprout; after which they proceed on to the Eastward, to the barren grounds; and the does that have been on the barren ground all the Winter, are taught by instinct to advance to the Westward to meet them, in order to propagate their species. Immediately after the rutting season is over, they separate, as hath been mentioned above. The old vulgar saying, so generally[217] received among the lower class of people in England, concerning the bucks shedding their yards, or more properly the glands of the {200} *penis*, yearly, whether it be true in England or not, is certainly not true in any of the countries bordering on Hudson's Bay. A long residence among the Indians has enabled me to confirm this assertion with great confidence, as I have seen deer killed every day throughout the year; and when I have mentioned this circumstance to the Indians, either Northern or Southern, they always assured me that they never observed any such symptoms. With equal truth I can assert, and that from ocular demonstration, that the animal which is called the Alpine Hare in Hudson's Bay, actually undergoes something similar to that which is vulgarly ascribed to the English deer. I have seen and handled several of them, who had been killed just after they had coupled in the Spring, with the *penises* hanging out, dried up, and shrivelled, like the navel-string of young animals; and on examination I always found a passage through them for the urine to pass. I have thought proper to give this remark a place in my Journal, because, in all probability, it is not generally known, even to those gentlemen who have made natural history their chief study; and if their researches are of any real utility to mankind, it is surely to be regretted that Providence should have placed the greatest part of them too remote from want to be obliged to travel for ocular proofs of what they assert in their publications; they are therefore wisely content to stay at home, and enjoy the blessings with which they are endowed, resting satisfied to collect such information for their own amusement, and the gratification of the public, as those {201} who are necessitated to be travellers are able or willing to give them. It is true, and I am sorry it is so, that I come under the latter description; but hope I have not, or shall not, in the course of this Journal, advance any thing that will not stand the test of experiment, and the skill of the most competent judges.[218]

1771. September.

After leaving White Stone Lake, we continued our course in the South West quarter, seldom walking more than twelve miles a day, and frequently not half that distance.

> 3d.

On the third of September, we arrived at a small river belonging to Point Lake, but the weather at this time proved so boisterous, and there was so much rain, snow, and frost, alternately, that we were obliged to wait several days before we could cross it in our canoes; and the water was too deep, and the current too rapid, to attempt fording it. During this interruption, however, our time was not entirely lost, as deer were so plentiful that the Indians killed numbers of them, as well for the sake of their skins, as for their flesh, which was at present in excellent order, and the skins in proper season for the sundry uses for which they are destined.

> 7th.

> 8th.

In the afternoon of the seventh, the weather became fine and moderate, when we all were ferried across the river; and the next morning shaped our course to the {202} South West, by the side of Point Lake. After three days journey, which only consisted of about eighteen miles, we came to a few small scrubby woods,[88] which were the first that we had seen from the twenty-fifth of May, except those we had perceived at the Copper-mine River.

> 1771. September.

One of the Indian's wives, who for some time had been in a consumption, had for a few days past become so weak as to be incapable of travelling, which, among those people, is the most deplorable state to which a human being can possibly be brought. Whether she had been given over by the doctors, or that it was for want of friends among them, I cannot tell, but certain it is, that no expedients were taken for her recovery; so that, without much ceremony, she was left unassisted, to perish above-ground.

[219]

Though this was the first instance of the kind I had seen, it is the common, and indeed the constant practice of those Indians; for when a grown person is so ill, especially in the Summer, as not to be able to walk, and too heavy to be carried, they say it is better to leave one who is past recovery, than for the whole family to sit down by them and starve to death; well knowing that they cannot be of any service to the afflicted. On those occasions, therefore, the friends or relations of the sick generally leave them some victuals and water; and, if the situation of the place will afford it, a little firing. When {203} those articles are provided, the person to be left is acquainted with the road which the others intend to go; and then, after covering them well up with deer skins, &c. they take their leave, and walk away crying.

Sometimes persons thus left, recover; and come up with their friends, or wander about till they meet with other Indians, whom they accompany till they again join their relations. Instances of this kind are seldom known. The poor woman above mentioned, however, came up with us three several times, after having been left in the manner described. At length, poor creature! she dropt behind, and no one attempted to go back in search of her.

A custom apparently so unnatural is perhaps not to be found among any other of the human race: if properly considered, however, it may with justice be ascribed to necessity and self-preservation, rather than to the want of humanity and social feeling, which ought to be the characteristic of men, as the noblest part of the creation. Necessity, added to national custom, contributes principally to make scenes of this kind less shocking to those people, than they must appear to the more civilized part of mankind.[220]

During the early part of September, the weather was in general cold with much sleet and snow; which seemed to {204} promise that the Winter would set in early. Deer at this time being very plentiful, and the few woods we met with affording tent-poles and firing, the Indians proposed to remain where we were some time, in order to dress skins, and provide our Winter clothing; also to make snow-shoes and temporary sledges, as well as to prepare a large quantity of dried meat and fat to carry with us; for by the accounts of the Indians, they have always experienced a great scarcity of deer, and every other kind of game, in the direction they proposed we should go when we left Point Lake.

28th.

30th.

Toward the middle of the month, the weather became quite mild and open, and continued so till the end of it; but there was so much constant and incessant rain, that it rotted most of our tents. On the twenty-eighth, however, the wind settled in the North West quarter, when the weather grew so cold, that by the thirtieth all the ponds, lakes, and other standing waters, were frozen over so hard that we were enabled to cross them on the ice without danger.

Among the various superstitious customs of those people, it is worth remarking, and ought to have been mentioned in its proper place, that immediately after my companions had killed the Esquimaux at the Copper River, they considered themselves in a state of uncleanness, which induced them to practise some very curious and unusual ceremonies. {205} In the first place, all who were absolutely concerned in the murder were prohibited from cooking any kind of victuals, either for themselves or others. As luckily there were two in company who had not shed blood, they were employed always as cooks till we joined the women. This circumstance was exceedingly favourable on my side; for had there been no persons of the above description in company, that task, I was told, would have fallen on me; which would have been no less fatiguing and troublesome, than humiliating and vexatious.[221]

1771. September.

When the victuals were cooked, all the murderers took a kind of red earth, or oker, and painted all the space between the nose and chin, as well as the greater part of their cheeks, almost to the ears, before they would taste a bit, and would not drink out of any other dish, or smoke out of any other pipe, but their own; and none of the others seemed willing to drink or smoke out of theirs.

We had no sooner joined the women, at our return from the expedition, than there seemed to be an universal spirit of emulation among them, vying who should first make a suit of ornaments for their husbands, which consisted of bracelets for the wrists, and a band for the forehead, composed of porcupine quills and moose-hair, curiously wrought on leather.

The custom of painting the mouth and part of the cheeks before each meal, and drinking and smoking out {206} of their own utensils, was strictly and invariably observed, till the Winter began to set in; and during the whole of that time they would never kiss any of their wives or children. They refrained also from eating many parts of the deer and other animals, particularly the head, entrails, and blood; and during their uncleanness, their victuals were never sodden in water, but dried in the sun, eaten quite raw, or broiled, when a fire fit for the purpose could be procured.

When the time arrived that was to put an end to these ceremonies, the men, without a female being present, made a fire at some distance from the tents, into which they threw all their ornaments, pipe-stems, and dishes, which were soon consumed to ashes; after which a feast was prepared, consisting of such articles as they had long been prohibited from eating; and when all was over, each man was at liberty to eat, drink, and smoke as he pleased; and also to kiss his wives and children at discretion, which they seemed to do with more raptures than I had ever known them do it either before or since.

October. 6th.

1771. October.

October came in very roughly, attended with heavy falls of snow, and much drift. On the sixth at night, a heavy[222] gale of wind from the North West put us in great disorder; for though the few woods we passed had furnished us with tent-poles and fewel, yet they did not afford us the least shelter whatever. The wind blew with such {207} violence, that in spite of all our endeavours, it overset several of the tents, and mine, among the rest, shared the disaster, which I cannot sufficiently lament, as the but-ends of the weather tent-poles fell on the quadrant,[89] and though it was in a strong wainscot case, two of the bubbles, the index, and several other parts were broken, which rendered it entirely useless. This being the case, I did not think it worth carriage, but broke it to pieces, and gave the brass-work to the Indians, who cut it into small lumps, and made use of it instead of ball.

23d.

On the twenty-third of October, several Copper and a few Dog-ribbed Indians came to our tents laden with furrs, which they sold to some of my crew for such iron-work as they had to give in exchange. This visit, I afterwards found, was by appointment of the Copper Indians whom we had seen at Congecathawhachaga, and who, in their way to us, had met the Dog-ribbed Indians, who were also glad of so favourable an opportunity of purchasing some of those valuable articles, though at a very extravagant price: for one of the Indians in my company, though not properly of my party, got no less than forty beaver skins, and sixty martins, for one piece of iron which he had stole when he was last at the Fort.[AV]

[223]

1771. October.

{208} One of those strangers had about forty beaver skins, with which he intended to pay Matonabbee an old debt; but one of the other Indians seized the whole, notwithstanding he knew it to be in fact Matonabbee's property. This treatment, together with many other insults, which he had received during my abode with him, made him renew his old resolution of leaving his own country, and going to reside with the Athapuscow Indians.

1771. October.

As the most interesting part of my journey was now over, I did not think it necessary to interfere in his private affairs; and therefore did not endeavour to influence him either one way or the other: out of complaisance, therefore, rather than any thing else, I told him, that I thought such behaviour very uncourteous, especially in a man of his rank and dignity. As to the reason of his determination, I did not think it worth while to enquire into it; but, by his discourse with the other Indians, I soon understood that they all intended to make an excursion into the country of the Athapuscow Indians, in order to kill moose and beaver. The former of those animals are never found in the Northern Indian territories; and the latter are so scarce in those Northern parts, that during the whole Winter of one thousand seven hundred and seventy, {209} I did not see more than two beaver houses. Martins are also scarce in those parts; for during the above period, I do not think that more than six or eight were killed by all the Indians in my company. This exceedingly small number, among so many people, may with great truth be attributed to the indolence of the Indians, and the wandering life which they lead, rather than to the great scarcity of the martins. It is true, that our moving so frequently from place to place, did at times make it not an object worth while to build traps; but had they taken the advantage of all favourable opportunities, and been possessed of half the industry of the Company's servants in the Bay, they might with great ease have caught as many hundreds, if not some thousands; and when we[224] consider the extent of ground which we walked over in that time, such a number would not have been any proof of the martins being very plentiful.

Except a few martins; wolves, quiquehatches, foxes, and otters, are the chief furrs to be met with in those parts, and few of the Northern Indians chuse to kill either the wolf or the quiquehatch, under a notion that they are something more than common animals. Indeed, I have known some of them so bigotted to this opinion, that having by chance killed a quiquehatch by a gun which had been set for a fox, they have left it where it was killed, and would not take off its skin. Notwithstanding this {210} silly notion, which is too frequently to be observed among those people, it generally happens that there are some in every gang who are less scrupulous, so that none of those furrs are ever left to rot; and even those who make a point of not killing the animals themselves, are ready to receive their skins from other Indians, and carry them to the Fort for trade.

30th.

November. 1st.

By the thirtieth of October, all our clothing, snowshoes, and temporary sledges, being completed, we once more began to prepare for moving, and on the following day set out, and walked five or six miles to the Southward.

5th.

From the first to the fifth of November we walked on the ice of a large lake, which, though very considerable both in length and breadth, is not distinguished by any general name; on which account I gave it the name of No Name Lake.[90] On the South side of this lake we found some wood, which was very acceptable, being the first that we had seen since we left Point Lake.

[225]

No Name Lake is about fifty miles long from North to South, and, according to the account of the Indians, is thirty-five miles wide from East to West. It is said to abound with fine fish; but the weather at the time we crossed it was so cold, as to render it impossible to sit on the ice any {211} length of time to angle. A few exceedingly fine trout, and some very large pike, however, were caught by my companions.

When we arrived on the South side of the above lake, we shaped our course to the South West; and though the weather was in general very cold, yet as we every night found tufts of wood, in which we could pitch our tents, we were enabled to make a better defence against the weather, than we had had it in our power to do for some time past.

10th.

On the tenth of November, we arrived at the edge of the main woods; at which time the Indians began to make proper sledges, some snow-shoes, &c. after which we proceeded again to the South West. But deer and all other kinds of game were so scarce the whole way, that, except a few partridges, nothing was killed by any in company: we had, nevertheless, plenty of the provision which had been prepared at Point Lake.

> 20th.

> 1771. November.

On the twentieth of the same month, we arrived at[226] Anaw'd Whoie,[91] or the Indian Lake. In our way we crossed part of Methy Lake,[92] and walked near eighty miles on a small river belonging to it, which empties itself into the Great Athapuscow[93] Lake.[AW] While we were walking {212} on the above little river, the Indians set fishing-nets under the ice every night; but their labour was attended with so little success, that all they caught served only as a delicacy, or to make a little change in our diet; for the quantity was too trifling to occasion any considerable saving of our other provisions.

Anaw'd Lake, though so small as not to exceed twenty miles wide in the broadest part, is celebrated by the natives for abounding with plenty of fish during the Winter; accordingly the Indians set all their nets, which were not a few, and met with such success, that in about ten days the roes only were as much as all the women could haul after them.

Tittimeg and barble, with a few small pike, were the only fish caught at this part; the roes of which, particularly those of the tittimeg, are more esteemed by the Northern Indians, to take with them on a journey, than the fish itself; for about two pounds weight of these roes, when well bruised, will make near four gallons of broth, as thick as common burgoe; and if properly managed, will be as white as rice, which makes it very pleasing to the eye, and no less agreeable to the palate.

> 1771. November.

[227]

The land round this lake is very hilly, though not mountainous, and chiefly consists of rocks and loose stones; there must, however, be a small portion of soil {213} on the surface, as it is in most parts well clothed with tall poplars, pines, fir, and birch; particularly in the vallies, where the poplars, pine, and birch seem to thrive best; but the firs were as large, and in as flourishing a state, on the very summit of the hills, as in any other part.

Rabbits[94] were here so plentiful, particularly on the South and South East side of the lake, that several of the Indians caught twenty or thirty in a night with snares; and the wood-partridges[95] were so numerous in the fir trees, and so tame, that I have known an Indian kill near twenty of them in a day with his bow and arrows. The Northern Indians call this species of the partridge Day; and though their flesh is generally very black and bitter, occasioned by their feeding on the brush of the fir tree, yet they make a variety, or change of diet, and are thought exceedingly good, particularly by the natives, who, though capable of living so hard, and at times eating very ungrateful food, are nevertheless as fond of variety as any people whom I ever saw; and will go as great lengths, according to their circumstances, to gratify their palates, as the greatest epicure in England. As a proof of this assertion, I have frequently known Matonabbee, and others who could afford it, for the sake of variety only, send some of their young men to kill a few partridges at the expence of more ammunition than would have killed deer sufficient to have maintained their families many days; whereas the partridges were always eaten up at one meal: and to {214} heighten the luxury on these occasions, the partridges are boiled in a kettle of sheer fat, which it must be allowed renders them beyond all description finer flavoured than when boiled in water or common broth. I have also eat deer-skins boiled in fat, which were exceedingly good.

1771. November.

[228]

As during our stay at Anaw'd Lake several of the Indians were sickly, the doctors undertook to administer relief; particularly to one man, who had been hauled on a sledge by his brother for two months. His disorder was the dead palsey, which affected one side, from the crown of his head to the sole of his foot. Besides this dreadful disorder, he had some inward complaints, with a total loss of appetite; so that he was reduced to a mere skeleton, and so weak as to be scarcely capable of speaking. In this deplorable condition, he was laid in the center of a large conjuring-house, made much after the manner as that which has been already described. And that nothing might be wanting toward his recovery, the same man who deceived me in swallowing a bayonet in the Summer, now offered to swallow a large piece of board, about the size of a barrel-stave, in order to effect his recovery. The piece of board was prepared by another man, and painted according to the direction of the juggler, with a rude representation of some beast of prey on one side, and on the reverse was painted, according to their rude method, a resemblance of the sky.

{215} Without entering into a long detail of the preparations for this feat, I shall at once proceed to observe, that after the conjurer had held the necessary conference with his invisible spirits, or shadows, he asked if I was present; for he had heard of my saying that I did not see him swallow the bayonet fair; and on being answered in the affirmative, he desired me to come nearer; on which the mob made a lane for me to pass, and I advanced close to him, and found him standing at the conjuring-house door as naked as he was born.

1771. November.

When the piece of board was delivered to him, he proposed at first only to shove one-third of it down his throat, and then walk round the company afterward to shove down another third; and so proceed till he had swallowed the whole, except a small piece of the end, which was left behind to haul it up again. When he put it to his mouth it apparently slipped down his throat like lightning, and only left about three inches sticking without his lips; after walking backwards and[229] forwards three times, he hauled it up again, and ran into the conjuring-house with great precipitation. This he did to all appearance with great ease and composure; and notwithstanding I was all attention on the occasion, I could not detect the deceit; and as to the reality of its being a piece of wood that he pretended to swallow, there is not the least reason to doubt of it, for I had it in my hand, both before and immediately after the ceremony.

{216} To prevent a variety of opinions on this occasion, and to lessen the apparent magnitude of the miracle, as well as to give some colour to my scepticism, which might otherwise perhaps appear ridiculous, it is necessary to observe, that this feat was performed in a dark and excessively cold night; and although there was a large fire at some distance, which reflected a good light, yet there was great room for collusion: for though the conjurer himself was quite naked, there were several of his fraternity well-clothed, who attended him very close during the time of his attempting to swallow the board, as well as at the time of his hauling it up again.

For these reasons it is necessary also to observe, that on the day preceding the performance of this piece of deception, in one of my hunting excursions, I accidentally came across the conjurer as he was sitting under a bush, several miles from the tents, where he was busily employed shaping a piece of wood exactly like that part which stuck out of his mouth after he had pretended to swallow the remainder of the piece. The shape of the piece which I saw him making was this, ; which exactly resembled the forked end of the main piece, the shape of which was this, . So that when his attendants had concealed the main piece, it was easy for him to stick the small point into his mouth, as it was reduced at the small end to a proper size for the purpose.

1771. November.

{217} Similar proofs may easily be urged against his swallowing the bayonet in the Summer, as no person less[230] ignorant than themselves can possibly place any belief in the reality of those feats; yet on the whole, they must be allowed a considerable share of dexterity in the performance of those tricks, and a wonderful deal of perseverance in what they do for the relief of those whom they undertake to cure.

Not long after the above performance had taken place, some of the Indians began to ask me what I thought of it. As I could not have any plea for saying that I was far off, and at the same time not caring to affront them by hinting my suspicions of the deceit, I was some time at a loss for an answer: I urged, however, the impossibility of a man's swallowing a piece of wood, that was not only much longer than his whole back, but nearly twice as broad as he could extend his mouth. On which some of them laughed at my ignorance, as they were pleased to call it; and said, that the spirits in waiting swallowed, or otherwise concealed, the stick, and only left the forked end apparently sticking out of the conjurer's mouth. My guide, Matonabbee, with all his other good sense, was so bigotted to the reality of those performances, that he assured me in the strongest terms, he had seen a man, who was then in company, swallow a child's cradle, with as much ease as he could fold up a piece of paper, and put it into his mouth; and that when he hauled it up again, not the {218} mark of a tooth, or of any violence, was to be discovered about it.

1771. November.

This story so far exceeded the feats which I had seen with the bayonet and board, that, for the sake of keeping up the farce, I began to be very inquisitive about the spirits which appear to them on those occasions, and their form; when I was told that they appeared in various shapes, for almost every conjurer had his peculiar attendant; but that the spirit which attended the man who pretended to swallow the piece of wood, they said, generally appeared to him in the shape of a cloud. This I thought very apropos to the present occasion; and I must confess that I never had so thick a cloud thrown before[231] my eyes before or since; and had it not been by accident, that I saw him make a counterpart to the piece of wood said to be swallowed, I should have been still at a loss how to account for so extraordinary a piece of deception, performed by a man who was entirely naked.

As soon as our conjurer had executed the above feat, and entered the conjuring-house, as already mentioned, five other men and an old woman, all of whom were great professors of that art, stripped themselves quite naked and followed him, when they soon began to suck, blow, sing, and dance, round the poor paralytic; and continued so to do for three days and four nights, without taking the least rest or refreshment, not even so much as a drop of water. {219} When these poor deluding and deluded people came out of the conjuring-house, their mouths were so parched with thirst as to be quite black, and their throats so sore, that they were scarcely able to articulate a single word, except those that stand for *yes* and *no* in their language.

1771. November.

After so long an abstinence they were very careful not to eat or drink too much at one time, particularly for the first day; and indeed some of them, to appearance, were almost as bad as the poor man they had been endeavouring to relieve. But great part of this was feigned; for they lay on their backs with their eyes fixed, as if in the agonies of death, and were treated like young children; one person sat constantly by them, moistening their mouths with fat, and now and then giving them a drop of water. At other times a small bit of meat was put into their mouths, or a pipe held for them to smoke. This farce only lasted for the first day; after which they seemed to be perfectly well, except the hoarseness, which continued for a considerable time afterwards. And it is truly wonderful, though the strictest truth, that when the poor sick man was taken from the conjuring-house, he had not only recovered his appetite to an amazing degree, but was able to move all the fingers and toes of the side that had been so long[232] dead. In three weeks he recovered so far as to be capable of walking, and at the end of six weeks went a hunting for his family. He was one of the persons[AX] {220} particularly engaged to provide for me during my journey; and after his recovery from this dreadful disorder, accompanied me back to Prince of Wales's Fort in June one thousand seven hundred and seventy-two; and since that time he has frequently visited the Factory, though he never had a healthy look afterwards, and at times seemed troubled with a nervous complaint. It may be added, that he had been formerly of a remarkable lively disposition; but after his last illness he always appeared thoughtful, sometimes gloomy, and, in fact, the disorder seemed to have changed his whole nature; for before that dreadful paralytic stroke, he was distinguished for his good-nature and benevolent disposition; was entirely free from every appearance of avarice; and the whole of his wishes seemed confined within the narrow limits of possessing as many goods as were absolutely necessary, with his own industry, to enable him to support his family from season to season; but after this event, he was the most fractious, quarrelsome, discontented, and covetous wretch alive.

Though the ordinary trick of these conjurers may be easily detected, and justly exploded, being no more than the tricks of common jugglers, yet the apparent good effect of their labours on the sick and diseased is not so easily accounted for. Perhaps the implicit confidence placed in them by the sick may, at times, leave the mind so perfectly at rest, as to cause the disorder to take a favourable turn; and a few successful cases are quite sufficient to establish the doctor's character and reputation: {221} But how this consideration could operate in the case I have just mentioned I am at a loss to say; such, however, was the fact, and I leave it to be accounted for by others.

A WINTER VIEW IN THE ATHAPUSCOW LAKE
By Samuel Hearne, 1771

[233]

1771. November.

When these jugglers take a dislike to, and threaten a secret revenge on any person, it often proves fatal to that person; as, from a firm belief that the conjurer has power over his life, he permits the very thoughts of it to prey on his spirits, till by degrees it brings on a disorder which puts an end to his existence:[AY] and sometimes a threat of this {222} kind causes the death of a whole family; and that without any blood being shed, or the least apparent molestation being offered to any of the parties.

December. 1st.

1771. December.

Having dried as many fish and fish-roes as we could conveniently take with us, we once more packed up our stores, and, on the first day of December, set out, and continued our course to the South West, leaving Anaw'd Lake on the South West. Several of the Indians being out of order, we made but short days journies.

[234]

From the first to the thirteenth, we walked along a course of small lakes, joined to each other by small rivers, or creeks, that have communication with Anaw'd Lake.

In our way we caught daily a few fish by angling, and saw many beaver houses; but these were generally in so difficult a situation, and had so many stones in the composition of them, that the Indians killed but few, and that at a great expence of labour and tools.

13th.

On the thirteenth, one of the Indians killed two deer, which were the first that we had seen since the twentieth {223} of October. So that during a period of near two months, we had lived on the dried meat that we had prepared at Point Lake, and a few fish; of which the latter was not very considerable in quantity, except what was caught at Anaw'd Lake. It is true, we also caught a few rabbits, and at times the wood-partridges were so plentiful, that the Indians killed considerable numbers of them with their bows and arrows; but the number of mouths was so great, that all which was caught from our leaving Point Lake, though if enumerated, they might appear very considerable, would not have afforded us all a bare subsistence; for though I and some others experienced no real want, yet there were many in our company who could scarcely be said to live, and would not have existed at all, had it not been for the dry meat we had with us.

> 24th.

> 1771. December.

When we left the above-mentioned lakes we shaped a course more to the Southward, and on the twenty-fourth, arrived at the North side of the great Athapuscow Lake.[196] In our way[235] we saw many Indian deer,[97] and beaver were very plentiful, many of which the Indians killed; but the days were so short, that the Sun only took a circuit of a few points of the compass above the horizon, and did not, at its greatest altitude, rise half-way up the trees. The brilliancy of the *Aurora Borealis*, however, and of the Stars, even without the assistance of the Moon, made some amends for that deficiency; for it was frequently so light all night, that I could see to read a very small print. {224} The Indians make no difference between night and day when they are hunting of beaver; but those *nocturnal* lights are always found insufficient for the purpose of hunting deer or moose.

Photo: J. P. Tyrrell, July 30, 1893.
HERD OF CARIBOU ON THE BANKS OF DUBAWNT RIVER

Photo: J. P. Tyrrell, July 31, 1893.
DRYING CARIBOU MEAT

1771. December.

I do not remember to have met with any travellers into high Northern latitudes, who remarked their having heard the Northern Lights make any noise in the air as they vary their colours or position; which may probably be owing to the want of perfect silence at the time they made their observations on those meteors. I can positively affirm, that in still nights I have frequently heard them make a rustling and crackling noise, like the waving of a large flag in a fresh gale of wind. This is not peculiar to the place of which I am now writing, as I have heard the same noise very plain at Churchill River; and in all probability it is only for want of attention that it has not been heard in every part of the Northern hemisphere where they have been known to shine with any considerable degree of lustre. It is, however, very probable that these lights are sometimes much nearer the Earth than they are at others, according to the state of the atmosphere, and this may have a great effect on the sound: but the truth or falsehood of this conjecture I leave to the determinations of those who are better skilled in natural philosophy than I can pretend to be.[236]

1771. December.

Indian deer (the only species found in those parts, except the moose) are so much larger than those which {225} frequent the barren grounds to the North of Churchill River, that a small doe is equal in size to a Northern buck. The hair of the former is of a sandy red during the Winter; and their horns, though much stronger, are not so long and branchy as are those of the latter kind. Neither is the flesh of those deer so much esteemed by the Northern Indians, as that of the smaller kind, which inhabit the more Eastern and Northern parts of the country. Indeed, it must be allowed to be much coarser, and of a different flavour; inasmuch as the large Lincolnshire mutton differs from grass lamb. I must acknowledge, however, that I always thought it very good. This is that species of deer which are found so plentiful near York Fort and Severn River. They are also at times found in considerable numbers near Churchill River; and I have seen them killed as far North, near the sea-side, as Seal River: But the small Northern Indian deer are seldom known to cross Churchill River, except in some very extraordinary cold seasons, and when the Northern winds have prevailed much in the preceding fall; for those visits are always made in the Winter. But though I own that the flesh of the large Southern deer is very good, I must at the same time confess that the flesh of the small Northern deer, whether buck or doe, in their proper season, is by far more delicious and the finest I have ever eaten, either in this country or any other; and is of that peculiar quality, that it never cloys. I can affirm this from my own experience; {226} for after living on it entirely, as it may be said, for twelve or eighteen months successively, I scarcely[237] ever wished for a change of food; though when fish or fowl came in my way, it was very agreeable.

The beaver[93] being so plentiful, the attention of my companions was chiefly engaged on them, as they not only furnished delicious food, but their skins proved a valuable acquisition, being a principal article of trade, as well as a serviceable one for clothing, &c.

The situation of the beaver-houses is various. Where the beavers are numerous they are found to inhabit lakes, ponds, and rivers, as well as those narrow creeks which connect the numerous lakes with which this country abounds; but the two latter are generally chosen by them when the depth of water and other circumstances are suitable, as they have then the advantage of a current to convey wood and other necessaries to their habitations, and because, in general, they are more difficult to be taken, than those that are built in standing water.

There is no one particular part of a lake, pond, river, or creek, of which the beavers make choice for building their houses on, in preference to another; for they sometimes build on points, sometimes in the hollow of a bay, and often on small islands; they always chuse, however, {227} those parts that have such a depth of water as will resist the frost in Winter, and prevent it from freezing to the bottom.

1771. December.

The beaver that build their houses in small rivers or creeks, in which the water is liable to be drained off when the back supplies are dried up by the frost, are wonderfully taught by instinct to provide against that evil, by making a dam quite across the river, at a convenient distance from their houses. This I look upon as the most curious piece of workmanship that is performed by the beaver; not so much for the neatness of the work, as for its strength and real service; and at the same time it discovers such a degree of sagacity and foresight in the animal, of approaching evils, as is little inferior to that of the human species, and is certainly peculiar to those animals.

[238]

The beaver-dams differ in shape according to the nature of the place in which they are built. If the water in the river or creek have but little motion, the dam is almost straight; but when the current is more rapid, it is always made with a considerable curve, convex towards the stream. The materials made use of in those dams are drift-wood, green willows, birch, and poplars, if they can be got; also mud and stones, intermixed in such a manner as must evidently contribute to the strength of the dam; but in these dams there is no other order or method observed, {228} except that of the work being carried on with a regular sweep, and all the parts being made of equal strength.

In places which have been long frequented by beaver undisturbed, their dams, by frequent repairing, become a solid bank, capable of resisting a great force both of water and ice; and as the willow, poplar, and birch generally take root and shoot up, they by degrees form a kind of regular-planted hedge, which I have seen in some places so tall, that birds have built their nests among the branches.

Though the beaver which build their houses in lakes and other standing waters, may enjoy a sufficient quantity of their favourite element without the assistance of a dam, the trouble of getting wood and other necessaries to their habitations without the help of a current, must in some measure counterbalance the other advantages which are reaped from such a situation; for it must be observed, that the beaver which build in rivers and creeks, always cut their wood above their houses, so that the current, with little trouble, conveys it to the place required.

1771. December.

The beaver-houses are built of the same materials as their dams, and are always proportioned in size to the number of inhabitants, which seldom exceed four old, and six or eight[239] young ones; though, by chance, I have seen above double that number.

{229} These houses, though not altogether unworthy of admiration, fall very short of the general description given of them; for instead of order or regulation being observed in rearing them, they are of a much ruder structure than their dams.

Those who have undertaken to describe the inside of beaver-houses, as having several apartments appropriated to various uses; such as eating, sleeping, store-houses for provisions, and one for their natural occasions, &c. must have been very little acquainted with the subject; or, which is still worse, guilty of attempting to impose on the credulous, by representing the greatest falsehoods as real facts. Many years constant residence among the Indians, during which I had an opportunity of seeing several hundreds of those houses, has enabled me to affirm that every thing of the kind is entirely void of truth; for, notwithstanding the sagacity of those animals, it has never been observed that they aim at any other conveniencies in their houses, than to have a dry place to lie on; and there they usually eat their victuals, which they occasionally take out of the water.

> 1771. December.

It frequently happens, that some of the large houses are found to have one or more partitions, if they deserve that appellation; but that is no more than a part of the main building, left by the sagacity of the beaver to support the roof. On such occasions it is common for those {230} different apartments, as some are pleased to call them, to have no communication with each other but by water; so that in fact they may be called double or treble houses, rather than different apartments of the same house. I have seen a large beaver-house built in a small island, that had near a dozen apartments under one roof: and, two or three of these only excepted, none of them had any communication with each other but by water. As there were beaver enough to inhabit[240] each apartment, it is more than probable that each family knew its own, and always entered at their own door, without having any farther connection with their neighbours than a friendly intercourse; and to join their united labours in erecting their separate habitations, and building their dams where required. It is difficult to say whether their interest on other occasions was anyways reciprocal. The Indians of my party killed twelve old beaver, and twenty-five young and half-grown ones out of the house above mentioned; and on examination found that several had escaped their vigilance, and could not be taken but at the expence of more trouble than would be sufficient to take double the number in a less difficult situation.[AZ]

Travellers who assert that the beaver have two doors to their houses, one on the land-side, and the other next the {231} water, seem to be less acquainted with those animals than others who assign them an elegant suite of apartments. Such a proceeding would be quite contrary to their manner of life, and at the same time would render their houses of no use, either to protect them from their enemies, or guard them against the extreme cold in Winter.

The quiquehatches, or wolvereens, are great enemies to the beaver; and if there were a passage into their houses on the land-side, would not leave one of them alive wherever they came.

1771. December.

I cannot refrain from smiling, when I read the accounts of different Authors who have written on the œconomy of those animals, as there seems to be a contest between them, who shall most exceed in fiction. But the Compiler of the Wonders of Nature and Art seems, in my opinion, to have succeeded best in this respect; as he has not only collected all the fictions into which other writers on the subject have run, but has so greatly improved on them, that little remains to be added to his account of the beaver, beside a vocabulary of their language, a code of their laws, and a sketch of their religion, to make it the most complete natural history of that animal which can possibly be offered to the public.

[241]

There cannot be a greater imposition, or indeed a grosser insult, on common understanding, than the wish {232} to make us believe the stories of some of the works ascribed to the beaver; and though it is not to be supposed that the compiler of a general work can be intimately acquainted with every subject of which it may be necessary to treat, yet a very moderate share of understanding is surely sufficient to guard him against giving credit to such marvellous tales, however smoothly they may be told, or however boldly they may be asserted, by the romancing traveller.

To deny that the beaver is possessed of a very considerable degree of sagacity, would be as absurd in me, as it is in those Authors who think they cannot allow them too much. I shall willingly grant them their full share; but it is impossible for any one to conceive how, or by what means, a beaver, whose full height when standing erect does not exceed two feet and a half, or three feet at most, and whose fore-paws are not much larger than a half-crown piece, can "drive stakes as thick as a man's leg into the ground three or four feet deep." Their "wattling those stakes with twigs," is equally absurd; and their "plaistering the inside of their houses with a composition of mud and straw," and "swimming with mud and stones on their tails," are still more incredible. The form and size of the animal, notwithstanding all its sagacity, will not admit of its performing such feats; and it would be as impossible for a beaver to use its tail as a trowel, except on the surface of the ground on which it walks, as it {233} would have been for Sir James Thornhill to have painted the dome of St. Paul's cathedral without the assistance of scaffolding. The joints of their tail will not admit of their turning it over their[242] backs on any occasion whatever, as it has a natural inclination to bend downwards; and it is not without some considerable exertion that they can keep it from trailing on the ground. This being the case, they cannot sit erect like a squirrel, which is their common posture: particularly when eating, or when they are cleaning themselves, as a cat or squirrel does, without having their tails bent forward between their legs; and which may not improperly be called their trencher.

So far are the beaver from driving stakes into the ground when building their houses, that they lay most of the wood crosswise, and nearly horizontal, and without any other order than that of leaving a hollow or cavity in the middle; when any unnecessary branches project inward, they cut them off with their teeth, and throw them in among the rest, to prevent the mud from falling through the roof. It is a mistaken notion, that the wood-work is first completed and then plaistered; for the whole of their houses, as well as their dams, are from the foundation one mass of wood and mud, mixed with stones, if they can be procured. The mud is always taken from the edge of the bank, or the bottom of the creek or pond, near the door of the house; and though their fore-paws are so small, yet it is held close up between them, under their throat, {234} that they carry both mud and stones; while they always drag the wood with their teeth.

All their work is executed in the night; and they are so expeditious in completing it, that in the course of one night I have known them to have collected as much mud at their houses as to have amounted to some thousands of their little handfuls; and when any mixture of grass or straw has appeared in it, it has been, most assuredly, mere chance, owing to the nature of the ground from which they had taken it. As to their designedly making a composition for that purpose, it is entirely void of truth.

1771. December.

It is a great piece of policy in those animals, to cover, or plaister, as it is usually called, the outside of their houses[243] every fall with fresh mud, and as late as possible in the Autumn, even when the frost becomes pretty severe; as by this means it soon freezes as hard as a stone, and prevents their common enemy, the quiquehatch, from disturbing them during the Winter. And as they are frequently seen to walk over their work, and sometimes to give a flap with their tail, particularly when plunging into the water, this has, without doubt, given rise to the vulgar opinion that they use their tails as a trowel, with which they plaister their houses; whereas that flapping of the tail is no more than a custom, which they always preserve, even when they become tame and domestic, and more particularly so when they are startled.

{235} Their food chiefly consists of a large root, something resembling a cabbage-stalk, which grows at the bottom of the lakes and rivers. They eat also the bark of trees, particularly that of the poplar, birch, and willow; but the ice preventing them from getting to the land in Winter, they have not any barks to feed upon during that season, except that of such sticks as they cut down in Summer, and throw into the water opposite the doors of their houses; and as they generally eat a great deal, the roots above mentioned constitute a chief part of their food during the Winter. In Summer they vary their diet, by eating various kinds of herbage, and such berries as grow near their haunts during that season.

When the ice breaks up in the Spring, the beaver always leave their houses, and rove about the whole Summer, probably in search of a more commodious situation; but in case of not succeeding in their endeavours, they return again to their old habitations a little before the fall of the leaf, and lay in their Winter stock of woods. They seldom begin to repair the houses till the frost commences, and never finish the outer-coat till the cold is pretty severe, as hath been already mentioned.

1771. December.

When they shift their habitations, or when the increase of their number renders it necessary to make some addition to their houses, or to erect new ones, they begin felling[244] {236} the wood for these purposes early in the Summer, but seldom begin to build till the middle or latter end of August, and never complete their houses till the cold weather be set in.

Notwithstanding what has been so repeatedly reported of those animals assembling in great bodies, and jointly erecting large towns, cities, and commonwealths, as they have sometimes been called, I am confident, from many circumstances, that even where the greatest numbers of beaver are situated in the neighbourhood of each other, their labours are not carried on jointly in the erection of their different habitations, nor have they any reciprocal interest, except it be such as live immediately under the same roof; and then it extends no farther than to build or keep a dam which is common to several houses. In such cases it is natural to think that every one who receives benefit from such dams, should assist in erecting it, being sensible of its utility to all.

Persons who attempt to take beaver in Winter should be thoroughly acquainted with their manner of life, otherwise they will have endless trouble to effect their purpose, and probably without success in the end; because they have always a number of holes in the banks, which serve them as places of retreat when any injury is offered to their houses; and in general it is in those holes that they are taken.

> 1771. December.

{237} When the beaver which are situated in a small river or creek are to be taken, the Indians sometimes find it necessary to stake the river across, to prevent them from passing; after which, they endeavour to find out all their holes or places of retreat in the banks. This requires much practice and experience to accomplish, and is performed in the following manner: Every man being furnished with an ice-chisel, lashes it to the end of a small staff about four or five feet long; he then walks along the edge of the banks, and keeps knocking his chisels against the ice. Those who are well acquainted with that kind of work well know by the sound of the ice when they are opposite to any of the beavers' holes or vaults.[245]

As soon as they suspect any, they cut a hole through the ice big enough to admit an old beaver; and in this manner proceed till they have found out all their places of retreat, or at least as many of them as possible. While the principal men are thus employed, some of the understrappers, and the women, are busy in breaking open the house, which at times is no easy task; for I have frequently known these houses to be five and six feet thick; and one in particular, was more than eight feet thick on the crown. When the beaver find that their habitations are invaded, they fly to their holes in the banks for shelter; and on being perceived by the Indians, which is easily done, by attending to the motion of the water, they block up the entrance with stakes of wood, and then haul the beaver out of its hole, either by hand, if they can reach it, or with a large hook {238} made for that purpose, which is fastened to the end of a long stick.

In this kind of hunting, every man has the sole right to all the beaver caught by him in the holes or vaults; and as this is a constant rule, each person takes care to mark such as he discovers, by sticking up the branch of a tree, or some other distinguishing post, by which he may know them. All that are caught in the house also are the property of the person who finds it.

The same regulations are observed, and the same process used in taking beaver that are found in lakes and other standing waters, except it be that of staking the lake across, which would be both unnecessary and impossible. Taking beaver-houses in these situations is generally attended with less trouble and more success than in the former.

1771. December.

The beaver is an animal which cannot keep under water long at a time; so that when their houses are broke open, and all their places of retreat discovered, they have but one choice left, as it may be called, either to be taken in their houses or their vaults: in general they prefer the latter; for where there is one beaver caught in the house, many thousands are taken[246] in their vaults in the banks. Sometimes they are caught in nets, and in the Summer very frequently in traps. In Winter they are very fat and {239} delicious; but the trouble of rearing their young, the thinness of their hair, and their constantly roving from place to place, with the trouble they have in providing against the approach of Winter, generally keep them very poor during the Summer season, at which time their flesh is but indifferent eating, and their skins of so little value, that the

Indians generally singe them, even to the amount of many thousands in one Summer. They have from two to five young, at a time. Mr. Dobbs, in his Account of Hudson's Bay, enumerates no less than eight different kinds of beaver[90]; but it must be understood that they are all of one kind and species; his distinctions arise wholly from the different seasons of the year in which they are killed, and the different uses to which their skins are applied, which is the sole reason that they vary so much in value.

[247]

1771. December.

Joseph Lefranc, or Mr. Dobbs for him, says, that a good hunter can kill six hundred beaver in one season, and can only carry one hundred to market. If that was really the case in Lefranc's time, the canoes must have been much smaller than they are at present; for it is well known that the generality of the canoes which have visited the Company's Factories for the last forty or fifty years, are capable of carrying three hundred beaver-skins with great ease, exclusive of the Indians luggage, provisions, &c.[100]

1771. December.

{240} If ever a particular Indian killed six hundred beaver in one Winter, (which is rather to be doubted), it is more than probable that many in his company did not kill twenty, and perhaps some none at all, so that by distributing them among those who had bad success, and others who had no abilities for that kind of hunting, there would be no necessity of leaving them to rot, or for singing them in the fire, as related by that Author. During my residence among the Indians I have known some individuals kill more beaver, and other heavy furrs, in the course of a Winter, than their wives could manage; but the overplus was never wantonly destroyed, but always given to their relations, or to those who had been less successful; so that the whole of the great hunters' labours were always brought to the

Factory. It is indeed too frequently a custom among the Southern Indians to singe many otters, as well as beaver; but this is seldom done, except in Summer, when their skins are of so little value as to be scarcely worth the duty; on which account it has been always thought impolitic to encourage the natives to kill such valuable animals at a time when their skins are not in season.

[248]

The white beaver, mentioned by Lefranc, are so rare, that instead of being "blown upon by the Company's Factors," as he asserts, I rather doubt whether one-tenth of them ever saw one during the time of their residence in this country. In the course of twenty years experience in the countries {241} about Hudson's Bay, though I travelled six hundred miles to the West of the sea-coast, I never saw but one white beaver-skin, and it had many reddish and brown hairs along the ridge of the back, and the sides and belly were of a glossy silvery white. It was deemed by the Indians a great curiosity; and I offered three times the usual price for a few of them, if they could be got; but in the course of ten years that I remained there afterward, I could not procure another; which is a convincing proof there is no such thing as a breed of that kind, and that a variation from the usual colour is very rare.

Black beaver, and that of a beautiful gloss, are not uncommon: perhaps they are more plentiful at Churchill than at any other Factory in the Bay; but it is rare to get more than twelve or fifteen of their skins in the course of one year's trade.

Lefranc, as an Indian, must have known better than to have informed Mr. Dobbs that the beaver have from ten to fifteen young at a time; or if he did, he must have deceived him wilfully; for the Indians, by killing them in all stages of gestation, have abundant opportunities of ascertaining the usual number of their offspring. I have seen some hundreds of them killed at the seasons favourable for those observations, and never could discover more than six young in one female, and that only in two {242} instances; for the usual number, as I have before observed, is from two to five.[249]

Besides this unerring method of ascertaining the real number of young which any animal has at a time, there is another rule to go by, with respect to the beaver, which experience has proved to the Indians never to vary or deceive them, that is by dissection; for on examining the womb of a beaver, even at a time when not with young, there is always found a hardish round knob for every young she had at the last litter. This is a circumstance I have been particularly careful to examine, and can affirm it to be true, from real experience.

Most of the accounts, nay I may say all the accounts now extant, respecting the beaver, are taken from the authority of the French who have resided in Canada; but those accounts differ so much from the real state and œconomy of all the beaver to the North of that place, as to leave great room to suspect the truth of them altogether. In the first place, the assertion that they have two doors to their houses, one on the land-side, and the other next the water, is, as I have before observed, quite contrary to fact and common sense, as it would render their houses of no use to them, either as places of shelter from the inclemency of the extreme cold in Winter, or as a retreat from their common enemy the quiquehatch. The only thing {243} that could have made M. Du Pratz, and other French writers, conjecture that such a thing did exist, must have been from having seen some old beaver houses which had been taken by the Indians; for they are always obliged to make a hole in one side of the house before they can drive them out; and it is more than probable that in so mild a climate as Canada, the Indians do generally make those holes on the land-side,[BA] which without doubt gave rise to the suggestion.

[250]

1771. December.

In respect to the beaver dunging in their houses, as some persons assert, it is quite wrong, as they always plunge into the water to do it. I am the better enabled to make this assertion, from having kept several of them till they became so domesticated as to answer to their name, and follow those to whom they were accustomed, in the same manner as a dog would do; and they were as much pleased at being fondled, as any animal I ever saw. I had a house built for them, and a small piece of water before the door, into which they always plunged when they wanted to ease nature; and their dung being of a light substance, immediately rises and floats on the surface, {244} then separates and subsides to the bottom. When the Winter sets in so as to freeze the water solid, they still continue their custom of coming out of their house, and dunging and making water on the ice; and when the weather was so cold that I was obliged to take them into my house, they always went into a large tub of water which I set for that purpose; so that they made not the least dirt, though they were kept in my own sitting-room, where they were the constant companions of the Indian women and children, and were so fond of their company, that when the Indians were absent for any considerable time, the beaver discovered great signs of uneasiness, and on their return shewed equal marks of pleasure, by fondling on them, crawling into their laps, laying on their backs, sitting erect like a squirrel, and behaving to them like children who see their parents but seldom. In general, during the Winter they lived on the same food as the women did, and were remarkably fond of rice and plum-pudding: they would eat partridges and fresh venison very freely, but I never tried them with fish, though I have heard they will at times prey on them. In fact, there are few of the granivorous animals that may not be brought to be carnivorous. It is well known that our domestic poultry will eat animal food: thousands of geese that come to London market are fattened on tallow-craps; and our horses in[251] Hudson's Bay would not only eat all kinds of animal food, but also drink freely of the wash, or pot-liquor, intended for the

{245} hogs. And we are assured by the most authentic Authors, that in Iceland, not only black cattle, but also the sheep, are almost entirely fed on fish and fish-bones during the Winter season. Even in the Isles of Orkney, and that in Summer, the sheep attend the ebbing of the tide as regular as the Esquimaux curlew, and go down to the shore which the tide has left, to feed on the sea-weed. This, however, is through necessity, for even the famous Island of Pomona[BB] will not afford them an existence above high-water-mark.

With respect to the inferior, or slave-beaver, of which some Authors speak, it is, in my opinion, very difficult for those who are best acquainted with the œconomy of this animal to determine whether there are any that deserve that appellation or not. It sometimes happens, that a beaver is caught, which has but a very indifferent coat, and which has broad patches on the back, and shoulders almost wholly without hair. This is the only foundation for asserting that there is an inferior, or slave-beaver, among them. And when one of the above description is taken, it is perhaps too hastily inferred that the hair is worn off from those parts by carrying heavy loads: whereas it is most probable that it is caused by a disorder that attacks them somewhat similar to the mange; for {246} were that falling off of the hair occasioned by performing extra labour, it is natural to think that instances of it would be more frequent than there are; as it is rare to see one of them in the course of seven or ten years. I have seen a whole house of those animals that had nothing on the surface of their bodies but the fine soft down; all the long hairs having molted off. This and every other deviation from the general run is undoubtedly owing to some particular disorder.

FOOTNOTES:

[86] Sir John Richardson says of Thaye-chuck-gyed Lake that it lies a short way to the northward of Point Lake.

[87] These are larvæ of a fly (*Hypoderma liniata?*), the eggs of which are laid in the skins of the deer in the early part of the summer. Here they

develop to the size of buckshot or larger, and those portions of the skin covering them become very thin, so that when the hide is taken off and tanned it is so full of holes, a quarter of an inch or more in diameter, as to be almost entirely useless.

[88] Sir John Franklin crossed Point Lake in 1821, and the "small scrubby woods" on its banks were noted by him, when he descended and surveyed the Coppermine River from it to the sea. Hearne places the south side of this lake on his map in North latitude 65° 45', only about thirty-five miles north of its true position. Caspar Whitney crossed Point Lake in the spring of 1895, and calls it Ecka tua (Fat-Water Lake). ("On Snowshoes to the Barren Grounds." By Caspar Whitney, p. 209.) Russell, in speaking of the Coppermine River which he crossed in April 1894, says, "It takes its rise in a large lake, called Ek-a Tooh, which is two days' journey in length." ("Explorations in the Far North." By Frank Russell, p. 112.)

[89] There is no evidence that any observations for latitude had been taken since he left Congecathawhachaga. Possibly the quadrant had been left behind with the women at that place, to be picked up again when he returned. But now, with the destruction of the quadrant, all uncertainty as to the character of the remainder of his survey is set at rest. His distances were estimated, and the general directions were doubtless taken with a magnetic compass, while observations for latitude were impossible.

[AV] The piece of iron above mentioned was the coulter of a new-fashioned plough, invented by Captain John Fowler, late Governor of Churchill River, with which he had a large piece of ground ploughed, and afterwards sowed with oats: but the part being nothing but a hot burning sand, like the Spanish lines at Gibraltar, the success may easily be guessed; which was, that it did not produce a single grain.

[90] This lake is identified by Sir John Richardson as the Providence Lake of Franklin and of the present maps, but it is more likely to be Mackay Lake, which is much more nearly the size of lake here described, and the description of the woods on the south shore agrees closely with the description of Lake Mackay given by Mr. Warburton Pike, who visited that region in 1890. This determination agrees also with the statement of Hearne, that No Name Lake lies but a short distance north of the edge of the "main woods," for the northern edge of the forest crosses the country from east to west, a few miles south of this lake. On Caspar Whitney's map

of his trip through the barren grounds this lake is called King or Grizzly Bear Lake. Mr. C. Harding, the officer in charge of Fort Resolution, the Hudson Bay Company's post on Great Slave Lake, has sent me the following Chipewyan Indian names of lakes, &c., in this region:—

ENGLISH.	CHIPEWYAN.	MEANING.
Mackay Lake.	Clayki thua.	White Sand Lake.
Le Gras Lake.	A ka thua.	Fat Lake.

(doubtless the same as Point Lake).

Aylmer Lake.	Chlueata thua.	Caribou swimming among the ice Lake.
Artillery Lake.	Atacho thua.	Caribou crossing in the middle of

		the lake Lake.
Coppermine River.	Sankataza.	Copper River.
Musk Ox Mountain.	Edegadaniyatha.	

[91] Mr. Harding informs me this is a lake lying a short distance south of Mackay Lake, and now known as "Lake of the Enemy." Anaw'd is doubtless the same word as Enna, which is the Chipewyan name for a Cree Indian.

Away to the west of this another large lake is indicated on the map, doubtless from the reports of the Indians, but no name is attached to it. On the Cook map this western lake is called Edlande Lake.

[92] L'abbé Petitot states (*op. cit.*, p. 143) that there are five rivers flowing into the north side of McLeod Bay of Great Slave Lake, and the little stream which flows from Methy Lake is doubtless one of these, and possibly Hoarfrost River. In that case Methy Lake is almost certainly Cook Lake, which agrees with Hearne's description inasmuch as it lies just within the edge of the woods.

[93] Great Slave Lake.

[AW] The course of this river is nearly South West.

[94] *Lepus americanus* (Erxl.).—E. A. P.

[95] *Canachites canadensis* (Linn.).—E. A. P.

[AX] His name was Cos-abyagh, the Northern Indian name for the Rock Partridge.

[AY] As a proof of this, Matonabbee, (who always thought me possessed of this art,) on his arrival at Prince of Wales's Fort in the Winter of 1778, informed me, that a man whom I had never seen but once, had treated him in such a manner that he was afraid of his life; in consequence of which he pressed me very much to kill him, though I was then several hundreds of miles distant: On which, to please this great man to whom I owed so much, and not expecting that any harm could possibly arise from it, I drew a rough sketch of two human figures on a piece of paper, in the attitude of wrestling: in the hand of one of them, I drew the figure of a bayonet pointing to the breast of the other. This is me, said I to Matonabbee, pointing to the figure which was holding the bayonet; and the other, is your enemy. Opposite to those figures I drew a pine-tree, over which I placed a large human eye, and out of the tree projected a human hand. This paper I gave to Matonabbee, with instructions to make it as publicly known as possible. Sure enough, the following year, when he came in to trade, he informed me that the man was dead, though at that time he was not less than three hundred miles from Prince of Wales's Fort. He assured me that the man was in perfect health when he heard of my design against him; but almost immediately afterwards became quite gloomy, and refusing all kind of sustenance, in a very few days died. After this I was frequently applied to on the same account, both by Matonabbee and other leading Indians, but never thought proper to comply with their requests; by which means I not only preserved the credit I gained on the first attempt, but always kept them in awe, and in some degree of respect and obedience to me. In fact, strange as it may appear, it is almost absolutely necessary that the chiefs at this place should profess something a little supernatural, to be able to deal with those people. The circumstance here recorded is a fact well known to Mr. William Jefferson, who succeeded me at Churchill Factory, as well as to all the officers and many of the common men who were at Prince of Wales's Fort at the time.

[96] The lake which he has now reached and which he calls Athapuscow Lake, Arathapescow Lake of the Cook and Pennant maps, is Great Slave Lake of the present maps, or the Slave Lake of Alexander Mackenzie, and not the lake now known as Athabasca Lake; and the point at which he reached it was somewhere east of the entrance to the North Arm. According to l'Abbé Petitot, the name Athabasca is a Cree word, referring

to a reedy, grassy mouth of a river, and means "The Herbaceous Network." It does not appear to have been the original name of any particular place or lake, but was doubtless applied to this lake by Hearne on account of the great marsh which covers much of the delta of Slave River, and later it was applied to the lake now known as Athabasca Lake on account of the character of the delta at the mouth of Athabasca River, near which Peter Pond, a trader from Montreal, established in 1778 the first trading-post on the Mackenzie waters. His map of 1785 designates the lake Arabasca Lake. Petitot states (Royal Geographical Society, vol. v. N.S. 1883, p. 728) that Great Slave Lake is called "'Thu-tué,' or 'Lake of the Breasts,' by the Chipewyans, because its eastern part is terminated by two extensive bays, in outline fancifully resembling the female bosom."

[97] Indian Deer = Wood Caribou (*Rangifer caribou* (Gmel.)).—E. A. P.

[98] *Castor canadensis* Kuhl.

[AZ] The difficulty here alluded to, was the numberless vaults the beaver had in the sides of the pond, and the immense thickness of the house in some parts.

[99] The eight different kinds of beavers referred to by Mr. Dobbs are rather eight different grades of beaver-skins classified on a strictly commercial basis. His statement is:

"There are eight kinds of Beavers received at the Farmer's Office.

"The first is the fat Winter Beaver, kill'd in Winter, which is worth 5s. 6d. per Pound.

"The Second is the fat Summer Beaver, killed in Summer, and is worth 2s. 9d.

"The third the dry Winter Beaver, and fourth the Bordeau, is much the same, and are worth 3s. 6d.

"The fifth the dry Summer Beaver is worth very little, about 1s. 9d. per Pound.

"The sixth is the Coat Beaver, which is worn till it is half greased, and is worth 4s. 6d. per Pound.

"The 7th the Muscovite dry Beaver, of a fine Skin, covered over with a silky Hair; they wear it in Russia, and comb away all the short Down, which they make into Stuffs and other Works, leaving nothing but the silky Hair; this is worth 4s. 6d. per Pound.

"The eighth is the Mittain Beaver, cut out for that Purpose to make Mittains, to preserve them from the Cold, and are greased by being used, and are worth 1s. 9d. per Pound." ("An Account of the Countries adjoining to Hudson's Bay." By Arthur Dobbs, London, 1744, pp. 25-26.)

On a later page, quoting Joseph Lefranc: "The Beavers, he says, are of three Colours; the brown reddish Colour, the black, and the white; the first is the cheapest; the black is most valued by the Company, and in England; the white, tho' most valued in Canada, giving 18 Shillings, when others gave 5 or 6 Shillings, is blown upon by the Company's Factors at the Bay, they not allowing so much for these as for the others; and therefore the Indians use them at home, or burn off the Hair, when they roast the Beavers like Pigs, at an Entertainment when they feast together; he says these Skins are extremely white, and have a fine Lustre, no Snow being whiter, and have a fine long Fur or Hair; he has seen 15 taken of that Colour out of one Lodge or Pond." (Ibid., pp. 39-40.)

White Beavers are not often caught. One skin which I obtained from the vicinity of the Winnipeg River, in Eastern Manitoba, had a decidedly pinkish tint.

[100] As dried Beaver skins weigh on an average from one and a half to two pounds, 300 skins would weigh on an average from 450 to 600 lbs., which is a heavier load than most of the birch-bark canoes made by the Chipewyans will carry in addition to the Indians and their necessary baggage and provisions. Dobbs's statement that 100 Beaver skins is a load for an Indian canoe is more nearly correct.

[BA] The Northern Indians think that the sagacity of the beaver directs them to make that part of their house which fronts the North much thicker than any other part, with a view of defending themselves from the cold winds which generally blow from that quarter during the Winter; and for this reason the Northern Indians generally break open that side of the beaver-houses which exactly front the South.

[BB] This being the largest of the Orkney Islands, is called by the inhabitants the Main Land.

[252]

Transactions and Remarks from our Arrival on the South Side of the Athapuscow Lake, till our Arrival at Prince of Wales's Fort on Churchill River.

Cross the Athapuscow Lake—Description of it and its productions, as far as could be discovered in Winter, when the snow was on the ground—Fish found in the lake—Description of the buffalo;—of the moose or elk, and the method of dressing their skins—Find a woman alone that had not seen a human face for more than seven months—Her account how she came to be in that situation; and her curious method of procuring a livelihood—Many of my Indians wrestled for her—Arrive at the Great Athapuscow River—Walk along the side of the River for several days, and then strike off to the Eastward—Difficulty in getting through the woods in many places—Meet with some strange Northern Indians on their return from the Fort—Meet more strangers, whom my companions plundered, and from whom they took one of their young women—Curious manner of life which those strangers lead, and the reason they gave for roving so far from their usual residence—Leave the fine level country of the Athapuscows, and arrive at the Stony Hills of the Northern Indian Country—Meet some strange Northern Indians, one of whom carried a letter for me to Prince of Wales's Fort, in March one thousand seven hundred and seventy-one, and now gave me an answer to it, dated twentieth of June following—Indians begin preparing wood-work and birch-rind for canoes—The equinoctial gale very severe—Indian method of running the moose deer down by speed of foot—Arrival at Theeleyaza River—See some strangers—The brutality of my companions—A tremendous gale and snow-drift—Meet with more strangers;—Remarks on it—Leave all the elderly people and children, {248} and proceed directly to the Fort—Stop to build canoes, and then advance—Several of the Indians die through hunger, and many others are obliged to decline the journey for want of ammunition—A violent storm and inundation, that forced us to the top of a high hill, where we suffered great distress [253] *for more than two days—Kill several deer—The Indians method of preserving the flesh without the assistance of salt—See several Indians that were going to Knapp's Bay—Game of all kinds remarkably plentiful—Arrive at the Factory.*

1772. January.

9th.

After expending some days in hunting beaver, we proceeded to cross the Athapuscow Lake; but as we had lost much time in hunting deer and beaver, which were very plentiful on some of the islands, it was the ninth of January before we arrived on the South side.

This lake, from the best information which I could get from the natives, is about one hundred and twenty leagues long from East to West, and twenty wide from North to South. The point where we crossed it is said to be the narrowest. It is full of islands; most of which are clothed with fine tall poplars, birch, and pines, and are well stocked with Indian deer. On some of the large islands we also found several beaver; but this must be understood only of such islands as had large ponds in them; for not one beaver-house was to be seen on the margin of any of them.[101]

1772. January.

[254]

The lake is stored with great quantities of very fine fish; particularly between the islands, which in some {249} parts are so close to each other as to form very narrow channels, like little rivers, in which I found (when angling for fish) a considerable current setting to the Eastward.

The fish that are common in this lake, as well as in most of the other lakes in this country, are pike, trout, perch, barble, tittameg, and methy[102]; the two last are names given by the natives to two species of fish which are found only in this country. Besides these, we also caught another kind of fish, which is said by the Northern Indians to be peculiar to this lake; at least none of the same kind have been met with in any other. The body of this fish much resembles a pike in shape; but the scales, which are very large and stiff, are of a beautifully bright silver colour; the mouth is large, and situated like that of a pike; but when open, much resembles that of a sturgeon; and though not provided with any teeth, takes a bait as ravenously as a pike or a trout. The sizes we caught were from two feet long to four feet. Their flesh, though delicately white, is very soft, and has so rank a taste, that many of the Indians, except they are in absolute want, will not eat it. The Northern Indians call this fish Shees.[103] The trout in this lake are of the largest size I ever saw; some that were caught by my companions could not, I think, be less than thirty-five or forty pounds weight. Pike are also of an incredible size in this extensive water; here they are seldom {250} molested, and have multitudes of smaller fish to prey upon. If I say that I have seen some of these fish that were upwards of forty pounds weight, I am sure I do not exceed the truth.

[255]

1772. January.

Immediately on our arrival on the South side of the Athapuscow Lake, the scene was agreeably altered, from an entire jumble of rocks and hills, for such is all the land on the North side, to a fine level country, in which there was not a hill to be seen, or a stone to be found: so that such of my companions as had not brass kettles, loaded their sledges with stones from some of the last islands, to boil their victuals with in their birch-rind kettles, which will not admit of being exposed to the fire. They therefore heat stones and drop them into the water in the kettle to make it boil.

Buffalo,[104] moose, and beaver were very plentiful; and we could discover, in many parts through which we passed, the tracks of martins, foxes, quiquehatches, and other animals of the furr kind: so that they were by no means scarce: but my companions never gave themselves the least trouble to catch any of the three last mentioned animals; for the buffalo, moose, and beaver engaged all their attention; perhaps principally so on account of the excellency of their flesh; whereas the flesh of the fox and quiquehatch are never eaten by those people, except when they are in the greatest distress, and then merely to save {251} life. Their reasons for this shall be given in a subsequent part of my Journal.

> 1772. January.

The buffalo in those parts, I think, are in general much larger than the English black cattle; particularly the bulls, which, though they may not in reality be taller than the largest size of the English oxen, yet to me always appeared to be much larger. In fact, they are so heavy, that when six or eight Indians are in company at the skinning of a large bull, they never attempt to turn it over while entire, but when the upper side is skinned, they cut off the leg and shoulder, rip up the belly, take out all the intestines, cut off the head, and make it as light as possible, before they turn it to skin the under side. The skin is in some places of an incredible thickness, particularly about the neck, where it often exceeds an inch. The horns are short, black, and almost straight, but very thick at the roots or base.

[256]

The head of an old bull is of a great size and weight indeed: some which I have seen were so large, that I could not without difficulty lift them from the ground;[BC] {252} but the heads of the cows are much smaller. Their tails are, in general, about a foot long, though some appear to be, exclusive of the long brush of hair at the end, longer. The hair on the tails of the bulls is generally of a fine glossy black; but the brush at the end of the cows' tails is always of a rusty brown, probably owing to being stained with their urine.

The hair of the body is soft and curled, somewhat approaching to wool; it is generally of a sandy brown, and of an equal length and thickness all over the body: but on the head and neck it is much longer than it is on any other part.

1772. January.

The Indians, after reducing all the parts of the skin to an equal thickness by scraping, dress them in the hair for clothing; when they are light, soft, warm, and durable. They also dress some of those skins into leather without the hair, of which they make tents and shoes; but the grain is remarkably open and spungy, by no means equal in goodness to that of the skin of the moose: nor am I certain that the curriers or tanners in Europe could manufacture these skins in such a manner as to render them of any considerable value; for, to appearance, they are of the same quality with the skins of the musk-ox, which are held in so little estimation in England, that when a number of them was sent home from Churchill Factory, the Company issued out orders the year following, that unless they could be purchased from the Indians at the rate of four {253} skins for one beaver, they would not answer the expence of sending home; a great proof of their being of very little value.

[257]

1772. January.

The buffalos chiefly delight in wide open plains, which in those parts produce very long coarse grass, or rather a kind of small flags and rushes, upon which they feed; but when pursued they always take to the woods. They are of such an amazing strength, that when they fly through the woods from a pursuer, they frequently brush down trees as thick as a man's arm; and be the snow ever so deep, such is their strength and agility that they are enabled to plunge through it faster than the swiftest Indian can run in snow-shoes. To this I have been an eye-witness many times, and once had the vanity to think that I could have kept pace with them; but though I was at that time celebrated for being particularly fleet of foot in snow-shoes, I soon found that I was no match for the buffalos, notwithstanding they were then plunging through such deep snow, that their bellies made a trench in it as large as if many heavy sacks had been hauled through it. Of all the large beasts in those parts the buffalo is easiest to kill, and the moose are the most difficult; neither are the deer very easy to come at, except in windy weather: indeed it requires much practice, and a great deal of patience, to slay any of them, as they will by no means suffer a direct approach, unless the hunter be entirely sheltered by woods or willows. The flesh of the buffalo {254} is exceedingly good eating; and so entirely free from any disagreeable smell or taste, that it resembles beef as nearly as possible: the flesh of the cows, when some time gone with calf, is esteemed the finest; and the young calves, cut out of[258] their bellies, are reckoned a great delicacy indeed. The hunch on their backs, or more properly on their shoulders, is not a large fleshy lump, as some suppose, but is occasioned by the bones that form the withers being continued to a greater length than in most other animals. The flesh which surrounds this part being so equally intermixed with fat and lean, is reckoned among the nicest bits. The weight, however, is by no means equal to what has been commonly reported. The tongue is also very delicate; and what is most extraordinary, when the beasts are in the poorest state, which happens regularly at certain seasons, their tongues are then very fat and fine; some say, fatter than when they are in the best order; the truth of which, I will not confirm. They are so esteemed here, however, that many of them are brought down to the Company's Factory at York as presents, and are esteemed a great luxury, probably for no other reason but that they are far-fetched; for they are by no means so large, and I think them not so fine, as a neat's tongue in England.

The moose[105] deer is also a large beast, often exceeding the largest horse both in height and bulk; but the length of the legs, the bulk of the body, the shortness of the neck, {255} and the uncommon length of the head and ears, without any appearance of a tail, make them have a very awkward appearance. The males far exceed the females in size, and differ from them in colour. The hair of the male, which is long, hollow, and soft, like that of a deer, is at the points nearly black, but a little way under the surface it is of an ash colour, and at the roots perfectly white. The hair of the female is of a sandy brown, and in some parts, particularly under the throat, the belly, and the flank, is nearly white at the surface, and most delicately so at the root.

1772. January.

---

[259]

Their legs are so long, and their necks so short, that they cannot graze on level ground like other animals, but are obliged to brouze on the tops of large plants and the leaves of trees during the Summer; and in Winter they always feed on the tops of willows, and the small branches of the birch-tree; on which account they are never found during that season but in such places as can afford them a plentiful supply of their favourite food: and though they have no fore-teeth in the upper-jaw, yet I have often seen willows and small birch-trees cropped by them, in the same manner as if they had been cut by a gardener's sheers, though some of them were not smaller than common pipe-stems; they seem particularly partial to the red willow.

In Summer they are generally found to frequent the banks of rivers and lakes, probably with no other view {256} than to have the benefit of getting into the water, to avoid the innumerable multitudes of muskettos and other flies that pester them exceedingly during that season. There is also a variety of water-plants, of which the moose are very fond, and which are adapted to their necessities in a peculiar manner during the Summer season, as they can easily brouze on them when nearly emerged in water, to avoid the torment of the flies.

1772. January.

The head of the moose is, as I have observed, remarkably long and large, not very unlike that of a horse; but the nose and nostrils are at least twice as large. The ears are about a foot long, and large; and they always stand erect. Their faculty of hearing is supposed to be more acute than either their sight or scent; which makes it very difficult to kill them, especially as the Indians in those parts have no other method of doing it but by creeping after them, among the trees and bushes, till they get within gun-shot; taking care always to keep to leeward of the moose, for fear of being overheard. In Summer, when they frequent the margins of rivers and lakes, they are often killed by the Indians in the water, while they are crossing rivers, or swimming from the main to islands, &c. When pursued in this manner, they are the[260] most inoffensive of all animals, never making any resistance; and the young ones are so simple, that I remember to have seen an Indian paddle his canoe up to one of them, and take it by the poll without the least opposition: the poor {257} harmless animal seeming at the same time as contented along-side the canoe, as if swimming by the side of its dam, and looking up in our faces with the same fearless innocence that a house-lamb would, making use of its fore-foot almost every instant to clear its eyes of muskettos, which at that time were remarkably numerous.

I have also seen women and boys kill the old moose in this situation, by knocking them on the head with a hatchet; and in the Summer of one thousand seven hundred and seventy-five, when I was on my passage from Cumberland House to York Fort, two boys killed a fine buck moose in the water, by forcing a stick up its fundament; for they had neither gun, bow, nor arrows with them. The common deer are far more dangerous to approach in canoes, as they kick up their hind legs with such violence as to endanger any birch-rind canoe that comes within their reach; for which reason all the Indians who kill deer upon the water are provided with a long stick that will reach far beyond the head of the canoe.

The moose are also the easiest to tame and domesticate of any of the deer kind. I have repeatedly seen them at Churchill as tame as sheep,[BD] and even more so; for they {258} would follow their keeper any distance from home, and at his call return with him, without the least trouble, or ever offering to deviate from the path.[BE]

[261]

1772. January.

The flesh of the moose is very good, though the grain is but coarse, and it is much tougher than any other kind of venison. The nose is most excellent, as is also the tongue, though by no means so fat and delicate as that of the common deer. It is perhaps worth remarking, that the livers of the moose are never found, not even at any time of the year; and, like the other deer, they have no gall. The fat of the intestines is hard, like suet; but all the external fat is soft, like that of a breast of mutton, and when put into a bladder, is as fine as marrow. In this they differ from all the other species of deer, of which the external fat is as hard as that of the kidnies.

{259} The moose in all their actions and attitudes appear very uncouth, and when disturbed, never run, only make a kind of trot, which the length of their legs enables them to do with great swiftness, and apparently with much ease; but were the country they inhabit free from under-wood, and dry underfoot, so that horsemen and dogs might follow them, they would become an easy prey, as they are both tender-footed and short-winded: But of this more hereafter.[BF]

1772. January.
---

[262]

The skins of the moose, when dressed by the natives, make excellent tent-covers and shoe-leather; and in fact every other part of their clothing. These, like the skins of the buffalo, are of very unequal thickness. Some of the Indian women, who are acquainted with the manufacture of them, will, by means of scraping, render them as even as a piece of thick cloth, and when well dressed they are very soft; but not being dressed in oil, they always grow hard after being wet, unless great care be taken to keep rubbing them all the time they are drying. The same may be said of all the Indian-dressed leather, except that of the wewaskish,[106] which will wash as well as shammoy-leather, and always preserve its softness.

{260} The female moose never have any horns, but the males have them of a prodigious size and weight, and very different in shape from those of the common deer. The extremity of each horn is palmated to the size of a common shovel, from which a few short branches shoot out; and the shaft of the horn is frequently as large as a common man's wrist. They shed them annually like the common deer. The horns of the moose are frequently found to exceed sixty pounds weight; and their texture, though of a large size and of such rapid growth, is much harder than any other species of deer-horns in those parts.

Though the flesh of the moose is esteemed by most Indians both for its flavour and substance, yet the Northern Indians of my crew did not reckon either it or the flesh of the buffalo substantial food. This I should think entirely proceeded from prejudice, especially with respect to the moose; but the flesh of the buffalo, though so fine to the eye, and pleasing to the taste, is so light and easy of digestion, as not to be deemed substantial food by any Indian in this country, either Northern or Southern. The moose have from one to three young at a time, and generally bring them forth in the latter end of April, or beginning of May.

1772. January. 11th.

Soon after our arrival on the South-side of Athapuscow Lake, Matonabbee proposed continuing our course in the {261} South West quarter, in hopes of meeting some of the Athapuscow Indians; because I wished, if possible, to purchase a tent, and other ready-dressed skins from them; as a supply of those articles would at this time have been of material service to us, being in great want both of tents and shoe-leather: and though my companions were daily killing either moose or buffalo, the weather was so excessively cold, as to render dressing their skins not only very troublesome, but almost impracticable, especially to the generality of the Northern Indians, who are not well acquainted with the manufacture of that kind of leather.

[263]

To dress those skins according to the Indian method, a lather is made of the brains and some of the softest fat or marrow of the animal, in which the skin is well soaked, when it is taken out, and not only dried by the heat of a fire, but hung up in the smoke for several days; it is then taken down, and well soaked and washed in warm water, till the grain of the skin is perfectly open, and has imbibed a sufficient quantity of water, after which it is taken out and wrung as dry as possible, and then dried by the heat of a slow fire; care being taken to rub and stretch it as long as any moisture remains in the skin. By this simple method, and by scraping them afterwards, some of the moose skins are made very delicate both to the eye and the touch.

> 1772. January.

{262} On the eleventh of January, as some of my companions were hunting, they saw the track of a strange snow-shoe, which they followed; and at a considerable distance came to a little hut, where they discovered a young woman sitting alone. As they found that she understood their language, they brought her with them to the tents. On examination, she proved to be one of the Western Dog-ribbed Indians, who had been taken prisoner by the Athapuscow Indians in the Summer of one thousand seven hundred and seventy; and in the following Summer, when the Indians that took her prisoner were near this part, she had eloped from them, with an intent to return to her own country; but the distance being so great,[264] and having, after she was taken prisoner, been carried in a canoe the whole way, the turnings and windings of the rivers and lakes were so numerous, that she forgot the track; so she built the hut in which we found her, to protect her from the weather during the Winter, and here she had resided from the first setting in of the fall.

From her account of the moons passed since her elopement, it appeared that she had been near seven months without seeing a human face; during all which time she had supported herself very well by snaring partridges, rabbits, and squirrels; she had also killed two or three beaver, and some porcupines. That she did not seem to have been in want is evident, as she had a small stock of {263} provisions by her when she was discovered; and was in good health and condition, and I think one of the finest women, of a real Indian, that I have seen in any part of North America.

> 1772. January.

The methods practised by this poor creature to procure a livelihood were truly admirable, and are great proofs that necessity is the real mother of invention. When the few deer-sinews that she had an opportunity of taking with her were all expended in making snares, and sewing her clothing, she had nothing to supply their place but the sinews of the rabbits legs and feet; these she twisted together for that purpose with great dexterity and success. The rabbits, &c. which she caught in those snares, not only furnished her with a comfortable subsistence, but of the skins she made a suit of neat and warm clothing for the Winter. It is scarcely possible to conceive that a person in her forlorn situation could be so composed as to be capable of contriving or executing any thing that was not absolutely necessary to her existence; but there were sufficient proofs that she had extended her care much farther, as all her clothing, beside being calculated for real service, shewed great taste, and exhibited no little variety of ornament. The materials, though rude, were very curiously wrought, and so judiciously placed, as to make the whole[265] of her garb have a very pleasing, though rather romantic appearance.

{264} Her leisure hours from hunting had been employed in twisting the inner rind or bark of willows into small lines, like net-twine, of which she had some hundred fathoms by her; with this she intended to make a fishing-net as soon as the Spring advanced. It is of the inner bark of willows, twisted in this manner, that the Dog-ribbed Indians make their fishing-nets; and they are much preferable to those made by the Northern Indians.[BG]

Five or six inches of an iron hoop, made into a knife, and the shank of an arrow-head of iron, which served her as an awl, were all the metals this poor woman had with her when she eloped; and with these implements she had made herself complete snow-shoes, and several other useful articles.

Her method of making a fire was equally singular and curious, having no other materials for that purpose than two hard sulphurous stones. These, by long friction and hard knocking, produced a few sparks, which at length communicated to some touchwood; but as this method was attended with great trouble, and not always with success, she did {265} not suffer her fire to go out all the Winter. Hence we may conclude that she had no idea of producing fire by friction, in the manner practised by the Esquimaux, and many other uncivilized nations; because if she had, the above-mentioned precaution would have been unnecessary.

> 1772. January.

The singularity of the circumstance, the comeliness of her person, and her approved accomplishments, occasioned a strong contest between several of the Indians of my party, who should have her for a wife; and the poor girl was actually won and lost at wrestling by near half a score different men the same evening. My guide, Matonabbee, who at that time had no less than seven wives, all women grown, besides a young girl of eleven or twelve years old, would have put in for the prize also, had not one of his wives made him ashamed of it, by telling him that he had already more wives than he could properly attend. This piece of satire, however true, proved fatal to the poor girl who dared to make so open a declaration; for the great man, Matonabbee, who would willingly have been thought equal to eight or ten men in every respect, took it as such an affront, that he fell on her with both hands and feet, and bruised her to such a degree, that after lingering some time she died.

[266]

When the Athapuscow Indians took the above Dog-ribbed Indian woman prisoner, they, according to the universal custom of those savages, surprised her and her party in {266} the night, and killed every soul in the tent, except herself and three other young women. Among those whom they killed, were her father, mother, and husband. Her young child, four or five months old, she concealed in a bundle of clothing, and took with her undiscovered in the night; but when she arrived at the place where the Athapuscow Indians had left their wives (which was not far distant), they began to examine her bundle, and finding the child, one of the women took it from her, and killed it on the spot.

1772. January.

This last piece of barbarity gave her such a disgust to those Indians, that notwithstanding the man who took care of her treated her in every respect as his wife, and was, she said, remarkably kind to, and even fond of her; so far was she from being able to reconcile herself to any of the tribe, that she rather chose to expose herself to misery and want, than live in ease and affluence among persons who had so cruelly murdered her infant.[811] The {267} poor woman's relation of this shocking story, which she delivered in a very affecting manner, only excited laughter among the savages of my party.

[267]

In a conversation with this woman soon afterward, she told us, that her country lies so far to the Westward, that she had never seen iron, or any other kind of metal, till she was taken prisoner. All of her tribe, she observed, made their hatchets and ice-chisels of deer's horns, and their knives of stones and bones; that their arrows were shod with a kind of slate, bones, and deer's horns; and the instruments which they employed to make their wood-work were nothing but beavers' teeth. Though they had frequently heard of the useful materials which the nations or tribes to the East of them were supplied with from the English, so far were they from drawing nearer, to be in the way of trading for iron-work, &c. that they were obliged to retreat farther back, to avoid the Athapuscow Indians, who made surprising slaughter among them, both in Winter and Summer.

16th.

1772. January.

On the sixteenth, as we were continuing our course in the South West quarter, we arrived at the grand {268} Athapuscow River,[107] which at that part is about two miles wide, and empties itself into the great lake of the same name we had so lately crossed, and which has been already described.

[268]

The woods about this river, particularly the pines and poplars, are the tallest and stoutest I have seen in any part of North America. The birch also grows to a considerable size, and some species of the willow are likewise tall: but none of them have any trunk, like those in England.

The bank of the river in most parts is very high, and in some places not less than a hundred feet above the ordinary surface of the water. As the soil is of a loamy quality, it is very subject to moulder or wash away by heavy rains, even during the short Summer allotted to this part of the globe. The breaking up of the ice in the Spring is annually attended with a great deluge, when, I am told, it is not uncommon to see whole points of land washed away by the inundations; and as the wood grows close to the edge of the banks, vast quantities of it are hurried down the stream by the irresistible force of the water and ice, and conveyed into the great lake already mentioned; on the shores and islands of which, there lies the greatest quantity of drift wood I ever saw. Some of this wood is large enough to make masts for the largest ships that are built. The banks of the river in general are so steep as to be inaccessible to either man or beast, except in some slacks, or gulleys, that have been wore down by heavy rains, {269} backwaters, or deluges; and even those slacks are, for the most part, very difficult to ascend, on account of the number of large trees which lie in the way.

There are several low islands in this river, which are much frequented by the moose, for the sake of the fine willows they produce, which furnish them with a plentiful supply of their favourite food during the Winter. Some of those islands are also frequented by a number of rabbits; but as larger game could be procured in great plenty, those small animals were not deemed worthy our notice at present.

1772. January.

Beside the grand river already mentioned, there are several[269] others of less note, which empty themselves into the great Athapuscow Lake: There are also several small rivers and creeks on the North East side of the Lake that carry off the superfluous waters, some of which, after a variety of windings through the barren grounds to the North of Churchill River, are lost in the marshes and low grounds, while others, by means of many small channels and rivulets, are discharged into other rivers and lakes, and at last, doubtless, find their way into Hudson's Bay. These rivers, though numberless, are all so full of shoals and stones, as not to be navigable for an Indian canoe to any considerable distance; and if they were, it would be of little or no use to the natives, as none of them lead within several hundred miles of Churchill River.

{270} Agreeably to Matonabbee's proposal, we continued our course up the Athapuscow River for many days, and though we passed several parts which we well knew to have been the former Winter-haunts of the Athapuscow Indians, yet we could not see the least trace of any of them having been there that season. In the preceding Summer, when they were in those parts, they had set fire to the woods; and though many months had elapsed from that time till our arrival there, and notwithstanding the snow was then very deep, the moss was still burning in many places, which at first deceived us very much, as we took it for the smoke of strange tents; but after going much out of our way, and searching very diligently, we could not discover the least track of a stranger.

27th.

Thus disappointed in our expectations of meeting the Southern Indians, it was resolved (in Council, as it may be called) to expend as much time in hunting buffalo, moose, and beaver as we could, so that we might be able to reach Prince of Wales's Fort a little before the usual time of the ships arrival from England. Accordingly, after having walked upwards of forty miles by the side of Athapuscow River, on the twenty-seventh of January we struck off to the Eastward,[270] and left the River at that part where it begins to tend due South.

1772. January.

In consequence of this determination of the Indians, we continued our course to the Eastward; but as game of all kinds was very plentiful, we made but short days {271} journies, and often remained two or three days in one place, to eat up the spoils or produce of the chace. The woods through which we were to pass were in many places so thick, that it was necessary to cut a path before the women could pass with their sledges; and in other places so much of the woods had formerly been set on fire and burnt, that we were frequently obliged to walk farther than we otherwise should have done, before we could find green brush enough to floor our tents.

> **February. 15th-24th.**

From the fifteenth to the twenty-fourth of February, we walked along a small river that empties itself into the Lake Clowey,[108] near the part where we built canoes in May one thousand seven hundred and seventy-one. This little river is that which we mentioned in the former part of this Journal, as having communication with the Athapuscow Lake: but, from appearances, it is of no consequence whence it takes its rise, or where it empties itself, as one half of it is nearly dry three-fourths of the year. The intervening ponds, however, having sufficient depth of water, are, we may suppose, favourable situations for beaver, as many of their houses are to be found in those parts.

> **24th.**

> **1772. February.**

On the twenty-fourth, a strange Northern Indian leader, called Thlew-sa-nell-ie, and several of his followers, joined us from the Eastward. This leader presented Matonabbee and myself with a foot of tobacco each, and a two-quart {272} keg of brandy, which he intended as a present for the Southern Indians; but being informed by my companions, that there was not the least probability of meeting any, he did not think it worth any farther carriage. The tobacco was indeed very acceptable, as our stock of that article had been expended some time. Having been so long without tasting spirituous liquors, I would not partake of the brandy, but left it entirely to the Indians, to whom, as they were numerous, it was scarcely a taste for each. Few of the Northern Indians are fond of spirits, especially those who keep at a distance from the Fort: some who are near, and who usually shoot geese for us in the Spring, will drink it at free cost as fast as the Southern Indians, but few of them are ever so imprudent as to buy it.

[271]

The little river lately mentioned, as well as the adjacent lakes and ponds, being well-stocked with beaver, and the land abounding with moose and buffalo, we were induced to make but slow progress in our journey. Many days were spent in hunting, feasting, and drying a large quantity of flesh to take with us, particularly that of the buffalo; for my companions knew by experience, that a few days walk to the Eastward of our present situation would bring us to a part where we should not see any of those animals.

The strangers who had joined us on the twenty-fourth informed us, that all were well at Prince of Wales's Fort {273} when they left it last; which, according to their account of the Moons past since, must have been about the fifth of November one thousand seven hundred and seventy-one. These strangers only remained in our company one night before the Leader and part of his crew left us, and proceeded on their journey to the North Westward; but a few of them having procured some furrs in the early part of the Winter, joined our party, with an intent to accompany us to the Factory.

28th.

Having a good stock of dried meat, fat, &c. prepared in the best manner for carriage, on the twenty-eighth we shaped[272] our course in the South East quarter, and proceeded at a much greater rate than we had lately done, as little or no time was now lost in hunting. The next day we saw the tracks of some strangers; and though I did not perceive any of them myself, some of my companions were at the trouble of searching for them, and finding them to be poor inoffensive people, plundered them not only of the few furrs which they had, but took also one of their young women from them.

Every additional act of violence committed by my companions on the poor and distressed, served to increase my indignation and dislike; this last act, however, displeased me more than all their former actions, because it was committed on a set of harmless creatures, whose general manner of life renders them the most secluded from society of any of the human race.

{274} Matonabbee assured me, that for more than a generation past one family only, as it may be called, (and to which the young men belonged who were plundered by my companions,) have taken up their Winter abode in those woods,[109] which are situated so far on the barren ground as to be quite out of the track of any other Indians. From the best accounts that I could collect, the latitude of this place must be about 63½° or 63° at least; the longitude is very uncertain. From my own experience I can affirm, that it is some hundreds of miles both from the sea-side and the main woods to the Westward. Few of the trading Northern Indians have visited this place; but those who have, give a pleasing description of it, all agreeing that it is situated on the banks of a river which has communication with several fine lakes. As the current sets to the North Eastward, it empties itself, in all probability, into some part of Hudson's Bay;

and, from the latitude, no part seems more likely for this communication, than Baker's Lake, at the head of Chesterfield's inlet. This, however, is mere conjecture; nor is it of any consequence, as navigation on any of the rivers in those parts is not only impracticable, but would be also unprofitable, as they do not lead into a country that produces any thing for trade, or that contains any inhabitants worth visiting.

[273]

The accounts given of this place, and the manner of life of its inhabitants, would, if related at full length, fill a volume: let it suffice to observe, that the situation {275} is said to be remarkably favourable for every kind of game that the barren ground produces at the different seasons of the year; but the continuance of the game with them is in general uncertain, except that of fish and partridges. That being the case, the few who compose this little commonwealth, are, by long custom and the constant example of their forefathers, possessed of a provident turn of mind, with a degree of frugality unknown to every other tribe of Indians in this country except the Esquimaux.

> 1772. February.

Deer is said to visit this part of the country in astonishing numbers, both in Spring and Autumn, of which circumstances the inhabitants avail themselves, by killing and drying as much of their flesh as possible, particularly in the fall of[274] the year; so that they seldom are in want of a good Winter's stock.

Geese, ducks, and swans visit here in great plenty during their migrations both in the Spring and Fall, and by much art, joined to an insurmountable patience, are caught in considerable numbers in snares,[B1] and, {276} without doubt, make a very pleasing change in the food. It is also reported, (though I confess I doubt the truth of it,) {277} that a remarkable species of partridges as large as English fowls, are found in that part of the country only. Those, as well as the common partridges, it is said, are killed in considerable numbers, with snares, as well as with bows and arrows.

1772. February.

The river and lakes near the little forest where the family above mentioned had fixed their abode, abound with fine fish, particularly trout and barble, which are easily caught; the former with hooks, and the latter in nets. In fact, I have not seen or heard of any part of this country which seems to possess half the advantages requisite for a constant residence, that are ascribed to this little spot. The descendents, however, of the present inhabitants must in time evacuate it for want of wood, which is of so slow a growth in those regions, that what is used in one year, exclusive of what is cut down and carried away by the Esquimaux, must cost many years to replace.

[275]

1772. March.

It may probably be thought strange that any part of a community, apparently so commodiously situated, and happy within themselves, should be found at so great a distance from the rest of their tribe, and indeed nothing but necessity could possibly have urged them to undertake a journey of so many hundred miles as they have done; but no situation is without its inconveniences, and as their woods contain no birch-trees of sufficient size, or perhaps none of any size, this party had come so far to the {278} Westward to procure birch-rind for making two canoes, and some of the fungus that grows on the outside of the birch-tree, which is used by all the Indians in those parts for tinder. There are two sorts of these funguses which grow on the birch-trees; one is hard, the useful part of which much resembles rhubarb; the other is soft and smooth like velvet on the outside, and when laid on hot ashes for some time, and[276] well beaten between two stones, is something like spunk. The former is called by the Northern Indians Jolt-thee, and is known all over the country bordering on Hudson's Bay by the name of Pesogan,[BJ] it being so called by the Southern {279} Indians. The latter is only used by the Northern tribes, and is called by them Clalte-ad-dee.

> 1st.

By the first of March we began to leave the fine level country of the Athapuscows, and again to approach the stony mountains or hills which bound the Northern Indian country. Moose and beaver still continued to be plentiful; but no buffaloes could be seen after the twenty-ninth of February.

> 14th.

> 1772. March.

As we were continuing our course to the East South East, on the fourteenth we discovered the tracks of more strangers, and the next day came up with them. Among those Indians was the man who had carried a letter for me in March one thousand seven hundred and seventy-one, to the Chief at Prince of Wales's Fort, and to which he had brought an answer, dated the twenty-first of June. When this Indian received the letter from me, it was very uncertain what route we should take in our return from the Copper River, and, in all probability, he himself had not then determined on what spot he would pass the present Winter; consequently our meeting each other was merely accidental.

[277]

These Indians having obtained a few furrs in the course of the Winter, joined our party, which now consisted of twenty tents, containing in the whole about two {280} hundred persons; and indeed our company had not been much less during the whole Winter.

From the strangers who last joined us we received some ready-dressed moose-skins for tenting and shoe-leather; also some other skins for clothing, for all of which the Chief at the Factory was to pay on our arrival.

I cannot sufficiently lament the loss of my quadrant, as the want of it must render the course of my journey from Point Lake, where it was broken, very uncertain; and my watch stopping while I was at the Athapuscow Lake, has contributed greatly to the misfortune, as I am now deprived of every means of estimating the distances which we walked with any degree of accuracy, particularly in thick weather, when the Sun could not be seen.

16th.

1772. March.

The Indians were employed at all convenient times in procuring birch-rind and making wood-work ready for building canoes; also in preparing small staffs of birch-wood, to take with them on the barren ground, to serve as tent-poles all the Summer; and which, as hath been already observed, they convert into snow-shoe frames when the Winter sets in. Here it may be proper to observe, that none of those incidental avocations interfere with, or retard the Indians in their journey; for they always take the advantage of every {281} opportunity which offers, as they pass along, and when they see a tree fit for their purpose, cut it down, and either strip off the bark, if that be what they want, or split the trunk in pieces; and after hewing it roughly with their hatchet, carry it to the tent,[278] where in the evenings, or in the morning before they set out, they reduce it with their knives to the shape and size which is required.

> 19th.

Provisions being plentiful, and the weather fine, we advanced a little each day; and on the nineteenth took up our lodgings by the side of Wholdyeah-chuck'd Whoie, or Large Pike Lake. In our way we crossed another small lake, where we caught some trout by angling, and killed a few deer and one moose.

> 20th.

On the twentieth we crossed Large Pike Lake, which at that part was not more than seven miles wide; but from North North West to the South South East is much longer. The next day we arrived at Bedodid Lake,[1111] which in general is not more than three miles wide, and in several places much less; but it is upward of forty miles long, which gives it the appearance of a river. It is said by the Indians to be shut up on all sides, and entirely surrounded with high land, which produces vast quantity of fir trees, but none of them grow to a great height in those parts: their branches, however, spread wider than those of firs of three times their height and thickness do in Europe; so that they resemble an apple-tree in shape, {282} more than any species of the pine. They seem rich in tar, as the wood of them will burn like a candle, and emit as strong a smell, and as much black smoke, as the staves of an old tar-barrel; for which reason no Indians chuse to burn it in their tents, or even out of doors, for the purpose of cooking their victuals.

> 1772. March.

[279]

The thaws began now to be very considerable, and the under-woods were so thick in these parts as to render travelling through them very difficult; we therefore took the advantage of walking on the ice of the above-mentioned Lake, which lay nearly in the direction of our course; but after proceeding about twenty-two miles on it, the Lake turned more toward the North, on which account we were obliged to leave it, striking off to the Eastward; and after walking fourteen miles farther, we arrived at Noo-shetht Whoie,[112] or the Hill-Island Lake, so called from a very high island which stands in it.

> 31st.

From the twenty-eighth to the thirty-first of March, we had so hard a gale of wind from the South, as to render walking on lakes or open plains quite impossible, and the violence with which the trees were blown down made walking in the woods somewhat dangerous; but though several had narrow escapes, no accident happened.

> April. 1st.

> 1772. April.

From the middle to the latter end of March, and in the beginning of April, though the thaw was not general, {283} yet in the middle of the day it was very considerable: it commonly froze hard in the nights; and the young men took the advantage of the mornings, when the snow was hard crusted over, and ran down many moose; for in those situations a man with a good pair of snow-shoes will scarcely make any impression on the snow, while the moose, and even the deer, will break through it at every step up to the belly. Notwithstanding this, however, it is very seldom that the Indians attempt to run deer down. The moose are so tender-footed, and so short-winded, that a good runner will generally tire them in less than a day, and very frequently in six or eight hours; though I have known some of the Indians continue the chace for two days, before they could come up with, and kill the game. On those occasions the Indians, in general, only take with them a knife or bayonet, and a little bag containing a set of fire-tackle, and are as lightly clothed as possible; some of them will carry a bow and two or three arrows, but I never knew any of them take a gun unless such as had been blown or bursted, and the barrels cut quite short, which, when reduced to the least possible size to be capable of doing any service, must be too great a weight for a man to run with in his hand for so many hours together.

[280]

When the poor moose are incapable of making farther speed, they stand and keep their pursuers at bay with {284} their head and fore-feet; in the use of which they are very dexterous, especially the latter; so that the Indians who have neither a bow nor arrows, nor a short gun, with them, are generally obliged to lash their knives or bayonets to the end of a long stick, and stab the moose at a distance. For want of this necessary precaution, some of the boys and fool-hardy young men, who have attempted to rush in upon them, have frequently received such unlucky blows from their fore-feet, as to render their recovery very doubtful.

The flesh of the moose, thus killed, is far from being well-tasted, and I should think must be very unwholesome, from being over-heated; as by running so many hours together, the animal must have been in a violent fever; the flesh being soft and clammy, must have a very disagreeable taste, neither resembling fish, flesh, nor fowl.[BK]

The Southern Indians use dogs for this kind of hunting, which makes it easier and more expeditious; but the Northern tribes having no dogs trained to that exercise, are under the necessity of doing it themselves.

[281]

1772. April. 7th.

{285} On the seventh we crossed a part of Thee-lee-aza River: at which time the small Northern deer were remarkably plentiful, but the moose began to be very scarce, as none were killed after the third.

> 12th.

On the twelfth, we saw several swans flying to the Northward; they were the first birds of passage we had seen that Spring, except a few snow-birds, which always precede the migrating birds, and consequently are with much propriety called the harbingers of Spring. The swans also precede all the other species of water-fowl, and migrate so early in the season, that they find no open water but at the falls of rivers, where they are readily met, and sometimes shot, in considerable numbers.

> 14th.

On the fourteenth, we arrived at another part of Thee-lee-aza River,[113] and pitched our tents not far from some families of strange Northern Indians, who had been there some time snaring deer, and who were all so poor as not to have one gun among them.

> 1772. April.

The villains belonging to my crew were so far from administering to their relief, that they robbed them of almost every useful article in their possession; and to complete their cruelty, the men joined themselves in parties of six, eight, or ten in a gang, and dragged several of their young women to a little distance from their tents, {286} where they not only ravished them, but otherwise ill-treated them, and that in so barbarous a manner, as to endanger the lives of one or two of them. Humanity on this, as well as on several other similar occasions during my residence among those wretches, prompted me to upbraid them with their barbarity; but so far were my remonstrances from having the desired effect, that they afterwards made no scruple of telling me in the plainest terms, that if any female relation of mine had been there, she should have been served in the same manner.

[282]

Deer being plentiful, we remained at this place ten days, in order to dry and prepare a quantity of the flesh and fat to carry with us; as this was the last time the Indians expected to see such plenty until they met them again on the barren ground. During our stay here, the Indians completed the wood-work for their canoes, and procured all their Summer tent-poles, &c.; and while we were employed in this necessary business, the thaw was so great that the bare ground began to appear in many places, and the ice in the rivers, where the water was shallow and the current rapid, began to break up; so that we were in daily expectation of seeing geese, ducks, and other birds of passage.

> 25th.

On the twenty-fifth, the weather being cool and favourable for travelling, we once more set out, and that {287} day walked twenty miles to the Eastward; as some of the women had not joined us, we did not move on the two following days.

> 28th.

On the twenty-eighth, having once more mustered all our forces, early in the morning we set out, and the next day passed by Thleweyaza Yeth,[114] the place at which we had prepared wood-work for canoes in the Spring one thousand seven hundred and seventy-one.

> May. 1st.

> 1772. May.

As the morning of the first of May was exceedingly fine and pleasant, with a light air from the South, and a great thaw, we walked eight or nine miles to the East by North, when a heavy fall of snow came on, which was followed, or indeed more properly accompanied, by a hard gale of wind from the North West. At the time the bad weather began, we were on the top of a high barren hill, a considerable distance from any woods; judging it to be no more than a squall, we sat down, in expectation of its soon passing by. As the night, however, advanced, the gale increased to such a degree, that it was impossible for a man to stand upright; so that we were obliged to lie down, without any other defence against the weather, than putting our sledges and other lumber to windward of us, which in reality was of no real service, as it only harboured a great drift of snow, with which in some places we were covered to the depth of two or three feet; and as the night was not very cold, I found myself, {288} and many others who were with me, long before morning in a puddle of water, occasioned by the heat of our bodies melting the snow.

[283]

2d.

3d.

The second proved fine pleasant weather, with warm sunshine. In the morning, having dried all our clothing, we proceeded on our journey. In the afternoon we arrived at the part at which my guide intended we should build our canoes; but having had some difference with his countrymen, he altered his mind, and determined to proceed to the Eastward, as long as the season would permit, before he attempted to perform that duty. Accordingly, on the third, we pursued our way, and as that and the following day were very cold, which made us walk briskly, we were enabled to make good days' journies; but the fifth was so hot and sultry, that we only walked about thirteen miles in our old course to the East by North, and then halted about three-quarters of a mile to the South of Black Bear Hill;[115] a place which I had seen in the Spring of one thousand seven hundred and seventy-one.

> 6th.

[284]

On the sixth, the weather was equally hot with the preceding day; in the morning, however, we moved on eleven miles to the East, and then met several strange Indians, who informed us that a few others, who had a tolerable cargo of furrs, and were going to the Factory that Summer, were not far distant.

> 1772. May.

{289} On receiving this intelligence, my guide, Matonabbee, sent a messenger to desire their company. This was soon complied with, as it is an universal practice with the Indian Leaders, both Northern and Southern, when going to the Company's Factory, to use their influence and interest in canvassing for companions; as they find by experience that a large gang gains them much respect. Indeed, the generality of Europeans who reside in those parts, being utterly unacquainted with the manners and customs of the Indians, have conceived so high an opinion of those Leaders, and their authority, as to imagine that all who accompany them on those occasions are entirely devoted to their service and command all the year; but this is so far from being the case, that the authority of those great men, when absent from the Company's Factory, never extends beyond their own family; and the trifling respect which is shown them by their countrymen during their residence at the Factory, proceeds only from motives of interest.

> 1772. May.

The Leaders have a very disagreeable task to perform on those occasions; for they are not only obliged to be the mouthpiece, but the beggars for all their friends and relations for whom they have a regard, as well as for those whom at other times they have reason to fear. Those unwelcome commissions, which are imposed on them by their followers, joined to their own desire of being thought men of great consequence and interest with the English, {290} make them very troublesome. And if a Governor deny them any thing which they ask, though it be only to give away to the most worthless of their gang, they immediately turn sulky and impertinent to the highest degree; and however rational they may be at other[285] times, are immediately divested of every degree of reason, and raise their demands to so exorbitant a pitch, that after they have received to the amount of five times the value of all the furrs they themselves have brought, they never cease begging during their stay at the Factory; and, after all, few of them go away thoroughly satisfied.[BL]

| 1772. May. 11th. |

{291} After stopping four days at this place, Matonabbee, and all the Indians who were to accompany me to the Fort, agreed to leave the elderly people and young children here, in the care of some Indians who were capable of providing for them, and who had orders to proceed to a place called Cathawhachaga, on the barren grounds, and there wait the return of their relations from the Factory. Matters of this kind being settled, apparently to the entire satisfaction of all parties, we resumed our journey on the eleventh of May, and that at a much brisker pace than we could probably have done when all the old people and young children were with us. In the afternoon of the same day we met some other Northern Indians, who were also going to the Fort with furrs; those joined our party, and at night we all pitched our tents by the side of a river that empties itself into Doobaunt Lake. This day all of us threw away our snow-shoes, as the ground was so bare in most places as not to require any such assistance; but sledges were occasionally serviceable for some time, particularly when we walked on the ice of rivers or lakes.

[286]

12th.

18th.

{292} The weather on the twelfth was so exceedingly hot and sultry, and the water so deep on the top of the ice of the above-mentioned river, as to render walking on it not only very troublesome, but dangerous; so after advancing about five miles we pitched our tents, and the warm weather being likely to continue, the Indians immediately began to build their canoes, which were completed with such expedition, that in the afternoon of the eighteenth we again set forward on our journey, but the day being pretty far spent, we only walked about four miles, and put up for the night.

19th.

1772. May.

The morning of the nineteenth was fine pleasant weather; and as all the water was drained off from the top of the ice, it rendered walking on it both safe and easy; accordingly we set out pretty early, and that day walked upwards of twenty miles to the East North East on the above-mentioned river.[110] The next day proved so cold, that after walking about fifteen miles, we were obliged to put up; for having left Doo-baunt River, we were frequently obliged to wade above the knees through swamps of mud, water, and wet snow; which froze to our stockings and shoes in such a thick crust, as not only rendered walking very laborious, but at the same time subjected us to the danger of having our legs and feet frozen.

[287]

21st.

The weather on the twenty-first was more severe than on the preceding day; but the swamps and ponds being {293} by that time frozen over, it was tolerable walking: we proceeded therefore on our journey, but the wind blew so fresh, that we had not walked sixteen miles, before we found that those who carried the canoes could not possibly keep up with us, so that we put up for the night. In the course of this day's journey we crossed the North West Bay of Wholdyah'd Lake; which, at that part, is called by the Northern Indians A Naw-nee-tha'd Whoie.[117] This day several of the Indians turned back, not being able to proceed for want of provisions. Game of all kinds indeed were so scarce, that, except a few geese, nothing had been killed by any of our party, from our leaving the women and children on the eleventh instant, nor had we seen one deer the whole way.

22d.

The twenty-second proved more moderate, when all our party having joined, we again advanced to the North East, and after walking about thirteen miles, the Indians killed four deer. Our number, however, had now so increased, that four small Northern deer would scarcely afford us all a single meal.

23d.

25th.

1772. May.

[288]

The next day we continued our journey, generally walking in the North East quarter; and on the twenty-fifth, crossed the North bay of They-hole-kye'd Whoie, or Snow-bird Lake; and at night got clear of all woods, and lay on the barren ground. The same day several of the Indians struck off another way, not being able to {294} proceed to the Fort for want of ammunition. As we had for some days past made good journies, and at the same time were all heavy-laden, and in great distress for provisions, some of my companions were so weak as to be obliged to leave their bundles of furrs;[BM] and many others were so reduced as to be no longer capable of proceeding with us, having neither guns nor ammunition; so that their whole dependence for support was on the fish they might be able to catch; and though fish was pretty plentiful in most of the rivers and lakes hereabout, yet they were not always to be depended on for such an immediate supply of food as those poor people required.

Though I had at this time a sufficient stock of ammunition to serve me and all my proper companions to the Fort, yet self-preservation being the first law of Nature, it was thought advisable to reserve the greatest part of it for our own use; especially as geese and other smaller birds were the only game now to be met with, and which, in times of scarcity, bears hard on the articles of powder and shot. Indeed most of the Indians who actually accompanied me the whole way to the Factory had some little ammunition remaining, which enabled them to travel in times of real scarcity better than those whom we left behind; and though {295} we assisted many of them, yet several of their women died for want. It is a melancholy truth, and a disgrace to the little humanity of which those people are possessed, to think, that in times of want the poor women always come off short; and when real distress approaches, many of them are permitted to starve, when the males are amply provided for.

Photo: J. B. Tyrrell, December 5, 1894.

WOODS OF SPRUCE AND LARCH, SOUTH-WEST OF CHURCHILL

Photo: J. B. Tyrrell, August 2, 1893.
STONY SURFACE OF BARREN LANDS BESIDE DUBAWNT RIVER

[289]

> 1772. May. 26th.

The twenty-sixth was fine and pleasant. In the morning we set out as usual, and after walking about five miles, the Indians killed three deer; as our numbers were greatly lessened, these served us for two or three meals, at a small expence of ammunition.

> 30th.

> June. 3d.

In continuing our course to the Eastward, we crossed Cathawhachaga River, on the thirtieth of May,[118] on the ice, which broke up soon after the last person had crossed it. We had not been long on the East side of the river before we perceived bad weather near at hand, and began to make every preparation for it which our situation would admit, and that was but very indifferent, being on entire barren ground. It is true, we had complete sets of Summer tent-poles, and such tent-cloths as are generally used by the Northern Indians in that season; these were arranged in the best manner, and in such places as were most likely to afford us shelter from the threatening storm. The rain soon began to descend in such torrents as to make the river overflow to such a degree as soon to convert our first {296} place of retreat into an open sea, and oblige us in the middle of the night to assemble at the top of an adjacent hill, where the violence of the wind would not permit us to pitch a tent; so that the only shelter we could obtain was to take the tent-cloth about our shoulders, and sit with our backs to the wind; and in this situation we were obliged to remain without the least refreshment, till the morning of the third of June: in the course of which time the wind shifted all round the compass, but the bad weather still continued, so that we were constantly obliged to shift our position as the wind changed.

[290]

> 1772. June.

The weather now became more moderate, though there was still a fresh gale from the North West, with hard frost and frequent showers of snow. Early in the morning, however, we proceeded on our journey, but the wet and cold I had experienced the two preceding days so benumbed my lower extremities, as to render walking for some time very troublesome. In the course of this day's journey we saw great numbers of geese flying to the Southward, a few of which we killed; but these were very disproportionate to the number of mouths we had to feed, and to make up for our long fasting.

> 8th.

> 1772. June.

From that time to the eighth we killed every day as many geese as were sufficient to preserve life; but on that day we perceived plenty of deer, five of which the Indians killed, which put us all into good spirits, and the {297} number of deer we then saw afforded great hopes of more plentiful times during the remainder of our journey.

It is almost needless to add, that people in our distressed situation expended a little time in eating, and slicing some of the flesh ready for drying; but the drying it occasioned no delay, as we fastened it on the tops of the women's bundles, and dried it by the sun and wind while we were walking; and, strange as it may appear, meat thus prepared is not only very substantial food, but pleasant to the taste, and generally much esteemed by the natives. For my own part I must acknowledge, that it was not only agreeable to my palate, but after eating a meal of it, I have always found that I could travel longer without victuals, than after any other kind of food. All the dried meat prepared by the Southern Indians is performed by exposing it to the heat of a large fire, which soon exhausts all the fine juices from it, and when sufficiently dry to prevent putrefaction, is no more to be compared with that cured by the Northern Indians in the Sun, or by the heat of a very slow fire, than meat that has been boiled down for the sake of the soup, is to that which is only sufficiently boiled for eating: the latter has all the juices remaining, which, being easily dissolved[291] by the heat and moisture of the stomach, proves a strong and nourishing food; whereas the former being entirely deprived of those qualities, can by no means have an equal claim to that character. Most of the Europeans, however, are fonder of it than they are of that cured by the {298} Northern Indians. The same may be said to the lean parts of the beast, which are first dried, and then reduced into a kind of powder. That done by the Northern Indians is entirely free from smoke, and quite soft and mellow in the mouth: whereas that which is prepared by the Southern tribes is generally as bitter as soot with smoke, and is as hard as the scraps of horn, &c. which are burnt to make hardening for the cutlers. I never knew, that any European was so fond of this as they are of that made by the Northern Indians.

9th.

On the ninth, as we were continuing our course to the Factory, which then lay in the South East quarter, we saw several smokes to the North East, and the same day spoke with many Northern Indians, who were going to Knapp's Bay to meet the Churchill sloop. Several of those Indians had furrs with them, but having some time before taken up goods on trust at Prince of Wales's Fort, were taking that method to delay the payment of them. Defrauds of this kind have been practised by many of those people with great success, ever since the furr-trade has been established with the Northern Indians at Knapp's Bay; by which means debts to a considerable amount are annually lost to the Company, as well as their Governor in the Bay.

Being desirous of improving every opportunity that the fine weather afforded, we did not lose much time in conversation with those Indians, but proceeded on our course {299} to the South East, while they continued theirs to the North East.

> 1772. June.

For many days after leaving those people, we had the good fortune to meet with plenty of provisions; and as the weather was for a long time remarkably fine and pleasant, our circumstances were altered so much for the better, that[292] every thing seemed to contribute to our happiness, as if desirous to make some amends for the severe hunger, cold, and excessive hardships that we had suffered long before, and which had reduced us to the greatest misery and want.

Deer was so plentiful a great part of the way, that the Indians killed as many as were wanted, without going out of their road; and every lake and river to which we came seemed willing to give us a change of diet, by affording us plenty of the finest fish, which we caught either with hooks or nets. Geese, partridges, gulls, and many other fowls, which are excellent eating, were also in such plenty, that it only required ammunition, in skilful hands, to have procured as many of them as we could desire.

The only inconvenience we now felt was from frequent showers of heavy rain; but the intervals between these showers being very warm, and the Sun shining bright, that difficulty was easily overcome, especially as the belly was plentifully supplied with excellent victuals. Indeed the {300} very thoughts of being once more arrived so near home, made me capable of encountering every difficulty, even if it had been hunger itself in the most formidable shape.

> 18th.

On the eighteenth, we arrived at Egg River, from which place, at the solicitation of my guide Matonabbee, I sent a letter post-haste to the Chief at Prince of Wales's Fort, advising him of my being so far advanced on my return. The weather at this time was very bad and rainy, which caused us to lose near a whole day; but upon the fine weather returning, we again proceeded at our usual rate of eighteen or twenty miles a day, sometimes more or less, according as the road, the weather, and other circumstances, would admit.[119]

[293]

> 1772. June.

Deer now began to be not quite so plentiful as they had been, though we met with enough for present use, which was all we wanted, each person having as much dried meat as he could conveniently carry, besides his furrs and other necessary baggage.

> 26th.

> 1772. June.

> 29th.

Early in the morning of the twenty-sixth we arrived at Seal River;[BN] but the wind blowing right up it, made {301} so great a sea, that we were obliged to wait near ten hours before we could venture to cross it in our little canoes. {302} In the afternoon the weather grew more moderate, so that we were enabled to ferry over the river; after which we resumed our journey, and at night pitched our tents in some tufts of willows in sight of the woods of Po-co-thee-kis-co River, at which we arrived early in the morning of the twenty-eighth; but the wind again blowing very hard in the North East quarter, it was the afternoon of the twenty-ninth before we could attempt to cross it.

[294]

1772. June.

Just at the time we were crossing the South branch of Po-co-thee-kis-co River, the Indians that were sent from Egg River with a letter to the Chief at Churchill, joined us on their return, and brought a little tobacco and some other articles which I had desired. Though it was late in the afternoon before we had all crossed the river, yet we walked that evening till after ten o'clock, and then put up on one of the Goose-hunting Islands, as they are generally called, about ten miles from the Factory. The next morning I arrived in good health at Prince of Wales's Fort, after having been absent eighteen months and twenty-three {303} days on this last expedition; but from my first setting out with Captain Chawchinaha, it was two years seven months and twenty-four days.

[295]

Though my discoveries are not likely to prove of any material advantage to the Nation at large, or indeed to the Hudson's Bay Company, yet I have the pleasure to think that I have fully complied with the orders of my Masters, and that it has put a final end to all disputes concerning a North West Passage through Hudson's Bay. It will also wipe off, in some measure, the ill-grounded and unjust aspersions of Dobbs, Ellis, Robson, and the American Traveller; who have all taken much pains to condemn the conduct of the Hudson's Bay Company, as being averse from discoveries, and from enlarging their trade.[121] [296]

Photo: J. B. Tyrrell, August 10, 1894.
TWO CHIPEWYAN INDIANS FROM KAZAN RIVER

Photo: J. B. Tyrrell, August 1, 1894.
VALLEY OF THLEWIAZA RIVER

FOOTNOTES:

[101] Great Slave Lake is 288 miles long from east to west, very irregular in width, and its area is about 10,400 square miles, being the fifth in size among the great lakes of America. However, no reasonably complete survey has yet been made of it. The place where he crossed it from north to south is on the regular Indian route through the Simpson Islands. A fish peculiar to this lake is the inconnu (see p. 254, note 103), which does not ascend the McKenzie River above the rapids at Fort Smith, and is not found in Athabasca Lake, so that if any confirmation were needed of the identity of his lake with Great Slave Lake, Hearne's reference to this fish would in itself be quite convincing. Hearne was the first white man to visit this lake, for it was not till 1785, between thirteen and fourteen years after his visit, that the traders of the North-West Company from Montreal reached and built a trading-post on it, east of the mouth of the Slave River. On Peter Pond's map of 1785, republished by L. J. Burpee, in his "Search for the Western Sea," 1908, page 182, the following interesting note is written across the space N.E. of Great Slave Lake: "Orchipoins Country et Road to Churchill," showing clearly that Pond knew of the trade carried on by the northern Indians with the Hudson's Bay Company at Churchill.

[102] Pike=*Esox lucius* Linn.; trout=*Cristivomer namaycush* Walbaum; perch=*Stizostedion vitreum* Mitchill; barble=*Catastomus*; tittameg=whitefish (*Coregonus*); methy=*Lota macuiosa* (Le Sueur).—E. A. P.

[103] Shees. This is probably the earliest notice of the inconnu, *Stenodus Mackenzii* (Richardson). This anadromous species inhabits in summer the principal rivers of Northern Alaska and Mackenzie, east to and including the Anderson. It is present in Great Slave Lake throughout the year, this being, as far as I know, the only inland lake thus distinguished.—E. A. P.

[104] Buffalo. This is the earliest notice of the northern race of the bison, the so-called Wood Bison, *Bison bison Athabasca* Rhoads. It was formerly very numerous and inhabited an extensive region (see Preble's "North Am. Fauna," No. 27, p. 144, 1908), but is now reduced to a few small herds, aggregating a few hundred individuals, which roam over a limited area south of Great Slave Lake.—E. A. P.

[BC] It is remarked by Mr. Catesby, in his description of this animal, that no man can lift one of their heads. Those I saw in the Athapuscow country are such as I have described; and I am assured by the Company's servants, as well as the Indians who live near Hudson's House, that the buffalos there are much smaller; so that the species Mr. Catesby saw, or wrote of, must have been much larger, or have had very large heads; for it is well known that a man of any tolerable strength can lift two and a half, or three hundred pounds weight. I think that the heads of his buffalos are too heavy for the bodies, as the bodies of those I saw in the Athapuscow country appear to have been of equal weight with his.

[105] *Alces Americanus* (Clinton), still common throughout the region.—E. A. P.

[BD] The moose formerly sent to his Majesty was from that place. A young male was also put on board the ship, but it died on the passage, otherwise it is probable they might have propagated in this country.

[BE] Since the above was written, the same Indian that brought all the above-mentioned young moose to the Factory had, in the year 1777, two others, so tame, that when on his passage to Prince of Wales's Fort in a canoe, the moose always followed him along the bank of the river; and at night, or on any other occasion when the Indians landed, the young moose generally came and fondled on them, in the same manner as the most domestic animal would have done, and never offered to stray from the tents. Unfortunately, in crossing a deep bay in one of the lakes (on a fine day), all the Indians that were not interested in the safe-landing of those engaging creatures, paddled from point to point; and the man that owned them, not caring to go so far about by himself, accompanied the others, in hopes they would follow him round as usual; but at night the young moose did not arrive; and as the howling of some wolves was heard in that quarter, it was supposed they had been devoured by them, as they were never afterward seen.

[BF] Mr. Du Pratz, in his description of this animal, says, it is never found farther North than Cape Breton and Nova Scotia; but I have seen them in great numbers in the Athapuscow Country, which cannot be much short of 60° North latitude.

[106] The deer here meant is the Wapati or Canadian Elk, the Cree name of which is Waskasū, or Wewaskasū.

[BG] The Northern Indians make their fishing-nets with small thongs cut from raw deer-skins; which when dry appear very good, but after being soaked in water some time, grow so soft and slippery, that when large fish strike the net, the hitches are very apt to slip and let them escape. Beside this inconvenience, they are very liable to rot, unless they be frequently taken out of the water and dried.

[BH] It is too common a case with most of the tribes of Southern Indians for the women to desire their husbands or friends, when going to war, to bring them a slave, that they may have the pleasure of killing it; and some of these inhuman women will accompany their husbands, and murder the women and children as fast as their husbands do the men.

When I was at Cumberland House, (an inland settlement that I established for the Hudson's Bay Company in the year 1774,) I was particularly acquainted with a very young lady of this extraordinary turn; who, when I desired some Indians that were going to war to bring me a young slave, which I intended to have brought up as a domestic, Miss was equally desirous that one might be brought to her, for the cruel purpose of murdering it. It is scarcely possible to express my astonishment, on hearing such an extraordinary request made by a young creature scarcely sixteen years old; however, as soon as I recovered from my surprise, I ordered her to leave the settlement, which she did, with those who were going to war; and it is therefore probable she might not be disappointed in her request. The next year I was ordered to the command of Prince of Wales's Fort, and therefore never saw her afterward.

[107] The map is very indefinite in this part of his course, and little dependence can be placed on his positions. The place where he came to the Slave (Athapuscow) River must have been some distance south of Great Slave Lake, and as he followed it upwards for forty miles to where it turned to the south, he probably reached some place not far from the rapids at Fort Smith, in latitude 60° north, which is 15' south of the point indicated on his map as the place where he left the river and struck into the country to the east.

[108] When the geography of the country between Athabasca and Great Slave Lakes becomes known, it may be possible to follow him here, but his map gives no indication of any stream in this vicinity flowing into Lake Clowey. He appears to have thought so little of the small river that he did not take the trouble to map it.

[109] The reference here and on the following pages is certainly to the belt of forest which occurs on the banks of Thelon River and its tributary above its junction with the Dubawnt River. J. W. Tyrrell, who explored and surveyed this river in 1900, refers to it as follows:—

"The investigations of the present expedition have, however, established both the existence and location of such an oasis; but, as predicted by Hearne, the primitive settlers have long since departed, although for some other reasons than lack of fuel.

"In support of Hearne's story, and my belief that his reference was to the valley of the Thelon, it may be noted that some very old choppings were observed, as well as the decayed, moss-grown remains of some very old camps, whilst scarcely any recent signs of habitation exist.

"The wooded, or partially-wooded, banks of the Thelon extend for a distance of about one hundred and seventy miles below the forks of the Hanbury. This distance is not to be understood as a continuous stretch of timber, but over that distance many fine spruce groves, as well as more or less continuous thinly-scattered trees are found. The largest trees measured from twelve to fifteen inches in diameter, but the average diameter would be about six inches." (Append. 26, Pt. III. Annual Report, Department of the Interior, Canada, 1901, pp. 7, 27.)

[B1] To snare swans, geese, or ducks, in the water, it requires no other process than to make a number of hedges, or fences, project into the water, at right angles, from the banks of a river, lake, or pond; for it is observed that those birds generally swim near the margin, for the benefit of feeding on the grass, &c. Those fences are continued for some distance from the shore, and separated two or three yards from each other, so that openings are left sufficiently large to let the birds swim through. In each of those openings a snare is hung and fastened to a stake, which the bird, when intangled, cannot drag from the bottom; and to prevent the snare from being wafted out of its proper place by the wind, it is secured to the stakes which form the opening, with tender grass, which is easily broken.

This method, though it has the appearance of being very simple, is nevertheless attended with much trouble, particularly when we consider the smallness of their canoes, and the great inconveniency they labour under in performing works of this kind in the water. Many of the stakes used on those occasions are of a considerable length and size, and the small branches which form the principal part of the hedges, are not arranged without much caution, for fear of oversetting the canoes, particularly where the water is deep, as it is in some of the lakes; and in many of the rivers the current is very swift, which renders this business equally troublesome. When the lakes and rivers are shallow, the natives are frequently at the pains to make fences from shore to shore.

To snare those birds in their nests requires a considerable degree of art, and, as the natives say, a great deal of cleanliness; for they have observed, that when snares have been set by those whose hands were not clean, the birds would not go into the nest.

Even the goose, though so simple a bird, is notoriously known to forsake her eggs, if they are breathed on by the Indians.

The smaller species of birds which make their nest in the ground, are by no means so delicate, of course less care is necessary to snare them. It has been observed that all birds which build in the ground go into their nest at one particular side, and out of it on the opposite. The Indians, thoroughly convinced of this, always set the snares on the side on which the bird enters the nest; and if care be taken in setting them, seldom fail of seizing their object. For small birds, such as larks, and many others of equal size, the Indians only use two or three hairs out of their head; but for larger birds, particularly swans, geese, and ducks, they make snares of deer-sinews, twisted like packthread, and occasionally of a small thong cut from a parchment deer-skin.

[BJ] The Indians, both Northern and Southern, have found by experience, that by boiling the pesogan in water for a considerable time, the texture is so much improved, that when thoroughly dried, some parts of it will be nearly as soft as spunge.

Some of those funguses are as large as a man's head; the outside, which is very hard and black, and much indented with deep cracks, being of no use, is always chopped off with a hatchet. Besides the two sorts of touchwood already mentioned, there is another kind of it in those parts, that I think is infinitely preferable to either. This is found in old decayed poplars, and lies in flakes of various sizes and thickness; some is not thicker than shammoy leather, others are as thick as a shoe-sole. This, like the fungus of the birch-tree, is always moist when taken from the tree, but when dry, it is very soft and flexible, and takes fire readily from the spark of a steel; but it is much improved by being kept dry in a bag that has contained gunpowder. It is rather surprising that the Indians, whose mode of life I have just been describing, have never acquired the method of making fire by friction, like the Esquimaux. It is also equally surprising that they do not make use of the skin-canoes. Probably deer-skins cannot be manufactured to withstand the water;[110] for it is well known that the Esquimaux use always seal-skins for that purpose, though they are in the habit of killing great numbers of deer.

[110] The Eskimos met with on the banks of the Kasan River in 1894 make their canoes entirely of deer-skin parchment.

[111] The positions of these two lakes are not exactly known, but they doubtless lie near the regular Indian canoe route from the north Bay of Lake Athabasca to Great Slave Lake. The latter lake lies fourteen miles W. or S.W. of Noo-shetht Lake.

[112] On Hearne's map the position of Noo-shetht Whoie or Newstheth tooy Lake in relation to the streams in the country is very indefinite, but on the Pennant map it is shown on a stream which flows northward into Great Slave Lake. In King's "Journey to the Shores of the Arctic Ocean," vol. ii. p. 289, a copy of an Indian map of a canoe route northward from Lake Athabasca is published. Most of this route is down the Copper Indian (Yellow Knife or Rock) River, which flows into Great Slave Lake a short

distance east of the mouth of Slave River, and one of the lakes there shown is Tazennatooy or Muddy Water Lake, while another is Newstheth tooy, the lake here referred to.

[BK] Though I was a swift runner in those days, I never accompanied the Indians in one of those chaces, but have heard many of them say, that after a long one, the moose, when killed, did not produce more than a quart of blood, the remainder being all settled in the flesh; which, in that state, must be ten times worse tasted, than the spleen or milt of a bacon hog.

[113] Thee-lee-aza River is called Theetinah River (Blue Fish River?) on the Pennant map, and Petitot speaks of it as a tributary of T'ezus or Snowdrift River, which also empties into the south side of Great Slave Lake.

[114] The latitude of this lake had been determined by Hearne as 61° 30' north, as previously stated on p. 127, and he had placed it on his map in latitude 61° 15' north. In making the journey to the Coppermine River and back to the lake, he had occupied a little more than a year, having left it on April 18th, 1771, and returned to it on April 29th, 1772.

[115] On the 8th of March 1771 they "lay a little to the E.N.E. of Black Bear Hill" (see p. 125), while now they are three quarters of a mile south of it. As this hill is but a short distance (two days' journey) west of Wholdiah Lake, the two routes laid down on the map are evidently incorrect, for the map shows his route home at this place at least thirty-five miles north of the route out, instead of south of it as indicated by the text.

[BL] As a proof of this assertion I take the liberty, though a little foreign to the narrative of my journey, to insert one instance, out of many hundreds of the kind that happen at the different Factories in Hudson's Bay, but perhaps no where so frequently as at Churchill. In October 1776, my old guide, Matonabbee, came at the head of a large gang of Northern Indians, to trade at Prince of Wales's Fort; at which time I had the honour to command it. When the usual ceremonies had passed, I dressed him out as a Captain of the first rank, and also clothed his six wives from top to toe: after which, that is to say, during his stay at the Factory, which was ten days, he begged seven lieutenants' coats, fifteen common coats, eighteen hats, eighteen shirts, eight guns, one hundred and forty pounds weight of gunpowder, with shot, ball, and flints in proportion; together with many hatchets, ice chissels, files, bayonets, knives, and a great quantity of tobacco, cloth, blankets, combs, looking-glasses, stockings, handkerchiefs, &c. besides numberless small articles, such as awls, needles, paint, steels, &c. in all to the amount of upwards of seven hundred beaver in the way of trade, to give away among his followers. This was exclusive of his own present, which consisted of a variety of goods to the value of four hundred beaver more. But the most extraordinary of his demands was twelve pounds of powder, twenty-eight pounds of shot and ball, four pounds of tobacco, some articles of clothing, and several pieces of iron-work, &c. to give to two men who had hauled his tent and other lumber the preceding Winter. This demand was so very unreasonable, that I made some scruple, or at least hesitated to comply with it, hinting that he was the person who ought to satisfy those men for their services; but I was soon answered, that he did not expect to have been *denied such a trifle as that was*; and for the future he would carry his goods where he could get his own price for them. On my asking him where that was? he replied, in a very insolent tone, "To the Canadian Traders." I was glad to comply with his demands; and I here insert the anecdote, as a specimen of an Indian's conscience.

[116] The river down which the party was travelling at this time would appear to have been a tributary of the Dubawnt River from the west. Unfortunately when I descended the Dubawnt River there were no Chipewyan Indians in the party, so that I was not able to learn the local names of the various lakes and natural features encountered, nor anything of the geography of the country beyond the range of vision, so that doubtless many streams joined the main river without being noticed by me. This is probably one of them.

[117] The north end of Wholdiah Lake of the present maps is in latitude 60° 49' north, whereas the part crossed by Hearne, which he calls A Naw-nee-tha'd Whoie, is placed by him in latitude 61° 50' north. It remains for some future explorer to account for this discrepancy, and give the exact situation of this place. That Hearne's position is much too far north is clear, for they were then in the woods, and the northern limit of the woods crosses the Dubawnt River about latitude 61° 30' N., twenty-three miles south of Hearne's course as indicated on his map.

[BM] All the furrs thus left were properly secured in caves and crevices of the rocks, so as to withstand any attempt that might be made on them by beasts of prey, and were well shielded from the weather; so that, in all probability, few of them were lost.

[118] As they were then on the barren lands, they probably crossed the Kazan River, somewhere about the north end of Ennadai Lake. There is a lake marked on the Mackenzie map as Nipach Lake which may possibly be intended to represent this latter lake. Although there are a few groves of spruce along the banks of this stream, north of the limit of the forest, no attempts seem to have been made by Hearne or his party to camp at them. The date here given is interesting as naming a time when one, at least, of the streams through the barren lands breaks up in spring.

[119] In the text no indication is given of the course which he followed after crossing Kazan River, but his map shows that he followed the route of his journey outwards, crossing Fat, Island, Whiskey Jack, and Baralzoa Lakes. The Cook map, however, shows that he went round to the north of Island Lake, and doubtless he also went round the largest of the other lakes, for he would hardly dare to cross them in the little canoes which he and the Indians were using for crossing the streams.

[BN] Mr. Jérémie is very incorrect in his account of the situation of this River, and its course. It is not easy to guess, whether the Copper or Dog-ribbed Indians be the nation he calls *Platscotez de Chiens*: if it be the former, he is much mistaken; for they have abundance of beaver, and other animals of the furr kind, in their country: and if the latter, he is equally wrong to assert that they have copper-mines in their country; for neither copper nor any other kind of metal is in use among them.

Mr. Jérémie was not too modest when he said, (see Dobb's Account of Hudson's Bay, p. 19,) "he could not say any thing positively in going farther North;" for in my opinion he never was so far North or West as he pretends, otherwise he would have been more correct in his description of those parts.

The Strait he mentions is undoubtedly no other than what is now called Chesterfield's Inlet, which, in some late and cold seasons, is not clear of ice the whole Summer: for I will affirm, that no Indian, either Northern or Southern, ever saw either Wager Water or Repulse Bay, except the two men who accompanied Captain Middleton; and though those men were selected from some hundreds for their universal knowledge of those parts, yet they knew nothing of the coast so far North as Marble Island.

As a farther proof, that no Indians, except the Esquimaux, ever frequent such high latitudes, unless at a great distance from the sea, I must here mention, that so late as the year 1763, when Captain Christopher went to survey Chesterfield's Inlet, though he was furnished with the most intelligent and experienced Northern Indians that could be found, they did not know an inch of the land to the North of Whale Cove.

Mr. Jérémie is also as much mistaken in what he says concerning Churchill River, as he was in the direction of Seal River; for he says that no woods were found but in some islands which lie about ten or twelve miles up the river. At the time he wrote, which was long before a settlement was made there, wood was in great plenty on both sides the river; and that within five miles of where Prince of Wales's Fort now stands. But as to the islands of which he speaks, if they ever existed, they have of late years most assuredly disappeared; for since the Company have had a settlement on that river, no one ever saw an island in it that produced timber, or wood of any description, within forty miles of the Fort. But the great number of stumps now remaining, from which, in all probability, the trees have been cut for firing, are sufficient to prove that when Churchill River was first settled, wood was then in great plenty; but in the course of seventy-six years residence in one place, it is natural to suppose it was much thinned near the Settlement. Indeed for some years past common fewel is so scarce near that Factory, that it is the chief employment of most of the servants for upward of seven months in the year, to procure as much wood as will supply the fires for a Winter, and a little timber for necessary repairs.[120]

[120] Mr. Jérémie was in charge of York Factory for six years, from 1708 to 1714, while it was in the hands of the French. His reference to the presence of native copper among the *Plascôtez de Chiens*, or Dog Rib Indians, who inhabit the country between the mouth of the Mackenzie and the Coppermine River, is particularly interesting:—

"Ils ont dans leur Pays une *Mine de Cuivre rouge*, si abondante & si pure, que, sans le passer par la forge, tel qu'ils le ramassent à la Mine, ils ne font que le frapper entre deux pièrres, & en font tout ce qu'ils veulent. J'en ai vû fort souvent, parce que nos Sauvages en apportoient toutes les fois qu'ils alloient en guerre de ces côtez là." (*Jérémie*. "Relation du Detroit et de la Baie de Hudson," in "Recueil de Voyages au Nord." Par J. F. Bernard. 10 vols. 12mo. Amsterdam. 1724. Tom. v. p. 404.)

[121] Of the life at Fort Prince of Wales under Moses Norton in 1771, during the year of Hearne's absence on the Coppermine River, we have the following interesting account by Andrew Graham, one of the factors of the Hudson's Bay Company:—

"Prince of Wales Fort. On a peninsula at the entrance of the Churchill River. Most northern settlement of the Company. A stone fort, mounting forty-two cannon [an error, as there are embrasures for only forty cannon in the parapet of the fort], from six to twenty-four pounders. Opposite, on the south side of the river, Cape Merry Battery, mounting six twenty-four pounders, with lodge-house and powder magazine. The river 1006 yards wide. A ship can anchor six miles above the fort. Tides carry salt water twelve miles up the river. No springs near; drink snow water nine months of the year. In summer keep three draught horses to haul water and draw stones to finish building the forts.

"Staff:—A chief factor and officers, with sixty servants and tradesmen. The council, with discretionary power, consists of chief factor, second factor, surgeon, sloop and brig masters, and captain of Company's ship when in port. These answer and sign the general letter, sent yearly to directors. The others are accountant, trader, steward, armourer, ship-wright, carpenter, cooper, blacksmith, mason, tailor, and labourers. These must not trade with natives, under penalties for so doing. Council mess together, also servants. Called by bell to duty, work from six to six in summer, eight to four in winter. Two watch in winter, three in summer. In emergencies, tradesmen must work at anything. Killing of partridges the most pleasant duty.

"Company signs contract with servants for three or five years, with the remarkable clause: 'Company may recall them home at any time without satisfaction for the remaining time. Contract may be renewed, if servants or labourers wish, at expiry of term. Salary advanced forty shillings, if men have behaved well in first term. The land and sea officers' and tradesmen's salaries do not vary, but seamen's are raised in time of war.'

"A ship of 200 tons burden, bearing provisions, arrives yearly in August or early September. Sails again in ten days, wind permitting, with cargo and those returning. Sailors alone get pay when at home.

"The annual trade sent home from this fort is from ten to four thousand made beaver, in furs, pelts, castorum, goose feathers, and quills, and a small quantity of train oil and whale bone, part of which they receive from the Eskimos, and the rest from the white whale fishery. A black whale fishery is in hand, but it shows no progress." ("The Remarkable History of the Hudson's Bay Company." By George Bryce, 1900, pp. 108-9.)

[297]

{304} CHAP. IX.

A short Description of the Northern Indians, also a farther Account of their Country, Manufactures, Customs, &c.

An account of the persons and tempers of the Northern Indians—They possess a great deal of art and cunning—Are very guilty of fraud when in their power, and generally exact more for their furrs than any other tribe of Indians,—Always dissatisfied, yet have their good qualities—The men in general jealous of their wives—Their marriages—Girls always betrothed when children, and their reasons for it—Great care and confinement of young girls from the age of eight or nine years old—Divorces common among those people—The women are less prolific than in warmer countries—Remarkable piece of superstition observed by the women at particular periods—Their art in making it an excuse for a temporary separation from their husbands on any little quarrel—Reckoned very unclean on those occasions—The Northern Indians frequently, for the want of firing, are obliged to eat their meat raw—Some through necessity obliged to boil it in vessels made of the rind of the birch-tree—A remarkable dish among those people—The young animals always cut out of their dams eaten, and accounted a great delicacy—The parts of generation of all animals eat by the men and boys—Manner of passing their time, and method of killing deer in Summer with bows and arrows—Their tents, dogs, sledges, &c.—Snow-shoes—Their partiality to domestic vermin—Utmost extent of the Northern Indian country—Face of the country—Species of fish—A peculiar kind of moss useful for the support of man—Northern Indian method of catching fish, either with hooks or nets—Ceremony observed when two parties of those people meet—Diversions in common use—A singular disorder which attacks some of those people—Their {305} superstition with respect to the death of their friends—Ceremony observed on those occasions—Their ideas of the first inhabitants of the world—No form of religion among them—Remarks on that circumstance—The extreme misery to which old age [298] *is exposed—Their opinion of the Aurora*

Borealis, &c.—Some Account of Matonabbee, and his services to his country, as well as to the Hudson's Bay Company.

As to the persons of the Northern Indians, they are in general above the middle size; well-proportioned, strong, and robust, but not corpulent. They do not possess that activity of body, and liveliness of disposition, which are so commonly met with among the other tribes of Indians who inhabit the West coast of Hudson's Bay.

Their complexion is somewhat of the copper cast, inclining rather toward a dingy brown; and their hair, like all the other tribes in India, is black, strong, and straight.[BO] Few of the men have any beard; this seldom makes its appearance till they are arrived at middle-age, and then is by no means equal in quantity to what is observed on the faces of the generality of Europeans; the little they have, however, is exceedingly strong and bristly. Some of them take but little pains to eradicate their beards, though it is considered as very unbecoming; and those {306} who do, have no other method than that of pulling it out by the roots between their fingers and the edge of a blunt knife. Neither sex have any hair under their armpits, and very little on any other part of the body, particularly the women; but on the place where Nature plants the hair, I never knew them attempt to eradicate it.

Their features are peculiar, and different from any other tribe in those parts; for they have very low foreheads, small eyes, high cheek-bones, Roman noses, full cheeks, and in general long broad chins. Though few of either sex are exempt from this national set of features, yet Nature seems to be more strict in her observance of it among the females, as they seldom vary so much as the men. Their skins are soft, smooth, and polished; and when they are dressed in clean clothing, they are as free from an offensive smell as any of the human race.

[299]

Every tribe of Northern Indians, as well as the Copper and Dog-ribbed Indians, have three or four parallel black strokes marked on each cheek; which is performed by entering an awl or needle under the skin, and, on drawing it out again, immediately rubbing powdered charcoal into the wound.

Their dispositions are in general morose and covetous, and they seem to be entirely unacquainted even with the name of gratitude. They are for ever pleading poverty, {307} even among themselves; and when they visit the Factory, there is not one of them who has not a thousand wants.

When any real distressed objects present themselves at the Company's Factory, they are always relieved with victuals, clothes, medicines, and every other necessary, *gratis*; and in return, they instruct every one of their countrymen how to behave, in order to obtain the same charity. Thus it is very common to see both men and women come to the Fort half-naked, when either the severe cold in Winter, or the extreme troublesomeness of the flies in Summer, make it necessary for every part to be covered. On those occasions they are seldom at a loss for a plausible story, which they relate as the occasion of their distress (whether real or pretended), and never fail to interlard their history with plenty of sighs, groans, and tears, sometimes affecting to be lame, and even blind, in order to excite pity. Indeed, I know of no people that have more command of their passions on such occasions; and in this respect the women exceed the men, as I can affirm with truth I have seen some of them with one side of the face bathed in tears, while the other has exhibited a significant smile. False pretences for obtaining charity are so common among those people, and so often detected, that the Governor is frequently obliged to turn a deaf ear to many who apply for relief; for[300] if he did not, he might give away the whole of the Company's goods, and by degrees all the Northern {308} tribe would make a trade of begging, instead of bringing furrs, to purchase what they want. It may truly be said, that they possess a considerable degree of deceit, and are very complete adepts in the art of flattery, which they never spare as long as they find that it conduces to their interest, but not a moment longer. They take care always to seem attached to a new Governor, and flatter his pride, by telling him that they look up to him as the father of their tribe, on whom they can safely place their dependance; and they never fail to depreciate the generosity of his predecessor, however extensive that might have been, however humane or disinterested his conduct; and if aspersing the old, and flattering the new Governor, has not the desired effect in a reasonable time, they represent him as the worst of characters, and tell him to his face that he is one of the most cruel of men; that he has no feeling for the distresses of their tribe, and that many have perished for want of proper assistance, (which, if it be true, is only owing to want of humanity among themselves,) and then they boast of having received ten times the favours and presents from his predecessor. It is remarkable that those are most lavish in their praises, who have never either deserved or received any favours from him. In time, however, this language also ceases, and they are perfectly reconciled to the man whom they would willingly have made a fool, and say, "he is no child, and not to be deceived by them."

{309} They differ so much from the rest of mankind, that harsh uncourteous usage seems to agree better with the generality of them, particularly the lower class, than mild treatment; for if the least respect be shown them, it makes them intolerably insolent; and though some of their leaders may be exempt from this imputation, yet there are but few even of them who have sense enough to set a proper value on the favours and indulgences which are granted to them while they[301] remain at the Company's Factories, or elsewhere within their territories. Experience has convinced me, that by keeping a Northern Indian at a distance, he may be made serviceable both to himself and the Company; but by giving him the least indulgence at the Factory, he will grow indolent, inactive, and troublesome, and only contrive methods to tax the generosity of an European.

The greatest part of these people never fail to defraud Europeans whenever it is in their power, and take every method to over-reach them in the way of trade. They will disguise their persons and change their names, in order to defraud them of their lawful debts, which they are sometimes permitted to contract at the Company's Factory; and all debts that are outstanding at the succession of a new Governor are entirely lost, as they always declare, and bring plenty of witnesses to prove, that they were paid long before, but that their names had been forgotten to be struck out of the book.

{310} Notwithstanding all those bad qualities, they are the mildest tribe of Indians that trade at any of the Company's settlements; and as the greatest part of them are never heated with liquor, are always in their senses, and never proceed to riot, or any violence beyond bad language.

The men are in general very jealous of their wives, and I make no doubt but the same spirit reigns among the women; but they are kept so much in awe of their husbands, that the liberty of thinking is the greatest privilege they enjoy. The presence of a Northern Indian man strikes a peculiar awe into his wives, as he always assumes the same authority over them that the master of a family in Europe usually does over his domestic servants.

Their marriages are not attended with any ceremony; all matches are made by the parents, or next of kin. On those occasions the women seem to have no choice, but implicitly obey the will of their parents, who always endeavour to marry[302] their daughters to those that seem most likely to be capable of maintaining them, let their age, person, or disposition be ever so despicable.

The girls are always betrothed when children, but never to those of equal age, which is doubtless sound policy with people in their situation, where the existence of a family {311} depends entirely on the abilities and industry of a single man. Children, as they justly observe, are so liable to alter in their manners and disposition, that it is impossible to judge from the actions of early youth what abilities they may possess when they arrive at puberty. For this reason the girls are often so disproportionably matched for age, that it is very common to see men of thirty-five or forty years old have young girls of no more than ten or twelve, and sometimes much younger. From the early age of eight or nine years, they are prohibited by custom from joining in the most innocent amusements with children of the opposite sex; so that when sitting in their tents, or even when travelling, they are watched and guarded with such an unremitting attention as cannot be exceeded by the most rigid discipline of an English boarding-school. Custom, however, and constant example, make such uncommon restraint and confinement sit light and easy even on children, whose tender ages seem better adapted to innocent and cheerful amusements, than to be cooped up by the side of old women, and constantly employed in scraping skins, mending shoes, and learning other domestic duties necessary in the care of a family.

Notwithstanding those uncommon restraints on the young girls, the conduct of their parents is by no means uniform or consistent with this plan; as they set no bounds to their conversation, but talk before them, and even to them, on the most indelicate subjects. As their ears are accustomed {312} to such language from their earliest youth, this has by no means the same effect on them, it would have on girls born and educated in a civilized country, where every care is taken to prevent[303] their morals from being contaminated by obscene conversation. The Southern Indians are still less delicate in conversation, in the presence of their children.

The women among the Northern Indians are in general more backward than the Southern Indian women; and though it is well known that neither tribe lose any time, those early connections are seldom productive of children for some years.

Divorces are pretty common among the Northern Indians; sometimes for incontinency, but more frequently for want of what they deem necessary accomplishments or for bad behaviour. This ceremony, in either case, consists of neither more nor less than a good drubbing, and turning the woman out of doors; telling her to go to her paramour, or relations, according to the nature of her crime.

Providence is very kind in causing these people to be less prolific than the inhabitants of civilized nations; it is very uncommon to see one woman have more than five or six children; and these are always born at such a distance from one another, that the youngest is generally two or {313} three years old before another is brought into the world. Their easy births, and the ceremonies which take place on those occasions, have already been mentioned; I shall therefore only observe here, that they make no use of cradles, like the Southern Indians, but only tie a lump of moss between their legs, and always carry their children at their backs, next the skin, till they are able to walk. Though their method of treating young children is in this respect the most uncouth and awkward I ever saw, there are few among them that can be called deformed, and not one in fifty who is not bow-legged.

There are certain periods at which they never permit the women to abide in the same tent with their husbands. At such times they are obliged to make a small hovel for themselves at some distance from the other tents. As this is an universal custom among all the tribes, it is also a piece of[304] policy with the women, upon any difference with their husbands, to make that an excuse for a temporary separation, when, without any ceremony, they creep out (as is their usual custom on those occasions) under the eves of that side of the tent at which they happen to be sitting; for at those times they are not permitted to go in or out through the door. This custom is so generally prevalent among the women, that I have frequently known some of the sulky dames leave their husbands and tent for four or five days at a time, and repeat the farce twice or thrice in a month, while the poor men have never suspected the deceit, or if they {314} have, delicacy on their part has not permitted them to enquire into the matter. I have known Matonabbee's handsome wife, who eloped from him in May one thousand seven hundred and seventy-one, live thun-nardy, as they call it, (that is, alone,) for several weeks together, under this pretence; but as a proof he had some suspicion, she was always carefully watched, to prevent her from giving her company to any other man. The Southern Indians are also very delicate in this point; for though they do not force their wives to build a separate tent, they never lie under the same clothes during this period. It is, however, equally true, that the young girls, when those symptoms make their first appearance, generally go a little distance from the other tents for four or five days, and at their return wear a kind of veil or curtain, made of beads, for some time after, as a mark of modesty; as they are then considered marriageable, and of course are called women, though some at those periods are not more than thirteen, while others at the age of fifteen or sixteen have been reckoned as children, though apparently arrived at nearly their full growth.

On those occasions a remarkable piece of superstition prevails among them; women in this situation are never permitted to walk on the ice of rivers or lakes, or near the part where the men are hunting beaver, or where a fishing-net is set, for fear of averting their success. They are also prohibited[305] at those times from partaking of the {315} head of any animal, and even from walking in, or crossing the track where the head of a deer, moose, beaver, and many other animals, have lately been carried, either on a sledge or on the back. To be guilty of a violation of this custom is considered as of the greatest importance; because they firmly believe that it would be a means of preventing the hunter from having an equal success in his future excursions.

Those poor people live in such an inhospitable part of the globe, that for want of firing, they are frequently obliged to eat their victuals quite raw, particularly in the Summer season, while on the barren ground; but early custom and frequent necessity make this practice so familiar to them, that so far from finding any inconvenience arise from it, or having the least dislike to it, they frequently do it by choice, and particularly in the article of fish; for when they do make a pretence of dressing it, they seldom warm it through. I have frequently made one of a party who has sat round a fresh-killed deer, and assisted in picking the bones quite clean, when I thought that the raw brains and many other parts were exceedingly good; and, however strange it may appear, I must bestow the same epithet on half-raw fish: even to this day I give the preference to trout, salmon, and the brown tittemeg, when they are not warm at the bone.

{316} The extreme poverty of those Indians in general will not permit one half of them to purchase brass kettles from the Company; so that they are still under the necessity of continuing their original mode of boiling their victuals in large upright vessels made of birch-rind. As those vessels will not admit of being exposed to the fire, the Indians, to supply the defect, heat stones red-hot and put them into the water, which soon occasions it to boil; and by having a constant succession of hot stones, they may continue the process as long as it is necessary. This method of cooking, though very expeditious, is attended with one great evil; the victuals which are thus[306] prepared are full of sand: for the stones thus heated, and then immerged in the water, are not only liable to shiver to pieces, but many of them being of a coarse gritty nature, fall to a mass of gravel in the kettle, which cannot be prevented from mixing with the victuals which are boiled in it. Besides this, they have several other methods of preparing their food, such as roasting it by a string, broiling it, &c.; but these need no farther description.

The most remarkable dish among them, as well as all the other tribes of Indians in those parts, both Northern and Southern, is blood mixed with the half-digested food which is found in the deer's stomach or paunch, and boiled up with a sufficient quantity of water, to make it of the consistence of pease-pottage. Some fat and scraps {317} of tender flesh are also shred small and boiled with it. To render this dish more palatable, they have a method of mixing the blood with the contents of the stomach in the paunch itself, and hanging it up in the heat and smoke of the fire for several days; which puts the whole mass into a state of fermentation, and gives it such an agreeable acid taste, that were it not for prejudice, it might be eaten by those who have the nicest palates. It is true, some people with delicate stomachs would not be easily persuaded to partake of this dish, especially if they saw it dressed; for most of the fat which is boiled in it is first chewed by the men and boys, in order to break the globules that contain the fat; by which means it all boils out, and mixes with the broth: whereas, if it were permitted to remain as it came from the knife, it would still be in lumps, like suet. To do justice, however, to their cleanliness in this particular, I must observe, that they are very careful that neither old people with bad teeth, nor young children, have any hand in preparing this dish. At first, I must acknowledge that I was rather shy in partaking of this mess, but when I was sufficiently convinced of the truth of the above remark, I no longer made any scruple, but always thought it exceedingly good.[307]

The stomach of no other large animal beside the deer is eaten by any of the Indians that border on Hudson's Bay. In Winter, when the deer feed on fine white moss, the contents of the stomach is so much esteemed by them, {318} that I have often seen them sit round a deer where it was killed, and eat it warm out of the paunch. In Summer the deer feed more coarsely, and therefore this dish, if it deserve that appellation, is then not so much in favour.

The young calves, fawns, beaver, &c. taken out of the bellies of their mothers, are reckoned most delicate food; and I am not the only European who heartily joins in pronouncing them the greatest dainties that can be eaten. Many gentlemen who have served with me at Churchill, as well as at York Fort, and the inland settlements, will readily agree with me in asserting, that no one who ever got the better of prejudice so far as to taste of those young animals, but has immediately become excessively fond of them; and the same may be said of young geese, ducks, &c. in the shell. In fact, it is almost become a proverb in the Northern settlements, that whoever wishes to know what is good, must live with the Indians.

The parts of generation belonging to any beast they kill, both male and female, are always eaten by the men and boys; and though those parts, particularly in the males, are generally very tough, they are not, on any account, to be cut with an edge-tool, but torn to pieces with the teeth; and when any part of them proves too tough to be masticated, it is thrown into the fire and burnt. For the Indians believe firmly, that if a dog should eat any part of them, it would have the same effect on their {319} success in hunting, that a woman crossing their hunting-track at an improper period would have. The same ill-success is supposed also to attend them if a woman eat any of those parts.

They are also remarkably fond of the womb of the buffalo, elk, deer, &c. which they eagerly devour without washing, or any other process but barely stroking out the contents. This,[308] in some of the larger animals, and especially when they are some time gone with young, needs no description to make it sufficiently disgusting; and yet I have known some in the Company's service remarkably fond of the dish, though I am not one of the number. The womb of the beaver and deer is well enough, but that of the moose and buffalo is very rank, and truly disgusting.[BP]

{320} Our Northern Indians who trade at the Factory, as well as all the Copper tribe, pass their whole Summer on the barren ground, where they generally find plenty of deer; and in some of the rivers and lakes, a great abundance of fine fish.

Their bows and arrows, though their original weapons, are, since the introduction of fire-arms among them, become of little use, except in killing deer as they walk or run through a narrow pass prepared for their reception, where several Indians lie concealed for that purpose. This method of hunting is only practicable in Summer, and on the barren ground, where they have an extensive prospect, and can see the herds of deer at a great distance, as well as discover the nature of the country, and make every {321} necessary arrangement for driving them through the narrow defiles. This method of hunting is performed in the following manner:

[309]

When the Indians see a herd of deer, and intend to hunt them with bows and arrows, they observe which way the wind blows, and always get to leeward, for fear of being smelled by the deer. The next thing to which they attend, is to search for a convenient place to conceal those who are appointed to shoot. This being done, a large bundle of sticks, like large ramrods, (which they carry with them the whole Summer for the purpose,) are ranged in two ranks, so as to form the two sides of a very acute angle, and the sticks placed at the distance of fifteen or twenty yards from each other. When those necessary arrangements are completed, the women and boys separate into two parties, and go round on both sides, till they form a crescent at the back of the deer, which are drove right forward; and as each of the sticks has a small flag, or more properly a pendant, fastened to it, which is easily waved to and fro by the wind, and a lump of moss stuck on each of their tops, the poor timorous deer, probably taking them for ranks of people, generally run straight forward between the two ranges of sticks, till they get among the Indians, who lie concealed in small circular fences, made with loose stones, moss, &c. When the deer approach very near, the Indians who are thus concealed start up and shoot; but as the deer generally pass along at {322} full speed, few Indians have time to shoot more than one or two arrows, unless the herd be very large.

This method of hunting is not always attended with equal success; for sometimes after the Indians have been at the[310] trouble of making places of shelter, and arranging the flag-sticks, &c. the deer will make off another way, before the women and children can surround them. At other times I have seen eleven or twelve of them killed with one volley of arrows; and if any gun-men attend on those occasions, they are always placed behind the other Indians, in order to pick up the deer that escape the bow-men. By these means I have seen upwards of twenty fine deer killed at one broadside, as it may be termed.

Though the Northern Indians may be said to kill a great number of deer in this manner during the Summer, yet they have so far lost the art of shooting with bows and arrows, that I never knew any of them who could take those weapons only, and kill either deer, moose, or buffalo, in the common, wandering, and promiscuous method of hunting. The Southern Indians, though they have been much longer used to fire-arms, are far more expert with the bow and arrow, their original weapons.

The tents made use of by those Indians, both in Summer and Winter, are generally composed of deer-skins in the hair; and for convenience of carriage, are always {323} made in small pieces, seldom exceeding five buck-skins in one piece. These tents, as also their kettles, and some other lumber, are always carried by dogs, which are trained to that service, and are very docile and tractable. Those animals are of various sizes and colours, but all of the fox and wolf breed, with sharp noses, full brushy tails, and sharp ears standing erect. They are of great courage when attacked, and bite so sharp, that the smallest cur among them will keep several of our largest English dogs at bay, if he can get up in a corner. These dogs are equally willing to haul in a sledge, but as few of the men will be at the trouble of making sledges for them, the poor women are obliged to content themselves with lessening the bulk of their load, more than the weight, by making the dogs carry these articles only, which are always lashed on their backs, much after the same manner as packs are, or used formerly to be, on pack-horses.

INDIAN IMPLEMENTS
A Bow
An Arrow
A left foot Snowshoe 4½ foot long
& 13 Inches broad
A Sledge
A kettle made of Burch rinde

[311]

In the fall of the year, and as the Winter advances, those people sew the skins of the deer's legs together in the shape of long portmanteaus, which, when hauled on the snow as the hair lies, are as slippery as an otter, and serve them as temporary sledges while on the barren ground; but when they arrive at any woods, they then make proper sledges, with thin boards of the larch-tree, generally known in Hudson's Bay by the name of Juniper.[122]

{324} Those sledges are of various sizes, according to the strength of the persons who are to haul them: some I have seen were not less than twelve or fourteen feet long, and fifteen or sixteen inches wide, but in general they do not exceed eight or nine feet in length, and twelve or fourteen inches in breadth.

The boards of which those sledges are composed are not more than a quarter of an inch thick, and seldom exceed five or six inches in width; as broader would be very unhandy for the Indians to work, who have no other tools than an ordinary knife, turned up a little at the point, from which it acquires the name of Bafe-hoth among the Northern Indians, but among the Southern tribes it is called Mo-co-toggan. The boards are sewed together with thongs of parchment deer-skin, and several cross bars of wood are sewed on the upper side, which serves both to strengthen the sledge and secure the ground-lashing, to which the load is always fastened by other smaller thongs, or stripes of leather. The head or fore-part of the sledge is turned up so as to form a semi-circle, of at least fifteen or twenty inches diameter. This prevents the carriage from diving into light snow, and enables it to slide over the inequalities and hard drifts of snow which are constantly met with on the open plains and barren grounds. The trace or draught-line to those sledges is a double string, or slip of leather, made fast to the head; and the bight is put across the shoulders of the person who {325} hauls the sledge, so as to rest against the breast. This contrivance, though so simple, cannot be improved by the most ingenious collar-maker in the world.

[312]

Their snow-shoes differ from all others made use of in those parts; for though they are of the galley kind, that is, sharp-pointed before, yet they are always to be worn on one foot, and cannot be shifted from side to side, like other snow-shoes; for this reason the inner-side of the frames are almost straight, and the outer-side has a very large sweep. The frames are generally made of birch-wood, and the netting is composed of thongs of deer-skin; but their mode of filling that compartment where the foot rests, is quite different from that used among the Southern Indians.

Their clothing, which chiefly consists of deer-skins in the hair, makes them very subject to be lousy; but that is so far from being thought a disgrace, that the best among them amuse themselves with catching and eating these vermin; of which they are so fond, that the produce of a lousy head or garment affords them not only pleasing amusement, but a delicious repast. My old guide, Matonabbee, was so remarkably fond of those little vermin, that he frequently set five or six of his strapping wives to work to louse their hairy deer-skin shifts, the produce of which being always very considerable, he eagerly received with both hands, and licked them in as fast, and with as good a grace, as {326} any European epicure would the mites in a cheese. He often assured me that such amusement was not only very pleasing, but that the objects of the search were very good; for which I gave him credit, telling him at the same time, that though I endeavoured to habituate myself to every other part of their diet, yet as I was but a sojourner among them, I had no inclination to accustom myself to such dainties as I could not procure in that part of the world where I was most inclined to reside.[313]

The Southern Indians and Esquimaux are equally fond of those vermin, which are so detestable in the eyes of an European; nay, the latter have many other dainties of a similar kind, for beside making use of train-oil as a cordial and as sauce to their meat, I have frequently seen them eat a whole handful of maggots that were produced in meat by fly-blows. It is their constant custom to eat the filth that comes from the nose; and when their noses bleed by accident, they always lick the blood into their mouths, and swallow it.

The tract of land inhabited by the Northern Indians is very extensive, reaching from the fifty-ninth to the sixty-eighth degree of North latitude; and from East to West is upward of five hundred miles wide. It is bounded by Churchill River on the South; the Athapuscow Indians' Country on the West; the Dog-ribbed and Copper Indians' Country on the North; and by Hudson's Bay on the East. {327} The land throughout that whole tract of country is scarcely anything but one solid mass of rocks and stones, and in most parts very hilly, particularly to the Westward among the woods. The surface, it is very true, is in most places covered with a thin sod of moss, intermixed with the roots of the Wee-sa-ca-pucca, cranberries, and a few other insignificant shrubs and herbage; but under it there is in general a total want of soil, capable of producing anything except what is peculiar to the climate. Some of the marshes, indeed, produce several kinds of grass, the growth of which is amazingly rapid; but this is dealt out with so sparing a hand as to be barely sufficient to serve the geese, swans, and other birds of passage, during their migrations in the Spring and Fall, while they remain in a moulting state.

The many lakes and rivers with which this part of the country abounds, though they do not furnish the natives with water-carriage, are yet of infinite advantage to them; as they afford great numbers of fish, both in Summer and Winter. The only species caught in those parts are trout, tittameg, (or[314] tickomeg,) tench, two sorts of barble, (called by the Southern Indians Na-may-pith,) burbot, pike, and a few perch. The four former are caught in all parts of this country, as well the woody as the barren; but the three latter are only caught to the Westward, in such lakes and rivers as are situated among the woods; and though some of those rivers lead to the barren ground, yet the {328} three last mentioned species of fish are seldom caught beyond the edge of the woods, not even in the Summer season.

There is a black, hard, crumply moss, that grows on the rocks and large stones in those parts, which is of infinite service to the natives, as it sometimes furnishes them with a temporary subsistence, when no animal food can be procured. This moss, when boiled, turns to a gummy consistence, and is more clammy in the mouth than sago; it may, by adding either moss or water, be made to almost any consistence. It is so palatable, that all who taste it generally grow fond of it. It is remarkably good and pleasing when used to thicken any kind of broth, but it is generally most esteemed when boiled in fish-liquor.

The only method practised by those people to catch fish either in Winter or Summer, is by angling and setting nets; both of which methods is attended with much superstition, ceremony, and unnecessary trouble; but I will endeavour to describe them in as plain and brief a manner as possible.

When they make a new fishing-net, which is always composed of small thongs cut from raw deer-skins, they take a number of birds bills and feet, and tie them, a little apart from each other, to the head and foot rope of the net, and at the four corners generally fasten some of the toes and jaws of the otters and jackashes. The birds feet {329} and bills made choice of on such occasions are generally those of the laughing goose, wavey, (or white goose,) gulls, loons, and black-heads[123]; and unless some or all of these be fastened to the net, they will not attempt to put it into the water, as they firmly believe it would not catch a single fish.

[315]

A net thus accoutred is fit for setting whenever occasion requires, and opportunity offers; but the first fish of whatever species caught in it, are not to be sodden in the water, but broiled whole on the fire, and the flesh carefully taken from the bones without dislocating one joint; after which the bones are laid on the fire at full length and burnt. A strict observance of these rules is supposed to be of the utmost importance in promoting the future success of the new net; and a neglect of them would render it not worth a farthing.[BQ]

When they fish in rivers, or narrow channels that join two lakes together, they could frequently, by tying two, three, or more nets together, spread over the whole breadth of the channel, and intercept every sizable fish that passed; but instead of that, they scatter the nets at a considerable distance from each other, from a {330} superstitious notion, that were they kept close together, one net would be jealous of its neighbour, and by that means not one of them would catch a single fish.

The methods used, and strictly observed, when angling, are equally absurd as those I have mentioned; for when they bait a hook, a composition of four, five, or six articles, by way of charm, is concealed under the bait, which is always sewed round the hook. In fact, the only bait used by those people is in their opinion a composition of charms, inclosed within a bit of fish skin, so as in some measure to resemble a small fish. The things used by way of charm, are bits of beavers tails and fat, otter's vents and teeth, musk-rat's guts and tails, loon's vents, squirrel's testicles, the cruddled milk taken out of the stomach of sucking fawns and calves, human hair, and numberless other articles equally absurd.

[316]

Every master of a family, and indeed almost every other person, particularly the men, have a small bundle of such trash, which they always carry with them, both in Summer and Winter; and without some of those articles to put under their bait, few of them could be prevailed upon to put a hook into the water, being fully persuaded that they may as well sit in the tent, as attempt to angle without such assistance. They have also a notion that fish of the same species inhabiting different parts of the country, are fond of different things; so that almost every {331} lake and river they arrive at, obliges them to alter the composition of the charm. The same rule is observed on broiling the first fruits of a new hook that is used for a new net; an old hook that has already been successful in catching large fish is esteemed of more value, than a handful of new ones which have never been tried.

Deer also, as well as fish, are very numerous in many parts of this country; particularly to the North of the sixtieth degree of latitude. Alpine hares are in some parts of the barren ground pretty plentiful, where also some herds of musk-oxen are to be met with; and to the Westward, among the woods, there are some rabbits and partridges.

With all those seeming sources of plenty, however, one half of the inhabitants, and perhaps the other half also, are frequently in danger of being starved to death, owing partly to their want of œconomy; and most of these scenes of distress happen during their journies to and from Prince of Wales's Fort, the only place at which they trade.

When Northern Indians are at the Factory, they are very liable to steal any thing they think will be serviceable; particularly iron hoops, small bolts, spikes, carpenters tools, and, in short, all small pieces of iron-work which they can turn to advantage, either for their own use, or for the purpose of[317] trading with such of their countrymen as seldom visit the Company's Settlement: {332} among themselves, however, the crime of theft is seldom heard of.

When two parties of those Indians meet, the ceremonies which pass between them are quite different from those made use of in Europe on similar occasions; for when they advance within twenty or thirty yards of each other, they make a full halt, and in general sit or lie down on the ground, and do not speak for some minutes. At length one of them, generally an elderly man, if any be in company, breaks silence, by acquainting the other party with every misfortune that has befallen him and his companions from the last time they had seen or heard of each other; and also of all deaths and other calamities that have befallen any other Indians during the same period, at least as many particulars as have come to his knowledge.

When the first has finished his oration, another aged orator, (if there be any) belonging to the other party relates, in like manner, all the bad news that has come to his knowledge; and both parties never fail to plead poverty and famine on all occasions. If those orations contain any news that in the least affect the other party, it is not long before some of them begin to sigh and sob, and soon after break out into a loud cry, which is generally accompanied by most of the grown persons of both sexes; and sometimes it is common to see them all, men, women, and children, in one universal howl. The young girls, in {333} particular, are often very obliging on those occasions; for I never remember to have seen a crying match (as I called it) but the greatest part of the company assisted, although some of them had no other reason for it, but that of seeing their companions do the same. When the first transports of grief subside, they advance by degrees, and both parties mix with each other, the men always associating with the men, and the women with the women. If they have any tobacco among them, the pipes are passed round pretty freely,[318] and the conversation soon becomes general. As they are on their first meeting acquainted with all the bad news, they have by this time nothing left but good, which in general has so far the predominance over the former, that in less than half an hour nothing but smiles and cheerfulness are to be seen in every face; and if they be not really in want, small presents of provisions, ammunition, and other articles, often take place; sometimes merely as a gift, but more frequently by way of trying whether they cannot get a greater present.

They have but few diversions; the chief is shooting at a mark with bow and arrows; and another out-door game, called Holl, which in some measure resembles playing with quoits; only it is done with short clubs sharp at one end. They also amuse themselves at times with dancing, which is always performed in the night. It is remarkable that those people, though a distinct nation, have never adopted any mode of dancing of their own, or any songs to which {334} they can dance; so that when anything of this kind is attempted, which is but seldom, they always endeavour to imitate either the Dog-ribbed or Southern Indians, but more commonly the former, as few of them are sufficiently acquainted either with the Southern Indian language, or their manner of dancing. The Dog-ribbed method is not very difficult to learn, as it only consists in lifting the feet alternately from the ground in a very quick succession, and as high as possible, without moving the body, which should be kept quite still and motionless; the hands at the same time being closed, and held close to the breast, and the head inclining forward. This diversion is always performed quite naked, except the breech-cloth, and at times that is also thrown off; and the dancers, who seldom exceed three or four at a time, always stand close to the music. The music may, by straining a point, be called both vocal and instrumental, though both are sufficiently humble. The former is no more than a frequent repetition of the words, hee, hee, hee, ho, ho, ho, &c. which, by a more or less frequent[319] repetition, dwelling longer on one word and shorter on another, and raising and lowering the voice, produce something like a tune, and has the desired effect. This is always accompanied by a drum or tabor; and sometimes a kind of rattle is added, made with a piece of dried buffalo skin, in shape exactly like an oil-flask, into which they put a few shot or pebbles, which, when shook about, produces music little inferior to the drum, though not so loud.

{335} This mode of dancing naked is performed only by the men; for when the women are ordered to dance, they always exhibit without the tent, to music which is played within it; and though their method of dancing is perfectly decent, yet it has still less meaning and action than that of the men: for a whole heap of them crowd together in a straight line, and just shuffle themselves a little from right to left, and back again in the same line, without lifting their feet from the ground; and when the music stops, they all give a little bend of the body and knee, somewhat like an awkward curtsey, and pronounce, in a little shrill tone, h-e-e, h-o-o-o-e.

Beside these diversions, they have another simple in-door game, which is that of taking a bit of wood, a button, or any other small thing, and after shifting it from hand to hand several times, asking their antagonist, which hand it is in? When playing at this game, which only admits of two persons, each of them have ten, fifteen, or twenty small chips of wood, like matches; and when one of the players guesses right, he takes one of his antagonist's sticks, and lays it to his own; and he that first gets all the sticks from the other in that manner, is said to win the game, which is generally for a single load of powder and shot, an arrow, or some other thing of inconsiderable value.

The women never mix in any of their diversions, not even in dancing; for when that is required of them, they {336} always exhibit without the tent, as has been already observed; nor are they allowed to be present at a feast. Indeed, the whole[320] course of their lives is one continued scene of drudgery, *viz.* carrying and hauling heavy loads, dressing skins for clothing, curing their provisions, and practising other necessary domestic duties which are required in a family, without enjoying the least diversion of any kind, or relaxation, on any occasion whatever; and except in the execution of those homely duties, in which they are always instructed from their infancy, their senses seem almost as dull and frigid as the zone they inhabit. There are indeed some exceptions to be met with among them, and I suppose it only requires indulgence and precept to make some of them as lofty and insolent as any women in the world. Though they wear their hair at full length, and never tie it up, like the Southern Indians; and though not one in fifty of them is ever possessed of a comb, yet by a wonderful dexterity of the fingers, and a good deal of patience, they make shift to stroke it out so as not to leave two hairs entangled; but when their heads are infested with vermin, from which very few of either sex are free, they mutually assist each other in keeping them under.

A scorbutic disorder, resembling the worst stage of the itch, consumptions, and fluxes, are their chief disorders. The first of these, though very troublesome, is never known to prove fatal, unless it be accompanied with some inward complaint; but the two latter, with a few {337} accidents, carries off great numbers of both sexes and all ages: indeed few of them live to any great age, probably owing to the great fatigue they undergo from their youth up, in procuring a subsistence for themselves and their offspring.

Though the scorbutic disorder above mentioned does appear to be infectious, it is rare to see one have it without the whole tent's crew being more or less affected with it; but this is by no means a proof of its being contagious; I rather attribute it to the effects of some bad water, or the unwholesomeness of some fish they may catch in particular places, in the course of their wandering manner of life. Were it otherwise, a single[321] family would in a short time communicate it to the whole tribe; but, on the contrary, the disease is never known to spread. In the younger sort it always attacks the hands and feet, not even sparing the palms and soles. Those of riper years generally have it about the wrists, insteps, and posteriors; and in the latter particularly, the blotches, or boils as they may justly be called, are often as large as the top of a man's thumb. This disorder most frequently makes its appearance in the Summer, while the Indians are out on the barren ground; and though it is by no means reckoned dangerous, yet it is so obstinate, as not to yield to any medicine that has ever been applied to it while at the Company's Factory. And as the natives themselves never make use of any medicines of their own preparing, Nature alone works the cure, which is never performed in {338} less than twelve or eighteen months; and some of them are troubled with this disagreeable and loathsome disorder for years before they are perfectly cured, and then a dark livid mark remains on those parts of the skin which have been affected, for many years afterwards, and in some during life.

When any of the principal Northern Indians die, it is generally believed that they are conjured to death, either by some of their own countrymen, by some of the Southern Indians, or by some of the Esquimaux: too frequently the suspicion falls on the latter tribe, which is the grand reason of their never being at peace with those poor and distressed people. For some time past, however, those Esquimaux who trade with our sloops at Knapp's Bay, Navel's Bay, and Whale Cove, are in perfect peace and friendship with the Northern Indians; which is entirely owing to the protection they have for several years past received from the Chiefs at the Company's Fort at Churchill River.[BR] But those of that tribe who live so far to the {339} North, as not to have any intercourse with our vessels, very often fall a sacrifice to the fury and superstition of the {340} Northern Indians; who are by no means a bold or warlike people; nor can I think from experience, that they are particularly guilty of committing acts of wanton cruelty on any other part of the human race beside the Esquimaux. Their hearts, however, are in general so unsusceptible of tenderness, that they can view the deepest distress in those who are not immediately related to them, without the least emotion; not even half so much as the generality of mankind feel for the sufferings of the meanest of the brute creation. I have been present when one of them, imitating the groans, distorted features, and contracted position, of a {341} man who had died in the most excruciating pain, put the whole company, except myself, into the most violent fit of laughter.

[323]

[322]

The Northern Indians never bury their dead, but always leave the bodies where they die, so that they are supposed to be devoured by beasts and birds of prey; for which reason they will not eat foxes, wolves, ravens, &c. unless it be through mere necessity.

The death of a near relation affects them so sensibly, that they rend all their cloths from their backs, and go naked, till some persons less afflicted relieve them. After the death of a father, mother, husband, wife, son, or brother, they mourn, as it may be called, for a whole year, which they measure by the moons and seasons. Those mournful periods are not distinguished by any particular dress, except that of cutting off the hair; and the ceremony consists in almost perpetually crying. Even when walking, as well as at all other intervals from sleep, eating, and conversation, they make an odd[324] howling noise, often repeating the relationship of the deceased. But as this is in a great measure mere form and custom, some of them have a method of softening the harshness of the notes, and bringing them out in a more musical tone than that in which they sing their songs. When they reflect seriously on the loss of a good friend, however, it has such an effect on them for the present, that they give an {342} uncommon loose to their grief. At those times they seem to sympathise (through custom) with each other's afflictions so much, that I have often seen several scores of them crying in concert, when at the same time not above half a dozen of them had any more reason for so doing than I had, unless it was to preserve the old custom, and keep the others in countenance. The women are remarkably obliging on such occasions; and as no restriction is laid on them, they may with truth be said to cry with all their might and main; but in common conversation they are obliged to be very moderate.

They have a tradition among them, that the first person upon earth was a woman, who, after having been some time alone, in her researches for berries, which was then her only food, found an animal like a dog, which followed her to the cave where she lived, and soon grew fond and domestic. This dog, they say, had the art of transforming itself into the shape of a handsome young man, which it frequently did at night, but as the day approached, always resumed its former shape; so that the woman looked on all that passed on those occasions as dreams and delusions. These transformations were soon productive of the consequences which at present generally follow such intimate connexions between the two sexes, and the mother of the world began to advance in her pregnancy.

{343} Not long after this happened, a man of such a surprising height that his head reached up to the clouds, came to level the land, which at that time was a very rude mass; and after he had done this, by the help of his walking-stick he marked[325] out all the lakes, ponds, and rivers, and immediately caused them to be filled with water. He then took the dog, and tore it to pieces; the guts he threw into the lakes and rivers, commanding them to become the different kinds of fish; the flesh he dispersed over the land, commanding it to become different kinds of beasts and land-animals; the skin he also tore in small pieces, and threw it into the air, commanding it to become all kinds of birds; after which he gave the woman and her offspring full power to kill, eat, and never spare, for that he had commanded them to multiply for her use in abundance. After this injunction, he returned to the place whence he came, and has not been heard of since.

RELIGION has not as yet begun to dawn among the Northern Indians; for though their conjurors do indeed sing songs, and make long speeches, to some beasts and birds of prey, as also to imaginary beings, which they say assist them in performing cures on the sick, yet they, as well as their credulous neighbours, are utterly destitute of every idea of practical religion. It is true, some of them will reprimand their youth for talking {344} disrespectfully of particular beasts and birds; but it is done with so little energy, as to be often retorted back in derision. Neither is this, nor their custom of not killing wolves and quiquehatches, universally observed, and those who do it can only be viewed with more pity and contempt than the others; for I always found it arose merely from the greater degree of confidence which they had in the supernatural power of their conjurors, which induced them to believe, that talking lightly or disrespectfully of any thing they seemed to approve, would materially affect their health and happiness in this world: and I never found any of them that had the least idea of futurity. Matonabbee, without one exception, was a man of as clear ideas in other matters as any that I ever saw: he was not only a perfect master of the Southern Indian language, and their belief, but could tell a better story of our Saviour's birth and life, than one half of[326] those who call themselves Christians; yet he always declared to me, that neither he, nor any of his countrymen, had an idea of a future state. Though he had been taught to look on things of this kind as useless, his own good sense had taught him to be an advocate for universal toleration; and I have seen him several times assist at some of the most sacred rites performed by the Southern Indians, apparently with as much zeal, as if he had given as much credit to them as they did: and with the same liberality of sentiment he would, I am persuaded, have assisted at the altar {345} of a Christian church, or in a Jewish synagogue; not with a view to reap any advantage himself, but merely, as he observed, to assist others who believed in such ceremonies.

Being thus destitute of all religious control, these people have, to use Matonabbee's own words, "nothing to do but consult their own interest, inclinations, and passions; and to pass through this world with as much ease and contentment as possible, without any hopes of reward, or painful fear of punishment, in the next." In this state of mind they are, when in prosperity, the happiest of mortals; for nothing but personal or family calamities can disturb their tranquillity, while misfortunes of the lesser kind sit light on them. Like most other uncivilized people, they bear bodily pain with great fortitude, though in that respect I cannot think them equal to the Southern Indians.

Old age is the greatest calamity that can befal a Northern Indian; for when he is past labour, he is neglected, and treated with great disrespect, even by his own children. They not only serve him last at meals, but generally give him the coarsest and worst of the victuals: and such of the skins as they do not chuse to wear, are made up in the clumsiest manner into clothing for their aged parents; who, as they had, in all probability, treated their fathers and mothers with the same neglect, in {346} their turns, submitted patiently to their lot, even without a murmur, knowing it to be the common[327] misfortune attendant on old age; so that they may be said to wait patiently for the melancholy hour when, being no longer capable of walking, they are to be left alone, to starve, and perish for want. This, however shocking and unnatural it may appear, is nevertheless so common, that, among those people, one half at least of the aged persons of both sexes absolutely die in this miserable condition.

The Northern Indians call the *Aurora Borealis*, Ed-thin; that is, Deer:[BN] and when that meteor is very bright, they say that deer is plentiful in that part of the atmosphere; but they have never yet extended their ideas so far as to entertain hopes of tasting those celestial animals.

Beside this silly notion, they are very superstitious with respect to the existence of several kinds of fairies, called by them Nant-e-na, whom they frequently say they see, and who are supposed by them to inhabit the different elements {347} of earth, sea, and air, according to their several qualities. To one or other of those fairies they usually attribute any change in their circumstances, either for the better or worse; and as they are led into this way of thinking entirely by the art of the conjurors, there is no such thing as any general mode of belief; for those jugglers differ so much from each other in their accounts of these beings, that those who believe any thing they say, have little to do but change their opinions according to the will and caprice of the conjuror, who is almost daily relating some new whim, or extraordinary event, which, he says, has been revealed to him in a dream, or by some of his favourite fairies, when on a hunting excursion.

[328]

{348} *Some Account of* MATONABBEE, *and of the eminent Services which he rendered to his Country, as well as to the Hudson's Bay Company.*

MATONABBEE was the son of a Northern Indian by a slave woman, who was formerly bought from some Southern Indians who came to Prince of Wales's Fort with furrs, &c. This match was made by Mr. Richard Norton, then Governor, who detained them at and near the Fort, for the same purpose as he did those Indians called Home-guard. As to Matonabbee's real age, it is impossible to be particular; for the natives of those parts being utterly unacquainted with letters, or the use of hieroglyphics, though their memories are not less retentive than those of other nations, cannot preserve and transmit to posterity the exact time when any particular event happens. Indeed, the utmost extent of their chronology reaches no farther, than to say, My son, or my daughter, was born in such a Governor's time, and such an event happened during such a person's life-time (though, perhaps, he or she has been dead many years). However, according to appearance, and some corroborating circumstances, Matonabbee was born about the year one thousand seven hundred and thirty-six, or one thousand seven hundred and thirty-seven; and his father dying while he was young, the Governor took the {349} boy, and, according to the Indian custom, adopted him as his son.

Soon after the death of Matonabbee's father, Mr. Norton went to England, and as the boy did not experience from his successor the same regard and attention which he had been accustomed to receive from Mr. Norton, he was soon taken from the Factory by some of his father's relations, and continued with the Northern Indians till

Mr. Ferdinand Jacobs succeeded to the command of Prince of Wales's Fort, in the year one thousand seven hundred and fifty-two; when out of regard to old Mr. Norton, (who was then dead,) Mr. Jacobs took the first opportunity that offered to detain Matonabbee at the Factory, where he was for several years employed in the hunting-service with some of the Company's servants, particularly with the late Mr. Moses Norton,[BT] (son of the late Governor,) and Mr. Magnus Johnston.[BU]

Photo: J. W. Tyrrell, 1905.
GATEWAY OF FORT PRINCE OF WALES

Photo: J. W. Tyrrell, October 1894.
INTERIOR OF FORT PRINCE OF WALES, SHOWING WALLS
OF OLD DWELLING-HOUSE

[329]

In the course of his long stay at and near the Fort, it is no wonder that he should have become perfect master of the Southern Indian language, and made some progress in the English. It was during this period, that he gained a knowledge of the Christian faith; and he always declared, that it was too deep and intricate for his comprehension. Though he was a perfect bigot with respect to {350} the arts and tricks of Indian jugglers, yet he could by no means be impressed with a belief of any part of our religion, nor of the religion of the Southern Indians, who have as firm a belief in a future state as any people under the Sun. He had so much natural good sense and liberality of sentiment, however, as not to think that he had a right to ridicule any particular sect on account of their religious opinions. On the contrary, he declared, that he held them all equally in esteem, but was determined, as he came into the world, so he would go out of it, without professing any religion at all. Notwithstanding his aversion from religion, I have met with few Christians who possessed more good moral qualities, or fewer bad ones.

[330]

It is impossible for any man to have been more punctual in the performance of a promise than he was; his scrupulous adherence to truth and honesty would have done honour to the most enlightened and devout Christian, while his benevolence and universal humanity to all the human race,[BV] according to his abilities and manner of life, could {351} not be exceeded by the most illustrious personage now on record; and to add to his other good qualities, he was the only Indian that I ever saw, except one, who was not guilty of backbiting and slandering his neighbours.

In stature, Matonabbee was above the common size, being nearly six feet high[BW]; and, except that his neck was rather (though not much) too short, he was one of the finest and best proportioned men that I ever saw. In complexion he was dark, like the other Northern Indians, but his face was not disfigured by that ridiculous custom of marking the cheeks with three or four black lines. His features were regular and agreeable, and yet so strongly marked and expressive, that they formed a complete index of his mind; which, as he never intended to deceive or dissemble, he never wished to conceal. In conversation he was easy, lively, and agreeable, but exceedingly modest; and at table, the nobleness and elegance of his manners might have been admired by the first personages in the world; for to the vivacity of a Frenchman, and the {352} sincerity of an Englishman, he added the gravity and nobleness of a Turk; all so happily blended, as to render his company and conversation universally pleasing to those who understood either the Northern or Southern Indian languages, the only languages in which he could converse.

[331]

He was remarkably fond of Spanish wines, though he never drank to excess; and as he would not partake of spirituous liquors, however fine in quality or plainly mixed, he was always master of himself. As no man is exempt from frailties, it is natural to suppose that as a man he had his share; but the greatest with which I can charge him, is jealousy, and that sometimes carried him beyond the bounds of humanity.

In his early youth he discovered talents equal to the greatest task that could possibly be expected from an Indian. Accordingly Mr. Jacobs, then Governor at Prince of Wales's Fort, engaged him, when but a youth, as an Ambassador and Mediator between the Northern Indians and the Athapuscow Tribe, who till then had always been at war with each other. In the course of this embassy Matonabbee not only discovered the most brilliant and solid parts, but shewed an extensive knowledge of every advantage that could arise to both nations from a total suppression of hostilities; and at times he displayed such instances of personal courage and magnanimity, as are rarely to be found among persons of superior condition and rank.

{353} He had not penetrated far into the country of the Athapuscow Indians, before he came to several tents with inhabitants; and there, to his great surprise, he found Captain Keelshies, (a person frequently mentioned in this Journal,[BX]) who was then a prisoner, with all his family and some of his friends, the fate of whom was then undetermined; but through the means of Matonabbee, though young enough to have[332] been his son, Keelshies and a few others were released, with the loss of his effects and all his wives, which were six in number. Matonabbee not only kept his ground after Keelshies and his small party had been permitted to return, but made his way into the very heart of the Athapuscow country, in order to have a personal conference with all or most of the principal inhabitants. The farther he advanced, the more occasion he had for intrepidity. At one time he came to five tents of those savages, which in the whole contained sixteen men, besides their wives, children, and servants, while he himself was entirely alone, except one wife and a servant boy. The Southern Indians, ever treacherous, and apparently the more kind when they are premeditating mischief, seemed to give him a hearty welcome, accepted the tenders of peace and reconciliation with apparent satisfaction, and, as a mark of their approbation, each tent in rotation made a feast, or entertainment, the {354} same night, and invited him to partake; at the last of which they had concerted a scheme to murder him. He was, however, so perfect a master of the Southern Indian language, that he soon discovered their design, and told them, he was not come in a hostile manner, but if they attempted any thing of the kind he was determined to sell his life as dear as possible. On hearing this, some of them ordered that his servant, gun, and snow-shoes, (for it was winter,) should be brought into the tent and secured; but he sprung from his seat, seized his gun and snow-shoes, and went out of the tent, telling them, if they had an intention to molest him, that was the proper place where he could see his enemy, and be under no apprehensions of being shot cowardly through the back. "I am sure (said he) of killing two or three of you, and if you chuse to purchase my life at that price, now is the time; but if otherwise, let me depart without any farther molestation." They then told him he was at liberty to go, on condition of leaving his servant; but to this he would not consent. He then rushed into the tent and took his servant by force from two men; when finding there was no appearance of farther danger, he set out on his return to the frontiers of his own country, and from thence to the Factory.

[333]

The year following he again visited the Athapuscow country, accompanied by a considerable number of chosen {355} men of his own nation, who were so far superior to such small parties of the Southern Indians as they had met, that they commanded respect wherever they came; and having traversed the whole country, and conversed with all the principal men, peace and friendship were apparently re-established. Accordingly, when the Spring advanced the Northern Indians began to disperse, and draw out to the Eastward on the barren ground; but Matonabbee, and a few others, chose to pass the Summer in the Athapuscow country. As soon as the

Southern Indians were acquainted with this design, and found the number of the Northern Indians so reduced, a superior number of them dogged and harassed them the whole Summer, with a view to surprise and kill them when asleep; and with that view twice actually approached so near their tents as fifty yards. But Matonabbee told them, as he had done when alone, that though there were but few of them, they were all determined to sell their lives as dear as possible: on which the Southern Indians, without making any reply, retired; for no Indians in this country have the courage to face their enemies when they find them apprized of their approach, and on their guard to receive them.

Notwithstanding all these discouragements and great dangers, Matonabbee persevered with courage and resolution to visit the Athapuscow Indians for several years successively; and at length, by an uniform display of his pacific disposition, and by rendering a long train of good {356} offices to those Indians, in return for their treachery and perfidy, he was so happy as to be the sole instrument of not only bringing about[334] a lasting peace, but also of establishing a trade and reciprocal interest between the two nations.

After having performed this great work, he was prevailed upon to visit the Copper-mine River, in company with a famous leader, called I-dat-le-aza; and it was from the report of those two men, that a journey to that part was proposed to the Hudson's Bay Company by the late Mr. Moses Norton, in one thousand seven hundred and sixty-nine. In one thousand seven hundred and seventy he was engaged as the principal guide on that expedition; which he performed with greater punctuality, and more to my satisfaction, than perhaps any other Indian in all that country would have done. At his return to the Fort in one thousand seven hundred and seventy-two, he was made head of all the Northern Indian nation; and continued to render great services to the Company during his life, by bringing a greater quantity of furrs to their Factory at Churchill River, than any other Indian ever did, or ever will do. His last visit to Prince of Wales's Fort was in the Spring of one thousand seven hundred and eighty-two, and he intended to have repeated it in the

Winter following; but when he heard that the French had destroyed the Fort, and carried off all the Company's servants, he never afterwards reared his head, but took an opportunity, when no one {357} suspected his intention, to hang himself. This is the more to be wondered at, as he is the only Northern Indian who, that I ever heard, put an end to his own existence. The death of this man was a great loss to the Hudson's Bay Company, and was attended with a most melancholy scene; no less than the death of six of his wives, and four children, all of whom were starved to death the same Winter, in one thousand seven hundred and eighty-three.

FOOTNOTES:

[BO] I have seen several of the Southern Indian men who were near six feet high, preserve a single lock of their hair, that, when let down, would trail on the ground as they walked. This, however, is but seldom seen; and some have suspected it to be false: but I have examined the hair of several of them, and found it to be real.

[BP] The Indian method of preparing this unaccountable dish is by throwing the filthy bag across a pole directly over the fire, the smoke of which, they say, much improves it, by taking off the original flavour; and when any of it is to be cooked, a large flake, like as much tripe, is cut off and boiled for a few minutes; but the many large nodes with which the inside of the womb is studded, make it abominable. These nodes are as incapable of being divested of moisture as the skin of a live eel; but when boiled, much resemble, both in shape and colour, the yolk of an egg, and are so called by the natives, and as eagerly devoured by them.

The tripe of the buffalo is exceedingly good, and the Indian method of cooking it infinitely superior to that practised in Europe. When opportunity will permit, they wash it tolerably clean in cold water, strip off all the honey-comb, and only boil it about half, or three-quarters of an hour: in that time it is sufficiently done for eating; and though rather tougher than what is prepared in England, yet is exceedingly pleasant to the taste, and must be much more nourishing than tripe that has been soaked and scrubbed in many hot waters, and then boiled for ten or twelve hours.

The lesser stomach, or, as some call it, the many-folds, either of buffalo, moose, or deer, are usually eat raw, and are very good; but that of the moose, unless great care be taken in washing it, is rather bitter, owing to the nature of their food.

The kidneys of both moose and buffalo are usually eat raw by the Southern Indians; for no sooner is one of those beasts killed, than the hunter rips up its belly, thrusts in his arm, snatches out the kidneys, and eats them warm, before the animal is quite dead. They also at times put their mouths to the wound the ball has made, and suck the blood; which they say quenches thirst, and is very nourishing.

[122] *Larix laricina* (Du Roi.).

[123] For fuller reference to these birds see pp. 396-405.

[BQ] They frequently sell new nets, which have not been wet more than once or twice, because they have not been successful. Those nets, when soaked in water, are easily opened, and then make most excellent heel and toe netting for snow-shoes. In general it is far superior to the netting cut by the Southern Indian women, and is not larger than common net-twine.

[BR] In the Summer of 1756, a party of Northern Indians lay in wait at Knapp's Bay till the sloop had sailed out of the harbour, when they fell on the poor Esquimaux, and killed every soul. Mr. John Bean, then Master of the sloop, and since Master of the Trinity yacht, with all his crew, heard the guns very plain; but did not know the meaning or reason of it till the Summer following, when he found the shocking remains of more than forty Esquimaux, who had been murdered in that cowardly manner; and for no other reason but because two principal Northern Indians had died in the preceding Winter.

No Esquimaux were seen at Knapp's Bay for several years after; and those who trade there at present have undoubtedly been drawn from the Northward, since the above unhappy transaction; for the convenience of being nearer the woods, as well as being in the way of trading with the sloop that calls there annually. It is to be hoped that the measures taken by the Governors at Prince of Wales's Fort of late years, will effectually prevent any such calamities happening in future, and by degrees be the means of bringing about a lasting, friendly, and reciprocal interest between the two nations.

Notwithstanding the pacific and friendly terms which begin to dawn between those two tribes at Knapp's Bay, Navel's Bay, and Whale Cove, farther North hostilities continue, and most barbarous murders are perpetrated: and the only protection the Esquimaux have from the fury of their enemies, is their remote situation in the Winter, and their residing chiefly on islands and peninsulas in Summer, which renders them less liable to be surprised during that Season. But even this secluded life does not prevent the Northern Indians from harassing them greatly, and at times they are so closely pursued as to be obliged to leave most of their goods and utensils to be destroyed by their enemy; which must be a great loss, as these cannot be replaced but at the expence of much time and labour; and the want of them in the meantime must create much distress both to themselves and their families, as they can seldom procure any part of their livelihood without the assistance of a considerable apparatus.

In 1756, the Esquimaux at Knapp's Bay sent two of their youths to Prince of Wales's Fort in the sloop, and the Summer following they were carried back to their friends, loaded with presents, and much pleased with the treatment they received while at the Fort. In 1767, they again sent one from Knapp's Bay and one from Whale Cove; and though during their stay at the Fort they made a considerable progress both in the Southern Indian and the English languages, yet those intercourses have not been any ways advantageous to the Company, by increasing the trade from that quarter. In fact, the only satisfaction they have found for the great expence they have from time to time incurred, by introducing those strangers, is, that through the good conduct of their upper servants at Churchill River, they have at length so far humanized the hearts of those two tribes, that at present they can meet each other in a friendly manner; whereas, a few years since, whenever they met, each party premeditated the destruction of the other; and what made their war more shocking was, they never gave quarter: so that the strongest party always killed the weakest, without sparing either man, woman, or child.

It is but a few years ago that the sloop's crew who annually carried them all their wants, durst not venture on shore among the Esquimaux unarmed, for fear of being murdered; but latterly they are so civilized, that the Company's servants visit their tents with the greatest freedom and safety, are always welcome, and desired to partake of such provisions as they have: and knowing now our aversion from train-oil, they take every means in their power to convince our people that the victuals prepared for them is entirely free from it. But the smell of their tents, cooking-utensils, and other furniture, is scarcely less offensive than Greenland Dock. However, I have eaten both fish and venison cooked by them in so cleanly a manner, that I have relished them very much, and partaken of them with a good appetite.

[BS] Their ideas in this respect are founded on a principle one would not imagine. Experience has shewn them, that when a hairy deer-skin is briskly stroked with the hand in a dark night, it will emit many sparks of electrical fire, as the back of a cat will. The idea which the Southern Indians have of this meteor is equally romantic, though more pleasing, as they believe it to be the spirits of their departed friends dancing in the clouds; and when the *Aurora Borealis* is remarkably bright, at which time they vary most in colour, form, and situation, they say, their deceased friends are very merry.

[BT] Afterwards Governor.

[BU] Master of the Churchill sloop.

[BV] I must here observe, that when we went to war with the Esquimaux at the Copper River in July 1771, it was by no means his proposal: on the contrary, he was forced into it by his countrymen. For I have heard him say, that when he first visited that river, in company with I-dot-le-aza, they met with several Esquimaux; and so far from killing them, were very friendly to them, and made them small presents of such articles as they could best spare, and that would be of most use to them. It is more than probable that the two bits of iron found among the plunder while I was there, were part of those presents. There were also a few long beads found among those people, but quite different from any that the Hudson's Bay Company had ever sent to the Bay; so that the only probable way they could have come by them, must have been by an intercourse with some of their tribe, who had dealings with the Danes in Davis's Straits. It is very probable, however, they might have passed through many hands before they reached this remote place. Had they had an immediate intercourse with the Esquimaux in Davis's Straits, it is natural to suppose that iron would not have been so scarce among them as it seemed to be; indeed the distance is too great to admit of it.

[BW] I have seen two Northern Indians who measured six feet three inches; and one, six feet four inches.

[BX] The same person was at Prince of Wales's Fort when the French arrived on the 8th of August 1782, and saw them demolish the Fort.

[335]

{358} CHAP. X.[124]

An Account of the principal Quadrupeds found in the Northern Parts of Hudson's Bay.—The Buffalo, Moose, Musk-ox, Deer, and Beaver—A capital Mistake cleared up respecting the We-was-kish.

Animals with Canine Teeth.—The Wolf—Foxes of various colours— Lynx, or Wild Cat—Polar, or White Bear—Black Bear—Brown Bear—Wolverene—Otter—Jackash—Wejack—Skunk—Pine Martin—Ermine, or Stote.

Animals with cutting Teeth.—The Musk Beaver—Porcupine— Varying Hare—American Hare—Common Squirrel—Ground Squirrel—Mice of various Kinds,—and the Castor Beaver.

The Pinnated Quadrupeds with finlike Feet, found in Hudson's Bay, are but three in number, viz. the Walrus, or Sea-Horse,—Seal,—and Sea-Unicorn.

The Species of Fish found in the Salt Water of Hudson's Bay are also few in number; being the Black Whale—White Whale—Salmon— and Kepling.

Shell-fish, and empty Shells of several kinds, found on the Sea Coast near Churchill River.

Frogs of various sizes and colours; also a great variety of Grubbs, and other Insects, always found in a frozen state during Winter, but when exposed to the heat of a slow fire, are soon re-animated.

An Account of some of the principal Birds found in the Northern Parts of Hudson's Bay; as well those that only migrate there in Summer, as those that are known to brave the coldest Winters:—Eagles of various {359} kinds—Hawks of various sizes and plumage—White or Snowy Owl—Grey or mottled Owl—Cob-a-dee-cooch—Raven—Cinerious Crow—Wood Pecker—Ruffed Grouse—Pheasant—Wood Partridge—Willow Partridge—Rock Partridge—Pigeon—Red-breasted Thrush—Grosbeak—Snow [336] Bunting—White-crowned Bunting—Lapland Finch, two sorts—Lark—Titmouse—Swallow—Martin—Hopping Crane—Brown Crane—Bitron—Carlow, two sorts—Jack Snipe—Red Godwart—Plover—Black Gullemet—Northern Diver—Black-throated Diver—Red-throated Diver—White Gull—Grey Gull—Black-head—Pellican—Goosander—Swans of two species—Common Grey Goose—Canada Goose—White or Snow Goose—Blue Goose—Horned Wavy—Laughing Goose—Barren Goose—Brent Goose—Dunter Goose—Bean Goose.

The Species of Water-Fowl usually called Duck, that resort to those Parts annually, are in great variety; but those that are most esteemed are, the Mallard Duck,—Long-tailed Duck,—Wigeon, and Teal.

Of the Vegetable Productions as far North as Churchill River, particularly the most useful; such as the Berry-bearing Bushes, &c.—Gooseberry—Cranberry—Heathberry—Dewater-berry—Black Currans—Juniper-berry—Partridge-berry—Strawberry—Eye-berry—Blue-Berry—and a small species of Hips.

Burridge—Coltsfoot—Sorrel—Dandelion.

Wish-a-capucca—Jackashey-puck—Moss of various sorts—Grass of several kinds—and Vetches.

The Trees found so far North near the Sea, consist only of Pines—Juniper—Small Poplar—Bush-willows—and Creeping Birch.

Before I conclude this work, it may not be improper to give a short account of the principal Animals that frequent the high Northern latitudes, though most of them are found also far to the Southward, and consequently {360} in much milder climates. The buffalo, musk-ox, deer, and the moose,[125] have been already described in this Journal. I shall therefore only make a few remarks on the latter, in order to rectify a mistake, which, from wrong information, has crept into Mr. Pennant's Arctic Zoology. In page 21 of that elegant work, he classes the Moose with the We-was-kish, though it certainly has not any affinity to it.

[337]

The We-was-kish,[126] or as some (though improperly) call it, the Waskesse, is quite a different animal from the moose, being by no means so large in size. The horns of the We-was-kish are something similar to those of the common deer, but are not palmated in any part. They stand more upright, have fewer branches, and want the brow-antler. The head of this animal is so far from being like that of the Moose, that the nose is sharp, like the nose of a sheep: indeed, the whole external appearance of the head is not very unlike that of an ass. The hair is usually of a sandy red; and they are frequently called by the English who visit the interior parts of the country, red deer. Their flesh is tolerable eating; but the fat is as hard as tallow, and if eaten as hot as possible, will yet chill in so short time, that it clogs the teeth, and sticks to the roof of the mouth, in such a manner as to render it very disagreeable. In the Spring of one thousand seven hundred and seventy-five, I had thirteen sledge-loads of this meat brought to Cumberland House in one day, and also two of the heads of this animal unskinned, but the horns {361} were chopped off; a proof of their wearing them the whole Winter. They are the most stupid of all the deer kind, and frequently make a shrill whistling, and quivering noise, not very unlike the braying of an ass, which directs the hunter to the very spot where they are. They generally keep in large herds, and when they find plenty of pasture, remain a long time in one place. Those deer are seldom an object of chace with the Indians bordering on Basquiau, except when moose and other game fail. Their skins, when dressed, very much resemble that of the moose, though they are much thinner, and have this peculiar quality, that they will wash as well as shamoy leather; whereas all the other leathers and pelts dressed by the Indians, if they get wet, turn quite hard, unless great care be taken to keep constantly rubbing them while drying.

[338]

The person who informed Mr. Pennant that the we-was-kish and the moose are the same animal, never saw one of them; and the only reason he had to suppose it, was the great resemblance of their skins: yet it is rather strange, that so indefatigable a collector of Natural History as the late Mr. Andrew Graham, should have omitted making particular enquiry about them: for any foreign Indian, particularly those that reside near Basquiau, could easily have convinced him to the contrary.

{362} *Animals with Canine Teeth.*

> Wolves.

WOLVES[123] are frequently met with in the countries West of Hudson's Bay, both on the barren grounds and among the woods, but they are not numerous; it is very uncommon to see more than three or four of them in a herd. Those that keep to the Westward, among the woods, are generally of the usual colour, but the greatest part of those that are killed by the Esquimaux are perfectly white. All the wolves in Hudson's Bay are very shy of the human race, yet when sharp set, they frequently follow the Indians for several days, but always keep at a distance. They are great enemies to the Indian dogs, and frequently kill and eat those that are heavy loaded, and cannot keep up with the main body. The Northern Indians have formed strange ideas of this animal, as they think it does not eat its victuals raw; but by a singular and wonderful sagacity, peculiar to itself, has a method of cooking them without fire. The females are much swifter than the males; for which reason the Indians, both Northern and Southern, are of opinion that they kill the greatest part of the game.

[339]

This cannot, however, always be the case; for to the North of Churchill they, in general, live a forlorn life all the Winter, and are seldom seen in pairs till the Spring, when they begin to couple; and generally keep in pairs all the Summer. They always burrow underground to bring forth their young; and though it is natural {363} to suppose them very fierce at those times, yet I have frequently seen the Indians go to their dens, and take out the young ones and play with them. I never knew a Northern Indian hurt one of them: on the contrary, they always put them carefully into the den again; and I have sometimes seen them paint the faces of the young Wolves with vermillion, or red ochre.

Foxes of various colours.

The ARCTIC FOXES[128] are in some years remarkably plentiful, but generally most so on the barren ground, near the sea-coast. Notwithstanding what has been said of this animal only visiting the settlements once in five or seven years,[129] I can affirm there is not one year in twenty that they are not caught in greater or less numbers at Churchill; and I have known that for three years running, not less than from two hundred to four hundred have been caught each year within thirty miles of the Fort. They always come from the North along the coast, and generally make their appearance at Churchill about the middle of October, but their skins are seldom in season till November; during that time they are never molested, but permitted to feed round the Fort, till by degrees they become almost domestic. The great numbers of those animals that visit Churchill River in some years do not all come in a body, as it would be impossible for the fourth part of them to find subsistence by the way; but when they come near the Fort, the carcasses of dead whales lying along the shores, and the skin and other offal, after boiling the oil, {364} afford them a plentiful repast, and prove the means of keeping them about the Fort till, by frequent reinforcements from the Northward, their numbers are so far increased as almost to exceed credibility.

[340]

When their skins are in season, a number of traps and guns are set, and the greatest part of them are caught in one month, though some few are found during the whole Winter. I have frequently known near forty killed in one night within half a mile of Prince of Wales's Fort; but this seldom happens after the first or second night. When Churchill River is frozen over near the mouth, the greatest part of the surviving white Foxes cross the river, and direct their course to the Southward, and in some years assemble in considerable numbers at York Fort and Severn River. Whether they are all killed, or what becomes of those which escape, is very uncertain; but it is well known that none of them ever migrate again to the Northward. Besides taking a trap so freely, they are otherwise so simple, that I have seen them shot off-hand while feeding, the same as sparrows in a heap of chaff, sometimes two or three at a shot. This sport is always most successful in moon-light nights; for in the daytime they generally keep in their holes among the rocks, and under the hollow ice at high-water-mark.

These animals will prey on each other as readily as on any other animals they find dead in a trap, or wounded by gun; which renders them so destructive, that I have known upwards of one hundred and twenty Foxes of different {365} colours eaten, and destroyed in their traps by their comrades in the course of one Winter, within half a mile of the Fort.

The Naturalists seem still at a loss to know their breeding-places, which are doubtless in every part of the coast they frequent. Several of them breed near Churchill, and I have[341] seen them in considerable numbers all along the West coast of Hudson's Bay, particularly at Cape Esquimaux, Navel's Bay, and Whale Cove, also on Marble Island; so that with some degree of confidence we may affirm, that they breed on every part of the coast they inhabit during the Summer season. They generally have from three to five young at a litter; more I never saw with one old one. When young they are all over almost of a sooty black, but as the fall advances, the belly, sides, and tail turn to a light ash-colour; the back, legs, some part of the face, and the tip of the tail, changes to a lead colour; but when the Winter sets in they become perfectly white: the ridge of the back and the tip of the tail are the last places that change to that colour; and there are few of them which have not a few dark hairs at the tip of the tail all the Winter. If taken young, they are easily domesticated in some degree, but I never saw one that was fond of being caressed; and they are always impatient of confinement.

The White Fox.

WHITE FOXES, when killed at any considerable distance from the sea coast, (where they cannot possibly get any {366} thing to prey upon, except rabbits, mice, and partridges,) are far from being disagreeable eating. And on Marble Island I have shot them when they were equal in flavour to a rabbit; probably owing to their feeding entirely on eggs and young birds; but near Churchill River they are as rank as train-oil.

The Lynx, or Wild Cat.

The LYNX, or WILD CAT,[136] is very scarce to the North of Churchill; but is exactly the same as those which are found in great plenty to the South West. I have observed the tracks of this animal at Churchill, and seen them killed, and have eaten of their flesh in the neighbourhood of York Fort. The flesh is white, and nearly as good as that of a rabbit. They are, I think, much larger than that which is described in the Arctic Zoology; they never approach near the settlements in Hudson's Bay, and are very destructive to rabbits;

they seldom leave a place which is frequented by rabbits till they have nearly killed them all.

[342]

The Polar or White Bear.

The POLAR or WHITE BEAR,[131] though common on the sea-coast, is seldom found in its Winter retreats by any of our Northern Indians, except near Churchill River; nor do I suppose that the Esquimaux see or kill any of them more frequently during that season; for in the course of many years residence at Churchill River, I scarcely ever saw a Winter skin brought from the Northward by the sloop. Probably the Esquimaux, if they kill any, may {367} reserve the skins for their own use; for at that season their hair is very long, with a thick bed of wool at the bottom, and they are remarkably clean and white. The Winter is the only season that so oily a skin as the Bear's can possibly be cleaned and dressed by those people, without greasing the hair, which is very unpleasant to them; for though they eat train-oil, &c. yet they are as careful as possible to keep their clothes from being greased with it. To dress one of those greasy skins in Winter, as soon as taken from the beast, it is stretched out on a smooth patch of snow, and there staked down, where it soon freezes as hard as a board: while in that state, the women scrape off all the fat, till they come to the very roots of the hair. It is sometimes permitted to remain in that position for a considerable time; and when taken from the snow, is hung up in the open air. The more intense the frost, the greater is its drying quality; and by being wafted about by the wind, with a little scraping, it in time becomes perfectly supple, and both pelt and hair beautifully white. Drying deer, beaver, and otter skins, in this manner render their pelts very white, but not supple; probably owing to the close texture and thickness of their skins; whereas the skin of the bear, though so large an animal, is remarkably thin and spungy.[BY]

[343]

The Black Bear.

{368} BLACK BEARS[132] are not very numerous to the North West of Churchill. Their manner of life is the same as the rest of the species, though the face of the country they {369} inhabit, differs widely from the more mild climates. In Summer they proul about in search of berries, &c. and as the Winter approaches, retire to their dens, which are always under-ground; and generally, if not always, on the side of a small hillock. The Bears that inhabit the Southern parts of America are said to take up their Winter abode in hollow trees; but I never saw any trees in my Northern travels, that could afford any such shelter.

[344]

The places of retreat of those Bears that burrow under-ground are easily discovered in Winter, by the rime that hangs about the mouth of the den; for let the snow be ever so deep, the heat and breath of the animal prevents the mouth of the den from being entirely closed up. They generally retire to their Winter quarters before the snow is of any considerable depth, and never come abroad again (unless disturbed) till the thaws are considerable, which in those high latitudes is seldom till the latter end of March, or the beginning of April; so that the few Black Bears that inhabit those cold regions may be said to subsist for four months at least without food. I have been present at the killing [of] two of them in Winter; and the Northern Indian method is similar to that said to be in use among the Kamtschatkans; for they always blocked up the mouth of the den with logs of wood, then broke open the top of it, and killed the animal either with a spear or a gun; but the latter method is reckoned both cowardly and wasteful, as it is not possible for the Bear either to make its escape, or to do the Indians the least injury. {370} Sometimes they put a snare about the Bear's neck, and draw up his head close to the hole, and kill him with a hatchet. Though those animals are but scarce to the North of Churchill, yet they are so numerous between York Fort and Cumberland House, that in one thousand seven hundred and seventy-four I saw eleven killed in the course of one day's journey, but their flesh was abominable. This was in the month of June, long before any fruit was ripe, for the want of which they then fed entirely on[345] water insects, which in some of the lakes we crossed that day were in astonishing multitudes.[BZ][133]

The method by which the Bears catch those insects is by swimming with their mouths open, in the same manner as the whales do, when feeding on the sea-spider. There was not one of the Bears killed that day, which had not its stomach as full of those insects (only) as ever a hog's was with grains, and when cut open, the stench from them was intolerable. I have, however, eaten of some killed at that early season which were very good; {371} but they were found among the woods, far from the places where those insects haunt, and had fed on grass and other herbage. After the middle of July, when the berries begin to ripen, they are excellent eating, and so continue till January or February following; but late in the Spring they are, by long fasting, very poor and dry eating.

The Southern Indians kill great numbers of those Bears at all seasons of the year; but no encouragement can prevent them from singeing almost every one that is in good condition: so that the few skins they do save and bring to the market, are only of those which are so poor that their flesh is not worth eating.[CA] In fact, the skinning of a Bear spoils the meat thereof, as much as it would do to skin a young porker, or a roasting pig. The same may be said of swans (the skins of which the Company have lately made an article of trade); otherwise thousands of their skins might be brought to market annually, by the Indians that trade with the Hudson's Bay Company's servants at the different settlements about the Bay.

[346]

The Brown Bear.

BROWN BEARS[134] are, I believe, never found in the North-Indian territories: but I saw the skin of an enormous {372} grizzled Bear at the tents of the Esquimaux at the Copper River;[135] and many of them are said to breed not very remote from that part.

The Wolverene.

The WOLVERENE[136] is common in the Northern regions, as far North as the Copper River, and perhaps farther. They are equally the inhabitants of woods and barren grounds; for the Esquimaux to the North of Churchill kill many of them when their skins are in excellent season: a proof of their being capable of braving the severest cold. They are very slow in their pace, but their wonderful sagacity, strength, and acute scent, make ample amends for that defect; for they are seldom killed at any season when they do not prove very fat: a great proof of their being excellent providers. With respect to the fierceness of this animal which some assert, I can say little, but I know them to be beasts of great courage and resolution, for I once saw one of them take possession of a deer that an Indian had killed, and though the Indian advanced within twenty yards, he would not relinquish his claim to it, but suffered himself to be shot standing on the deer. I once saw a similar instance of a lynx, or wild cat, which also suffered itself to be killed, before it would relinquish the prize. The Wolverenes have also frequently been seen to take a deer from a wolf before the latter had time to begin his repast after killing it. Indeed their amazing strength, and the length and sharpness of their claws, render them capable of making a strong resistance against {373} any other animal in those parts, the Bear not excepted. As a proof of their amazing strength, there was one at Churchill some years since, that overset the greatest part of a large pile of wood, (containing a whole Winter's firing, that measured upwards of seventy yards round,) to get at some provisions that had been hid there by the Company's servants, when going to the Factory to spend the Christmas holidays. The fact was, this animal had been lurking about in the neighbourhood of their tent (which was about eight miles from the Factory) for some weeks, and had committed many depredations on the game caught in their traps and snares, as well as eaten many foxes that were killed by guns set for that purpose: but the Wolverene was too cunning to take either trap or gun himself. The people knowing the mischievous disposition of those animals, took (as they thought) the most effectual method to secure the remains of their provisions, which they did not chuse to carry home, and accordingly tied it up in bundles and placed it on the top of the wood-pile, (about two miles from their tent,) little thinking the Wolverene would find it out; but to their great surprise, when they returned to their tent after the holidays, they found the pile of wood in the state already mentioned, though some of the trees that composed it were as much as two men could carry. The only reason the people could give for the animal doing so much mischief was, that in his attempting to carry off the booty, some of the small parcels of provisions had fallen down into the heart of the pile, and {374} sooner than lose half his prize, he pursued the above method till he had accomplished his ends. The bags of flour, oatmeal, and pease, though of no use to him, he tore all to pieces, and scattered the contents about on the snow; but every bit of animal food, consisting of beef, pork, bacon, venison, salt geese, partridges, &c. to a considerable amount, he carried away. These animals are great enemies to the Beaver, but the manner of life of the latter prevents them from falling into their clutches so frequently as many other animals; they commit vast depredations on the foxes during the Summer, while the young ones are small; their quick scent directs them to their dens, and if the entrance be too small, their strength enables them to widen it, and go in and kill the mother and all her cubs. In fact, they are the most destructive animals in this country.[CB]

[348]

[347]

The Otter.

OTTERS[137] are pretty plentiful in the rivers to the North of Churchill, as far as latitude 62°; farther North I do not recollect to have seen any. In Winter they generally frequent those parts of rivers where there are falls or rapids, which do not freeze in the coldest Winters;

because in {375} such situations they are most likely to find plenty of fish, and the open water gives them a free admission to the shore, where they sometimes go to eat the fish they have caught; but most commonly sit on the ice, or get on a great stone in the river. They are frequently seen in the very depth of Winter at a considerable distance from any known open water, both in woods and on open plains, as well as on the ice of large lakes; but it is not known what has led them to such places: perhaps merely for amusement, for they are not known to kill any game on the land during that season. If pursued when among the woods in Winter, (where the snow is always light and deep,) they immediately dive, and make considerable way under it, but are easily traced by the motion of the snow above them, and soon overtaken. The Indians kill numbers of them with clubs, by tracing them in the snow; but some of the old ones are so fierce when close pursued, that they turn and fly at their pursuer, and their bite is so severe that it is much dreaded by the Indians. Besides this method of killing them, the Indians have another, which is equally successful; namely, by concealing themselves within a reasonable gun-shot of the Otters usual landing-places, and waiting their coming out of the water. This method is more generally practised in moon-light nights. They also shoot many of them as they are sporting in the water, and some few are caught in traps.

[349]

The Otters in this, as well as every other part of the bay, vary in size and colour, according to age and season. {376} In Summer, when the hair is very short, they are almost black, but as the Winter advances, they turn to a beautiful dark auburn, except a small spot under the chin, which is of a silver gray. This colour they retain all the Winter; but late in the Spring (though long before they shed their coat) they turn to a dull rusty brown; so that a person who is acquainted with those changes can tell to a great nicety, by looking at the skins, (when offered for sale,) the very time they were killed, and pay for them according to their value. The number of their young is various, from three to five or six. They unite in copulation the same as a dog, and so do every other animal that has a bone in the *penis.* I will here enumerate all of that description that I[350] know of in those parts, *viz.* bears of all sorts, wolves, wolvereens, foxes, martins, otters, wejacks, jackashes, skunks, and ermines.[CC]

> The Jackash.

JACKASH.[138] This animal is certainly no other than the lesser Otter of Canada, as its colour, size, and manner of life entirely correspond with the description of that animal in Mr. Pennant's Arctic Zoology. They, like the larger Otter, are frequently found in Winter several miles from any water, and are often caught in traps built for martins. They are supposed to prey on mice and partridges, the same as the martin; but when by the side of rivers or {377} creeks, they generally feed on fish. They vary so much in size and colour, that it was very easy for Mr. Pennant to have mistaken the specimen sent home for another animal. They are the easiest to tame and domesticate of any animal I know, except a large species of field-mice, called the Hair-tailed Mouse; for in a very short time they are so fond, that it is scarcely possible to keep them from climbing up one's legs and body, and they never feel themselves happier than when sitting on the shoulder; but when angry, or frightened, (like the skunk,) they emit a very disagreeable smell. They sleep very much in the day, but prowl about and feed in the night; they are very fierce when at their meals, not suffering those to whom they are most attached to take it from them. I have kept several of them, but their over-fondness made them troublesome, as they were always in the way; and their so frequently emitting a disagreeable smell, rendered them quite disgusting.

[351]

> The Wejack, and Skunk.

Though the WEJACK[139][CD] and SKUNK[140] are never found in the Northern Indian country, yet I cannot help observing that fœtid smell of the latter has not been much exaggerated by any Author. When I was at Cumberland {378} House, in the Fall of one thousand seven hundred and seventy-four, some Indians that were tenting on the plantation killed two of those animals, and made a feast of them; when the spot where they were singed and gutted was so impregnated with that nauseous smell which they emit, that after a whole Winter had elapsed, and the snow had thawed away in the Spring, the smell was still intolerable. I am told, however, that the flesh is by no means tainted with the smell, if care be taken in gutting, and taking out the bag that contains this surprising effluvia, and which they have the power of emitting at pleasure; but I rather doubt their being capable of ejecting their urine so far as is reported; I do not think it is their urine which contains that pestilential effluvia, for if that was the case, all the country where they frequent would be so scented with it, that neither man nor beast could live there with any degree of comfort.

> **The Pine Martin.**

The COMMON PINE MARTIN[141] is found in most parts of this country, and though very scarce in what is absolutely called the Northern Indian territory, yet by the Indians strolling toward the borders of the Southern Indian country, are killed in great numbers, and annually traded for at Churchill Factory.

[352]

> **The Ermine, or Stote.**

The ERMINE, or STOTE,[142] is common in those parts, but generally more plentiful on the barren ground, and open plains or marshes, than in the woods; probably owing to {379} the mice being more numerous in the former situations than in the latter. In Summer they are of a tawney brown, but in Winter of a delicate white all over, except the tip of the tail, which is of a glossy black. They are, for their size, the strongest and most courageous animal I know: as they not only kill partridges, but even attack rabbits with great success. They sometimes take up their abode in the out-offices and provision-sheds belonging to the Factories; and though they commit some depredations, make ample amends by killing great numbers of mice, which are very numerous and destructive at most of the settlements in the Bay. I have taken much pains to tame and domesticate this beautiful animal, but never could succeed; for the longer I kept it the more restless and impatient it became.

Animals with Cutting Teeth.

The Musk Rat.

The MUSK RAT,[143] or MUSQUASH; or, as Naturalists call it, the MUSK BEAVER; is common in those parts; generally frequenting ponds and deep swamps that do not freeze dry in Winter. The manner of life of this species of animals is peculiar, and resembles that of the Beaver, as they are in some respects provident, and build houses to shelter themselves from the inclemency of the cold in Winter; but instead of making those houses on the banks of ponds or swamps, like the Beaver, they generally build them on the ice as soon as it is skinned over, and at a considerable {380} distance from the shore; always taking care to keep a hole open in the ice to admit them to dive for their food, which chiefly consists of the roots of grass: in the Southern parts of the country they feed much on a well-known root, called *Calamus Aromaticus.*[144] The materials made use of in building their houses are mud and grass, which they fetch up from the bottom. It sometimes happens in very cold Winters, that the holes in their houses freeze over, in spite of all their efforts to keep them open. When that is the case, and they have no provisions left in the house, the strongest preys on the weakest, till by degrees only one is left out of a whole lodge. I have seen several instances sufficient to confirm the truth of this assertion; for when their houses were broke open, the skeletons of seven or eight have been found, and only one entire animal. Though they occasionally eat fish and other animal food, yet in general they feed very clean, and when fat are good eating, particularly when nicely singed, scalded, and boiled. They are easily tamed, and soon grow fond; are very cleanly and playful, and smell exceedingly pleasant of musk; but their resemblance to a Rat is so great that few are partial to them. Indeed the only difference between them and a common Rat, exclusive of their superior size, is, that their hind-feet are large and webbed, and the tail, instead of being round, is flat and scaly.

[353]

Though I have before said, that the Musk Beaver generally build their houses on the ice, it is not always the case; for in the Southern parts of the country, particularly {381} about Cumberland House, I have seen, in some of the deep swamps that were over-run with rushes and long grass, many small islands that have been raised by the industry of those animals; on the tops of which they had built their houses, like the beaver, some of which were very large. The tops of those houses are favourite breeding-places for the geese, which bring forth their young brood there, without the fear of being molested by foxes, or any other destructive animal, except the Eagle.[354]

> The Porcupine.

PORCUPINES[145] are so scarce to the North of Churchill River, and I do not recollect to have seen more than six during almost three years' residence among the Northern Indians. Mr. Pennant observes in his Arctic Zoology,[146] that they always have two at a time; one brought forth alive and the other still-born;[CF] but I never saw an instance of this kind, though in different parts of the country I have seen them killed in all stages of pregnancy. The flesh of the porcupine is very delicious, and so much esteemed by the Indians, that they think it the greatest luxury that their country affords. The quills are in great request among the women; who make them into a variety of ornaments, such as shot-bags, belts, garters, bracelets, &c. Their mode of copulation is singular, for their {382} quills will not permit them to perform that office in the usual mode, like other quadrupeds. To remedy this inconvenience, they sometimes lie on their sides, and meet in that manner; but the usual mode is for the male to lie on his back, and the female to walk over him, (beginning at his head,) till the parts of generation come in contact. They are the most forlorn animal I know; for in those parts of Hudson's Bay where they are most numerous, it is not common to see more than one in a place. They are so remarkably slow and stupid, that our Indians going with packets from Fort to Fort often see them in the trees, but not having occasion for them at that time, leave them till their return; and should their absence be a week or ten days, they are sure to find them within a mile of the place where they had seen them before.

[355]

Foxes of various Colours.

FOXES[147] of various colours are not scarce in those parts; but the natives living such a wandering life, seldom kill many. It is rather strange that no other species of Fox, except the white, are found at any distance from the woods on the barren ground; for so long as the trade has been established with the Esquimaux to the North of Churchill, I do not recollect that Foxes of any other colour than white were ever received from them.

Varying Hares.

The VARYING HARES[148] are numerous to the North of Churchill River, and extend as far as latitude 72°, probably farther. They delight most in rocky and stony {383} places, near the borders of woods; though many of them brave the coldest Winters on entire barren ground. In Summer they are nearly the colour of our English wild rabbit; but in Winter assume a most delicate white all over, except the tips of the ears, which are black. They are, when full grown and in good condition, very large, many of them weighing fourteen or fifteen pounds; and if not too old, are good eating. In

Winter they feed on long rye-grass and the tops of dwarf willows, but in Summer eat berries, and different sorts of small herbage. They are frequently killed on the South-side of Churchill River, and several have been known to breed near the settlement at that place. They must multiply very fast, for when we evacuated Prince of Wales's Fort in one thousand seven hundred and eighty-two, it was rare to see one of them within twenty or thirty miles of that place; but at our return, in one thousand seven hundred and eighty-three, we found them in such numbers, that it was common for one man to kill two or three in a day within half a mile of the new settlement. But partly, perhaps, from so many being killed, and partly from the survivors being so frequently disturbed, they have shifted their situation, and are at present as scarce near the settlement as ever. The Northern Indians pursue a singular method in shooting those Hares; finding by long experience that these animals will not bear a direct approach, when the Indians see a hare sitting, they walk round it in circles, always drawing nearer at every revolution, till by degrees they get within gun-shot. The {384} middle of the day, if it be clear weather, is the best time to kill them in this manner; for before and after noon, the Sun's altitude being so small, makes a man's shadow so long on the snow, as to frighten the Hare before he can approach near enough to kill it. The same may be said of deer when on open plains, who are frequently more frightened at the long shadow than at the man himself.

[357]

[356]

> **The American Hare.**

The AMERICAN HARES,[149] or, as they are called in Hudson's Bay, RABBITS, are not plentiful in the Eastern parts of the Northern Indian country, not even in those parts that are situated among the woods; but to the Westward, bordering on the Southern Indian country, they are in some places pretty numerous, though by no means equal to what has been reported of them at York Fort, and some other settlements in the Bay.

The furr of those animals, when killed in the best part of the season, was for many years entirely neglected by the furriers; for some time past the Company have ordered as many of their skins to be sent home as can be procured; they are but of small value.

The flesh of those Hares is generally more esteemed than that of the former. They are in season all the Winter; and though they generally feed on the brush of pine and fir during that season, yet many of the Northern Indians eat the contents of the stomach. They are seldom sought after in Summer, as in that season they are not esteemed {385} good eating; but as the Fall advances they are, by feeding on berries, &c. most excellent. In Spring they shed their Winter coat, and during the Summer are nearly the colour of the English wild rabbit, but as the Winter advances they become nearly white. In thick weather they are easily shot with the gun; but the most usual method of killing them is by snares, set nearly in the manner described by Dragge in the First Volume of his North West Passage.

The Common Squirrel.

The COMMON SQUIRRELS[150] are plentiful in the woody parts of this country, and are caught by the natives in considerable numbers with snares, while the boys kill many of them with blunt-headed arrows. The method of snaring them is rather curious, though very simple, as it consists of nothing more than setting a number of snares all round the body of the tree in which they are seen, and arranging them in such a manner that it is scarcely possible for the squirrels to descend without being entangled in one of them. This is generally the amusement of the boys. Though small, and seldom fat, yet they are good eating.

[358]

The beauty and delicacy of this animal induced me to attempt taming and domesticating some of them, but without success; for though several of them were so familiar as to take any thing out of my hand, and sit on the table where I was writing, and play with the pens, &c. yet they never would bear to be handled, and were very mischievous; gnawing the chair-bottoms, window-curtains, sashes, &c. to pieces. They are an article of trade in the {386} Company's standard, but the greatest part of their skins, being killed in Summer, are of very little value.

| The Ground Squirrel. |

The GROUND SQUIRRELS[151] are never found in the woody parts of North America, but are very plentiful on the barren ground, to the North of Churchill River, as far as the latitude 71°, and probably much farther. In size they are equal to the American Grey Squirrel, though more beautiful in colour. They generally burrow among the rocks and under great stones, but sometimes on the sides of sandy ridges; and are so provident in laying up a Winter's stock during the Summer, that they are seldom seen on the surface of the snow in Winter. They generally feed on the tufts of grass, the tender tops of dwarf willows, &c. and are for the most part exceedingly fat, and good eating. They are easily tamed, and soon grow fond; by degrees they will bear handling as well as a cat; are exceeding cleanly, very playful, and by no means so restless and impatient of confinement as the Common Squirrel.

[359]

| Mice of various kinds. |

MICE are in great plenty and variety in all parts of Hudson's Bay; the marshes being inhabited by one species, and the dry ridges by another. The Shrew Mouse[152] is frequently found in Beaver houses during Winter, where they not only find a warm habitation, but also pick up a comfortable livelihood from the scraps left by the Beaver.

Most of the other species build or make nests of dry grass, {387} of such a size and thickness, that when covered with snow, they must be sufficiently warm. They all feed on grass in general, but will also eat animal food when they can get it. The Hair-tailed Mouse[183] is the largest in the Northern parts of the Bay, being little inferior in size to a common rat. They always burrow under stones, on dry ridges; are very inoffensive, and so easily tamed, that if taken when full-grown, some of them will in a day or two be perfectly reconciled, and are so fond of being handled, that they will creep about your neck, or into your bosom. In Summer they are grey, and in Winter change to white, but are by no means so beautiful as a white ermine. At that season they are infested with multitudes of small lice, not a sixth part so large as the mites in a cheese; in fact, they are so small, that at first sight they only appear like reddish-brown dust, but on closer examination are all perceived in motion. In one large and beautiful animal of this kind, caught in the depth of Winter, I found those little vermin so numerous about it, that almost every hair was covered with them as thick as ropes with onions, and when they approached near the ends of the hair they may be said to change the mouse from white to a faint brown. At that time I had an excellent microscope, and endeavoured to examine them, and to ascertain their form, but the weather was so exceedingly cold, that the glasses became damp with the moisture of my breath before I could get a single sight. The hind-feet of these Mice are exactly like those of a Bear, and the {388} fore-feet are armed with a horny substance, (that I never saw in any other species of the Mouse,) which is wonderfully adapted for scraping away the ground where they wish to take up their abode. They are plentiful on some of the stony ridges near Churchill Factory, but never approach the house, or any of the out-offices. From appearances they are very local, and seldom stray far from their habitations even in Summer, and in Winter they are seldom seen on the surface of the snow; a great proof of their being provident in Summer to lay by a stock for that season.

[360]

Pinnated Quadrupeds.

With respect to the Pinnated Quadrupeds with finlike feet, there are but few species in Hudson's Bay. The Walrus, or Sea-Horse, and Seals, are the only ones that I know.

The Walrus.

The WALRUS[154] are numerous about Merry and Jones's Islands, but more so on a small island called Sea-Horse Island, that lies in the fair way going to Whale Cove. In July one thousand seven hundred and sixty-seven, when on my voyage to the North of Churchill River, in passing Sea-Horse Island, we saw such numbers of those animals lying on the shore, that when some swivel guns loaded with ball were fired among them, the whole beach seemed to be in motion. The greatest part of them plunged into the water, and many of them swam round {389} the vessel within musket-shot. Every one on board exerted their skill in killing them, but it was attended with so little success, that the few which were killed sunk to the bottom, and those which were mortally wounded made off out of our reach.

[361]

With what propriety those animals are called Horses, I cannot see; for there is not the least resemblance in any one part. Their bodies, fins, &c. are exactly like those of an enormous Seal, and the head is not very unlike that animal, except that the nose is much broader, to give room for the two large tusks that project from the upper jaw. Those tusks, and their red sparkling eyes, make them have a very fierce and formidable appearance.

They are generally found in considerable numbers, which indicate their love of society; and their affection for each other is very apparent, as they always flock round those that are wounded, and when they sink, accompany them to the bottom, but soon rise to the surface, and make a hideous roaring, and of all amphibious animals, they are at times the least sensible of danger from man that I know.

They often attack small boats merely through wantonness, and not only put the people in great confusion, but subject them to great danger; for they always aim at staving the boat with their tusks, or endeavour to get in, but are never known to hurt the people. In the year one thousand seven hundred and sixty-six some of the sloop's {390} crew, who annually sail to the North to trade with the Esquimaux, were attacked by a great number of those animals; and notwithstanding their utmost endeavours to keep them off, one more daring than the rest, though a small one, got in over the stern, and after sitting and looking at the people some time, he again plunged into the water to his companions.[362] At that instant another, of an enormous size, was getting in over the bow; and every other means proving ineffectual to prevent such an unwelcome visit, the bowman took up a gun, loaded with goose-shot, put the muzzle into the Horse's mouth, and shot him dead; he immediately sunk, and was followed by all his companions. The people then made the best of their way to the vessel, and just arrived before the Sea-Horses were ready to make their second attack, which in all probability might have been worse than the first, as they seemed much enraged at the loss of their companion.

Those animals are of various sizes, according to age and other circumstances; some are not larger than an old Seal but there are those among them that are not less than two ton weight.

The skin and teeth are the most valuable parts to the natives; for the fat is hard and grisly, and the flesh coarse, black, and tough.

Those animals are seldom found on the continent which borders on Hudson's Bay, or far up, in bays, rivers, or inlets, but usually frequent small islands, and sea-girt {391} shoals, at some distance from the main land; but as those places are frozen over for many miles during Winter, it is natural to think they keep at the edge of the water among the driving ice during that season. They are supposed to feed chiefly on marine plants, and perhaps on shell-fish, for their excrement is exceedingly offensive.

> **Seals.**

SEALS of various sizes and colours are common in most parts of Hudson's Bay, but most numerous to the North. Some of those animals are beautifully speckled, black and white;[156] others are of a dirty grey. The former are generally small, but some of the latter arrive at an amazing size, and their skins are of great use to the Esquimaux; as it is of them they cover their canoes, make all their boot-legs and shoes, besides many other parts of their clothing. The Seal-skins are also of great use to those people as a substitute for casks, to preserve oil, &c. for Winter use; they are also blown full of wind and dried, and then used as buoys on the whale-fishery. The flesh and fat of the Seal is also more esteemed by the Esquimaux than those of any other marine animal, salmon not excepted.

[363]

> **Sea Unicorn.**

Besides these, the SEA-UNICORN[156] is known to frequent Hudson's Bay and Straits, but I never saw one of them. Their horns are frequently purchased from our friendly Esquimaux, who probably get them in the way of barter from those tribes that reside more to the North; but I {392} never could be informed by the natives whether their skins are like those of the Whale, or hairy like those of the Seal; I suppose the former.

Species of Fish.

The Fish that inhabit the salt water of Hudson's Bay are but few:— the Black Whale, White Whale, Salmon, and a small fish called Kepling, are the only species of sea-fish in those parts.[CT]

> **Black Whale.**

The BLACK WHALE[157] is sometimes found as far South as Churchill River, and I was present at the killing of three there; but this was in the course of twenty years. To the Northward, particularly near Marble Island, they are more plentiful; but notwithstanding the Company carried on a fishery in that quarter, from the year one thousand seven hundred and sixty-five till one thousand seven hundred and seventy-two, they were so far from making it answer their expectations, that they sunk upwards of twenty thousand pounds; which is the less to be wondered at, when we consider the great inconveniencies and expences {393} they laboured under in such an undertaking. For as it was impossible to prosecute it from England, all the people employed on that service were obliged to reside at their settlement all the year at extravagant wages, exclusive of their maintenance. The harpooners had no less than fifty pounds *per annum* standing wages, and none of the crew less than from fifteen to twenty-five pounds; which, together with the Captains' salaries, wear and tear of their vessels, and other contingent expences, made it appear on calculation, that if there were a certainty of loading the vessels every year, the Company could not clear themselves. On the contrary, during the seven years they persevered in that undertaking, only four Black Whales were taken near Marble Island; and, except one, they were so small, that they would not have been deemed payable fish in the Greenland service.[CG] But the Hudson's Bay Company, with a liberality that does honour to them, though perfectly acquainted with the rules observed in the Greenland service, gave the same premium for a sucking fish, as for one of the greatest magnitude.

[365]

[364]

White Whale.

WHITE WHALES[158] are very plentiful in those parts, particularly from Chesterfield's Inlet to York Fort, or Hay's {394} River, on the West side of the Bay; and from Cape Smith to Slude River on the East side. On the West coast they are generally found in the greatest numbers at the mouths of the principal rivers; such as Seal River, Churchill, Port Nelson, and Hay's Rivers. But the East side of the Bay not being so well known, Whale River is the only part they are known to frequent in very considerable numbers. Some years ago the Company had a settlement at this river, called Richmond Fort; but all their endeavours to establish a profitable fishery here proved ineffectual, and the few Indians who resorted to it with furrs proving very inadequate to the expences, the Company determined to evacuate it. Accordingly, after keeping up this settlement for upward of twelve years, and sinking many thousands of pounds, they ordered it to be burnt, for the more easily getting the spikes and other iron-work. This was in the year one thousand seven hundred and fifty-eight.

At the old established Factories on the West side of the Bay, the Company have been more successful in the White Whale fishery, particularly at Churchill, where such of the Company's servants as cannot be employed during that season to more benefit for the Company, are sent on that duty, and in some successful years they send home from eight to thirteen tons of fine oil. To encourage a spirit of industry among those employed on this service, the Company allows a gratuity, not only to the harpooners, but to every man that sails in the boats; and this {395} gratuity is so ample as to inspire them with emulation, as they well know that the more they kill, the greater will be their emolument.

[366]

Salmon.

SALMON[159] are in some seasons very numerous on the North West side of Hudson's Bay, particularly at Knapp's Bay and Whale Cove. At the latter I once found them so plentiful, that had we been provided with a sufficient number of nets, casks, and salt, we might soon have loaded the vessel with them. But this is seldom the case, for in some years they are so scarce, that it is with difficulty a few meals of them can be procured during our stay at those harbours. They are in some years so plentiful near Churchill River, that I have known upward of two hundred fine fish taken out of four small nets in one tide within a quarter of a mile of the Fort; but in other years they are so scarce, that barely that number have been taken in upward of twenty nets during the whole season, which generally begins the latter end of June, and ends about the middle or latter end of August.

Kepling.

Beside the fish already mentioned, I know of no other that inhabits the salt water except the KEPLING,[16th] which is a small fish about the size of a smelt, but most excellent eating. In some years they resort to the shores near Churchill River in such multitudes to spawn, and such numbers of them are left dry among the rocks, as at times to be {396} quite offensive. In other seasons they are so scarce, that hardly a meal can be procured.

The same remark may be made on almost every species of game, which constitutes the greatest part of the fare of the people residing in those parts. For instance, in some years, hundreds of deer may easily be killed within a mile of York Fort; and in others, there is not one to be seen within twenty or thirty miles. One day thousands and tens of thousands of geese are seen, but the next they all raise flight, and go to the North to breed. Salmon, as I have lately observed, is so plentiful in some years at Churchill River, that it might be procured in any quantity; at others, so scarce as to be thought a great delicacy.

[367]

In fact, after twenty years residence in this country, I am persuaded that whoever relies much on the produce of the different seasons, will frequently be deceived, and occasionally expose himself and men to great want.

To remedy this evil, it is most prudent for those in command to avail themselves of plentiful seasons, and cure a sufficient quantity of the least perishable food, particularly geese.

Shell Fish.

Shell Fish.

SHELL FISH of a variety of kinds are also found in some parts of Hudson's Bay. Muscles[161] in particular are in great abundance on the rocky shores near Churchill River, and what is vulgarly called the Periwinkle are very plentiful {397} on the rocks which dry at low-water. Small Crabs[162] and Starfish[163] are frequently thrown on the shore by the surf in heavy gales of wind; and the empty shells of Wilks, small Scallops, Cockles, and many other kinds, are to be found on the beaches in great plenty. The same may be said of the interior parts of the country, where the banks of the lakes and rivers abound with empty shells of various kinds; but the fish themselves have never been discovered by the natives.

[368]

Frogs, Grubs, and other Insects.

Frogs.

Spiders and Grubs.

FROGS[164] of various colours are numerous in those parts as far North as the latitude 61°. They always frequent the margins of lakes, ponds, rivers, and swamps: and as the Winter approaches, they burrow under the moss, at a considerable distance from the water, where they remain in a frozen state till the Spring. I have frequently seen them dug up with the moss, (when pitching tents in Winter,) frozen as hard as ice; in which state the legs are as easily broken off as a pipe-stem, without giving the least sensation to the animal; but by wrapping them up in warm skins, and exposing them to a slow fire, they soon recover life, and the mutilated animal gains its usual activity; but if they are permitted to freeze again, they are past all recovery, and are never more known to come to life. The same may be said of the various species of {398} Spiders, and all the Grub kind, which are very numerous in those parts. I have seen thousands of them dug up with the moss, when we were pitching our tents in the Winter; all of which were invariably enclosed in a thick web, which Nature teaches them to spin on those occasions; yet they were apparently all frozen as hard as ice. The Spiders, if let fall from any height on a hard substance, would rebound like a grey pea; and all the Grub kind are so hard frozen as to be as easily broken as a piece of ice of the same size; yet when exposed to a slow heat, even in the depth of Winter, they will soon come to life, and in a short time recover their usual motions.

Birds.

The feathered creation that resort to those parts in the different seasons are numerous, but such as brave the severe Winter are but few in number, and shall be particularly noticed in their proper places.

[369]

Eagles.

EAGLES of several sorts are found in the country bordering on Hudson's Bay during the Summer; but none, except the common brown Fishing Eagle,[165] ever frequent the Northern parts. They always make their appearance in those dreary regions about the latter end of March or beginning of April, and build their nests in lofty trees, in the crevices of inaccessible rocks near the {399} banks of rivers. They lay but two eggs, (which are white,) and frequently bring but one young. They generally feed on fish, which they catch as they are swimming near the surface; but they are very destructive to the musk rat and hares, as also to geese and ducks, when in a moulting state, and frequently kill young beaver. Their nests are very large, frequently six feet in diameter; and before their young can fly, are so provident, that the Indians frequently take a most excellent meal of fish, flesh, and fowl from their larder. Though they bring forth their young so early as the latter end of May, or the beginning of June, yet they never fly till September; a little after which they migrate to the Southward. They are the most ravenous of any bird I know; for when kept in confinement or in a tame state as it may be called, I have known two of them eat more than a bushel of fish in a day. They are never known to breed on the barren grounds to the North of Churchill River, though many of the lakes and rivers in those parts abound with variety of fish. This is probably owing to the want of trees or high rocks to build in. The Northern Indians are very partial to the quill-feathers of the Eagle, as well as to those of the hawk, to wing or plume their arrows with, out of a superstitious notion that they have a greater effect than if winged with the feathers of geese, cranes, crows, or other birds, that in fact would do equally as well. The flesh of the Eagle is usually eaten by most of the Indians, but is always black, hard, and fishy; even the {400} young ones, when in a callow state, though the flesh is delicate white, are so rank as to render them very unpleasant to some persons, except in times of necessity.

[370]

> **Hawks of various sizes.**

HAWKS of various sizes and plumage frequent the different parts of the country round Hudson's Bay during Summer. Some of those Hawks are so large as to weigh three pounds, and others so small as not to exceed five or six ounces. But the weight of those, as well as every other species of Birds, is no standard for the Naturalist to go by; for at different seasons, and when in want of food, they are often scarcely half the weight they are when fat and in good order. Notwithstanding the variety of Hawks that resort to those parts in

Summer, I know but one species that brave the intense cold of the long Winters to the North of Churchill River; and that is what Mr. Pennant calls the Sacre Falcon.[166] They, like the other large species of Hawks, prey much on the white grouse or partridge, and also on the American hare, usually called here Rabbits. They are always found to frequent those parts where partridges are plentiful, and are detested by the sportsmen, as they generally drive all the game off the ground near their tents; but, in return, they often drive thither fresh flocks of some hundreds. Notwithstanding this, they so frequently baulk those who are employed on the hunting service, that the Governors generally give a reward of a quart of brandy for each of their heads. Their flesh is always eaten by the Indians, and sometimes by the {401} English; but it is always black, hard, and tough, and sometimes has a bitter taste.

The Indians are fond of taming those birds, and frequently keep them the whole Summer; but as the Winter approaches they generally take flight, and provide for themselves. When at Cumberland House I had one of them, of which my people were remarkably fond; and as it never wanted for food, would in all probability have remained with us all the Winter, had it not been killed by an Indian who did not know it to be tame.

[371]

> White or Snowy Owl.

The beautiful species of WHITE or SNOWY OWL[167] is common in all parts of Hudson's Bay, as far North as the Copper-mine River. These birds, when flying or sitting, appear very large, but when killed, seldom weigh more than three and a half, or four pounds, and sometimes scarcely half that weight. They generally feed on mice and partridges, and are at times known to kill rabbits. They are, like the hawk, very troublesome to the sportsmen; and, contrary to any other bird that I know, have a great propensity to follow the report of a gun, and frequently follow the hunters (as they are usually called in Hudson's Bay) the whole day. On those occasions they usually perch on high trees, and watch till a bird is killed, when they skim down and carry it off before the hunter can get near it; but in return, the hunters, when they see them on the watch, frequently decoy them within gun-shot, by throwing up a dead bird, which {402} the Owl seldom refuses to accept; but the sportsman being fully provided for this visit, and on his guard, generally shoots them before they can carry off the partridge. They are, however, so great a hindrance to those employed on the hunting service, that the same premium is given for one of their heads as for that of a hawk.

In Winter they are frequently very fat, their flesh delicately white, and generally esteemed good eating, both by English and Indians. Those Owls always make their nests on the ground, generally lay from three to four eggs, but seldom hatch more than two; and in the extreme North the young ones do not fly till September. They never migrate, but brave the coldest Winters, even on the barren ground, far remote from any woods; and in those situations perch on high rocks and stones, and watch for their prey.

[372]

> Grey or Mottled Owl.

The species of GREY or MOTTLED OWL[168] are by no means so numerous as the former, are something inferior in size, and always frequent the woods. They never go in search of their prey in the day time, but perch on the tops of lofty pines, and are easily approached and shot. Their food is generally known to be mice and small birds, yet their flesh is delicately white, and nearly as good as a barn-door fowl; of course it is much esteemed both by the English and Indians. This species of Owl is called by the Southern Indians Ho-ho, and the former Wap-a-kee-thow.

> Cob-a-dee-cooch.

{403} Besides those two species of Owls, there is another that remains in Hudson's Bay all the year, and is called by the Indians COB-A-DEE-COOCH.[169] It is so far inferior in size to the two former, that it seldom weighs half a pound; is of a mottled brown, the feathers long, and of a most delicate soft and silky quality. In general this species feed on mice, and birds they find dead; and are so impudent at times, that they light on a partridge when killed by the hunter, but not being able to carry it off, are often obliged to relinquish the prize. Like the White Owl, at times, though but seldom, they follow the report of a gun, and by so frequently skimming round the sportsmen, frighten the game nearly as much as the hawk. They seldom go far from the woods, build in trees, and lay from two to four eggs. They are never fat, and their flesh is eaten only by the Indians.

[373]

> Ravens.

RAVENS[179] of a most beautiful glossy black, richly tinged with purple and violet colour, are the constant inhabitants of Hudson's Bay; but are so far inferior in size to the English Raven, that they are usually called Crows. They build their nests in lofty pine-trees, and generally lay four speckled eggs; they bring forth their young so early as the latter end of May, or the beginning of June. In Summer many of them frequent the barren grounds, several hundred miles from any woods; probably invited there by the multitudes of deer and musk-oxen that are killed by the Northern Indians during that season, merely for their {404} skins, and who leave their flesh to rot, or be devoured by beasts or birds of prey. At those times they are very fat, and the flesh of the young ones is delicately white, and good eating. But in Winter they are, through necessity, obliged to feed on a black moss that grows on the pine-trees, also on deer's dung, and excrements of other animals. It is true, they kill some mice, which they find in the surface of the snow, and catch many wounded partridges and hares; in some parts of the country they are a great nuisance to the hunter, by eating the game that is either caught in snares or traps. With all this assistance, they are in general so poor during the severe cold in Winter, as to excite wonder how they possibly can exist.

Their faculty of scent must be very acute; for in the coldest days in Winter, when every kind of effluvia is almost instantaneously destroyed by the frost, I have frequently known buffaloes and other beasts killed where not one of those birds were seen; but in a few hours scores of them would gather about the spot to pick up the dung, blood, and other offal. An unarmed man may approach them very near when feeding, but they are shy of those that have a gun; a great proof that they smell the gunpowder. They are, however, frequently shot by guns set for foxes; and sometimes caught in traps built for martins. Though, on the whole, they may be called a shy bird, yet their necessities in Winter are so great, that, like the White Owl, they frequently follow the report of a gun, keep prudently at a distance from the sportsman, and frequently {405} carry off many wounded birds. Their quills make most excellent pens for drawing, or for ladies to write with.

[374]

Cinereous Crow.

The CINEREOUS CROW,[171] or, as it is called by the Southern Indians, Whisk-e-jonish, by the English Whiskey-jack, and by the Northern Indians Gee-za, but as some pronounce it, and that with more propriety, Jee-za, though classed among the Crows, is in reality so small, as seldom to weigh three ounces; the plumage grey, the feathers very long, soft, and silky, and in general entirely unwebbed, and in some parts much resembles hair. This bird is very familiar, and fond of frequenting habitations, either houses or tents; and so much given to pilfering, that no kind of provisions it can come at, either fresh or salt, is safe from its depredation. It is so bold as to come into tents, and sit on the edge of the kettle when hanging over the fire, and steal victuals out of the dishes. It is very troublesome to the hunters, both English and Indian, frequently following them a whole day; it will perch on a tree while the hunter is baiting his martin-traps, and as soon as his back is turned go and eat the baits. It is a kind of mock bird, and of course has a variety of notes; it is easily tamed, but never lives long in confinement. It is well known to be a provident bird, laying up great quantities of berries in Summer for a Winter stock; but its natural propensity to pilfer at all seasons makes it much detested both by the {406} English and Indians. It builds its nest in trees, exactly like that of the blackbird and thrush; lays four blue eggs, but seldom brings more than three young ones.

[375]

Wood-pecker.

I know of only one sort of WOOD-PECKER that frequents the remote Northern parts of Hudson's Bay; and this is distinguished by Mr. Pennant by the name of the Golden Winged Bird;[172] but to the South West that beautiful species of Wood-pecker with a scarlet crown is very frequent.[173] The manner of life of this species is nearly alike, always building their nests in holes in trees, and feeding on worms and insects. They generally have from four to six young at a time. They are said to be very destructive to fruit-trees that are raised in gardens in the more Southern parts of America; but the want of those luxuries in Hudson's Bay renders them very harmless and inoffensive birds. The red feathers of the larger sort, which frequent the interior and Southern parts of the Bay, are much valued by some of the Indians, who ornament their pipe-stems with them, and at times use them as ornaments to their children's clothing. Neither of the two species here mentioned ever migrate,[174] but are constant inhabitants of the different climates in which they are found.

Grouse.

There are several species of GROUSE in the different parts of Hudson's Bay; but two of the largest, and one of them the most beautiful, never reach so far North {407} as the latitude 59°: but as I have seen them in great plenty near Cumberland House, I shall take the liberty to describe them.

The Ruffed Grouse.

The RUFFED GROUSE.[175] This is the most beautiful of all that are classed under that name. They are of a delicate brown, prettily variegated with black and white: tail large and long, like that of a hawk, which is usually of an orange-colour, beautifully barred with black, chocolate, and white; and the tail is frequently expanded like a fan. To add to their beauty, they have a ruff of glossy black feathers, richly tinged with purple round the neck, which they can erect at pleasure: this they frequently do, but more particularly so when they spread their long tail, which gives them a noble appearance. In size they exceed a partridge, but are inferior to a pheasant. In Winter they are usually found perched on the branches of the pine-trees; and in that season are so tame as to be easily approached, and of course readily shot.

[376]

They always make their nests on the ground, generally at the root of a tree, and lay to the number of twelve or fourteen eggs. In some of the Southern parts of America several attempts have been made to tame those beautiful birds, by taking their eggs and hatching them under domestic hens, but it was never crowned with success; for when but a few days old, they always make their escape into the woods, where they probably pick up a subsistence. Their flesh is delicately white and firm, and {408} though they are seldom fat, they are always good eating, and are generally esteemed best when larded and roasted, or nicely boiled with a bit of bacon.

There is something very remarkable in those birds, and I believe peculiar to themselves, which is that of clapping their wings with such a force, that at half a mile distance it resembles thunder. I have frequently heard them make that noise near Cumberland House in the month of May, but it was always before Sun-rise, and a little after Sun-set. It is said by Mr. Barton and Le Hontan, that they never clap in this manner but in the Spring and Fall, and I must acknowledge that I never heard them in Winter, though I have killed many of them in that season. The Indians informed me they never make that noise but when feeding, which is very probable; for it is notoriously known that all the species of Grouse feed very early in the mornings, and late in the afternoons.[377] This species is called by some of the Indians bordering on Hudson's Bay, Pus-pus-kee, and by others Pus-pus-cue.

Sharp-tailed Grouse.

SHARP-TAILED GROUSE,[176] or as they are called in Hudson's Bay, Pheasant. Those birds are always found in the Southern parts of the Bay, are very plentiful in the interior parts of the country, and in some Winters a few of them are shot at York Fort, but never reach so far North as Churchill. In colour they are not very unlike that of the English hen pheasant; but the tail is short and pointed, like that of the common duck; and there is no perceivable {409} difference in plumage between the male and female. When full-grown, and in good condition, they frequently weigh two pounds, and though the flesh is dark, yet it is juicy, and always esteemed good eating, particularly when larded and roasted. In Summer they feed on berries, and in Winter on the tops of the dwarf birch, and the buds of the poplar. In the Fall they are tolerably tame, but in the severe cold more shy; frequently perch on the tops of the highest poplars, out of moderate gun-shot, and will not suffer a near approach. They sometimes, when disturbed in this situation, dive into the snow; but the sportsman is equally baulked in his expectations, as they force their way so fast under it as to raise flight many yards distant from the place they entered, and very frequently in a different direction to that from which the sportsman expects.[CH] They, like the other species of grouse, make their nests on the ground, and lay from ten to thirteen eggs. Like the Ruffed Grouse, they are not to be tamed, as many trials have been made at York Fort, but without success; for though they never made their escape, yet they always died, probably for the want of proper food; for the hens that hatched them were equally fond of them, as they could possibly have been had they been the produce of their own eggs. This species of Grouse is called by the Southern Indians Aw-kis-cow.

[378]

Wood Partridge.

{410} The WOOD PARTRIDGES[177] have acquired that name in Hudson's Bay from their always frequenting the forests of pines and fir; and in Winter feeding on the brush of those trees, though they are fondest of the latter. This species of Grouse is inferior in size and beauty to the Ruffed, yet may be called a handsome bird; the plumage being of a handsome brown, elegantly spotted with white and black. The tail is long, and tipped with orange; and the legs are warmly covered with short feathers, but the feet are naked. They are generally in the extreme with respect to shyness; sometimes not suffering a man to come within two gun-shots, and at others so tame that the sportsman may kill five or six out of one tree without shifting his station. They are seen in some years in considerable numbers near York Fort. They are very scarce at Churchill, though numerous in the interior parts, particularly on the borders of the Athapuscow Indians country, where I have seen my Indian companions kill many of them with blunt-headed arrows. In Winter their flesh is black, hard and bitter, probably owing to the resinous quality of their food during that season; but this is not observed in the rabbits, though they feed exactly in the same manner in Winter: on the contrary, their flesh is esteemed more delicate than that of the English rabbit. The Southern Indians call this species of Partridge, Mistick-a-pethow; and the Northern Indians call it, Day.

[379]

{411} The WILLOW PARTRIDGES[1751] have a strong black bill, with scarlet eye-brows, very large and beautiful in the male, but less conspicuous in the female. In Summer they are brown, elegantly barred and mottled with orange, white, and black; and at that season the males are very proud and handsome, but the females are less beautiful, being of one universal brown. As the Fall advances they change to a delicate white, except fourteen black feathers in the tail, which are also tipped with white; and their legs and feet, quite down to the nails, are warmly covered with feathers. In the latter end of September and beginning of October they gather in flocks of some hundreds, and proceed from the open plains and barren grounds, (where they usually breed,) to the woods and brush-willows, where they hord together in a state of society, till dispersed by their common enemies, the hawks, or hunters. They are by far the most numerous of any of the Grouse species that are found in Hudson's Bay; and in some places when permitted to remain undisturbed for a considerable time, their number is frequently so great, as almost to exceed credibility. I shall by no means exceed truth, if I assert that I have seen upward of four hundred in one flock near Churchill River; but the greatest number I ever saw was on the North side of Port Nelson River, when returning with a packet in March one thousand seven hundred and sixty-eight: at that time I saw thousands flying to the North, and the whole surface of the snow seemed to be in motion by those that were feeding on the tops of the short willows. Sir {412} Thomas Button mentions, that when he wintered in Port Nelson River in one thousand six hundred and twelve, his crew killed eighteen hundred dozen of those birds, which I have no reason to doubt; and Mr. Jérémie, formerly Governor at York Fort, when that place was in the possession of the French, and then called Fort Bourbon, asserts, that he and seventy-nine others eat no less than ninety thousand partridges and twenty-five thousand hares in the course of one Winter; which, considering the quantity of venison, geese, ducks, &c. enumerated in his account, that were killed that year, makes the number so great, that it is scarcely possible to conceive what eighty men could do with them; for on calculation, ninety thousand partridges and twenty-five thousand hares divided by eighty, amounts to no less than one thousand one hundred and twenty-five partridges, and three hundred and twelve hares per man. This is by far too great a quantity, particularly when it is considered that neither partridges nor hares are in season, or can be procured in any numbers, more than seven months in the year. Forty thousand partridges and five thousand hares would, I think, be much nearer the truth, and will be found, on calculation, to be ample provision for eighty men for seven months, exclusive of any change. The common weight of those birds is from eighteen to twenty-two ounces when first killed; there are some few that are nearly that weight when fit for the spit, but they are so scarce as by no means to serve as a standard; and as they always hord with the common {413} size, there is no room to suspect them of another species. As all those over-grown partridges are notoriously known to be males, it is more than probable that they are imperfect, and grow large and fat like capons; and every one that has had an opportunity of tasting those large partridges, will readily allow that they excel the common sort as much in flavour as they do in size. It is remarked in those birds, as well as the Rock Partridge, that they are provided with additional clothing, as it may be called; for every feather, from the largest to the smallest, except the quills and tail, are all double. The under-feather is soft and downy, shooting from the shaft of the larger; and is wonderfully adapted to their situation, as they not only brave the coldest Winters, but the species now under consideration always burrow under the snow at nights, and at day-light come forth to feed. In Winter they are always found to frequent the banks of rivers and creeks, the sides of lakes and ponds, and the plains which abound with dwarf willows; for it is on the buds and tops of that tree they always feed during the Winter. In summer they eat berries and small herbage. Their food in Winter being so dry and harsh, makes it necessary for them to swallow a considerable quantity of gravel to promote digestion; but the great depth of snow renders it very scarce during that season. The Indians having considered this point, invented the method now in use among the English, of catching them in nets by means of that simple allurement, a heap of gravel. The nets for this purpose are from eight {414} to twelve feet square, and are stretched in a frame of wood, and usually set on the ice of rivers, creeks, ponds, and lakes, about one hundred yards from the willows, but in some situations not half that distance. Under the center of the net a heap of snow is thrown up to the size of one or two bushels, and when well packed is covered with gravel. To set the nets, when thus prepared, requires no other trouble than lifting up one side of the frame, and supporting it with two small props, about four feet long: a line is fastened to those props, and the other end being conveyed to the neighbouring willows, is always so contrived that a man can get to it without being seen by the birds under the net. When every thing is thus prepared, the hunters have nothing to do but go into the adjacent willows and woods, and when they start game, endeavour to drive them into the net, which at times is no hard task, as they frequently run before them like chickens; and sometimes require no driving, for as soon as they see the black heap of gravel on the white snow they fly straight towards it. The hunter then goes to the end of the line to watch their motions, and when he sees there are as many about the gravel as the net can cover, or as many as are likely to go under at that time, with a sudden pull he hauls down the stakes, and the net falls horizontally on the snow, and encloses the greatest part of the birds that are under it. The hunter then runs to the net as soon as possible, and kills all the birds by biting them at the back of the head. He then sets up the net, {415} takes away all the dead game, and repeats the operation as often as he pleases, or as long as the birds are in good humour. By this simple contrivance I have known upwards of three hundred partridges caught in one morning by three persons; and a much greater number might have been procured had it been thought necessary. Early in the morning, just at break of day, and early in the afternoon, is the best time for this sport. It is common to get from thirty to seventy at one hawl; and in the Winter of one thousand seven hundred and eighty-six, Mr. Prince, then Master of a sloop at Churchill River, actually caught two hundred and four at two hawls. They are by no means equally plentiful every year; for in some Winters I have known them so scarce, that it was impossible to catch any in nets, and all that could be procured with the gun would hardly afford one day's allowance per week to the men during the season; but in the Winter one thousand seven hundred and eighty-five, they were so plentiful near Churchill, and such numbers were brought to the Factory, that I gave upward of two thousand to the hogs. In the latter end of March, or the beginning of April, those birds begin to change from white to their beautiful Summer plumage, and the first brown feathers make their appearance on the neck,[C] and by degrees {416} spread over the whole body; but their Summer dress is seldom complete till July. The feathers of those birds make excellent beds, and as they are the perquisite of the hunters, are usually sold to the Captains and Mates of the Company's ships, at the easy rate of three pence per pound.

[383]

[382]

[381]

[380]

Rock Partridges.

ROCK PARTRIDGES.[179] This species of Grouse are in Winter of the same colour as the former, but inferior in size; being in general not more than two-thirds of the weight. They have a black line from the bill to the eye, and differ in nature and manner from the Willow Partridge. They never frequent the woods or willows, but brave the severest cold on the open plains. They always feed on the buds and tops of the dwarf birch, and after this repast, generally sit on the high ridges of snow, with their heads to windward. They are never caught in nets, like the Willow Partridge; for when in want of gravel, their bills are of such an amazing strength, that they pick a sufficient quantity out of the rocks. Beside, being so much inferior in size to the former species, their flesh is by no means so good, being black, hard, and bitter. They are in general, like the Wood Partridge, either exceeding wild or very tame; and when in the latter humour, I have {417} known one man kill one hundred and twenty in a few hours; for as they usually keep in large flocks, the sportsmen can frequently kill six or eight at a shot. These, like the Willow Partridge, change their plumage in Summer to a beautiful speckled brown; and at that season are so hardy, that, unless shot in the head or vitals, they will fly away with the greatest quantity of shot of any bird I know. They discover great fondness for their young; for during the time of incubation, they will frequently suffer themselves to be taken by hand off their eggs.[CJ] Pigeons[180] of a small size, not larger than a thrush, are in some Summers found as far North as Churchill River. The bill is of a flesh-colour, legs red, and the greatest part of the plumage of a light lilac or blush. In the interior parts of the country they fly in large flocks, and perch on the poplar trees in such numbers that I have seen twelve of them killed at one shot. They usually feed on {418} poplar buds, and are good eating, though seldom fat. They build their nests in trees, the same as the Wood Pigeons do; never lay but two eggs, and are very scarce near the sea-coast in the Northern parts of Hudson's Bay.

[384]

Red-breasted Thrush.

The RED-BREASTED THRUSHES, commonly called in Hudson's Bay the Red Birds,[181] but by some the Black Birds, on account of their note, and by others the American Fieldfares usually make their appearance at Churchill River about the middle of May, build their nests of mud, like the English Thrush, and lay four beautiful blue eggs. They have a very loud and pleasing note, which they generally exercise most in the mornings and evenings, when perched on some lofty tree near their nest; but when the young can fly they are silent, and migrate to the South early in the Fall. They are by no means numerous, and are generally seen in pairs; they are never sought after as an article of food, but when killed by the Indian boys, are esteemed good eating, though they always feed on worms and insects.

[385]

Grosbeak.

GROSBEAK.[182] These gay birds visit Churchill River in some years so early as the latter end of March, but are by no means plentiful; they are always seen in pairs, and generally feed on the buds of the poplar and willow. The male is in most parts of its plumage of a beautiful crimson, but the female of a dull dirty green. In form they much resemble the English bullfinch, but are near {419} double their size. They build their nests in trees, sometimes not far from the ground; lay four white eggs, and always hatch them in June. They are said to have a pleasing note in Spring, though I never heard it, and are known to retire to the South early in the Fall. The English residing in Hudson's Bay generally call this bird the American Red Bird.

Snow Bunting.

SNOW BUNTINGS,[183] universally known in Hudson's Bay by the name of the Snow Birds, and in the Isles of Orkney by the name of Snow Flakes, from their visiting those parts in such numbers as to devour the grain as soon as sown, in some years are so destructive as to oblige the farmer to sow his fields a second, and occasionally a third time. These birds make their appearance at the Northern settlements in the Bay about the latter end of May, or beginning of April, [*sic*] when they are very fat, and not inferior in flavour to an ortolan. On their first arrival they generally feed on grass-seeds, and are fond of frequenting dunghills. At that time they are easily caught in great numbers under a net baited with groats or oatmeal; but as the Summer advances, they feed much on worms, and are then not so much esteemed. They sometimes fly in such large flocks, that I have killed upwards of twenty at one shot, and have known others who have killed double that number. In the Spring their plumage is prettily variegated, black and white; but their Summer dress may be called elegant, though not gay. They live {420} long in confinement, have naturally a pleasing note, and when in company with Canary birds soon imitate their song. I have kept many of them in cages in the same room with Canary birds, and always found they sung in Winter as well as in Summer; but even in confinement they change their plumage according to the season, the same as in a wild state. This species of bird seem fond of the coldest regions, for as the Spring advances they fly so far North that their breeding-places are not known to the inhabitants of Hudson's Bay. In Autumn they return to the South in large flocks, and are frequently shot in considerable numbers merely as a delicacy; at that season, however, they are by no means so good as when they first make their appearance in Spring.

[386]

White-crowned Bunting.

WHITE-CROWNED BUNTING.[184] This species is inferior in size to the former, and seldom make their appearance till June. They breed in most parts of the Bay, always make their nests on the ground, at the root of a dwarf willow or a gooseberry-bush. During the time their young are in a callow state they have a delightful note, but as soon as they are fledged they become silent, and retire to the South early in September.

[387]

Lapland Finch.

LAPLAND FINCH.[185] This bird is common on Hudson's Bay, and never migrates Southward in the coldest Winters. During that season it generally frequents the juniper plains, and feeds on the small buds of that tree, also on grass-seeds; {421} but at the approach of

Summer it flies still farther North to breed. A variety of this bird is also common, and is beautifully marked with a red forehead and breast.[186] It is most common in the Spring, and frequently caught in nets set for the Snow Bunting; and when kept in cages has a pleasing note, but seldom lives long in confinement, though it generally dies very fat.

> **Larks.**

LARKS[187] of a pretty variegated colour frequent those parts in Summer, and always make their appearance in May; build their nests on the ground, usually by the side of a stone at the root of a small bush, lay four speckled eggs, and bring forth their young in June. At their first arrival, and till the young can fly, the male is in full song; and, like the sky-lark, soars to a great height, and generally descends in a perpendicular direction near their nest. Their note is loud and agreeable, but consists of little variety, and as soon as the young can fly they become silent, and retire to the Southward early in the Fall. They are impatient of confinement, never sing in that state, and seldom live long.

> **Titmouse.**

The TITMOUSE[188] is usually called in Hudson's Bay, Blackcap. This diminutive bird braves the coldest Winter, and during that season feeds on the seeds of long rye-grass, but in Summer on insects and berries. The Southern Indians call this bird Kiss-kiss-heshis, from a twittering noise they make, which much resembles that word in sound.

[388]

> **Swallows.**

{422} SWALLOWS[189] visit these parts in considerable numbers in Summer, and are very domestic; building their nests in necessaries, stables, and other out-offices that are much frequented. They seldom make their appearance at Churchill River till June, and retire South early in August. They, like the European Swallow, gather in large flocks on the day of their departure, make several revolutions round the breeding-places, and then take their leave till the next year. I do not recollect to have seen any of those birds to the North of Seal River.

Martins.

MARTINS[190] also visit Hudson's Bay in great numbers, but seldom so far North as Churchill River. They usually make their nests in holes formed in the steep banks of rivers; and, like the Swallow, lay four or five speckled eggs; and retire Southward in August. At the Northern settlements they are by no means so domestic as the Swallow.

Hooping Crane.

HOOPING CRANE.[191] This bird visits Hudson's Bay in the Spring, though not in great numbers. They are generally seen only in pairs, and that not very often. It is a bird of considerable size, often equal to that of a good turkey, and the great length of the bill, neck, and legs, makes it measure, from the bill to the toes, near six feet in common, and some much more. Its plumage is of a pure white, except the quill-feathers, which are black; the crown is covered with a red skin, {423} thinly beset with black bristles, and the legs are large and black. It usually frequents open swamps, the sides of rivers, and the margins of lakes and ponds, feeds on frogs and small fish, and esteemed good eating. The wing-bones of this bird are so long and large, that I have known them made into flutes with tolerable success. It seldom has more than two young, and retires Southward early in the fall.

[389]

> **Brown Crane.**

The BROWN CRANE.[192] This species is far inferior in size to the former, being seldom three feet and a half in length, and on an average not weighing seven pounds. Their haunts and manner of life are nearly the same as that of the Hooping Crane, and they never have more than two young, and those seldom fly till September. They are found farther North than the former, for I have killed several of them on Marble Island, and have seen them on the Continent as high as the latitude 65°. They are generally esteemed good eating, and, from the form of the body when fit for the spit, they acquire the name of the North West Turkey. There is a circumstance respecting this bird that is very peculiar; which is, that the gizzard is larger than that of a swan, and remarkably so in the young birds. The Brown Cranes are frequently seen in hot calm days to soar to an amazing height, always flying in circles, till by degrees they are almost out of sight, yet their note is so loud, that the sportsman, before he sees their situation, often fancies they are very near him. They visit {424} Hudson's Bay in far greater numbers than the former, and are very good eating.

> **Bitterns.**

BITTERNS[193] are common at York Fort in Summer, but are seldom found so far North as Churchill River. I have seen two species of this bird; some having ash-coloured legs, others with beautiful grass-green legs, and very gay plumage. They always frequent marshes and swamps, also the banks of rivers that abound with reeds and long grass. They generally feed on insects that are bred in the water, and probably on small frogs; and though seldom fat, they are generally good eating. They are by no means numerous even at York Fort, nor in fact in the most Southern parts of the Bay that I have visited.

[390]

Curlew.

CURLEWS.[194] There are two species of this bird which frequent the coasts of Hudson's Bay in great numbers during Summer, and breed in all parts of it as far North as the latitude 72°; the largest of this species is distinguished by that great Naturalist Mr. Pennant, by the name of the Esquimaux Curlew. They always keep near the sea coast; attend the ebbing of the tide, and are frequently found at low-water-mark in great numbers, where they feed on marine insects, which they find by the sides of stones in great plenty; but at high-water they retire to the dry ridges and wait the receding of the tide. They fly as steady as a woodcock, answer to a whistle that resembles their note; lay long on their wings, and are a {425} most excellent shot, and at times are delicious eating. The other species of Curlew are in colour and shape exactly like the former, though inferior in size, and differ in their manner of life, as they never frequent the water's-edge, but always keep among the rocks and dry ridges, and feed on berries and small insects. The flesh of this bird is generally more esteemed than that of the former, but they are by no means so numerous. This species of Curlew are seldom found farther North than Egg River.

[391]

Jack Snipe.

JACK SNIPES.[195] Those birds visit Hudson's Bay in Summer in considerable numbers, but are seldom seen to the North of Whale Cove. They do not arrive till the ice of the rivers is broke up, and they retire to the South early in the Fall. During their stay, they always frequent marshes near the sea coast, and the shores of great rivers. In manner and flight they exactly resemble the European Jack Snipe; and when on the wing, fly at such a distance from each other, that it is but seldom the best sportsman can get more than one or two at a shot. Their flesh is by no means so delicate as that of the English Snipe.

Red Godwait.

RED GODWAITS,[196] usually called at the Northern settlements in Hudson's Bay, Plovers. Those birds visit the shores of that part in very large flocks, and usually frequent the marshes and the margins of ponds. They also frequently attend the tide, like the Esquimaux Curlews; fly down to low-water-mark, and feed on a small fish, {426} not much unlike a shrimp; but as the tide flows, they retire to the marshes. They fly in such large flocks, and so close to each other, that I have often killed upwards of twelve at one shot; and Mr. Atkinson, long resident at York Fort, actually killed seventy-two at one shot; but that was when the birds were sitting. Near Churchill River they are seldom fat, though tolerably fleshy, and are generally good eating. They usually weigh from ten to thirteen ounces; the female is always larger than the male, and differs in colour, being of a much lighter brown. They retire to the South long before the frost commences; yet I have seen this bird as far North as the latitude 71° 50'.

Spotted Godwait.

SPOTTED GODWAIT,[197] known in Hudson's Bay by the name of Yellow Legs. This bird also visits that country in considerable numbers, but more so in the interior parts; and usually frequents the flat muddy banks of rivers. In summer it is generally very poor, but late in the Fall is, as it may be called, one lump of fat. This bird, with many others of the migratory tribe, I saw in considerable numbers as far North as the latitude 71° 54'; and at York Fort I have known them shot so late as the latter end of October: at which time they are in the greatest perfection, and most delicious eating, more particularly so when put into a bit of paste, and boiled like an apple-dumpling; for in fact they are generally too fat at that season to be eaten either roasted or boiled.

[392]

Hebridal Sandpipers.

{427} HEBRIDAL SANDPIPERS,[198] but more commonly known in Hudson's Bay by the Name of Whale Birds, on account of their feeding on the carcases of those animals which frequently lie on the shores, also on maggots that are produced in them by fly-blows. These birds frequent those parts in considerable numbers, and always keep near the margin of the sea. They may, in fact, be called beautiful birds, though not gay in their plumage; they are usually very fat, but even when first killed they smell and taste so much like train-oil as to render them by no means pleasing to the palate, yet they are frequently eaten by the Company's servants. As the Summer advances they fly so far North of Churchill River, that their breeding-places are not known, though they remain at that part till the beginning of July, and return early in the Fall. They are by no means large birds, as they seldom weigh four ounces. The bill is black, plumage prettily variegated black and white, and the legs and feet are of a beautiful orange colour.[CK]

[393]

Plover.

PLOVERS,[199] commonly called Hawk's Eyes, from their watchfulness to prevent a near approach when sitting. When these birds are on the wing, they fly very swift and irregular, particularly when single or in small flocks. At Churchill River they are by no means numerous, but I have seen them in such large flocks at York Fort in the Fall of one {428} thousand seven hundred and seventy-three, that Mr. Ferdinand Jacobs then Governor, Mr. Robert Body Surgeon, and myself, killed in one afternoon as many as two men could conveniently carry. They generally feed on insects, and are at all times good eating, but late in the Fall are most excellent. They are by no means equally plentiful in all years; and at the Northern settlements in the Bay they are not classed with those species of game that add to the general stock of provisions, being only killed as a luxury; but I am informed that at Albany Fort, several barrels of them are annually salted for Winter use, and are esteemed good eating. This bird during Summer resorts to the remotest Northern parts; for I have seen them at the Copper River, though in those dreary regions only in pairs. The young of those birds always leave their nests as soon as hatched, and when but a few days old run very fast; at night, or in rainy weather, the old ones call them together, and cover them with their wings, in the same manner as a hen does her chickens.

Black Gullemots.

BLACK GULLEMOTS,[200] known in Hudson's Bay by the name of Sea Pigeons. Those birds frequent the shores of Hudson's Bay and Straits in considerable numbers; but more particularly the Northern parts, where they fly in large flocks; to the Southward they are only seen in pairs. They are of a fine black, but not glossy, with scarlet legs and feet; and the coverets of the wings are marked with white. They are in weight equal to a Widgeon, {429} though to appearance not so large. They usually make their nests in the holes of rocks, and lay two white eggs, which are delicate eating, but not proportionably large for the size of the bird. My friend Mr. Pennant says, they brave the coldest Winters in those parts, by keeping at the edge of the ice near the open water; but as the sea at that season is frozen over for several miles from the shore, I believe no one's curiosity ever tempted him to confirm the truth of this; and it is well known they never make their appearance near the land after the frost becomes severe.

[394]

Northern Divers.

NORTHERN DIVERS.[201] These birds, though common in Hudson's Bay, are by no means plentiful; they are seldom found near the sea coast, but more frequently in fresh water lakes, and usually in pairs. They build their nests at the edge of small islands, or the margins of lakes or ponds; they lay only two eggs, and it is very common to find only one pair and their young in one sheet of water; a great proof of their aversion to society. They are known in Hudson's Bay by the name of Loons. They differ in species from the Black and Red throated Divers, having a large black bill near four inches long; plumage on the back of a glossy black, elegantly barred with white; the belly of a silver white; and they are so large as at times to weigh fifteen or sixteen pounds. Their flesh is always black, hard, and fishy, yet it is generally eaten by the Indians.

Black-throated Divers.

{430} BLACK-THROATED DIVERS.[202] This species are more beautiful than the former; having a long white bill, plumage on the back and wings black, elegantly tinged with purple and green, and prettily marked with white spots. In size they are equal to the former; but are so watchful as to dive at the flash of a gun, and of course are seldom killed but when on the wing. Their flesh is equally black and fishy with the former, but it is always eaten by the Indians. The skins of those birds are very thick and strong, and they are frequently dressed with the feathers on, and made into caps for the Indian men. The skins of the Eagle and Raven, with their plumage complete, are also applied to that use, and are far from being an unbecoming head-dress for a savage.

[395]

Red-throated Divers.

RED-THROATED DIVERS.[203] This species are also called Loons in Hudson's Bay; but they are so far inferior to the two former, that they seldom weigh more than three or four pounds. They, like the other species of Loon, are excellent divers; they always feed on fish, and when in pursuit of their prey, are frequently entangled in fishing-nets, set at the mouths of creeks and small rivers. They are more numerous than either of the former, as they frequently fly in flocks; but like them make their nests at the edge of the water, and only lay two eggs, which, though very rank and fishy, are always eaten by Indians and English. The legs of those three species of Loon are placed so near {431} the rump as to be of no service to them on the land, as they are perfectly incapable of walking; and when found in that situation (which is but seldom) they are easily taken, though they make a strong resistance with their bill, which is very hard and sharp.

White Gulls.

WHITE GULLS.[204] These birds visit Hudson's Bay in great numbers, both on the sea coasts and in the interior parts, and probably extend quite across the continent of America. They generally make their appearance at Churchill River about the middle of May; build their nests on the islands in lakes and rivers; lay two speckled eggs, and bring forth their young in June. Their eggs are generally esteemed good eating, as well as the flesh of those in the interior parts of the country, though they feed on fish and carrion. They make their stay on Hudson's Bay as long in the Fall as the frost will permit them to procure a livelihood.

[396]

Grey Gulls.

GREY GULLS. These birds, though common, are by no means plentiful; and I never knew their breeding-places, as they seldom make their appearance at Churchill River till the Fall of the year, and remain there only till the ice begins to be formed about the shores. They seldom frequent the interior parts of the country. They are not inferior in size to the former, and in the Fall of the year are generally fat. The flesh is white and very good eating; and, like {432} most other Gulls, they are a most excellent shot when on the wing.

Black Gulls.

BLACK GULLS,[205] usually called in Hudson's Bay, Men of War, from their pursuing and taking the prey from a lesser species of Gull, known in that country by the name of Black-head. In size they are much inferior to the two former species; but, like them, always make their nests on islands, or at the margins of lakes or ponds; they lay only two eggs, and are found at a considerable distance from the sea coast. The length of their wings is very great in proportion to the body; the tail is uniform, and the two middle feathers are four or five inches longer than the rest. Their eggs are always eaten, both by the Indians and English; but the bird itself is generally rejected, except when other provisions are very scarce.

[397]

Black-heads.

BLACK-HEADS.[206] These are the smallest species of Gull that I know. They visit the sea coast of Hudson's Bay in such vast numbers, that they are frequently seen in flocks of several hundreds; and I have known bushels of their eggs taken on an island of very small circumference. These eggs are very delicate eating, the yolks being equal to that of a young pullet, and the whites of a semi-transparent azure, but the bird itself is always fishy. Their affection for their young is so strong, that when any person attempts to rob their nests, they fly at him, and sometimes {433} approach so near as to touch him with their pinions; and when they find their loss, will frequently follow the plunderer to a considerable distance, and express their grief by making an unusual screaming noise.

This bird may be ranked with the elegant part of the feathered creation, though it is by no means gay. The bill, legs, and feet are of a rich scarlet; crown black, and the remainder of the plumage of a light ash-colour, except the quill feathers, which are prettily barred, and tipped with black, and the tail much forked. The flight, or extent of wing, in this bird, is very great, in proportion to the body. They are found as far North as has hitherto been visited, but retire to the South early in the Fall.

> Pelicans.

PELICANS.[207] Those birds are numerous in the interior parts of the country, but never appear near the sea-coast. They generally frequent large lakes, and always make their nests on islands. They are so provident for their young, that great quantities of fish lie rotting near their nests, and emit such a horrid stench as to be smelt at a considerable distance. The flesh of the young Pelican is frequently eaten by the Indians; and as they are always very fat, great quantities of it is melted down, and preserved in bladders for Winter use,[CL] to mix with pounded {434} flesh; but by keeping, it grows very rank. The Pelicans in those parts are about the size of a common goose; their plumage is of a delicate white, except the quill-feathers, which are black. The bill is near a foot long; and the bag, which reaches from the outer-end of the under-mandible to the breast, is capable of containing upwards of three quarts. The skins of those birds are thick and tough, and are frequently dressed by the Indians and converted into bags, but are never made into clothing, though their feathers are as hard, close, and durable, as those of a Loon.

[398]

> Goosanders.

GOOSANDERS,[208] usually called in Hudson's Bay, Shell-drakes. Those birds are very common on the sea-coast, but in the interior parts fly in very large flocks. The bill is long and narrow, and toothed like a saw; and they have a tuft of feathers at the back of the head, which they can erect at pleasure. They are most excellent divers, and such great destroyers of fish, that they are frequently obliged to vomit some of them before they can take flight. Though not much larger than the Mallard Duck, they frequently swallow fish of six or seven inches {435} long and proportionably thick. Those that frequent the interior parts of the country prey much on crawfish, which are very numerous in some of the shallow stony rivers. In the Fall of the year they are very fat, and though they always feed on fish, yet their flesh at that season is very good; and they remain in those parts as long as the frost will permit them to procure a subsistence.

[399]

Swans.

SWANS.[200] There are two species of this bird that visit Hudson's Bay in summer; and only differ in size, as the plumage of both are perfectly white, with black bill and legs. The smaller sort are more frequent near the sea-coast, but by no means plentiful, and are most frequently seen in pairs, but sometimes single, probably owing to their mates having been killed on their passage North. Both species usually breed on the islands which are in lakes; and the eggs of the larger species are so big, that one of them is a sufficient meal for a moderate man, without bread, or any other addition. In the interior parts of the country the larger Swan precedes every other species of water-fowl, and in some years arrive so early as the month of March, long before the ice of the rivers is broken up. At those times they always frequent the open waters of falls and rapids, where they are frequently shot by the Indians in considerable numbers. They usually weigh upwards of thirty pounds, and the lesser species from eighteen to twenty-four. The flesh of both are excellent {436} eating, and when roasted, is equal in flavour to young heifer-beef, and the cygnets are very delicate.

Notwithstanding the size of this bird, they are so swift on the wing as to make them the most difficult to shoot of any bird I know, it being frequently necessary to take sight ten or twelve feet before their bills. This, however, is only when flying before the wind in a brisk gale, at which time they cannot fly at a less rate than an hundred miles an hour; but when flying across the wind, or against it, they make but a slow progress, and are then a noble shot. In their moulting state they are not easily taken, as their large feet, with the assistance of their wings, enables them to run on the surface of the water as fast as an Indian canoe can be paddled, and therefore they are always obliged to be shot; for by diving and other manœuvres they render it impossible to take them by hand. It has been said that the swans whistle or sing before their death, and I have read some elegant descriptions of it in some of the poets; but I have never heard any thing of the kind, though I have been at the deaths of several. It is true, in serene evenings, after Sun-set, I have heard them make a noise not very unlike that of a French-horn, but entirely divested of every note that constituted melody, and have often been sorry to find it did not forebode their death. Mr. Lawson, who, as Mr. Pennant justly remarks, was no inaccurate observer, properly enough calls the largest species Trumpeters, and the lesser, Hoopers. Some years ago, when I built Cumberland House, the Indians killed those {437} birds in such numbers, that the down and quills might have been procured in considerable quantities at a trifling expence; but since the depopulation of the natives by the small-pox, which has also driven the few survivors to frequent other parts of the country, no advantage can be made of those articles, though of considerable value in England.[CM]

[400]

Geese.

GEESE. There are no less than ten different species of Geese that frequent the various parts of Hudson's Bay during Summer, and are as follow: First, The Common Grey Goose.[401] Second, The

Canada Goose. Third, The White, or Snow Goose. Fifth, The Blue Goose. Sixth, The Laughing Goose. Seventh, The Barren Goose. Eighth, The Brent Goose. Ninth, The Dunter; and Tenth, the Bean Goose.

Common Grey Goose.

COMMON GREY GOOSE.[210] This bird precedes every other species of Goose in those parts, and in some forward Springs arrives at Churchill River so early as the latter {438} end of April, but more commonly from the eleventh to the sixteenth of May; and in one year it was the twenty-sixth of May before any Geese made their appearance. At their first arrival they generally come in pairs, and are so fond of society, that they fly straight to the call that imitates their note; by which means they are easily shot. They breed in great numbers in the plains and marshes near Churchill River; and in some years the young ones can be taken in considerable numbers, and are easily tamed; but will never learn to eat corn, unless some of the old ones are taken with them, which is easily done when in a moulting state. On the ninth of August one thousand seven hundred and eighty-one, when I resided at Prince of Wales's Fort, I sent some Indians up Churchill River in canoes to procure some of those Geese, and in the afternoon they were seen coming down the river with a large flock before them; the young ones not more than half-grown, and the old ones so far in a moulting state as not to be capable of flying; so that, with the assistance of the English and the Indians then residing on the plantation, the whole flock, to the amount of forty-one, was drove within the stockade which incloses the Fort, where they were fed and fattened for Winter use. Wild Geese taken and fattened in this manner are much preferable to any tame Geese in the world. When this species of Geese are full-grown, and in good condition, they often weigh twelve pounds, but more frequently much less.

[402]

Canada Goose.

{439} CANADA GOOSE,[211] or Pisk-a-sish, as it is called by the Indians, as well as the English in Hudson's Bay. This species do not differ in plumage from the former, but are inferior in size; the bill is much smaller in proportion, and the flesh being much whiter, of course is more esteemed. They are by no means so numerous as the former, and generally fly far North to breed; but some few of their eggs are found near Churchill River. It is seldom that either of these species lay more than four eggs; but if not robbed, they usually bring them all forth.

White or Snow Goose.

WHITE or SNOW GOOSE.[212] These are the most numerous of all the species of birds that frequent the Northern parts of the Bay, and generally make their appearance about a week or ten days after the Common Grey Goose. In the first part of the season they come in small parties, but in the middle, and toward the latter end, they fly in such amazing flocks, that when they settle in the marshes to feed, the ground for a considerable distance appears like a field of snow. When feeding in the same marsh with the Grey Geese, they never mix. Like the Grey Geese, they fly to the call that resembles their note; and in some years are killed and salted in great numbers for Winter provision; they are almost universally thought good eating, and will, if proper care be taken in curing them, continue good for eighteen months or two years. The Indians are far more expert in killing Geese, as well as every other species of game, than any European I ever saw in Hudson's Bay; {440} for some of them frequently kill upward of a hundred Geese in a day, whereas the most expert of the English think it a good day's work to kill thirty. Some years back it was common for an Indian to kill from a thousand to twelve hundred Geese in one season; but latterly he is reckoned a good hunter that kills three hundred. This is by no means owing to the degeneracy of the natives; for the Geese of late years do not frequent those parts in such numbers as formerly. The general breeding-place of this bird is not known to any Indian in Hudson's Bay, not even to the Esquimaux who frequent the remotest North. The general route they take in their return to the South in the Fall of the year, is equally unknown; for though such multitudes of them are seen at Churchill River in the Spring, and are frequently killed to the amount of five or six thousand; yet in the Fall of the year, seven or eight hundred is considered a good hunt. At York Fort, though only two degrees South of Churchill River, the Geese seasons fluctuate so much, that in some Springs they have salted forty hogsheads, and in others not more than one or two: and at Albany Fort, the Spring season is by no means to be depended on; but in the fall they frequently salt sixty hogsheads of Geese, besides great quantities of Plover. The retreat of those birds in Winter is equally unknown, as that of their breeding-places. I observe in Mr. Pennant's Arctic Zoology, that about Jakutz, and other parts of Siberia, they are caught in great numbers, both in nets, and by decoying them into hovels; but if {441} these are the same birds, they must at times vary as much in manner as they do in situation, for in Hudson's Bay they are the shyest and most watchful of all the species of Geese, never suffering an open approach, not even within two or three gun-shots: yet in some of the rivers near Cumberland House, and at Basquiau, the Indians frequently kill twenty at one shot; but this is only done in moon-light nights, when the Geese are sitting on the mud, and the sportsmen are perfectly concealed from their view. Though the plumage of those Geese are perfectly white, except the quill-feathers, which are black, the skin is of a dark lead-colour, and the flesh is excellent eating, either fresh or salt. They are much inferior in size to the Common Grey Geese, but equal to the Canada Geese.

[404]

[403]

Blue Geese.

BLUE GEESE.[213] This species are of the same size as the Snow Geese; and, like them, the bill and legs are of a deep flesh-colour, but the whole plumage is of a dirty blue, resembling old lead. The skin, when stripped of its feathers, is of the same colour as the Snow Goose, and they are equally good eating. This species of Geese are seldom seen to the North of Churchill River, and not very common at York Fort; but at Albany Fort they are more plentiful than the White or Snow Geese. Their breeding-places are as little known to the most accurate observer as those of the Snow Geese; for I never knew any of their eggs taken, and their Winter haunts have {442} hitherto been undiscovered. Those birds are frequently seen to lead a flock of the White ones; and, as they generally fly in angles, it is far from unpleasant to see a bird of a different colour leading the van. The leader is generally the object of the first sportsman who fires, which throws the whole flock into such confusion, that some of the other hunters frequently kill six or seven at a shot.

Horned Wavey.

HORNED WAVEY.[214] This delicate and diminutive species of the Goose is not much larger than the Mallard Duck. Its plumage is delicately white, except the quill-feathers, which are black. The bill is not more than an inch long, and at the base is studded round with little knobs about the size of peas, but more remarkably so in the males. Both the bill and feet are of the same colour with those of the Snow Goose. This species is very scarce at Churchill River, and I believe are never found at any of the Southern settlements; but about two or three hundred miles to the North West of Churchill, I have seen them in as large flocks as the Common Wavey, or Snow Goose. The flesh of this bird is exceedingly delicate; but they are so small, that when I was on my journey to the North I eat two of them one night for supper. I do not find this bird described by my worthy friend Mr. Pennant in his Arctic Zoology. Probably a specimen of it was not sent home, for the person that commanded at Prince of Wales's Fort[CN] at {443} the time the collection was making, did not pay any attention to it.

[405]

Laughing Goose.

LAUGHING GOOSE.[215] This elegant species has a white bill, and the legs and feet are of a fine yellow colour; the upper part of the plumage is brown, the breast and belly white, the former prettily blotched with black. In size they are equal to the Snow Goose, and their skins, when stripped of their feathers, are delicately white, and the flesh excellent. They visit Churchill River in very small numbers; but about two hundred miles to the North West of that river I have seen them fly in large flocks, like the Common Waveys, or Snow Geese; and near Cumberland House and Basquiau they are found in such numbers, that the Indians in moon-light nights frequently kill upwards of twenty at a shot. Like the Horned Wavey, they never fly with the lead of the coast, but are always seen to come from the Westward. Their general breeding-places are not known, though some few of their eggs are occasionally found to the North of Churchill; but I never heard any Indian say that he had seen any eggs of the Horned Wavey: it is probable they retire to North Greenland to breed; and their route in the Fall of the year, as they return Southward, is equally unknown. They are, I believe, seldom seen on the coast of Hudson's Bay to the Southward of latitude 59° North.

[406]

Barren Geese.

{444} BARREN GEESE.[216] These are the largest of all the species of Geese that frequent Hudson's Bay, as they frequently weigh sixteen or seventeen pounds. They differ from the Common Grey Goose in nothing but in size, and in the head and breast being tinged with a rusty brown. They never make their appearance in the Spring till the greatest part of the other species of Geese are flown Northward to breed, and many of them remain near Churchill River the whole

Summer. This large species are generally found to be males, and from the exceeding smallness of their testicles, they are, I suppose, incapable of propagating their species. I believe I can with truth say, that I was the first European who made that remark, though they had always been distinguished by the name of the Barren Geese; for no other reason than that of their not being known to breed. Their flesh is by no means unpleasant, though always hard and tough; and their plumage is so thick before they begin to moult, that one bird usually produces a pound of fine feathers and down, of a surprising elasticity.

Brent Geese.

BRENT GEESE.[217] This species certainly breed in the remotest parts of the North, and seldom make their appearance at Churchill River till late in August or September. The route they take in Spring is unknown, and their breeding-places have never been discovered by any Indian in Hudson's Bay. When they make their appearance at {445} Churchill River, they always come from the North, fly near the margin of the coast, and are never seen in the interior parts of the country. In size they are larger than a Mallard Duck, but inferior to the Snow Goose; and though their flesh appears delicate to the eye, it is not much esteemed. In some years they pass the mouth of Churchill River in prodigious numbers, and many of them are killed and served to the Company's servants as provisions; but, as I have just observed, they are not much relished. When migrating to the South, they generally avail themselves of a strong North or North Westerly wind, which makes them fly so swift, that when I have killed four or five at a shot, not one of them fell less than from twenty to fifty yards from the perpendicular spot where they were killed. Like the White, or Snow Geese, when in large flocks they fly in the shape of a wedge, and make a great noise. Their flight is very irregular, sometimes being forty or fifty yards above the water, and in an instant after they skim close to the surface of it, and then rise again to a considerable height; so that they may justly be said to fly in festoons.

[407]

> Dunter Geese.

The DUNTER GEESE,[218] as it is called in Hudson's Bay, but which is certainly the Eider Duck. They are common at the mouth of Churchill River as soon as the ice breaks up, but generally fly far North to breed; and the few that do remain near the settlement are so scattered among small islands, and sea-girt rocks and shoals, as to {446} render it not worth while to attempt gathering their down. Their eggs, when found, are exceeding good eating; and in the Fall of the year the flesh is by no means unpleasant, though they are notoriously known to feed on fish.

> Bean Goose.

BEAN GOOSE.[219] This species is seldom found in any part of Hudson's Bay, as in all my travels I have only seen three that were killed. This bird never came under the inspection of Mr. Graham, or the late Mr. Hutchins, though they both contributed very largely to the collection sent home to the Royal Society.[CO]

[408]

Species of Water-Fowl.

> Ducks.

DUCKS of various kinds are found in those parts during Summer; some only frequenting the sea-coast, while others visit the interior parts of the country in astonishing numbers. The species of this bird which is found most commonly here are, the King Duck,[220] Black Duck,[221] Mallard {447} Duck,[222] Long-tailed Duck,[223] Widgeon,[224] and Teal.[225] The two first only visit the sea-coast, feed on fish and fish-spawn; and their flesh is by no means esteemed good, though their eggs are not disagreeable. The Mallard and Long-tailed Duck visit Hudson's Bay in great numbers, and extend from the sea-coast, to the remotest Western parts, and near Cumberland House are found in vast multitudes. At their first arrival on the sea-coast, they are exceeding good eating; but when in a moulting state, though very fat, they are in general so rank that few Europeans are fond of them. At those seasons the difference in flavour is easily known by the colour of the fat; for when that is white, the flesh is most assuredly good; but when it is yellow, or of an orange colour, it is very rank and fishy. This difference is only peculiar to those that frequent and breed near the sea-coast; for in the interior parts I never knew them killed but their flesh was very good; and the young Mallard Duck before it can fly is very fat, and most delicate eating. The same may be said of the Long-tailed Duck. Neither of those species lay more than six or eight eggs in common, and frequently bring them all forth.

[409]

Widgeon.

WIDGEON.[226] This species of Duck is very uncommon in Hudson's Bay; usually keeping in pairs, and being seldom seen in flocks. They are by no means so numerous as the two former, and are most frequently seen in rivers and marshes near the sea-coast. Their flesh is generally esteemed; and the down of those I have examined is little inferior in elasticity to that of the Eider, though much {448} shorter. The same may be said of several other species of Ducks that frequent those parts; but the impossibility of collecting the down in any quantity, prevents it from becoming an article of trade.

Teal.

TEAL.[227] Like the Mallard, they are found in considerable numbers near the sea-coast; but are more plentiful in the interior parts of the country, and fly in such large flocks that I have often killed twelve or fourteen at one shot, and have seen both English and Indians kill a much greater number. At their first arrival they are but poor, though generally esteemed good eating. This diminutive Duck is by far the most prolific of any I know that resorts to Hudson's Bay; for I have often seen the old ones swimming at the head of seventeen young, when not much larger than walnuts. This bird remains in those parts as long as the season will permit; for in the year one thousand seven hundred and seventy-five, in my passage from Cumberland House to York Fort, I, as well as my Indian companions, killed them in the rivers we passed through as late as the twentieth of October. At those times they are entirely involved in fat, but delicately white, and may truly be called a great luxury.

[410]

Besides the birds already described, there is a great variety of others, both of land and water fowl, that frequent those parts in Summer; but these came not so immediately under my inspection as those I have already described.

{449} *Of the Vegetable Productions.*

The vegetable productions of this country by no means engaged my attention so much as the animal creation; which is the less to be wondered at, as so few of them are useful for the support of man. Yet I will endeavour to enumerate as many of them as I think are worth notice.

Gooseberries.

The GOOSEBERRIES[228] thrive best in stony and rocky ground, which lies open and much exposed to the Sun. But in those situations few of the bushes grow to any height, and spread along the ground like vines. The fruit is always most plentiful and the finest on the under-side of the branches, probably owing to the reflected heat from the stones and gravel, and from being sheltered from all cold winds and fog by the leaves. I never saw more than one species of Gooseberry in any part of Hudson's Bay, which is the red one. When green, they make excellent pies or tarts; and when ripe are very pleasant eating, though by no means so large as those produced in England.

[411]

Cranberries.

CRANBERRIES[229] grow in great abundance near Churchill, and are not confined to any particular situation, for they {450} are as common on open bleak plains and high rocks as among the woods. When carefully gathered in the Fall, in dry weather, and as carefully packed in casks with moist sugar, they will keep for years, and are annually sent to England in considerable quantities as presents, where they are much esteemed. When the ships have remained in the Bay so late that the Cranberries are ripe, some of the Captains have carried them home in water with great success.

Heathberries.

The HEATHBERRIES[230] are in some years so plentiful near Churchill, that it is impossible to walk in many places without treading on thousands and millions of them. They grow close to the ground, and are a favourite repast of many birds that migrate to those parts in Summer, particularly the Grey Goose; on which account the Indians distinguish them by the name of Nishca-minnick, or the Grey Gooseberry. The juice of this berry makes an exceeding pleasant beverage, and the fruit itself would be more pleasing were it not for the number of small seeds it contains.

Bethago-tominick.

BETHAGO-TOMINICK,[231] as it is called by the Indians, or the Dewater-berry of Mr. Dragge. I have seen this berry as far North as Marble Island, and that in great abundance. It flourishes best, and is most productive, in swampy boggy ground covered with moss, and is seldom found {451} among grass. The plant itself is not very unlike that of a Strawberry, but the leaves are larger. Out of the center of the plant shoots a single stalk, sometimes to the height of seven or eight inches, and each plant only produces one berry, which at some distance resembles a Strawberry; but on examination they have not that conical form; and many of them are only composed of three or four lobes, while others consist of nearly twenty. The flavour of this berry is far from unpleasing, and it is eaten by our people in considerable quantities during the season, (which is August,) and, like all the other fruits in those parts, is supposed to be wholesome, and a great antiscorbutic.

[412]

Currans.

CURRANS,[232] both red and black, are common about Churchill River, but the latter are far more plentiful than the former, and are very large and fine. The bushes on which those currans grow, frequently exceed three feet in height, and generally thrive best in those parts that are moist but not swampy. Small vallies between the rocks, at some little distance from the woods, are very favourable to them; and I have frequently observed that the fruit produced in those situations is larger and finer than that which is found in the woods. Those berries have a very great effect on some people if eaten in any considerable quantities, by acting as a very powerful purgative, and in some as an emetic at the same {452} time; but if mixed with Cranberries, they never have that effect.

Juniper-berries.

JUNIPER-BERRIES[233] are frequently found near the new settlement at Churchill River, but by no means in such plenty as in the more Southern and interior parts of the country. The bush they grew on is so similar to the creeping pine, that one half of the Company's servants residing in Hudson's Bay do not know one from the other.

Like the Gooseberry bushes in those parts, the fruit is always most plentiful on the under side of the branches. They are not much esteemed either by the Indians or English, so that the few that are made use of are generally infused in brandy, by way of making a cordial, which is far from unpleasant.[CP]

[413]

Strawberries.

STRAWBERRIES,[CO][234] and those of a considerable size and excellent flavour, are found as far North as Churchill River; and what is most remarkable, they are frequently known to be more plentiful in such places as have formerly been set on fire. This is not peculiar to the Strawberry, but it is well known that in the interior parts of the country, as well as at Albany and Moose Forts, that after {453} the ground, or more properly the under-wood and moss, have been set on fire, that Raspberry-bushes and Hips have shot up in great numbers on spots where nothing of the kind had ever been seen before. This is a phænomenon that is not easily accounted for; but it is more than probable that Nature wanted some assistance, and the moss being all burnt away, not only admits the sun to act with more power, but the heat of the fire must, in some measure, loosen the texture of the soil, so as to admit the plants to shoot up, after having been deep-rooted for many years without being able to force their way to the surface.

Besides the Berries already mentioned, there are three others found as far North as Churchill; namely, what the Indians call the Eye-berry, and the other two are termed Blue-berry and Partridge-berry by the English.

Eye-berry.

The EYE-BERRY[235] grows much in the same manner as the Strawberry, and though smaller, is infinitely superior in flavour.

This berry is found in various situations; but near Churchill River they are most plentiful in small hollows among the rocks, which are situated some distance from the woods; but they are never known to grow in swampy ground, and I never saw them so plentiful in any part of Hudson's Bay as about Churchill River.

[414]

> ### Blue-berry.

{454} The BLUE-BERRY[236] is about the size of a Hurtle-berry, and grows on bushes which rise to eighteen inches or two feet, but in general are much lower. They are seldom ripe till September, at which time the leaves turn to a beautiful red; and the fruit, though small, have as fine a bloom as any plum, and are much esteemed for the pleasantness of their flavour.

> ### Partridge-berry.

The PARTRIDGE-BERRY[237] is nearly as large as the Cranberry imported from Newfoundland, and though of a beautiful transparent red, yet has a disagreeable taste. These berries are seldom taken, either by the Indians or English; and many of the latter call them Poison-berries, but several birds are fond of them. They grow close to the ground, like the Cranberry, and the plant that produces them is not very unlike small sage, either in shape or colour, but has none of its virtues.

I had nearly forgotten another species of Berry,[238] which is found on the dry ridges at Churchill in considerable numbers. In size and colour they much resemble the Red Curran, and grow on bushes so much like the Creeping Willow, that people of little observation scarcely know the difference; particularly as all the fruit is on the under-side of the branches, and entirely hid by the leaves. I never knew this Berry eaten but by a frolicksome Indian girl; and as it had no ill effect, it is a proof it is {455} not unwholesome, though exceedingly unpleasant to the palate, and not much less so to the smell.

Hips.

HIPS[239] of a small size, though but few in number, are also found on the banks of Churchill River, at some distance from the sea. But in the interior parts of the country they are frequently found in such vast quantities, that at a distance they make the spots they grow on appear perfectly red. In the interior parts of Hudson's Bay they are as large as any I ever remember to have seen, and when ripe, have a most delightful bloom; but at that season there is scarcely one in ten which has not a worm in it; and they frequently act as a strong purgative.

With[415] respect to the smaller productions of the vegetable world, I am obliged to be in a great measure silent, as the nature of my various occupations during my residence in this country gave me little leisure, and being unacquainted with botany, I viewed with inattention things that were not of immediate use: the few which follow are all that particularly engaged my attention.

Wish-a-ca-pucca.

The WISH-A-CA-PUCCA,[240] which grows in most parts of this country, is said by some Authors to have great medical virtues, applied, either inwardly as an alterative, or outwardly dried and pulverised, to old sores and gangrenes. The truth of this I much doubt, and could {456} never think it had the least medical quality. It is, however, much used by the lower class of the Company's servants as tea; and by some is thought very pleasant. But the flower is by far the most delicate, and if gathered at a proper time, and carefully dried in the shade, will retain its flavour for many years, and make a far more pleasant beverage than the leaves. There are several species of this plant, of which some of the leaves are nearly as large as that of the Creeping Willow, while others are as small and narrow as that of the Rosemary, and much resembles it in colour; but all the species have the same smell and flavour.

[416]

> Jackashey-puck.

JACKASHEY-PUCK.[241] This herb much resembles Creeping Box; and is only used, either by the Indians or English, to mix with tobacco, which makes it smoke mild and pleasant; and would, I am persuaded, be very acceptable to many smokers in England.

> Moss.

MOSS of various sorts and colours is plentiful enough in most parts of this country, and is what the deer usually feed on.

> Grass.

GRASS of several kinds is also found in those parts, and some of it amazingly rapid of growth, particularly that which is there called Rye-grass, and which, in our short Summer at Churchill, frequently grows to the height {457} of three feet. Another species of Grass, which is produced in marshes, and on the margins of lakes, ponds, and rivers, is particularly adapted for the support of the multitudes of the feathered creation which resort to those parts in Summer. The Marsh Grass at Churchill is of that peculiar nature, that where it is mowed one year, no crop can be procured the next Summer; whereas at York Fort, though the climate is not very different, they can get two crops, or harvests, from the same spot in one Summer. Vetches are plentiful in some parts as far North as Churchill River; and Burrage, Sorrel, and Coltsfoot, may be ranked among the useful plants. Dandelion is also plentiful at Churchill, and makes an early salad, long before any thing can be produced in the gardens.

In fact, notwithstanding the length of the Winter, the severity of the cold, and the great scarcity of vegetables at this Northern settlement, by proper attention to cleanliness, and keeping the people at reasonable exercise, I never had one man under me who had the least symptoms of the scurvy; whereas at York Fort, Albany, and Moose River, there were almost annual complaints that one half of the people were rendered incapable of duty by that dreadful disorder.

[417]

I do not wish to lay claim to any merit on this occasion, but I cannot help observing that, during ten years I had {458} the command at Churchill River, only two men died of that distemper, though my complement at times amounted in number to fifty-three.

Trees.

The Forest Trees that grow on this inhospitable spot are very few indeed; Pine,[242] Juniper,[243] small scraggy Poplar,[244] Creeping Birch,[245] and Dwarf Willows,[246] compose the whole catalogue. Farther Westward the Birch Tree[247] is very plentiful; and in the Athapuscow country, the Pines, Larch, Poplar, and Birch, grow to a great size; the Alder[248] is also found there.

[418]

FOOTNOTES:

[124] The notes to this chapter within brackets are by Mr. Edward A. Preble of the United States Biological Survey.

[125] See pages 255, 164, 235, and 254.

[126] This is the so-called elk or wapiti, *Cervus canadensis* Erx., formerly abundant from the west side of Lake Winnipeg north-westward to the Peace River region.

[127] The wolves of the wooded country belong to the species to which the name *Canis occidentalis* of Richardson seems applicable; those of the Barren Grounds, which are frequently white, may be considered as subspecifically separable under the name *Canis o. albus* Sabine (type locality, Fort Enterprise, North-West Territory).

[128] *Vulpes lagopus innuitus* Merriam. This name is applicable to the Arctic foxes of the American mainland. They are larger than and differ in cranial characters from the typical animal of Lapland.

[129] See Pennant, "Arct. Zool.," i. p. 43, 1784, where this statement is credited to Mr. Graham. While Hearne is probably right about the foxes appearing every season, yet at intervals of a few years there is an incursion of more than ordinary numbers, and on these occasions the species reaches farther south than usual.

[130] The Canada Lynx, *Lynx canadensis* Kerr, is of general distribution throughout the wooded country, and occasionally in summer extends its wanderings for a short distance into the Barren Grounds.

[131] *Thalarctos maritimus* (Phipps). This species, of circumpolar distribution, keeps closely to the sea-coasts, and reaches the southern extremity of Hudson Bay, probably the most southern point of its present distribution.

[BY] It is rather singular that the Polar Bears are seldom found on the land during the Winter, on which account it is supposed they go out on the ice, and keep near the edge of the water during that season, while the females that are pregnant seek shelter at the skirts of the woods, and dig themselves dens in the deepest drifts of snow they can find, where they remain in a state of inactivity, and without food, from the latter end of December or January, till the latter end of March; at which time they leave their dens, and bend their course towards the sea with their cubs; which, in general, are two in number. Notwithstanding the great magnitude of those animals when full grown, yet their young are not larger than rabbits, and when they leave their dens, in March, I have frequently seen them not larger than a white fox, and their steps on the snow not bigger than a crown-piece, when those of their dam measure near fifteen inches long and nine inches broad. They propagate when young, or at least before they are half-grown; for I have killed young females not larger than a London calf, with milk in their teats; whereas some of the full grown ones are heavier than the largest of our common oxen. Indeed I was once at the killing of one, when one of its hind feet being cut off at the ankle, weighed fifty-four pounds. The males have a bone in their *penis*, as a dog has, and of course unite in copulation; but the time of their courtship is, I believe, not exactly known: probably it may be in July or August, for at those times I have often been at the killing of them, when the males were so attached to their mistresses, that after the female was killed, the male would put his two fore-paws over, and suffer himself to be shot before he would quit her. I have frequently seen and killed those animals near twelve leagues from the land; but as the Fall of the year advances, they are taught by instinct to seek the shore. Though such a tremendous animal, they are very shy of coming near a man; but when closely pursued in the water, they frequently attack the boat, seize the oars, and wrest them from the hands of the strongest man, seeming desirous to get on board; but the people on those occasions are always provided with fire-arms and hatchets, to prevent such an unwelcome visit. The flesh of this animal, when killed in Winter, (if not too old,) is far from being unpleasant eating; and the young cubs, in the Spring, are rather delicate than otherwise. The teats of the female are only two in number, and are placed between the fore-legs. The best Drawing of this Animal I have seen, is that done by Mr. Webber, among the Plates of Cook's last Voyage.

[132] *Ursus americanus* Pallas. This species inhabits all the region west of Hudson Bay nearly or quite to the limit of trees, though it is rare near the border of the woods.

[BZ] The insects here spoken of are of two kinds; the one is nearly black, its skin hard like a beetle, and not very unlike a grasshopper, and darts through the water with great ease, and with some degree of velocity. The other sort is brown, has wings, and is as soft as the common cleg-fly. The latter are the most numerous; and in some of the lakes such quantities of them are forced into the bays in gales of wind, and there pressed together in such multitudes, that they are killed, and remain there a great nuisance; for I have several times, in my inland voyages from York Fort, found it scarcely possible to land in some of those bays for the intolerable stench of those insects, which in some places were lying in putrid masses to the depth of two or three feet. It is more than probable, that the Bears occasionally feed on these dead insects.

[133] The insects here referred to are mainly May-flies (Ephemeridæ), which are washed up along the shores of the lakes in this region in incredible quantities, and are eaten by the bears, as Hearne says.

[CA] It is common for the Southern Indians to tame and domesticate the young cubs; and they are frequently taken so young that they cannot eat. On those occasions the Indians oblige their wives who have milk in their breasts to suckle them. And one of the Company's servants, whose name is Isaac Batt, willing to be as great a brute as his Indian companions, absolutely forced one of his wives, who had recently lost her infant, to suckle a young Bear.

[134] By brown bears, Hearne probably refers to the brown or cinnamon phase of the black bear. This colour phase, which is often spoken of as if constituting a distinct species, is rare near the northern border of the range of the animal.

[135] *Ursus richardsoni* Swainson. See *ante*, p. 181.

[136] *Gulo luscus* (Linn.). This powerful freebooter ranges north to the extremity of the continent, and has been detected in a few instances on the islands of the Arctic Sea.

[CB] Mr. Graham says they take their lodging in the clefts of rocks, or in hollow trees. The former I acknowledge, but I believe that neither Mr. Graham nor any of the Company's servants ever saw an instance of the latter. In fact, during all my travels in the interior parts of Hudson's Bay, I never saw a hollow tree that was capable of affording shelter to any larger animal than martins, jackashes, or wejacks; much less the quiquehatch or Bear, as some have asserted.

[This statement is from Pennant, "Arct. Zool.," i. p. 68, 1784, and given on the authority of Mr. Graham.]

[137] *Lutra canadensis* (Schreber). This valuable fur-bearer is found throughout the wooded country, but is rare near the borders of the forest.

[CC] The Otter is very fond of play; and one of their favourite pastimes is, to get on a high ridge of snow, bend their fore-feet backward, and slide down the side of it, sometimes to the distance of twenty yards.

[138] *Lutreola vison lacustris* (Preble, North Am. Fauna, No. 22, p. 66, 1902). This race differs from the typical race of Eastern Canada in its larger size and some minor cranial characters. It inhabits the region west of Hudson Bay, north to the limit of trees.

[139] *Mustela pennanti* Erxleben. As far as known, this fur-bearer reaches its northern limit on the coast of Hudson Bay near Cape Tatnam.

[CD] Mr. Graham asserts that this animal frequents the banks of creeks, and feeds on fish; but these are by no means their usual haunts. I have, however, no doubt, but when they find fish on the land, that they may eat it, like other carnivorous animals; but they are as shy of taking the water as a domestic cat. They climb trees, and catch partridges, mice, and rabbits, with as much ease as a martin. They are easily tamed and domesticated, are very fond of tea-leaves, have a pleasant musky smell, and are very playful.

[This statement is apparently from Pennant ("Arct. Zool.," i. p. 82, 1784), who gives Mr. Graham as authority.]

[140] The Skunk, *Mephitis mephitis* (Schreber), has not been detected on the coast of Hudson Bay north of Fort Albany, but farther westward it reaches Oxford House and Great Slave Lake. The animal of the Cumberland House region is the Northern Plains Skunk, *Mephitis hudsonica* Richardson.

[141] *Mustela americana abieticola* Preble. A much larger race than typical *M. americana* of Eastern Canada is the form inhabiting the country west of Hudson Bay.

[142] The common weasel of the wooded parts of the Hudson Bay region is *Putorius richardsoni* (Bonaparte). North of the tree-limit is found a larger species, *P. arcticus* Merriam, which ranges north of the continent over the Arctic islands. Both species turn white in winter and are then known as ermine.

[143] *Fiber zibethicus hudsonius* Preble (North Am. Fauna, No. 22, p. 53, 1902; type locality, Fort Churchill). This race, which differs from the typical animal of Eastern Canada in smaller size and in cranial characters, inhabits the region west of Hudson Bay, north to the limit of trees.

[144] *Acorus calamus* Linn. A widely diffused herb abundant in the southern part of the Hudson Bay region. The Crees are said to style it *Wachusk mitsu-in*, i.e. that which the musk-rats eat.

[145] *Erethizon dorsatum* (Linn.). In Hearne's time the porcupine was rather common throughout the southern part of the Hudson Bay region, and ranged nearly or quite to the limit of trees. Hearne's journey to the Coppermine River was mainly through the Barren Grounds, or near the edge of the timber, where of course the animal was scarce, which accounts for the small number seen by him.

Now, throughout the region, constant persecution has reduced this species almost to the verge of extinction, so that a person may travel hundreds of miles through its range without encountering one.

[146] "Arctic Zool.," i. p. 110, 1784.

[CE] This information was given to Mr. Pennant from the authority of Mr. Graham; but the before-mentioned account of seeing them killed in all stages of pregnancy, when no symptoms of that kind appeared, will, I hope, be sufficient to clear up that mistake.

[147] By foxes of various colours, Hearne refers to the different colour-phases of the red fox, *Vulpes fulvus* (Desmarest). These are the cross-fox, in which there is a darkening of the colour, and a more or less plainly marked cross indicated on the back; the silver, in which the red tinge is nearly or wholly lost, the general colour being black, with many of the hairs showing a white subterminal zone; and the black, in which the white is absent, or very nearly so. In all these phases, now generally admitted to be varying degrees of melanism, the tip of the tail is white, as in the normal red phase. A perfect black fox is one of the most valuable furs known.

[148] *Lepus arcticus canus* Preble. Arctic hares are still found regularly as far south as Fort Churchill, and in winter reach still farther south, while to the north-west they occupy suitable localities throughout the Barren Grounds.

[149] *Lepus americanus* (Erxleben), based mainly on specimens from Churchill River and Severn River, which last place may be considered the type locality.

[150] *Sciurus hudsonicus* Erxleben. Common throughout the Hudson Bay region north to the tree-limit. The name was based on specimens from Hudson Bay, probably from the west coast, although no definite type locality has been assigned.

[151] *Citellus parryi* (Richardson). This species at the time of Hearne's writing was undescribed, but was later characterised by Richardson (App. to Parry's Second Voyage, p. 316, 1827), from specimens taken at Five Hawser Bay, Melville Peninsula. It inhabits the Barren Grounds from Hudson Bay north-westward to the Mackenzie, and is represented by related and intergrading forms nearly throughout Alaska, and southward in the Rocky Mountains to the northern United States.

[152] The shrew most often found in the beaver houses is the marsh shrew, *Neosorex palustris* (Rich.), whose aquatic habits admirably fit it for such situations. Two or three smaller shrews, less aquatic in habits, also inhabit the Hudson Bay region.

[153] *Dicrostonyx richardsoni* Merriam. This lemming, which is closely related to *D. hudsonius* of Labrador, was described from specimens taken at Fort Churchill, where it is abundant. Farther to the north it is represented by closely related forms whose ranges are among the most northerly of all land animals. Hearne's excellent account of this species has been confirmed in almost every particular by later observers.

[154] *Odobœnus rosmarus* (Linn.). This animal was formerly abundant in Hudson Bay, but is now far from common, and is confined to the northern and north-eastern parts.

[155] *Phoca vitulina* Linn. is one of the commonest seals about the Bay, while the ringed seal, *Phoca hispida* Schreber, is perhaps equally abundant about its northern shores. The grey species mentioned is the bearded seal, *Erignathus barbatus* (Erxleben), which is abundant in most parts of Hudson Bay.

[156] The narwhal, *Monodon monoceros* Linn., is still a rare inhabitant of Hudson Strait and the extreme northern part of the Bay.

[CF] In the Fall of the year 1768, a fine rock cod was drove on shore in a high gale of wind, and was eaten at the Governor's table; Messrs. William Wales and Joseph Dymond, who went out to observe the transit of Venus which happened on the 3d of June 1769, partook of it; but I never heard of one being caught with a hook, nor ever saw an entire fish of that description in those parts: their jaw-bones are, however, frequently found on the shores.

[The common cod, *Gadus callarius* Linn., enters Hudson Strait, and is economically important in Ungava Bay. An occasional one is reported in Hudson Bay, but whether or not the fish is abundant there is not known.]

[157] *Balœna mysticetus* Linn. This species, the principal object of pursuit by the northern whalers, was originally fairly common in the northern part of Hudson Bay, but is now rare there.

[CG] I have heard that no Whale caught by our Greenland ships is called a Pay-fish; that is, that no emolument arises to the harpooner that strikes it; unless the longest blade of the bone, usually called Whale-bone, measures six feet; whereas those killed in Hudson's Bay seldom measured more than four feet and an half.

[158] *Delphinapterus catodon* (Linn.). This toothed whale is still common in nearly all parts of Hudson Bay, and considerable numbers are taken by means of nets at Fort Churchill. The oil is exported and the meat utilized for food for dogs.

[159] The "Salmon" here spoken of is evidently some form of the widely distributed *Salvelinus alpinus* (Linn.), several supposed forms of which have been described from different parts of Arctic North America. The ordinary method of taking it on the coast of Hudson Bay is by stretching a net between stakes at low tide at right angles to the shore. The net being immersed at high tide intercepts the fish, which apparently follow the line of the shore. When the tide falls the catch is of course easily retrieved.

[160] *Mallotus villosus* (Müller). This is a kind of smelt of wide distribution in northern waters.

[161] Apparently referring to *Mytilus edulis* (Linn.), which is very abundant on the shore of Hudson Bay.

[162] *Hyas coarctatus* Leach, occurs on the west coast of Hudson Bay. Probably other species inhabit its waters.

[163] A common starfish on the west coast of Hudson Bay is a six-armed species, *Asterias polaris* (Müller and Troschel).

[164] The common frog of the Hudson Bay region is the northern wood frog, *Rana cantabrigensis latiremis* Cope, which is abundant north to the tree-limit. A smaller species, *Chorophilus septentrionalis* Boulenger, is abundant on the coast as far north at least as York Factory.

[165] From Hearne's description of its habits he evidently refers to the white-headed eagle, *Haliaetus leucocephalus alascanus* Townsend, which is the commoner of the two species of that region. The golden eagle, *Aquila chrysœtos* (Linn.), is rare near the Bay, but in places in the interior, where rocky ledges occur, is sometimes rather common.

[166] The Sacre Falcon of Pennant is generally identified as *Falco rusticolus gyrfalco* Linn.

[167] *Nyctea nyctea* (Linn.). This beautiful owl is common throughout the region, breeding on the Barren Grounds, and in winter moving southward into the wooded country. Occasionally a pair will nest far south of the normal range.

[168] The great horned owl, *Bubo virginianus subarcticus* (Hoy), found throughout the region north nearly to the limit of trees.

[169] This is the hawk owl, *Surnia ulula caparoch* (Müller). It is fairly abundant throughout the region north to the limit of trees.

[170] *Corvus corax principalis* (Ridgway). The raven is rare on the coast of Hudson Bay, but is rather common in the interior.

[171] *Perisoreus canadensis* (Linn.). Very abundant throughout the region north to the limit of trees. It nests in late winter, laying three or four bluish-grey eggs spotted with brownish.

[172] Besides the "Golden-winged Bird," *Colaptes auratus luteus* (Bangs), which reaches the limit of trees, several other woodpeckers inhabit that region.

[173] Referring to the pileated woodpecker, *Phlœotomus pileatus abieticola* (Bangs), which is found about the southern parts of Hudson Bay, and inland toward the south-west.

[174] Hearne is mistaken here, as the golden-winged woodpecker is well known to leave the northern parts of its summer habitat for several months.

[175] *Bonasa umbellus togata* (Linn.). Found about the southern shores of Hudson Bay, as far north as about 57°, and inland much farther north.

[176] *Pediœcetes phasianellus* (Linn.). Hearne's remarks on its range in this region are well founded, and agree with what is known of its present distribution.

[CII] This I assert from my own experience when at Cumberland House.

[177] *Canachites canadensis* (Linn.). This grouse inhabits all the region west of Hudson Bay north nearly to the limit of trees, but is scarce near the northern border of its range.

[178] *Lagopus lagopus* (Linn.) This beautiful ptarmigan is still abundant on the shores of Hudson Bay. It breeds abundantly throughout the Barren Grounds and in considerable numbers on the treeless areas which form an almost continuous fringe along the west coast of the Bay nearly to its southern extremity.

[CI] Mr. Dragge observes, in his North West Passage, that when the partridges begin to change colour, the first brown feathers appear in the rump; but this is so far from being a general rule, that an experienced Hudsonian must smile at the idea. That Mr. Dragge never saw an instance of this kind I will not say, but when Nature deviates so far from its usual course, it is undoubtedly owing to some accident; and nothing is more likely than that the feathers of the bird Mr. Dragge had examined, had been struck off by a hawk; and as the usual season for changing their plumage was near, the Summer feathers supplied their place; for out of the many hundreds of thousands that I have seen killed, I never saw or heard of a similar instance.

[179] *Lagopus rupestris* (Gmel.). This species, first described from specimens sent from Hudson Bay, is more northern in its range than the willow ptarmigan.

[CJ] Besides the birds already mentioned, which form a constant dish at our tables in Hudson's Bay, during their respective seasons, Mr. Jérémie asserts, that during the time he was Governor at York Fort, the bustard was common. But since that Fort was delivered up to the English at the peace of Utrecht in 1713, none of the Company's servants have ever seen one of those birds: nor does it appear by all the Journals now in the possession of the Hudson's Bay Company, that any such bird was ever seen in the most Southern parts of the Bay, much less at York Fort, which is in the latitude 57° North; so that a capital error, or a wilful design to mislead, must have taken place. Indeed, his account of the country immediately where he resided, and the productions of it, are so erroneously stated as to deserve no notice. His colleague, De le Potries, asserts the existence of the bustard in those parts, and with an equal regard to truth.

[This is explained by the fact that the early French writers referred to the Canada goose under the name *Outarde.*]

[180] *Ectopistes migratorius* (Linn.). This short account of the habits is evidently founded on Hearne's experience with the species in the Cumberland House region, where at that time it was doubtless abundant. The present record for Fort Churchill, as well as other early notices of its occurrence at York Factory, probably represent the northward wandering of flocks after the breeding season.

[181] *Planesticus migratorius* (Linn.). The American robin is rather common in the Hudson Bay region north to the tree-limit. At Fort Churchill, in late July 1900, I saw flocks composed of old birds and young just from the nests.

[182] *Pinicola enucleator leucura* (Müller). Found throughout the region north to the limit of trees, but, as Hearne intimates, not abundant.

[183] *Plectrophenax nivalis* (Linn.). This name was based on a Hudson Bay specimen. The bird is abundant throughout the region in migration, and breeds from the vicinity of Neville Bay (near lat. 62°), northward.

[184] *Zonotrichia leucophrys* (Forster). First described from specimens taken at Severn River, Hudson Bay. An abundant species throughout the region north to the limit of trees.

[185] *Calcarius lapponica* (Linn.). A common species, as Hearne says. It breeds from the tree-limit northward.

[186] Apparently referring to the Redpoll, *Acanthis linaria* (Linn.), which is, of course, not closely related to the Lapland longspur.

[187] Hearne apparently refers to the Shore Lark, *Otocoris alpestris hoyti* Bishop, which breeds abundantly on the small barrens along the west coast of Hudson Bay as well as on the main area of the Barren Grounds.

[188] *Penthestes hudsonicus*; first described by Forster from specimens taken at Severn River, Hudson Bay. It inhabits the region north to the limit of trees.

[189] This account of the nesting habits seems to refer to the Barn Swallow, *Hirundo erythrogastra* (Bodd). I am not aware that this bird now nests at Fort Churchill, though it is not unlikely that it did so formerly. The cliffs in the vicinity would afford ideal natural nesting sites.

[190] Here Hearne undoubtedly refers to the Bank Swallow, *Riparia riparia* (Linn.), which inhabits the region in myriads. As it nests only in banks of clay or sand its local abundance is dependent on their presence. The eggs are unspotted.

[191] *Grus americana* (Linn.). Though specimens from Hudson Bay figured in the original description of this magnificent species, it was rare even in Hearne's time, and is now probably extirpated in that region.

[192] The Brown Crane (*Grus canadensis*), was described by Linnæus from Hudson Bay specimens, and is still rather common on its marshy plains, and on the Barren Grounds.

[193] The American Bittern, *Botaurus lentiginosus* (Montagu), is fairly common in the marshes about Hudson Bay north to the vicinity of York Factory.

[194] The Esquimaux Curlew of Pennant ("Arct. Zool.," ii. p. 461, 1785) is really the Hudsonian Curlew, *Numenius hudsonicus* (Latham), and Hearne of course follows Pennant in this error. It is still a common species on the west coast of Hudson Bay. The smaller one, which is the real Eskimo Curlew, *Numenius borealis* (Forster), was formerly very abundant, but is now, unhappily, nearly or quite extinct.

[195] Apparently the common Snipe, *Gallinago delicata* (Ord.).

[196] The Hudsonian Godwit, *Limosa hæmastica* (Linn.). This name was based on the drawing of a specimen from Hudson Bay. It breeds in the

marshes on the west coast of the Bay, probably nearly throughout its length.

[197] The Spotted Godwit of Pennant ("Arct. Zool.," ii. p. 467, 1785) is the Greater Yellowlegs, *Totanus melanoleucus* (Gmel.).

[198] *Arenaria morinella* (Linn.). The Turnstone is abundant along the west coast of Hudson Bay in migration, and doubtless breeds about its northern shores, though I am not aware that its nest has actually been discovered there.

[CK] They exactly correspond with the bird described by Mr. Pennant, except that they are much longer.

[199] *Charadrius dominicus* Müller. Formerly very abundant, as Hearne intimates, but now very much reduced in numbers. It breeds about the northern shores of Hudson Bay.

[200] *Cepphus mandti* (Mandt). This Guillemot is abundant on Hudson Bay and the neighbouring waters to the northward.

[201] *Gavia immer* (Brünn.). This is perhaps the least abundant of the Loons found on Hudson Bay, though common in the lakes of the interior.

[202] *Gavia adamsi* (Gray). Hearne's statement that the bird has a white bill shows that he refers to the present species, though a Black-throated Loon, *Gavia pacifica* (Lawrence), is common there. Perhaps he confuses the two. At any rate, *G. adamsi* is abundant over much of the country traversed by him on his Coppermine journey, but I am not aware that it has been detected as far east as Hudson Bay.

[203] *Gavia stellata* (Pontoppidan). Abundant in the lake-studded country bordering Hudson Bay.

[204] Though in all probability several species are included under this heading, the commonest is the widely distributed Herring Gull, *Larus argentatus* Pontoppidan. The "Grey Gull" following is undoubtedly the young of the same species.

[205] Jaegers, *Stercorarius*, of which perhaps the commonest, and the one suggested by Hearne's description, is *S. pomarinus*. It is probable,

however, that both *S. parasiticus* and *S. longicaudus* (the former of which is the more abundant) also came under his observation.

[206] Plainly referring to the Arctic Tern, *Sterna paradisœa* Brünn. An excessively abundant species on the west coast of Hudson Bay.

[207] *Pelecanus erythrorhynchos* Gmel., has been taken on Hudson Bay only as a rare straggler, but is abundant in the Cumberland House region.

[CL] In the Fall of 1774, when I first settled at Cumberland House, the Indians imposed on me and my people very much, by selling us Pelican fat for the fat of the black bear. Our knowledge of the delicacy of the latter induced us to reserve this fat for particular purposes; but when we came to open the bladders, it was little superior to train oil, and was only eatable by a few of my crew, which at that time consisted only of eight Englishmen and two of the home Indians from York Fort.

Cumberland House was the first inland settlement the Company made from Hudson's Fort; and though begun on so small a scale, yet upon it and Hudson's House, which is situated beyond it, upwards of seventy men were now employed.

[208] *Mergus serrator* Linn. This species is still very abundant on the coast of Hudson Bay, as well as in the interior.

[209] The smaller Swan is *Olor columbianus* (Ord.), formerly very abundant on Hudson Bay, and still occurring in some numbers during migrations. It breeds on the islands in the northern parts of the Bay, and in other parts of the far North.

The larger Whooping Swan, *Olor buccinator* (Richardson), formerly bred about the southern part of the Hudson Bay region, and also far northward. In the wholesale destruction of these magnificent birds, this species has suffered most.

[CM] Mr. Pennant, in treating of the Whistling Swan, takes notice of the formation of the Windpipe; but on examination, the windpipes of both the species which frequent Hudson's Bay are found to be exactly alike, though their note is quite different. The breast-bone of this bird is different from any other I have seen; for instead of being sharp and solid, like that of a goose, it is broad and hollow. Into this cavity the windpipe passes from the valve, and reaching quite down to the abdomen, returns into the chest, and joins the lungs. Neither of the species of Swan that frequent Hudson's Bay are mute: but the note of the larger is much louder and harsher than that of the smaller.

[210] *Branta canadensis* (Linn.). This large goose is the earliest to arrive in spring, and is the most southern breeder, nesting throughout the wooded country.

[211] *Branta canadensis hutchinsi* (Richardson). This smaller form of the Canada Goose was named in honour of Thomas Hutchins, a Hudson's Bay Company officer who made natural history collections on Hudson Bay, and was the first to call attention to this race. It breeds on the Barren Grounds.

[212] *Chen hyperboreus nivalis* (Forster). This larger form of *C. hyperboreus* was first described from Severn River specimens. Though much reduced in numbers, it still breeds about the northern part of Hudson Bay, and is an important food species in the region.

[213] *Chen cærulescens* (Linn.). First described from a Hudson Bay specimen. According to the natives it breeds in the interior of northern Ungava; west of Hudson Bay, it is known only as a straggler. It winters in the Mississippi valley and on the Atlantic coast.

[214] This is the first account of *Chen rossi*, formally described by Cassin in 1861 from specimens taken on Great Slave Lake. It is almost unknown on Hudson Bay, but is abundant in migrations about Great Slave and Athabaska lakes. It breeds somewhere to the northward of this region, but its summer home is unknown.

[CN] Mr. Moses Norton.

[215] *Anser albifrons gambeli* Hartl. An inhabitant of the west coast of Hudson Bay, but more common in the Mackenzie valley.

[216] Probably referring, as Hearne suggests, to abnormally large and perhaps barren individuals of the Canada Goose (*Branta canadensis*).

[217] *Branta bernicla glaucogastra* (Brehm). Still occurring in some numbers along the west coast of Hudson Bay, in migrations, and breeding about its northern shores.

[218] Both *Somateria mollissima borealis* (Brehm), and *S. dresseri* Sharpe, occur about the north-west coast of Hudson Bay in summer, and doubtless both breed there. The King Eider also, *S. spectabilis* (Linn.), migrates down the coast, but probably breeds farther to the north.

[219] The Bean Goose, *Anser fabalis* (Latham), is of very doubtful occurrence in the Hudson Bay region.

[CO] It is, however, no less true, that the late Mr. Humphry Martin, many years Governor of Albany Fort, sent home several hundred specimens of animals and plants to complete that collection; but by some mistake, nothing of the kind was placed to the credit of his account. Even my respected friend Mr. Pennant, who with a candour that does him honour, has so generously acknowledged his obligations to all to whom he thought he was indebted for information when he was writing his Arctic Zoology, (see the Advertisement,) has not mentioned his name; but I am fully persuaded that it entirely proceeded from a want of knowing the person; and as Mr. Hutchins succeeded him at Albany in the year 1774, every thing that has been sent over from that part has been placed to his account.

[220] *Somateria spectabilis* (Linn.).

[221] Probably *Anas rubripes* Brewster.

[222] *Anas platyrhynchos* Linn.

[223] *Dafila acuta* (Linn.).

[224] *Mareca americana* (Gmel.).

[225] *Nettion carolinense* (Gmel.).

[226] *Mareca americana* (Gmel.). The American Widgeon occurs on the west coast of Hudson Bay north to the tree-limit, but is not common there.

[227] The Common Teal of the west coast of Hudson Bay is *Nettion carolinense* (Gmel.), which occurs in numbers well into the Barren Grounds. The Blue-winged Teal, *Querquedula discors* (Linn.), has been taken there, but is excessively rare.

[228] *Ribes oxyacanthoides* Linn. A species of very wide distribution in the north. It is usually common about the trading posts.

[229] *Vaccinium vitisidæa* Linn. An abundant species; reaches its greatest perfection near the northern border of the forest.

[230] *Empetrum nigrum* Linn. The crowberry is very abundant about Fort Churchill and northward.

[231] *Rubus chamæmorus* Linn. The cloudberry or baked-apple berry is abundant throughout the country treated by Hearne.

[232] The northern red currant, *Ribes rubrum* Linn., and the black currant, *Ribes hudsonianum* Richardson, are species of wide distribution in the north.

[233] Apparently Hearne refers to *Juniperus nana* Willd., the dwarf juniper, since Richardson gives the same Indian name as applied by the Crees to this shrub. Granting this, Hearne's creeping pine is *Juniperus sabina* Linn., shrubby red cedar. Both species extend northward to the tree-limit.

[CP] The Indians call the Juniper-berry Caw-caw-cue-minick, or the Crowberry.

[CQ] The Oteagh-minick of the Indians, is so called, because it in some measure resembles a heart.

[234] Probably *Fragaria canadensis* Michx.

[235] Probably *Rubus arcticus* Linn. A pretty little plant, similar in distribution to the cloudberry.

[236] *Vaccinium uliginosum* Linn. A low blueberry of wide distribution. The fruit is excellent.

[237] Probably *Comandra livida* Rich.

[238] Evidently, from his description, Hearne here refers to the Alpine bearberry, *Arctous alpina* (Linn.). It is abundant throughout the region.

[239] Apparently referring to the common rose of the region, *Rosa acicularis* Lindl. An abundant and very beautiful species.

[240] Hearne refers here to the two species of *Ledum. L. grœnlandicum* Œder is the broad-leaved sort, generally distributed through the wooded

country, and extending a little into the Barren Grounds. *L. palustre* Linn. is a smaller narrow-leaved species, which overlaps the range of the larger sort, and extends much farther north.

[241] This refers to the common bearberry, *Arctostaphylos uva-ursi* (Linn.). Its leaves are smoked both by the Indians and the Eskimo, and also by the white residents.

[242] *Picea alba* (Ait.) and *P. mariana* (Mill.).

[243] *Larix laricina* (Du Roi).

[244] *Populus balsamifera* Linn., and *P. tremuloides* Michx.

[245] *Betula nana* Linn.

[246] A number of dwarf willows, including *Salix anglorum* Cham., *S. phylicifolia* Linn., and *S. reticulata* Linn., grow on the coast of Hudson Bay to the northward of Fort Churchill.

[247] *Betula papyrifera* Marsh, from whose bark the Indians make their canoes.

[248] The common alder of the interior is *Alnus alnobetula* (Ehrh.).

[419]

BIBLIOGRAPHY

ANDERSON, JAMES. Letters from Chief Factor James Anderson to Sir George Simpson, Governor in chief of Rupert Land. Communicated by the Hudson's Bay Company. *Jour. Roy. Geog. Soc.*, vol. 26 (1856), pp. 18-25.

ANDERSON, JAMES. Extracts from Chief Factor James Anderson's Journal. Communicated by Sir John Richardson. *Jour. Roy. Geog. Soc.*, vol. 27 (1857), pp. 321-328.

ARROWSMITH, A. Map exhibiting all the new discoveries in the interior parts of North America, Jan. 1, 1795, with additions to 1811.

BACK, CAPTAIN (SIR GEORGE). Narrative of the Arctic Land Expedition to the mouth of the Great Fish River, &c., in the years 1833, 1834, and 1835. London, 1836. 8vo. Maps and plates. X., 663.

BRYCE, GEORGE. The Remarkable History of the Hudson's Bay Company. Toronto, 1900. 8vo. XXI., 501.

BURPEE, LAWRENCE J. The Search for the Western Sea. Toronto, 1908. 8vo. Maps and illustrations, IX., 651.

CLUNY, ALEXANDER. The American Traveller; or, Observations on the Present State, Culture and Commerce of the British Colonies in America, &c. By an Old and Experienced Trader. London, 1769. 4to. Map and plate, 122. Another edition. 12mo. New York, 1770.

DAWSON, GEORGE M. The Larger Unexplored Regions of Canada. *Ott. Nat.*, 1890, pp. 29-40, with map.

DAWSON, GEORGE M. Notes to accompany a geological map of the Northern portion of the Dominion of Canada, east of the Rocky Mountains. *Ann. Rep. Geol. and Nat. Hist. Survey Can.*, 1886. Pt. R. Montreal, 1887. 8vo, Map, 62.

DOBBS, ARTHUR. An Account of the Countries adjoining to Hudson's Bay, in the North-West Part of America. London, 1744. 4to. Map. II., 211.

[420]

DOUGLAS, DR. JOHN (Bishop of Salisbury). Introduction to "A Voyage to the Pacific Ocean, &c., performed under the direction of Captains Cook, Clerke and Gore." (Cook's 3rd Voyage.) 3 vols. and Atlas. London, 1784. 4to. Introduction, xcvi.

DRAGGE, T. S. An Account of a Voyage for the Discovery of a North-West Passage by Hudson's Streights to the Western and Southern Ocean of America. Performed in the year 1746 and 1747, in the ship *California*, Capt. *Francis Smith*, Commander. *By the* CLERK *of the* CALIFORNIA (T. S. Dragge). London, 1748-9. 2 vols. 12mo. Charts and plates, VII., 237 and 326, with Index.

DYMOND, JOSEPH, AND WALES, WILLIAM. Observations on the state of the Air, Winds, Weather, &c., made at Prince of Wales Fort, on the North-West Coast of Hudson's Bay, in the years 1768 and 1769. *Phil. Trans.*, vol. lx. for the year 1770. London, 1771. pp. 137-178.

ELLIS, HENRY. A Voyage to Hudson's Bay. By the *Dobbs Galley* and *California*, in the years 1746 and 1747. London, 1748. 8vo. XXVIII., 336.

FORSTER, J. R. Account of several quadrupeds sent from Hudson's Bay. *Phil. Trans.* (London), vol. lxii. 1772. pp. 370-381.

FORSTER, J. R. An account of the Birds sent from Hudson's Bay; with Observations relative to their Natural History, and Latin descriptions of some of the most uncommon. *Phil. Trans.* (London), vol. lxii. 1772. pp. 382-433.

FRANKLIN, SIR JOHN. Narrative of a Journey to the shores of The Polar Sea in the years 1819, 20, 21 and 22, with Appendix. London, 1823. 4to. Maps and plates. XV., 783. Another edition. 2 vols. 8vo, without Appendix. London, 1824. XIX., 370 and IV. 397.

FRANKLIN, SIR JOHN. Narrative of a Second Expedition to the shores of The Polar Sea, in the years 1825, 1826 and 1827, with Appendix. London, 1728. 4to. Maps and plates. XXIV., 319, clvii.

HANBURY, D. T. A Journey from Chesterfield Inlet to Great Slave Lake, 1898-9. *Geog. Jour.*, vol. xvi. pp. 63-77. London, 1900.

[421]

HANBURY, D. T. Through the Barren Ground of North-Eastern Canada to the Arctic Coast. *Geog. Jour.*, vol. xxi. pp. 178-191. London, 1903.

HANBURY, DAVID T. Sport and Travel in the Northland of Canada. New York, 1904. 8vo. Maps and plates. XXXII., 319.

HEARNE, SAMUEL. A Journey from Prince of Wales's Fort in Hudson's Bay, to the Northern Ocean. London, 1795. 4to. Maps and plates. XLIV., 458. Another edition. Dublin, 1796. 8vo. A French translation was published in Paris in 1799 in 1 vol. 4to and 2 vols. 12mo.

HEARNE, SAMUEL. Obituary. (Anon.) *European Magazine and London Review*, June 1797. 2 plates. pp. 371-2.

ISBISTER, A. K. On the Geology of the Hudson's Bay Territories, and of portions of the Arctic and North-Western Regions of America. *Quart. Jour. Geol. Soc.* (London), May 1855, vol. xi. pp. 497-520.

JÉRÉMIE, M. Relation du Detroit et de la baye d'Hudson. In Bernard's *Recueil de Voiages au Nord*. 12mo. Amsterdam, 1724.

JONES, C. J. (COLONEL "BUFFALO" JONES). Buffalo Jones' Forty Years of Adventure, compiled by Colonel Henry Inman. Topeka, 1899. 8vo. XII., 469.

KING, RICHARD. Narrative of a Journey to the Shores of the Arctic Ocean, in 1833, 1834 and 1835; under the Command of Capt. Back, R.N. London, 1836. 2 vols. 12mo. Map and plates. XV., 312 and VIII., 321.

KING, RICHARD. Temperature of Quadrupeds, Birds, Fishes, Plants, Trees, and Earth, as ascertained at different times and places in Arctic America during Captain Back's Expedition. *Edinb. New Philos. Journal*, xxi. pp. 150, 151. 1836.

KIRBY, WILLIAM. Fauna Boreali—Americana. Part Fourth. The Insects, pp. xxxix., 325. 4to. London, 1837.

LA PÉROUSE, COMTE DE. Expedition de la Baie d'Hudson. Extrait du Journal de Pierre-Bruno-Jean de la Mouneraye. *Bull. de la Société de Géographie.* 7th Ser. T. G. 1888.

[422]

LA PÉROUSE. A Voyage around the World performed in the Years 1785, 1786, 1787 and 1788. London, 1799. 4to. 2 vols, and Atlas. Translated from the French. (French edition published in 1797.)

LAUT, AGNES. Pathfinders of the West. Toronto, 1904. 8vo. XVII., 380.

LAUT, AGNES. Conquest of the Great North-West. New York, 1908. 8vo. 2 vols. XXI., 409 and IX., 415.

LOFTHOUSE, J. A Trip on the Tha-anné River, Hudson Bay. *The Geographical Journal*, vol. xiii. pp. 274-277. March 1899.

LOW, A. P. Cruise of the *Neptune*. Report on the Dominion Government Expedition to Hudson Bay and the Arctic Islands, on board the D.G.S. *Neptune*, 1903-1904. Ottawa, 1906. Maps and plates. XVII., 355.

MACFARLANE, R. R. Land and Sea Birds nesting within the Arctic Circle in the Lower Mackenzie District. *Hist. and Sci. Soc. Man. Trans.* 39. Winnipeg, 1890.

MACFARLANE, R. Notes on Mammals collected and observed in the Northern Mackenzie River District, North-West Territories of Canada, &c. *Proc. U.S. Nat. Mus.*, vol. xxviii. pp. 673-764. June 1905.

MACKENZIE, ALEXANDER. Voyages from Montreal, on the River St. Lawrence, through the Continent of North America, to the Frozen and Pacific Oceans; in the years 1789 and 1793. London, 1801. 4to. Maps and plates. VIII., cxxxii., 412.

M'KINLAY, JAMES. Narrative of a Journey in 1890, from Great Slave Lake to Beechy Lake, on the Great Fish River. (Edited by D. B. Dowling.) *Ott. Nat.*, 1893, pp. 85-92, and 101-114.

PELLETIER, E. A. Patrol Report Inspector E. A. Pelletier, Fort Saskatchewan, Alberta, to Chesterfield Inlet and Fullerton, Hudson Bay, and return to Regina, *viâ* Churchill, Hudson Bay. *Report of the R.N.W. Mounted Police*, 1909. pp. 141-168. App. O. Ottawa, 1909.

Pennant, Thomas. Vol. i., Quadrupeds. Advertisements, 6 pp.; Introduction, pp. cc. List of Quadrupeds, p. 185. London, 1784. Vol. ii., Birds, pp. 187-586. London, 1785.

[423]

PENNANT, THOMAS. Supplement to the Arctic Zoology. London, 1787. 4to. Maps. VIII., 163.

PETITOT, L'ABBÉ E. Géographie de L'Athabaskaw-Mackenzie. 2 Maps. *Bulletin de la Société de Géographie*, July, August and September 1875, pp. 5-42, 126-183, 242-290.

PIKE, WARBURTON. The Barren Ground of Northern Canada. 8vo. pp. 300. London and New York, 1892.

POND, PETER. Map in Burpee's "Search for the Western Sea," p. 182.

PREBLE, EDWARD A. A biological Investigation of the Hudson Bay Region. North American Fauna, No. 22. Washington, 1902. U.S. Dept. of Agriculture, Divn. of Biological Survey. 8vo. Map and plates, 140.

PREBLE, EDWARD A. A biological Investigation of the Athabaska-Mackenzie Region. North American Fauna, No. 27. Washington,

1908. U.S. Dept. of Agriculture, Divn. of Biological Survey. 8vo. Maps and plates, 574.

RAE, JOHN. Journey from Great Bear Lake to Wollaston Land. *Jour. Roy. Geog. Soc.*, vol. 22 (1852), pp. 73-96.

Report from the Committee appointed to inquire into the state and condition of the Countries adjoining to Hudson's Bay, and of the Trade carried on there. London, Government, 1749. Fol. pp. 215-286.

Report from the Select Committee on the Hudson's Bay Company. London, Government, 1857. Fol. Maps. XVIII., 547.

RICHARDSON, JOHN. Appendix to Captain Parry's Journal of a Second Voyage. 4to. London, 1825. (Contains many notes on Natural History of Coppermine region.)

RICHARDSON, JOHN. Short characters of a few Quadrupeds procured on Captain Franklin's late Expedition. *The Zool. Journal*, iii. No. 12. pp. 516-520. 1828.

RICHARDSON, JOHN. Fauna Boreali—Americana. Part First. Quadrupeds. pp. xlii, 300. 4to. London, 1829.

[424]

RICHARDSON, JOHN. Fauna Boreali—Americana. Part Third. The Fishes. 4to. London, 1836.

RICHARDSON, SIR JOHN. Arctic Searching Expedition; A Journey of a Boat-Voyage through Rupert's Land and the Arctic Sea. London, 1851. 8vo. 2 vols. Map, plates and woodcuts. VIII., 413 and VII., 426. Another edition. New York, 1854. 1 vol. 8vo, without plates. XI., 516.

RICHARDSON, SIR JOHN. The Polar Regions. Edinburgh, 1861. 8vo. Map. IX., 400.

ROBSON, JOSEPH. An Account of Six years Residence in Hudson's Bay from 1733 to 1736, and 1744 to 1747. London, 1752. 12mo. Charts and plans. 84-95.

RUSSELL, FRANK. Explorations in the Far North, being the Report of an expedition under the auspices of the University of Iowa during the years 1892, '93 and '94. (Des Moines), 1898. 8vo. Map and plates, IX., 290.

SETON, ERNEST THOMPSON. The Arctic Prairies. *Scribner's Magazine*, vol. xlviii., Nov. 1910, pp. 513-532; Dec. 1910, pp. 725-734; vol. xlix., Jan. 1911, pp. 61-72; Feb. 1911, pp. 207-223.

SIMPSON, THOMAS. Narrative of the Discoveries on the North Coast of America; effected by the Officers of the Hudson's Bay Company during the years 1836-39. London, 1843. 8vo. Map. XIX., 419.

SWAINSON, WILLIAM, and RICHARDSON, JOHN. Fauna Boreali—Americana. Part Second. The Birds. pp. lxvi, 524. 4to. London, 1831.

TYRRELL, J. B. Explorations in 1893 and 1894. *Ann. Rep. Geol. Sur. Can.*, 1894, vol. vii., Part A., pp. 38-48.

TYRRELL, J. B. Notes on the Pleistocene of the North-West Territories of Canada, north-west and west of Hudson's Bay. *Geol. Mag.* (London), Sept. 1894, pp. 394-399.

TYRRELL, J. B. An Expedition through the Barren Lands of Northern Canada. *Geog. Jour.* (London), vol. iv., Nov. 1894, pp. 437-450, and map.

[425]

TYRRELL, J. B. The Barren Lands. *The Ott. Nat.*, vol. x., Feb. 1897, pp. 203-207.

TYRRELL, J. B. A second Expedition through the Barren Lands of Northern Canada. *Geog. Jour.* (London), vol. vi., Nov. 1895, pp. 438-448, and map.

TYRRELL, J. B. Report on the Doobaunt, Kazan and Ferguson Rivers, and the North-West Coast of Hudson Bay, and on two overland routes from Hudson Bay to Lake Winnipeg. *Ann. Rep. Geol. Sur. Can.*, vol. ix., 1895, Pt. F. Ottawa, 1897. 8vo. Maps and plates, 218.

TYRRELL, J. B. The Glaciation of North-Central Canada. *Journal of Geology*, Feb. 1898, pp. 147-160.

TYRRELL, J. B. Natural Resources of the Barren Lands of Canada. *Scot. Geog. Mag.*, Mch. 1899, pp. 126-138.

TYRRELL, J. B. Minerals and Ores of Northern Canada. *Jour. Can. Min. Inst.*, vol. xi., 1908, pp. 348-365.

TYRRELL, J. W. Across the Sub-Arctics of Canada. A Journey of 3200 miles by canoe and snowshoe through the Barren Lands. Toronto, 1897. 8vo. Map and illustrations, 280.

TYRRELL, J. W. Report on an Exploratory Survey between Great Slave Lake and Hudson Bay. Ottawa, 1901. Annual Report, Dept. of Interior (Canada), App. 26, Part III. 23 maps and plates, 60.

UMFREVILLE, EDWARD. The Present State of Hudson's Bay, containing a full description of that settlement, and the adjacent country; and likewise of the Fur Trade. London, 1790. 12mo. VII., 230.

WALES, WILLIAM. Journal of a voyage made by order of the Royal Society, to Churchill River, on the North-West coast of Hudson's Bay; of Thirteen months residence in that country; and of the voyage back to England; in the years 1768 and 1769. *Phil. Trans.*, vol. ix., for the year 1770. London, 1771, pp. 100-136.

WHITNEY, CASPAR.[426] On Snow-shoes to the Barren Grounds. New York, 1896. 8vo. Maps and illustrations. X., 324.

WILLSON, BECKLES. The Great Company. London, 1899. 8vo. Maps and plates. XXII., 541.

For fuller bibliographies of Explorations in Hudson Bay and the North-West Territories of Canada, see Low's "Cruise of the Neptune," *and Burpee's "Search for the Western Sea."*

---

[427]

INDEX

Aberdeen Lake, 91

"Account of the Countries adjoining to Hudson's Bay, An," by Arthur Dobbs, 42, 246, 293

"Account of a Voyage for the Discovery of a North-West Passage Performed in the Years 1746 and 1747, An," by T. S. Dragge, 42, 166

Acres, ——, 137

Alarm Bird, 193

Albany Fort, 8, 44, 351, 393, 403, 404, 408, 413, 417

Albany Frigate, 44, 45

Albany River, 5

Alder, 417

Alpine bearberry, 414

America, 55, 396
—— North, 1, 23, 358
—— North-Western, 7

American Traveller (A. Cluny), 42, 43, 56, 295

Anaw'd Whoie (Lake of the Enemy), 226, 227, 233, 234

Anderson River, 254

Angikuni Lake (Titmeg Lake), 105

"Annual Report, Department of the Interior, Canada," 1901, App. 26, Pt. 3, by J. W. Tyrrell, 272

Arctic Circle, 30, 165, 192
—— Islands, 352
—— North America, 366
—— Ocean, 4, 151, 172, 201, 346

Artillery Lake (Atachothua = Caribou-crossing-in-the-middle-of-the-lake Lake), 23, 137, 139, 140, 225

Assiniboine River, 12

Athabasca Lake (Arabasca Lake), 119, 200, 201, 234, 235, 270, 278, 279, 404
River, 200, 201, 235

Athapuscow Country, 200, 256, 261, 276, 332, 333, 417
—— Indians. *See* *under* Indian
—— Lake (Arathapescow Lake, Great Slave Lake, or Slave Lake), 133, 234, 253, 255, 262, 269, 270, 277

Athapuscow River, 267, 269

Atkinson (Mr.), 391

Aurora Borealis (Ed-thin), 235, 327

Aylmer Lake (Chlueatathua = Caribou-swimming-among-the-ice Lake), 151, 225

Back, Sir George, 139, 140, 186, 419

Baker's Lake, 41, 55, 273

Barble,   88,   114,   254,   274,   314

Barlow,   Captain   George,   8,   9,   44-47

Barren Grounds, 137, 193, 338, 341, 354, 355, 358, 371, 378, 387, 389,   402,   409,   415

Barton   (Mr.),   376

Basquiau,   337,   338,   403,   405

Batt,   Isaac,   346

Bean,   John,   41,   46,   321

Bear,   169,   192,   343-345,   347,   348,   350
——   Black,   113,   343,   344,   398. _See_   _also_   Bear
——   Brown,   346.   _See_   _also_   Bear
——   Grizzled,   168.   _See_   _also_   Bear
——   Polar   (White),   342,   343. _See_   _also_   Bear

Beaver, 67, 78, 136, 223, 235, 237-251, 253, 255, 270, 271, 276, 305,   307,   308,   342,   348,   353,   355,   359,   369

Bedodid   Lake,   278

Beralzone   (Beralzoa,   Shoal   Lake),   81,   86,   292

Berens,   Herman,   50

Berrics,   413

Bethago-Tominick   (Dewater-berry),   411

Bimmester,   2

"Biological Investigation of the Athabaska-Mackenzie Region, A," by E. A. Preble, 23

"—— —— of the Hudson Bay Region, A," by E. A. Preble, 23

Birch, 417
—— Creeping, 417

Bitterns (American Bittern), 389

Black Bear Hill, 125, 283

Blackfeet Indians. *See* *under* Indian
[428]
Black-heads (Arctic Tern), 192, 314, 396, 397

Bloody Falls, 186, 187, 189, 195, 204

Blue-berry, 413, 414

Body, Robert, 393

Browne, Alexander, 10

Buffalo, 255-257, 263, 271, 276, 307, 308
—— (Musk-Ox) Lake, 164, 204

Bunting, Snow (Snow Bird, Snow Flake), 385
—— White-crowned, 386

Burbut, 114, 314

Burpee, L. J., 253, 419

Burrage, 416

Bustard, 384

Button, Sir Thomas, 379

Button's Bay, 105

California, 46

California (ship), 11

Calimut, 52

Canada, 44, 247, 249

—— Northern, 23

Canadian Indians. *See* Indian
—— traders, 285

Canadians, 44, 200, 201

Cape Esquimaux, 341
—— Merry Battery, 295
—— Smith, 365
—— Tatnam, 351

Caribou, 5, 87, 105

Carruthers, Captain, 9, 10

Cascathry, 153

Cassin, 404

Cat (Peshew) Lake, 139, 140, 151, 207

Catesby (Mr.), 256

Cathawhachaga, 285
—— (Kazan) River, 86-89, 92, 117, 137, 289

Charlotte (ship), 13, 48, 50, 56

Chawchinahaw, 52, 62, 64, 66, 68, 295

Cheesadawd Lake (Tchizè-ta, Gîte-du-Lynx, or Home-of-the-Wild-Cat Lake), 140

Chesterfield Inlet (Bowden's), 41, 55, 273, 293, 365

Chipewyan, Fort, 198
—— Indians (Northern Indians). *See under* Indian

Christie Bay, 132

Christmas, 112

Christopher, Captain, 41, 46, 48, 55, 293

Churchill, 6, 7, 9-14, 46, 50, 80, 87, 105, 112, 125, 140, 200, 201, 248, 253, 260, 285, 294, 307, 339-344, 346-348, 352, 355, 360, 365, 377, 378, 382, 405, 411, 413, 414, 416
—— River ('Tsan dézé, Iron or Metal River), 3, 8, 13, 43, 44, 57, 62, 95, 126, 183, 196-198, 201, 214, 215, 222, 235, 236, 269, 293, 294, 295, 313, 321, 323, 334, 339-342, 354-358, 360, 364-367, 369, 370, 379, 382, 384, 385, 388, 389, 391-393, 396, 401-407, 412-417

Churchill (sloop), 56, 329

Clinton-Colden Lake, 139, 140, 148, 150, 151, 207

Cloudberry (Baked-Appleberry), 411

Clowey, 29, 128, 130-137, 139, 140, 148, 149, 207, 270
—— River, 132

Cluny, Alexander, 42, 419

Cobadekoock, 193

Cockles, 367

Cod, Common, 363
—— Rock, 363

Cogead Lake (Contwoy-to or Rum Lake), 151, 152, 205, 207

Coltsfoot, 416

Conge-cathawhachaga, 29, 30, 152, 153, 155, 156, 161-163, 167,
170, 172, 173, 186, 204, 205, 222

Conjurers, 209, 228, 327

Conne-e-quese (Conreaquefé), 70, 77, 103

Contwoy-to or Rum Lake (Ko-ă-kă-tcai-tĭ, Cogead Lake), 152

Cook, Captain, 4

"Cook's Third Voyage," 18

Copper Indian (Yellow Knife or Rock) River, 279
—— Indians (Red Knives). See under Indian
—— mine, 1, 9, 50, 101, 109, 394
—— Mountains, 194-196

| Page

—— River, 30, 154, 170, 192, 204, 220, 277, 330, 346, 393. *See also* Coppermine River

Coppermine River (Tson-té, Sanka taza, Copper River), 7, 10, 11, 14, 15, 17, 18, 23, 43, 57, 90, 100, 109, 119, 127, 139, 146, 147, 149, 150, 151, 155, 169, 170, 172, 173, 186, 187, 204, 206, 207, 213, 218, 225, 282, 294, 295, 334, 354, 371. *See also* Copper River

Corbett's Inlet, 41
[429]
Cos-abyagh (Rock Partridge), 232

Cossadgath (Cassandgath) Lake, 139

Crabs, 367

Cranberry, 80, 188, 313, 411, 412, 414

Crane, Brown (North-West turkey), 389
—— Hooping, 388, 389

Crantz (Mr.), 189, 191

Crawfish, 398

Cree. *See* *under* Indian

Crow, Cinereous (Whisk-e-jonish)
—— (Whiskey-jack) (Geeza), 374

Crowberry, 411

Cumberland House, 5, 31, 86, 260, 267, 337, 344, 351, 354, 371, 375-377, 384, 397, 398, 400, 403, 405, 408, 410

Curlew, 192, 390

—— Esquimaux (Hudsonian Curlew), 390

Currant, Black, 412
—— Red, 412

Dalrymple (Mr.), 29, 30, 31

Dandelion, 416

Davis's Straits, 192, 330

Dawson (City), 148

Deer (Caribou), 58, 63, 64, 66, 67, 71, 78, 88, 90, 92, 98, 99, 102, 103, 111, 112, 116, 117, 119, 120-122, 125-127, 138, 147, 148, 152, 153, 156, 166, 167, 169-171, 174, 184, 192, 194, 213-216, 218, 220, 225, 227, 234, 235, 236, 253, 276, 282, 287, 289, 290, 293, 305, 306, 307-310, 316, 327, 336, 337, 342, 356, 366, 373

De le Potries, 384

Discovery (ship), 9, 11, 44, 45

Divers, Black-throated, 394
—— Northern (Loons), 394
—— Red-throated (Loons), 395

Dobbs, Arthur, 9, 41, 42, 246, 248, 295, 419

Dobbs (ship), 11

Dogribbed Indians. *See under* Indian

Dogs, 191, 310, 324, 325, 365

Doughty, Dr. Arthur G. (Archivist of the Dominion of Canada), 19

Douglas, Dr. John (Bishop of Salisbury), 18, 19, 139, 420

Dragge, T. S., 42, 166, 357, 382, 411

Dubawnt Lake (Doo-baunt Lake), 5, 91, 95, 105, 286

Dubawnt River (Doo-baunt River), 41, 91, 95, 105, 120, 272, 286, 287

Duck, 80, 83, 134, 274, 275, 307, 369, 380, 408, 409
—— Black, 408. See also Duck
—— Blue-winged Teal, 409. See also Duck
—— Common Teal, 409. See also Duck
—— Eider, 407. See also Duck
—— King, 408. See also Duck
—— Long-tailed, 408, 409. See also Duck
—— Mallard, 408, 409. See also Duck
—— Teal, 408, 409. See also Duck
—— Widgeon, 408, 409. See also Duck

Duncan, Captain, 32, 41

Dupetit-Thouars, ——, 20

Du Pratz (M.), 249, 261

Dymond, Joseph, 4, 363, 420

Eagle, 369, 395
—— Fishing, 369. See also Eagle
—— Golden, 369. See also Eagle
—— White-headed, 369. See also Eagle

E-arch-e-thinnew Indians (Blackfeet Indians). *See under* Indian

Edlande Lake, 226

Egg River, 103, 105, 110, 111, 292, 294, 390

Elk, 307, 337

Ellis, Henry, 41, 42, 46, 48, 55, 56, 113, 166, 295, 420

"English Chief," 201

Ennadai Lake (Nipach Lake), 289

Ermin (Stote), 192, 352

Eskimo Point, 21

Eskimos, or Esquimaux, 3, 5, 11, 13, 46-49, 86, 87, 135, 149, 150, 166, 174, 175, 176, 177, 178, 180-184, 186, 187, 189, 190, 191, 194-196, 220, 265, 273, 275, 276, 293, 296, 313, 321-323, 330, 338, 342, 346, 355, 361, 363, 403, 416

European Magazine and London Review, 1

"Explorations in the Far North," by Frank Russell, 152, 172, 218

Eye-berry, 413

Fairchild, ——, 137

Fairies, 327

[430]
Far Off Metal River, 54

Fatt (Twal-kai-tua or Fat-fish) Lake (Wiethen Lake), 117, 292

"First Journey," by Sir John Franklin, 152, 172, 187, 196, 198

Fish, 63, 72-74, 77, 79, 80, 82, 88, 114, 115, 116, 151, 183, 184, 225, 226, 234, 251, 253, 254, 273, 274, 288, 292, 305, 308, 313-316, 325

Fitz   Gerald,   James,   50,   191

Five   Hawser   Bay,   Melville   Peninsula,   358

Forest   trees,   417

Fort Albany, 8, 44, 351, 393, 403, 404, 408, 413, 417

Fort   Chipewyan,   198

Fort Churchill (*see* Fort Prince of Wales), 352, 355, 359, 365, 384, 388,   411,   417

Fort Cumberland, 5, 31, 86, 260, 267, 337, 344, 351, 354, 371, 375-377,   384,   397,   398,   400,   403,   405,   408,   410

Fort   Enterprise,   338

Fort   Hudson's,   398

Fort   Moose,   413

Fort Prince of Wales (*see* Fort Churchill), 2, 3, 4, 5, 16, 21, 46, 49, 51, 55, 57, 61, 68, 70, 75, 76, 79, 87, 100, 105, 106, 107, 110, 115, 124, 126-128, 137, 146, 147, 159, 162, 165, 166, 201, 202, 232, 233, 260, 267, 269, 271, 276, 285, 291, 292, 294, 295, 316, 322, 323, 328,   329,   331,   334,   340,   356,   401,   405

Fort Resolution, 225

Fort Richmond, 365

Fort Severn, 6

Fort Smith, 253, 267

Fort York, 5, 6, 8, 10, 13, 56, 160, 197, 236, 258, 260, 294, 307, 340, 341, 344, 345, 357, 365, 366, 368, 377, 378, 379, 384, 389, 390, 391, 392, 393, 398, 403, 404, 410, 416, 417

Fowler, Capt. John, 222

Fox, 192, 224, 255, 323, 348, 350, 355, 373
—— Arctic, 339
—— White, 340, 341

Franklin, Sir John, 23, 152, 153, 172, 186, 187, 196, 198, 218, 224, 420

Frobisher, Joseph, 5

Frogs, 368

Fullarton (Mr.), 44

Furnace, 11

Garbet (Mr.), 48

"Géographie de L'Athabaskaw Mackenzie," by A. Petitot, 132, 423

Geological Survey of Canada, 5

Godwait, Red (Plovers) (Hudsonian Godwit), 391
—— Spotted (Yellow Legs), 391

Godwit, Spotted (Greater Yellow Legs), 391

Goosanders (Shell-drakes), 398

Goose, 58, 80, 81, 83, 134, 192, 271, 274, 275, 287, 290, 292, 307, 313, 369, 380, 400, 403, 406
—— Barren, 406. See also Goose
—— Bean, 407. See also Goose
—— Blue, 404. See also Goose
—— Brent, 406. See also Goose
—— Canada (Pick-a-sish), 384, 402, 406. See also Goose
—— Common Grey, 401, 411. See also Goose
—— Common Wavey, 405. See also Goose
—— Dunter, 192, 407. See also Goose
—— Horned Wavey, 404, 405. See also Goose
—— Laughing, 405. See also Goose
—— White (Snow Goose), 402, 404, 405. See also Goose

Gooseberry, 410

Goose-hunting Islands, 294

"Governor, The, and Company of Adventurers of England," 8

Graham, A., 166, 295, 338, 339, 348, 351, 354, 408

Grant, Cuthbert, 200

Grass, 416
—— Marsh, 416
—— Rye, 416

"Great Company, The," 18

Great Slave Lake (Athapuscow Lake) ("Thu-tué" or "Lake of the Breasts"), 13, 132, 139, 151, 200, 225, 226, 235, 253, 254, 255, 267, 270, 278, 279, 281, 351, 404

Grizzled Bear Hill, 168

Grosbeak (American Red Bird), 385

Ground-squirrels, 169, 192

Grouse, 375, 383
—— Ruffed (Pus-pus-kee) (Pus-pus-cue), 375. *See also* Grouse
—— Sharp-Tailed (Pheasant) (Aw-kis-cow), 377. *See also* Grouse
—— White, 370. *See also* Grouse

Grubs, 368

Gull, 80, 83, 192, 292, 314
[431]
Gull, Arctic, 192. *See also* Gull
—— Black (Men of War), 396. *See also* Gull
—— Grey, 395, 396. *See also* Gull
—— White (Herring Gull), 395. *See also* Gull

Gullemots, Black (Sea Pigeons), 393

Ha-ha-wie, 192

Hanbury River, 139, 272

Harding, C., 224

Hare, 369, 379
—— Alpine, 192, 193, 217, 316. *See also* Hare

—— American, 357. *See also* Hare
—— Varying, 355. *See also* Hare

Hawks, 369, 370

Hawks-eyes, 192

Hay's River, 365

Hearne, Samuel, 1-7, 10, 12-19, 21, 51, 52, 87, 105, 107, 109, 113, 120, 139, 140, 151-153, 186, 187, 201, 218, 224, 235, 253, 272, 282, 287, 289, 339, 345, 346, 355, 375, 377, 384, 385, 387, 390, 393, 394, 406, 411, 412, 414, 415
—— (Mr.) (father of Samuel), 1
—— (Mrs.) (mother of Samuel), 1

Hearne's Journal, 6, 18, 255, 421

Heathberry (Nishca-minnick) (Grey Gooseberry), 188, 411

Hebridal Sandpipers (Whale Birds), 392

Hendry, Anthony, 12, 56

Hill Island Lake, 127

Hips, 413

"History of Greenland," 189

Hoarfrost River, 226

Holmes, Prof. W. H., 12

Hood, Lord, 2, 187

Hudson's Bay, 5, 7, 9, 11, 16, 29, 30, 32, 42, 43, 46, 47, 55-57, 73, 85, 107, 136, 139, 144, 158, 165, 183, 185, 189, 190-192, 217, 248, 251, 269, 273, 276, 285, 295, 298, 307, 311, 338, 341-343, 348, 350-355, 357-360, 362-373, 375, 377-379, 383-400, 402-404, 406-410, 412, 414, 415, 417
—— —— Committee, 191
—— —— Company, 2, 3, 6, 8, 9, 10, 18, 21, 31, 41, 42, 52, 54, 55, 109, 122, 147, 184, 186, 197, 199, 200, 253, 267, 295, 330, 334, 346, 364, 384
—— —— Report, 10, 11
—— House, or Fort, 256, 398
—— Straits, 30, 189, 191, 363, 393

Hutchins, Thomas, 32, 402, 408

I-dot-le-ezey (I-dot-le-aza), 100, 330, 334

Indian encampments, 5

Indian, or Indians, 9, 13, 14, 16, 45, 53, 54, 57, 67, 70, 71, 75, 76, 83, 96, 98, 105, 108, 111, 113, 119, 122, 124, 125, 127, 130, 133-136, 138, 147, 148, 151, 152, 155, 163, 168-171, 173-175, 178-180, 182-187, 189, 194-196, 198, 199, 201, 204-207, 209-213, 215, 218-220, 222, 223, 225-227, 230, 233, 234, 244-247, 249, 254-256, 259, 260, 262, 263, 265, 267, 273, 275-280, 282, 284-288, 293, 294, 306, 307, 309-311, 337-339, 346, 349, 352, 354, 365, 369-372, 375-377, 381, 394-403, 405-411, 412-414, 416, 417
—— Athapuscow, 146, 161, 200, 223, 263, 266, 267, 269, 331, 333. See also Indian
—— Blackfeet, 12, 56. See also Indian
—— Canadian, 158. See also Indian
—— Chipewyan (Northern), 5, 9, 17, 86, 107, 112, 118, 186, 200, 286. See also Indian and Northern Indian
—— Copper (Red Knives), 136, 149, 152-157, 162, 163, 168, 170, 171, 173, 193, 196, 198-201, 203-205, 222, 293, 299, 308. See also

Indian
—— Cree, 51, 353. *See also* Indian
—— Dogribbed, 136, 199, 200, 222, 263, 265, 293, 294, 299, 318. *See also* Indian
—— E-arch-e-thinnew (Blackfeet), 55, 56. *See also* Indian and Blackfeet Indians
—— Homeguard. *See also* Indian and Southern Indian
—— Mandan, 12. *See also* Indian
—— Neheaway, 161. *See also* Indian
—— Northern (Chipewyan), 9-11, 43, 49, 51, 52, 70, 71, 75, 87, 89, 92, 97, 98, 100-103, 113-115, 120, 125, 126, 128, 138, 144, 155, 158, 160, 161, 181, 197-203, 216, 224, 226, 227, 236, 239, 249, 253, 254, 263, 265, 271, 273, 276, 281, 285-287, 290, 291, 298, 299, 301, 303, 308, 310, 311, 313, 316, 317, 321-323, 325-327, 329-331, 333, 338, 339, 342, 344, 354, 356, 357, 369, 373, 374, 378. *See also* Indian and Chipewyan Indian
[432]
Indian, Southern (Homeguard), 51, 52, 70, 71, 85, 92, 97, 101, 103, 113, 114, 144, 158, 160, 161, 199, 248, 266, 269-271, 276, 280, 290, 291, 298, 303, 308, 310-313, 315, 318, 320, 321, 326-329, 332, 333, 338, 345, 372, 374, 378, 387. *See also* Indian

Isbester, William, 52, 57, 70, 421

Island Lake, 17, 105, 112-117, 292

Jack Snipe, 391

Jackashes, 314, 348, 350

Jackasheypuck (Common bearberry), 188, 416

Jacobs, Ferdinand, 160, 329, 331, 393

Jefferson, William, 233

Jérémie (Mr.), 293, 294, 379, 384, 421

Johnston, Magnus, 41, 46, 48, 329

Jones Island, 360

"Journey to the Shores of the Arctic Ocean," by Richard King, 279

Juniper, 417

Juniper-berry (Caw-caw-cue-minick) (Crowberry), 412

Kamtschatkans, 344

Kasba Lake (Cossed Whoie, Partridge Lake), 17, 117-119

Kazan River (Cathawhachaga), 86, 87, 91, 105, 113, 118, 276, 289, 292

Keelshies, 87, 136, 138, 139, 140, 145, 202, 203, 331, 332

Kelsey, Henry, 12

Kepling, 363, 366

King or Grizzly Bear Lake, 224

King, Richard, "Journey to the Shores of the Arctic Ocean," 279, 421

King William Island, 151

Knapp's Bay, 41, 165, 291, 321-323, 366

Knight,   Capt.   James,   8,   9,   11,   44-47

Labradore,   30,   192

Lake,   Bibye   (Dep.   Gov.),   50,   51

Lake,   James   Winter,   50

Lakes—
Aberdeen,   91
Anaw'd Whoie (Lake of the Enemy), 226, 227, 233, 234
Angikuni   (Titmeg),   105
Artillery (Atacho thua = Caribou-crossing-in-the-middle-of-the-lake Lake),   23,   137,   139,   140,   225
Athabasca (Arabasca), 119, 200, 201, 234, 235, 270, 278, 279, 404
Athapuscow (Arathapescow, Great Slave, or Slave), 133, 234, 253, 255,   262,   269,   270,   277
Aylmer (Chlueata thua = Caribou-swimming-among-the-ice Lake), 151,   225
Baker's,   41,   55,   273
Bedodid,   278
Beralzone (Beralzoa = Shoal Lake), 81, 86, 292
Buffalo   (Musk-Ox),   164,   204
Cat   (Peshew),   139,   140,   151,   207
Cheesadawd (Tchizè-ta, Gîte-du-Lynx, or Home-of-the-Wild-Cat Lake),   140
Clinton-Colden,   139,   140,   148,   150,   151,   207
Cogead (Contwoy-to or Rum Lake), 151, 152, 205, 207
Contwoy-to or Rum Lake (Ko-ă-kă-tcai-tĭ) (Cogead), 152
Cossadgath   (Cassandgath),   139
Dubawnt (Doo-baunt),   5,   91,   95,   105,   286
Edlande,   226
Ennadai   (Nipach),   289
Fatt (Twal-kai-tua = Fat-fish Lake) (Wiethen), 117, 292
Great Slave (Athapuscow) ("Thu-tué" or "Lake of the Breasts"), 13,

132, 139, 151, 200, 225, 226, 235, 253, 254, 255, 267, 270, 278, 279, 281, 351, 404
Hill Island, 127
Island, 17, 105, 112-117, 292
Kasba (Cossed Whoie = Partridge Lake), 17, 117-119
King or Grizzly Bear, 224
Large Pike (Wholdyeah-chuck'd Whoie), 278
Large White Stone, 188
Le Gras (A ka thua = Fat Lake), 225
Mackay (Clayki thua = White Sand Lake), 224, 225
Magnus, 105
Methy (Cook), 226
Muddy Water (Tazennatooy), 279
Napashish (Nutarawit), 91
No Name, 224
Noo-shetht (Newstheth tooy = Hill Island Lake), 278, 279
Nueltin (Frozen Island, North Lined, Menishtick, Island), 112
Partridge (Kasba), 118, 139, 140
Peshew (Cat, No Name), 139, 140, 147, 148
[433]Pike (Whooldyah'd Whoie or Pelican Lake), 120, 125
Point (Ecka tua = Fat-water Lake, Ek-a Tooh), 172, 186, 207, 213, 218, 220, 225, 234, 277
Providence, 224
Reindeer, 117
Scartack, 132
Shethnanei (She-than-nee), 75, 80, 85
Snow-bird (The-whole-kyed Whoie = Thel-wel-ky Lake), 29, 119, 287
Sussex, 151
Thaolintoa, 105
Thaye-chuck-gyed Whoie (Large Whitestone Lake), 213
Thoy-coy-lyned, 151
Thoy-noy-kyed (Tha-na-koi = Sand Hill Mount, Aylmer Lake), 150, 151
Tittameg, 132
Walmsley, 140, 151

Whiskey Jack, 292
White Stone, 218
Wholdiah (Wholdyah'd Lake or A Naw-nee-tha'd Whoie), 125, 127, 283, 287
Wild Cat, or Lynx (Seeza-tua), 140
Winnipeg, 337
Yath-kyed (White Snow, Haecoliguah), 86, 87, 89, 91

Lallemant, 19, 21

La Pérouse, Admiral, 5, 6, 19, 421

Lapland Finch, 387

Larch, 417

Large Pike Lake (Wholdyeah-chuck'd Whoie), 278

Large White Stone Lake, 188

Larks (Shore Lark), 387

Lawson (Mr.), 400

Lefranc, Joseph, 246, 248

Le Gras Lake (A ka thua = Fat Lake), 225

Le Hontan, 376

Leroux, Laurent, 200

Lice, 359

Linnæus, 389

Little Fish River (Nemace-a-seepee-a = fish), 115

Lofthouse, Rt. Rev. J., Bishop, 80, 140

Loons, 192, 314

Luc la Corne, 12

Lynx (Wild Cat), 341, 347

Mackachy, 65, 68, 71

Mackay Lake (Clayki thua = White Sand Lake), 224, 225

Mackenzie, 254
—— River, 13, 235, 253, 294, 358
—— Valley, 405

Mackenzie, Sir Alexander, 13, 16, 201, 422

Magnus Lake, 105

Mandan Indians. *See* *under* Indian

Marble Island, 9, 11, 47-49, 293, 341, 364, 389, 411

Marley (Mr.), 18

Martin (Bank Swallow), 76, 132, 223, 224, 255, 348, 350, 351, 388

Martin, Humphrey, 408

Matonabbee, 14, 53, 57, 100-103, 105-110, 113-115, 119, 128, 130, 132, 136, 137, 140, 141, 144-150, 153-155, 157, 169, 177, 203, 205, 207, 208, 223, 227, 230, 233, 262, 266, 269, 270, 272, 284, 285,

292,   312,   325,   328,   329,   330-333

May-flies   (Ephemeridæ),   345

McLeod   Bay,   226

Merle,   John   Anthony,   50

Merriman,   Thos.,   52,   57,   70

Merry   Island,   360

Merry,   Robert,   50

Methy,   73,   254
———   Lake   (Cook   Lake),   226

Middleton,   Captain,   11,   46,   48,   55

Monk,   Captain,   198

Montreal,   5,   200,   235,   253

Moor,   Captain,   11

Moos   River,   5,   417

Moose, 223, 235, 236, 255, 257-263, 268, 271, 276, 278-281, 305, 308,   310,   336-338

Moose   Fort,   413

Moss, 83, 90, 94, 122, 169, 183, 187, 193, 205, 309, 313, 314, 368, 416

Mouse,   192,   341,   352,   359

—— Hair-tailed, 350, 359. *See also* Mouse

—— Shrew, 359. *See also* Mouse

Muddy Water Lake (Tazennatooy), 279

Muscles, 367

Muskettoes, 169, 171, 259

Musk-ox, 64, 83, 84, 89, 164-167, 169, 172, 174, 184, 187, 192, 194, 196, 257, 316, 336, 373

Musk Ox Mountain (Edegadaniyatha), 225

Musk Rat (Musquash) (Musk Beaver), 352

Musquash (Musk Rat) (Musk Beaver), 352
[434]

Nabyah, 52

Napashish (Nutarawit), Lake, 91

"Narrative of Discoveries," by Thomas Simpson, 187

Navel's Bay, 321, 322, 341

"Naywatamee Poets" (Mandan Indians), 12

Neetha-san-san-dazey River, 54

Neheaway Indians. *See under* Indian

Nelson River, 8

Neville Bay, 385

No Name Lake, 224, 225

Noo-shetht Lake (Newstheth tooy Lake = Hill Island Lake), 278, 279

"North American Fauna," by E. A. Preble, 255, 350, 352

North Saskatchewan River, 12

Northern Indians (Chipewyan). *See under* Indian

North-West Company, 200, 201, 253
—— Passage, 1, 2, 11, 41, 46, 50, 295

"North-West Passage," by T. S. Dragge, 357, 382

Norton, Mary, 158
—— Moses, 3, 5, 10, 11, 13-15, 49-51, 57, 107, 108, 110, 158, 202, 295, 329, 334, 405
—— Richard, 10, 11, 107, 328, 329

Nueltin (Frozen Island) Lake or North Lined Lake, or Menishtick Lake (Island Lake), 112

Nutarawit River, 91

Old-wives, 192

"On Snowshoes to the Barren Grounds," by Caspar Whitney, 218

Otter, 224, 314, 342, 348-350

Oule-eye, 170

Owl, Cob-a-dee-cooch (Hawk Owl), 372
—— Grey or Mottled (Ho-ho) (Great Horned Owl), 372
—— White (Snowy) (Wap-a-kee-thow), 192, 371, 372, 374

Oxford House, 351

Pacific Ocean, 55

Paleluah, 87, 89

"Parry's Second Voyage," App. to, 358

Partridge, 63-66, 70, 72, 76-78, 83, 192, 193, 227, 273, 274, 292, 316, 341, 379, 382
—— Rock, 380, 383. *See also* Partridge

Partridge Willow, 378, 383. *See also* Partridge
—— Wood (Mistick-a-pethow) (Day), 227, 234, 378, 383. *See also* Partridge

Partridge-berry (Poison-berries), 413, 414

Partridge Lake (Kasba Lake), 118, 139, 140

Peace River, 337

Pelican, 397

Pemican, 89

Pennant (Mr.), 350, 354, 370, 375, 390-392, 394, 400, 405, 408

"Pennant's Arctic Zoology," 18, 32, 336, 339, 342, 348, 350, 351, 354, 391, 403, 405, 408, 422

"Pennant's Supplement to Arctic Zoology," 19, 423

Perch, 254, 314

Periwinkle, 367

Peshew Lake (Cat Lake) (No Name Lake), 139, 140, 147, 148

Petitot, L'Abbé, 132, 140, 226, 234, 235, 423

Pheasant, 376, 377

Pigeon, 384

Pike, 73, 114, 225, 314

Pike Lake (Whooldyah'd Whoie or Pelican Lake), 120, 125

Pike, Warburton, 139, 224, 423

Pine, 372
—— Creeping (Shrubby red cedar), 412

Pine Martin, 351

Platscotez de Chiens, 293, 294

Plover (Hawk's Eyes), 192, 393, 403

Po-co-ree-kis-co (Pauk-athakuskow, Beskai dézé or Knife) River (North River), 62, 293, 294

Point Lake (Ecka tua) (Fat-Water Lake) (Ek-a Tooh), 172, 186, 207, 213, 218, 220, 225, 234, 277

"Polar Regions," by Sir John Richardson, 153

Pond, Peter, 200, 235, 253, 423

Poplar, 417

Porcupine, 72, 264, 354

Port Nelson River, 365, 379

Postlethwayt, 157

Preble, Edward A., ix, 23, 335, 350-352, 355, 423

"Present State of Hudson's Bay, The," by E. Umfreville, 42

Prince (Mr.), 382

[435]
Prince of Wales Fort (*see* Fort Churchill), 2, 3, 4, 5, 16, 21, 46, 49, 51, 55, 57, 61, 68, 70, 75, 76, 79, 87, 100, 105, 106, 107, 110, 115, 124, 126, 127, 128, 137, 146, 147, 159, 162, 165, 166, 201, 202, 232, 233, 260, 267, 269, 271, 276, 285, 291, 292, 294, 295, 316, 322, 323, 328, 329, 331, 334, 340, 356, 401, 405

Providence Lake, 224

Ptarmigan, Willow, 383

Quadrant, Elton's, 29, 109, 117, 153
—— Hadley's, 29, 92, 94, 95, 98, 105, 109, 137, 222, 277

Quadrupeds, Pinnated, 360

Quiquehatch, 168, 224, 240, 243, 255, 325, 348

Rabbit, 65, 114, 227, 234, 268, 316, 341, 342, 357, 378

"Rabbit's Head," 198

Rankin Inlet, 41

Raspberry-bushes, 413

Ravens, 192, 323, 373, 395

Red Deer, 337. *See* *also* Wewaskish
—— —— River, 12

Reindeer Lake, 117

"Relation du Detroit et de la Baie de Hudson," by M. Jérémie, 294

Religion, 325

"Remarkable History of the Hudson's Bay Company, The," by George Bryce, 296

"Report on the Dubawnt, Kazan, and Ferguson Rivers," by J. B. Tyrrell, 5

Repulse Bay, 293

Richardson, Sir John, 139, 151-153, 172, 186, 187, 194, 213, 224, 338, 351, 358, 399, 412, 423

Richmond Fort, 365

Rivers—
Albany, 5
Anderson, 254
Assiniboine, 12

Athabasca, 200, 201, 235
Athapuscow, 267, 269
Churchill(Tsandézé=Iron or Metal River), 3, 8, 13, 43, 44, 57, 62, 95, 126, 183, 196, 197, 198, 201, 214, 215, 222, 235, 236, 269, 293, 294, 295, 313, 321, 323, 334, 339-342, 354-358, 360, 364-366, 367, 369, 370, 379, 382, 384, 385, 388, 389, 391-393, 396, 401-407, 412, 413, 414, 415, 416, 417
Clowey, 132
Copper, 30, 154, 170, 192, 204, 220, 277, 330, 346, 393. *See also* Coppermine
Copper Indians (Yellow Knife or Rock), 279
Coppermine (Tson-té) (Sanka taza=Copper River), 7, 10, 11, 14, 15, 17, 18, 23, 43, 57, 90, 100, 109, 119, 139, 146, 147, 149, 150, 151, 155, 169, 170, 172, 173, 186, 187, 204, 206, 207, 213, 218, 225, 282, 294, 295, 334, 354, 371. *See also* Copper
Dubawnt (Doo-baunt), 41, 91, 95, 105, 120, 272, 286, 287
Egg, 103, 105, 110, 111, 292, 294, 390
Far Off Metal, 54
Hanbury, 139, 272
Hay's, 365
Hoarfrost, 226
Kazan (Cathawhachaga), 86, 87, 91, 105, 113, 118, 276, 289, 292
Little Fish (Nemace-a-seepee-a-fish), 115
Mackenzie, 13, 235, 253, 294, 358
Moos, 5, 417
Neetha-san-san-dazey, 54
Nelson, 8
North Saskatchewan, 12
Nutarawit, 91
Peace, 337
Po-co-ree-kis-co (Pauk-athakuskow, Beskai dézé or Knife River, North River), 62, 293, 294
Port Nelson, 365, 379
Red Deer, 12
Saskatchewan, 5, 56
Seal, 62, 65, 66, 71, 72, 81, 104, 105, 110, 115, 138, 203, 236, 293,

365,   388

Severn,   236,   340,   357,   386,   387,   402

Slave   (Athapuscow),   200,   235,   253,   267,   279

Slude,   5,   365

South   Saskatchewan,   12

T'ézus-dèssé   or   Poudrerie   (Snowdrift),   132,   281

Thee-lee-aza   (Theetinah,   or   Blue   Fish?),   281

Theley-aza,   130,   134

Thelon,   132,   272

Thlewey-chuck   (Great-fish   River),   151

Thlewiaza,   105,   113

Whale,   31,   365

[436]

Roberts,   Henry,   18

Robin,   American,   384

Robson,   Joseph,   9,   21,   41,   42,   55,   295

Rocky   Defile,   196

——   Mountains,   358

Royal   Geographical   Society,   235

——   Society,   408

Russell   Frank,   152,   172,   218,   424

Sacre   Falcon,   370

Salmon,   182-184,   305,   363,   366,   367

Sandstone   Rapids,   172,   187

Saskatchewan   River,   5,   56

Scallops, 367

Scartack Lake, 132

Scatlif, Daniel, 29

Scroggs, Captain John, 9, 11, 46

Sea-horse (Walrus), 184, 360, 362

Sea-horse Island, 360

Seal, 184, 186, 192, 362

Seal River, 62, 65, 66, 71, 72, 81, 104, 105, 110, 115, 138, 203, 236, 293, 365, 388

"Search for the Western Sea," by L. J. Burpee, 253

Sea-unicorn, 363

Severn River, 236, 340, 357, 386, 387, 402

Sheep, 251

Shees, 254

Shell-fish, 367

Shethnanei Lake (She-than-nee), 75, 80, 85

Simpson Islands, 253

Simpson, Thomas, 187, 424

"Six Years' Residence in Hudson's Bay, An account of," by J.

Robson, 9, 42

Skunks, 351

Skylark, 387

Slave River (Athapuscow River), 200, 235, 253, 267, 279

Sloops Cove, 3

Slude River, 5, 365

Smith, Captain, 11

Snow-bird Lake (The-whole-kyed Whoie or Thel-wel-ky Lake), 29, 119, 287

Sorrel, 416

Sossop (Saw-sop-o-kishac), 79, 80

South Saskatchewan River, 12

Southern (Homeguard) Indians. *See under* Indian

Speedwell, 50

Spiders, 368

Spurrel, Joseph, 50

Squirrel, Common, 192, 357

Squirrel, Ground, 358

Starfish, 367

Stephens, Joseph, 48

Stony Mountains, 162-164, 181, 204

Stote (Ermine), 352

Straits of Anian, 45

Strawberry (Oteagh-minick), 413

Success (ship), 48

Suckers, 88

Sussex Lake, 151

Swallows (Barn Swallow), 388

Swan, 80, 134, 192, 274, 275, 281, 313, 346, 399, 400
—— Smaller (Hoopers), 399. *See also* Swan
—— Whistling, 400. *See also* Swan
—— Whooping (Trumpeters), 399. *See also* Swan

Tench, 114, 314

T'ézus-dèssé or Poudrerie (Snowdrift) River, 132, 281

Thaolintoa Lake, 105

Thaye-chuck-gyed Whoie (Large Whitestone Lake), 213

Thee-lee-aza River (Theetinah River, or Blue Fish River?), 281

Theley-aza River, 130, 134

Thelon River, 132, 272

Thelwey-aza-yeth (Little Fish Hill), 29, 127, 128, 132, 147, 282

Thlewey-chuck (Great-fish River), 151

Thlewiaza River, 105, 113

Thlew-sa-nell-ie, 270

Thompson, David, 6

Thoy-coy-lyned Lake, 151

Thoy-noy-kyed Lake (Tha-na-koi or Sand Hill Mount or Aylmer Lake), 150, 151

Thrush, Red-Breasted (Red Birds) (Black Birds) (American Fieldfares), 384

Titmouse (Blackcap) (Kiss-kiss-heshis), 387

Tittameg Lake, 132

Tittemeg (Tickomeg), 73, 88, 114, 254, 305, 313

Trout, 72, 73, 89, 114, 225, 274, 278, 305, 313

Turnstone, 392

Tyrrell, J. B., viii, 5, 424-5
—— J. W., ix, 23, 137, 138, 139, 272, 425

Umfreville, Edward, 13, 42, 425

Ungava, 404

—————— Bay, 363

[437]

Vaughan, Captain David, 8, 44, 45

Venison, 66, 67, 81, 104, 125, 164, 184, 380

Venus, 4

Vetches, 416

"Voyage" (Cook's), 21

"Voyage of La Pérouse," 19

"Voyage to Hudson's Bay by the *Dobbs* Galley and *California* in the Years 1746 and 1747, A," by Henry Ellis, 42, 166

"Voyages" (Alexander Mackenzie's), 19

Wager Strait, 55

—————— Water, 165, 293

Wales, William, 4, 22, 363, 425

Waller, 160

Walmsley Lake, 140, 151

Walrus (Sea-horse), 360

Wapoos, 86

Wapping, 29

Warbles, 215

Water insects, 345

Weasel, 352

Webber (Mr.), 343

Wee-sa-ca-pucca, 313

Wegg, Samuel, 18, 50

Wejacks, 348, 350, 351

Wewaskish (Canadian Elk), 262, 336-338

Whale, 340
—— Black, 363. *See also* Whale
—— White, 363, 365. *See also* Whale

Whale Cove, 41, 46, 293, 321-323, 341, 360, 366, 391

Whale River, 31, 365

Whale-Bone (sloop), 46

Whiskey Jack Lake, 292

White Stone Lake, 218

Whitefish, 88

Whitney, Caspar, 218, 224, 426

Wholdiah Lake (Wholdyah'd Lake or A Naw-nee-tha'd Whoie), 125, 127, 283, 287

Wild Cat (Lynx), 341, 347

Wild Cat or Lynx Lake (Seeza-tua), 140

Wilks, 367

Willicks, 192

Willow, Creeping, 414
———— Dwarf, 417

Willson, Beckles, 18, 50, 51, 426

Winnipeg, Lake, 337

Wish-a-capucca (Labrador Tea = Wishacumpuckey), 90, 188, 415

Wolf, 192, 224, 323, 325, 338, 347, 350

Wolvarine (Wolverene), 192, 240, 346, 350

Wood-pecker (Golden-winged Bird), 375

Yath-kyed Lake (White Snow Lake, Haecoliguah), 86, 87, 89, 91

Yellow-legs, 192

York Factory, 5, 6, 8, 10, 13, 56, 258, 294, 368, 384, 389
———— Fort (Fort Bourbon), 160, 197, 236, 260, 307, 340, 341, 344, 345, 357, 365, 366, 377, 378, 379, 384, 389, 390-393, 398, 403, 404, 410, 416, 417

Young, Dr., 94

[438]

[i]

THE PUBLICATIONS OF THE CHAMPLAIN SOCIETY

1. THE HISTORY OF NEW FRANCE. By MARC LESCARBOT. With an English Translation, Notes and Appendices by Professor W. L. GRANT of Queen's University, and an Introduction by H. P. BIGGAR. Vol. I., pp. xxi-331. (To be completed in Three Volumes.)

2. THE DESCRIPTION AND NATURAL HISTORY OF NORTH AMERICA (ACADIA). By NICOLAS DENYS. Translated and Edited, with a Memoir of the Author, Collateral Documents, and a Reprint of the Original, by Professor WILLIAM F. GANONG. Pp. xvi-625.

3. DOCUMENTS RELATING TO THE SEIGNIORIAL TENURE IN CANADA, 1598-1854. Edited, with a Historical Introduction and Explanatory Notes, by Professor WILLIAM BENNETT MUNRO of Harvard University. Pp. cxxiii-380.

4. THE LOGS OF THE CONQUEST OF CANADA. Edited, with a Historical Introduction, by Colonel WILLIAM WOOD. Author of "The Fight for Canada." Pp. xxvi-335.

5. NOUVELLE RELATION DE LA GASPÉSIE. Pa. CHRESTIEN LE CLERCQ. An English Translation with the French Text, edited, with Notes, by Professor W. F. GANONG. Pp. xvi-452.

6. JOURNEY FROM PRINCE OF WALES FORT IN HUDSON BAY TO THE NORTHERN OCEAN, 1769-1772. By SAMUEL HEARNE. A New Edition, edited, with Notes, by J. B. TYRRELL.

7. THE HISTORY OF NEW FRANCE. By MARC LESCARBOT. Edited by W. L. GRANT and H. P. BIGGAR. Vol. II.

[In the Press.

[iii]

The Champlain Society

His Honour L. W. SICOTTE, Stipendiary Magistrate, Montreal

A. H. U. COLQUHOUN, LL.D., Deputy Minister of Education for Ontario

Assistant Secretary-Treasurer

Miss ELEANOR CREIGHTON

NOTE.—*Correspondence should be addressed in care of The Canadian Bank of
Commerce, Toronto, Canada.*

[iv]

LIST OF MEMBERS

ABBOTT, H.	Vancouver
ADAMS, F. D.	Montreal
AIRD, JOHN	Winnipeg
ARDAGH, H. H.	Barrie
ARMOUR, ERIC N.	Toronto
ARMSTRONG, G. E.	Montreal
BAIN, J. WATSON	Toronto
BAIRD, Rev. Dr.	Winnipeg
BARKER, SAMUEL, M.P.	Hamilton
BARNETT, J. D.	Stratford
BECK, Mr. Justice	Edmonton
BELL, CHARLES N.	Winnipeg
BELL, A. J.	Toronto
BENNETT, R. B.	Calgary
BICKNELL, JAMES	Toronto
BIGGAR, O. M.	Edmonton
BIRKS, W. M.	Montreal

BLACK, J. C.	Toronto
BLAKE, HUME	Toronto
BLAKE, W. H.	Toronto
BONAR, JAMES	Ottawa
BONNER, G. T.	New York
BORDEN, Sir F. W.	Ottawa
BORDEN, R. L., M.P.	Ottawa
BOYCE, A. C., M.P.	{Sault Ste. Marie,
	{ Ont.
BOYD, Sir JOHN A.	Toronto
BOYD, MOSSOM M.	Bobcaygeon
BOYS, His Honour Judge	Barrie
BREBNER, JAMES	Toronto
BREITHAUPT, W. H.	Berlin, Ont.
BRITNELL, ALBERT	Toronto
BROUSE, W. H.	Toronto
BROWN, ADAM	Hamilton
BRUCE, ALEXANDER D.	Gormley, Ont.
BRUCE, HERBERT A.	Toronto

BRYCE, Rev. GEORGE	Winnipeg
BUCHANAN, A. W. P.	Montreal
BURKE, Rev. A. E.	Toronto
BURLAND, Lieut.-Col. J. H.	Montreal
BURPEE, LAWRENCE J.	Ottawa
BUSCOMBE, FREDERICK	Vancouver
CAMERON, D. A.	Toronto
CAMPBELL, GRAHAM	Toronto
CAMERON, I. H.	Toronto
CANTLEY, THOMAS	New Glasgow
CARSTAIRS, J. S.	Toronto
CARTWRIGHT, A. D.	Ottawa
CASSELMAN, A. C.	North Bay
CASSELS, HAMILTON	Toronto
CAVEN, JOHN	Toronto
CAVEN, W. P.	Toronto
CHAMBERS, E. T. D.	Quebec
CHIPMAN, C. C.	Winnipeg

CLARK, A. H., M.P.	Windsor, Ont.
CLARK, J. M.	Toronto
CLARKE, C. K.	Toronto
CLARKE, JOHN M.	Albany, N. Y.
CLOUSTON, Sir EDWARD, Bart.	} Montreal }
COCKBURN, F. J.	Quebec
COLBY, CHARLES W.	Montreal
COLDWELL, Hon. GEO. R.	Brandon
COLQUHOUN, A. H. U.	Toronto
CONOLLY, R. G. W.	St. Catharines
CORBET, J. B.	Toronto
COX, Hon. GEORGE A.	Toronto
COYNE, JAMES H.	St. Thomas
CRAICK, W. A.	Toronto
CRONYN, EDWARD	Toronto
CRONYN, V.	London, Ont.
CROSSLEY, FIELDEN	Woodstock
CROWE, W.	Sydney

CUMBERLAND, F. BARLOW	Port Hope
DAMPIER, L. H.	Strathroy
DARLING, FRANK	Toronto
DAVIDSON, WILLIAM	Toronto
DAVIES, WILLIAM	Toronto
DENNIS, J. S.	Calgary
DEWAR, D. B.	Hamilton
DEWART, H. H.	Toronto
DE WITT, JACOB	Montreal
DINGMAN, W. S.	Stratford
DONALDSON, A. G.	Toronto
DOUGLAS, JAMES	New York
DOUGLAS, W. M.	Toronto
DRUMMOND, G. E.	Montreal
DRUMMOND, GUY M.	Montreal
DWIGHT, H. P.	Toronto
DYMENT, A. E.	Toronto

EAKINS, W. G.	Toronto
EATON, Mrs. T.	Toronto
ECCLES, F. R.	London, Ont
EGERTON, HUGH E.	Oxford, Eng.
ENGLEHART, J. L.	Toronto
EWART, JOHN S.	Ottawa
FAIRCLOUGH, H. R.	Palo Alto, Cal. [v]
FALCONER, R. A.	Toronto
FISH, J. N.	Regina
FITTON, H. W.	Brantford
FLAVELLE, J. W.	Toronto
FLECK, A. W.	Ottawa
FLEMING, Sir SANDFORD,	} Ottawa
K.C.M.G.	}
FORGET, Hon. A. E.	Regina
FOSTER, F. APTHORP	Boston, Mass.
FOTHERINGHAM, J. T.	Toronto
FRASER, ALEXANDER	Toronto

FULTON, J. H.	New Orleans
GALT, GEORGE F.	Winnipeg
GARNEAU, Sir GEORGE	Quebec
GARNEAU, HECTOR	Montreal
GAUDET, PLACIDE	Ottawa
GAY, FREDERICK LEWIS	Brookline, Mass.
GILL, ROBERT	Ottawa
GOODERHAM, GEORGE H.	Toronto
GORDON, Rev. DANIEL M.	Kingston
GOULD, C. H.	Montreal
GOW, GEORGE	Toronto
GRANT, W. L.	Kingston
GREENSHIELDS, E. B.	Montreal
GREY, His Excellency Earl	Ottawa
GUNDY, W. P.	Toronto
HAMILTON, JOHN	Quebec

HANNA, D. B.	Toronto
HANNA, Hon. W. J.	Toronto
HANNAH, I. C.	{ Forest Row,
	{ Sussex, Eng.
HARCOURT, F. W.	Toronto
HART, JOHN S.	Toronto
HARVEY, Mr. Justice	Edmonton
HEATON, F. R.	Montreal
HEBDEN, E. F.	Montreal
HENRY, W. A.	Halifax
HILLE, F.	Port Arthur
HOBSON, R.	Hamilton
HOGG, WILLIAM	Toronto
HORNING, L. E.	Toronto
HOSKIN, JOHN	{ Tunbridge
	{ Wells, Eng.
HOWLAND, PELEG	Toronto
HUNTER, A. F.	Barrie
HUNTER, Mr. Justice	Victoria, B.C.

HUYCKE, His Honour Judge	Peterborough
INGERSOLL, J. H.	St. Catherines
JAFFRAY, Hon. ROBERT	Toronto
JAMES, C. C.	Toronto
JARVIS, AEMILIUS	Toronto
JEMMETT, F. G.	Toronto
JENNINGS, C. A. C.	Toronto
JETTÉ, Sir LOUIS A., K.C.M.G.	} Quebec }
JONES, F. C. L.	Toronto
JONES, H. V. F.	London, Eng.
JONES, Hon. L. MELVIN	Toronto
JOST, A. C.	Guysboro, N.S.
KAINS, ARCHIBALD	San Francisco
KEEFER, FRANK H.	Port Arthur
KEEFER T. C.	{ Rockliffe,

	{ Ottawa
KEMP, A. E.	Toronto
KENNEDY, GEORGE	Toronto
KENNEDY, T. J.	Sault Ste. Marie
KERALLAIN, RÉNÉ DE	Quimper, France
KERR, Hon. J. K.	Toronto
KILGOUR, JOSEPH	Toronto
KILGOUR, ROBERT	Toronto
KING, Hon. W. L. MACKENZIE	Ottawa
KINGMAN, ABNER	Montreal
KYLIE, EDWARD J.	Toronto
LAFLEUR, EUGÈNE	Montreal
LAIRD, ALEXANDER	Toronto
LANG, A. E.	Toronto
LANGLOIS, H.	Toronto
LANGTON, H. H.	Toronto
LANGTON, THOMAS	Toronto
LASH, J. F.	Toronto

LASH, MILLER	Toronto
LASH, Z. A.	Toronto
LAURIER, Rt. Hon. Sir	} Ottawa
WILFRID	}
LAUT, Miss AGNES C.	Wassaic, N.Y.
LEARMONT, J. B.	Montreal
LEE, JOHN T.	Madison, Wis.
LEFROY, H. B.	Toronto
LEFROY, W.	London, Eng.
LEGGAT, WILLIAM	Montreal
LEONARD, R. W.	St. Catherines
LE SUEUR, W. D.	Ottawa
LEVY, G. H.	Hamilton
LIGHTHALL, W. D.	Montreal
LINDSAY, G. G. S.	Toronto
LITTLE, H. A.	Woodstock, Ont.
LITTLE, Lieut.-Col. J. W.	London, Ont.
LOTBINIÈRE, E. G. JOLY DE	Quebec

McArthur, D. A.	Ottawa
McBride, Hon. Richard	Victoria, B.C.
McCorkell, Hon. J. C.	{ Cowansville,
	{ P.Q.
Macdonald, J. Bruce	Toronto
Macdonald, W. Campbell	Toronto
McDougall, John A.	Edmonton
Macfarlane, W. G.	{ Grand Rapids,
	{ Mich.
Macgillivray, D.	Halifax
Machar, Miss Agnes M.	Kingston
Machum, E. R.	St. John, N.B.
McInnes, Hector	Halifax
Mackenzie, Sir William	Toronto
McLaughlin, J. F.	Toronto
[vi]McLennan, Francis	Montreal
McLennan, John S.	Sydney, N.S.

MACMECHAN, A.	Halifax
MCMILLAN, Sir D. H.	Winnipeg
MACMURCHY, ANGUS	Toronto
MACPHERSON, W. M.	Quebec
MCPHILLIPS, L. G.	Vancouver
MACWATT, His Hon. Judge	Sarnia
MANNING, P. A.	Toronto
MASON, J. A. C.	{ New Orleans,
	{ La.
MASSEY, CHESTER D.	Toronto
MASSEY, JOHN	Toronto
MASSEY, VINCENT	Toronto
MASTEN, C. A.	Toronto
MEREDITH, Sir WILLIAM	Toronto
MERRETT, T. E.	Montreal
MILLER, Rev. J. O.	St. Catharines
MILLS, Lieut.-Col. D.	London, Eng.
MILLICHAMP, R.	Toronto
MORANG, GEORGE N.	Toronto

MORRIS, H. H.	Vancouver
MOSS, Sir CHARLES	Toronto
MOXON, A. E.	London, Eng.
MULVEY, THOMAS	Ottawa
MURRAY, WILLIAM	Vancouver
MURRAY, WALTER C.	Saskatoon
MUSSEN, R. T.	{ Summerside, { P.E.I.
MURTON, Sir WALTER	{ Langton, Kent, { Eng.
NEEDLER, G. H.	Toronto
NORTHRUP, W. B., M.P.	Belleville
NOYES, CHARLES WILLIAM	Castine, Maine
O'BRIAN, J. B.	Toronto
O'BRIEN, A. H.	Ottawa
OLIVER, E. H.	Saskatoon
OSBORNE, W. W.	Hamilton

OSLER, E. B., M.P.	Toronto
OSLER, Hon. F.	Toronto
OSLER, F. G.	Toronto
PARKER, Sir GILBERT	London, Eng.
PATTERSON, E. G.	Peterborough
PATTERSON, GEORGE	{ New Glasgow,
	{ N.S.
PEACOCK, E. R.	Toronto
PEARCE, WILLIAM	Calgary
PELL, S. H. P.	New York
PHIPPS, A. R.	London, Eng.
PONTON, Lieut.-Col. W. N.	Belleville
PRICE, H. M.	Quebec
PRIMROSE, A.	Toronto
READE, JOHN	Montreal
REEVE, R. A.	Toronto
RENNIE, GEORGE W.	Stratford

RIDDELL, Mr. Justice	Toronto
ROBARTS, A. W.	Port Arthur
ROBERTSON, JAMES F.	St. John, N.B.
ROBERTSON, W. J.	St. Catherines
ROSS, Sir GEORGE W.	Toronto
ROSS, J. F. W.	Toronto
ROWELL, N. W.	Toronto
ROWLEY, C. W.	Calgary
RUNDLE, W. E.	Toronto
RUSSELL, J. A.	Windsor, N.S.
SAUL, JOHN C.	Toronto
SAVARY, His Honour Judge	Annapolis Royal
SCOTT, C. S.	Hamilton
SCOTT, H. P.	Windsor, N.S.
SEWELL, FANE	Toronto
SHORT, WILLIAM	Edmonton
SHORTT, ADAM	Ottawa

SICOTTE, His Honour Judge	Montreal
SILCOX, SIDNEY	Stratford
SILVER, H. R.	Halifax
SKELTON, C. D.	Kingston
SOMERVILLE, C. R.	London, Ont.
SQUAIR, JOHN	Toronto
STARR, F. N. G.	Toronto
STEELE, J. J.	Dundas
STEPHENSON, R. H.	Leicester, Eng.
STONE, WILLIAM	Toronto
STRATHY, G. B.	Toronto
STRATHY, H. S.	Toronto
SUTHERLAND, Mr. Justice	Toronto
SWENY, Colonel G.	Toronto
SYMON, Sir J. H.	{ Adelaide, South { Australia
TAYLOR, H. C.	Edmonton

TIFFANY, E. H.	Alexandria, Ont.
TODD, J. L.	{ Macdonald College,
	{ P.Q.
TRIGGE, A. ST. L.	Toronto
TUNSTALL, SIMON J.	Vancouver
TUPPER, Sir C. HIBBERT	Vancouver
VAN HORNE, Sir WILLIAM	Montreal
WADE, F. C.	Vancouver
WALKER, Sir EDMUND	Toronto
WALKER, E. CHANDLER	Walkerville
WALKER, H. B.	Montreal
WARNER, C. M.	Napanee
WETHERELL, J. E.	Toronto
WHITE, E. N.	Winnipeg
WHITE, JAMES	Ottawa
WHITE, W. T.	Toronto

WILKIE, D. R.	Toronto
WILLISON, J. S.	Toronto
WITTON, H. B.	Hamilton
WOOD, E. R.	Toronto
WOOD, FRANK P.	Toronto
WRONG, GEORGE M.	Toronto
YOUNG, A. H.	Toronto

[vii]

SUBSCRIBING LIBRARIES

Adelaide, S. Australia	Public Library of South Australia
Albany, N.Y.	State Library
Ann Arbor, Mich.	University of Michigan
Baltimore, Md.	Enoch Pratt Free Library
"	Johns Hopkins University
Boston, Mass.	Athenæum Library
"	Public Library
Brampton, Ont.	Public Library
Brooklyn, N.Y.	Public Library
Buffalo, N.Y.	Buffalo Historical Society
Calgary, Alberta	Western Canada College
Cambridge, Eng.	University Library
Cambridge, Mass.	Harvard University
Chicago, Ill.	Newberry Library

"	Public Library
"	The John Crerar Library
"	University of Chicago
Cincinnati, Ohio	Public Library
Detroit, Mich.	Public Library
Dublin, Ireland	Trinity College
Edmonton, Alberta	Alberta Provincial Library
Fort William, Ont.	The Women's Canadian Club
Glasgow, Scotland	Mitchell Library
"	University of Glasgow
Halifax, N.S.	Presbyterian College
"	Nova Scotia Legislative Library
Hamilton, Ont.	Public Library
Hanover, N.H.	Dartmouth College
Kingston, Ont.	Queen's University

Lansing, Mich.	Michigan State Library
Lawrence, Kan.	University of Kansas
London, England	Royal Colonial Institute
"	Royal Geographical Society
"	The Colonial Office Library
London, Ont.	Public Library
Lynn, Mass.	Public Library
Madison, Wis.	State Historical Library of Wisconsin
Minneapolis, Minn.	Minneapolis Athenæum
Montpelier, Vt.	Vermont Historical Society
[viii]Montreal, P.Q.	Fraser Institute
"	Montreal College
"	Normal School Library
New Haven, Conn.	Yale University

Newcastle-upon-Tyne, England	Public Library
New York, N.Y.	Public Library
"	New York Historical Society
Northampton, Mass.	The Forbes Library
Ottawa, Ont.	Dominion Archives
"	Library of Parliament, Canada
Oxford, England	Bodleian Library
Paris, France	Bibliothèque de l'Université de Paris
"	Bibliothèque Nationale
Philadelphia, Pa.	The Library Company of Philadelphia
Poughkeepsie, N.Y.	Vassar College
Providence, R.I.	Brown University
"	The John Carter Brown Library
Quebec, P.Q.	Legislative Library of Quebec

"	Quebec Literary and Historical Society
Salem, Mass.	The Essex Institute
Sacramento, Cal.	State Library of California
St. John, N.B.	Free Public Library
St. Louis, Mo.	St. Louis Mercantile Library Association
St. Paul, Minn.	Minnesota Historical Society
St. Thomas, Ont.	Elgin Historical and Scientific Institute
Stratford, Ont.	Public Library
Toronto, Ont.	The Canadian Bank of Commerce
"	Department of Education, Ontario
"	Legislative Library, Ontario
"	Osgoode Hall
"	Provincial Archives
"	Public Library

"	University of Toronto
"	Victoria University
Urbana, Ill.	University of Illinois
Victoria, B.C.	Legislative Library of British Columbia
Washington, D.C.	{ Bureau of American Ethnology, Smithsonian
	{ Institution
"	Library of Congress
West Point, N.Y.	United States Military Academy
Winnipeg, Man.	Alpine Club of Canada
"	Women's Canadian Club
Worcester, Mass.	Free Public Library

**A Map
exhibiting M^R. HEARNE'S TRACKS in his
two Journies for the discovery of the
Copper Mine River
in the Years 1770, 1771 and 1772
under the direction of the
Hudson's Bay Company**

**A
Plan
of the
Copper-Mine River
Surveyed by
Samuel Hearne
July 1771**

A Plan of
ALBANY RIVER
in Hudson's Bay
Latitude 52°.12'.0" North
Longitude 82°.40'.0" W. from London

by S.H. 1774

Plan is laid down by Magnetical Compass. The three
hummocks of Wood on Sawpit Island can be seen in clear weather
over the Factory Island, in 3 fathom Water, and is a good
Mark. Saddle-back hummock bears due West from Albany
Roads and is a good Mark for laying the Buoys.

Plan

of

Moos River

in

Hudsons Bay, North America

Lat. 53°N. Lon. 83°W. from London

by S.H. 1774.

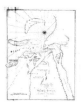

Plan
of
Slude River.
Lat. 52°.15' N. Lon. 83°.20' W.
by S.H.

A MAP EXHIBITING MR. HEARNE'S TRACKS IN HIS TWO JOURNEYS FOR THE DISCOVERY OF THE COPPERMINE RIVER IN THE YEARS 1770, 1771, AND 1772
Adjusted, as far as possible, in accordance with the latest maps by J. B. Tyrrell, 1909

MAP OF COPPERMINE RIVER as surveyed by SIR JOHN FRANKLIN IN

1821
Scale—14½ miles in 1 inch
References—t Observation for Latitude. O Observation for Longitude.
Y Variation. T Dip.
From Franklin's "Narrative of a Journey to the Shores of the Polar Sea"

Transcriber's Notes:

Except for the inline drawings on page 229, the maps and photos are low-resolution "thumbnails". Click on a thumbnail to display a high-resolution image.

The editor retained the page numbering of the original book in brackets [143]. These have been changed to braces {143} so as not to conflict with footnotes in the text version. In a few cases, page numbers within words have been moved to the following interword space.

Errors in punctuation and diacritical marks in French were fixed.

The following words appear in alternate spellings and have not been changed: "buffalos" / "buffaloes", "carcases" / "carcasses", "chisel" / "chissel", "dependence" / "dependance", "eat" / "eaten" / "ate", "fur" / "furr", "Prince of Wales Fort" / "Prince of Wales's Fort", "snowshoe(s)" / "snow-shoe(s)", "Stony" / "Stoney", "tittymeg" / "tittimeg" / "tittameg" / "tittemeg", "wolvarine" / "wolverene" / "wolvereen".

Inconsistent hyphenation and diacritics of place names and native names have not been changed.

Hyphen removed: "a[-]cross" (p. 129), "bear[-]berry" (p. 427), "day[-]break" (p. 94), "fin[-]like" (p. 360).

Hyphen added: "a[-]head" (pp. 181, 204), "fire[-]arms" (p. 86), "fire[-]wood" (p. 72), "gun[-]shot" (p. 181), "iron[-]work" (p. 285), "land[-]side" (p. 179), "sea[-]side" (p. 54), "tent[-]poles" (pp. 104, 163), "wood[-]work" (p. 191).

"Cheif" changed to "Chief" in the caption of the portrait of Hearne facing the original title page.

p. 56 (footnote): "exploded" changed to "explored" (it has so long been explored).

p. 64: duplicate "of" removed (one of which was).

p. 75: "eves" changed to "eaves" (over which the eaves of the tent).

p. 82: "aukwardness" changed to "awkwardness" (The awkwardness of my load).

p. 121: "of" inserted (on each side of the door).

p. 157: "haunts" changed to "hunt" (Their annual haunts).

p. 167: "scowring" changed to "scouring" (scouring the blade).

p. 168, Index: "Quequehatch" changed to "Quiquehatch".

p. 176: "differents" changed to "different" (inhabitants of the different elements).

p. 180: added "of" (on the East side the river).

p. 195: "oar" changed to "ore" (ballasted with the ore).

p. 246: "eight" changed to "eighth" (The eighth is the Mittain Beaver).

p. 246: "Joseph la France" changed to "Joseph Lefranc".

p. 258: "aukward" changed to "awkward" (very awkward appearance).

p. 292: added "a" (Deer was so plentiful a great part of the way).

p. 308, 315: "soked" changed to "soaked" (has been soaked and scrubbed, when soaked in water).

p. 313: "track" changed to "tract" (The track of land, that whole tract of country).

p. 343 (footnote [BY]): added "of" (often been at the killing of them).

p. 351: "patridges" changed to "partridges" (catch partridges, mice, and rabbits).

p. 373: "voilet" changed to "violet" (purple and violet colour).

p. 391 (sidenote): "Jacks Snipe" changed to "Jack Snipe).

p. 401: "streight" changed to "straight" (they fly straight to the call).

p. 406: "rout" changed to "route" (The route they take in Spring).

p. 423: "Sociétié de Géographie" changed to "Société de Géographie".

1700141

917.71

Author: Hearne, Samuel, 1745-1792
Title: Journey from...Hudson's
Bay...1769-1772

CPSIA information can be obtained
at www.ICGtesting.com
Printed in the USA
LVOW10s0048160317
527396LV00009B/149/P